972.01
H2785 Hassig
Aztec warfare

890433

DATE DUE

No 15 '90	OCT 14 '99		
Fe 20 '92			
Fe 4 '93	APR 24 '01		
Ap 8 '93	FEB 26 '02		
OCT 21 '93	MAR 15 '07		
MAR 03 '94			
NOV 10 '94	OCT 06 2010		
MAR 30 1995			
APR 13 1995			
OCT 05 1995			
OCT 19 1995			
NOV 16 '95			

Gift of T. Colbert

DISCA

D1171999

Learning Resources Center
Marshalltown Community College
Marshalltown, Iowa 50158

DEMCO

Aztec Warfare

The Civilization of the American Indian Series

Aztec Warfare

Imperial Expansion and Political Control

By Ross Hassig

COMMUNITY COLLEGE LRC
MARSHALLTOWN, IOWA 50158

890433

University of Oklahoma Press : Norman and London

By Ross Hassig

(Translator and editor, with J. Richard Andrews) Hernando Ruiz de Alarcón, *Treatise on the Heathen Superstitions and Customs That Today Live Among the Indians Native to This New Spain* (Norman, 1984)

Trade, Tribute, and Transportation: The Sixteenth-Century Political Economy of the Valley of Mexico (Norman, 1985)

Aztec Warfare: Imperial Expansion and Political Control (Norman, 1988)

Library of Congress Cataloging-in-Publication Data

Hassig, Ross, 1945–
Aztec warfare.
(The Civilization of the American Indian series; v. 188)
Bibliography: p. 361
Includes index.
1. Aztecs—Politics and government. 2. Aztecs—Wars. 3. Indians of Mexico—Politics and government. 4. Indians of Mexico—Wars. 5. Mexico—Antiquities. I. Title. II. Series.
F1219.76.P75H37 1988 972′.01 87–40553
ISBN 0–8061–2121–1 (alk. paper)

The paper in this book meets the guidelines for permanence and durability of the Committee on Production Guidelines for Book Longevity of the Council on Library Resources, Inc.

Copyright © 1988 by the University of Oklahoma Press, Norman, Publishing Division of the University. Manufactured in the U.S.A. First edition.

To J. Richard Andrews
Huei Nahuatlahtoh, Ixpetz, Nicniuhtzin

Contents

Illustrations and Maps

Figures

Chart

Maps

Preface

THE primary data for Aztec warfare are largely published accounts of sixteenth-century chronicles of Aztec conquests and lists of Aztec tributaries. The importance of this reconstruction is in the interpretation and analysis: many conquests have been recorded, but their significance is not always clear. Some towns fell after major combat, others accepted the barest suggestion that they become tributaries, others came into the empire when the towns to which they were subordinate were incorporated, and still others were conquered but remain unrecorded. Thus any attempt to reconstruct what really happened will necessarily be incomplete and inaccurate about specific events. My aim is an account of the main events and an interpretative analysis that informs the data.

Some attention must be directed to the way I have reconstructed the Aztec historical sequence in the latter half of the volume. Given the multiple sources detailing the sequence of conquests and the numerous lists of tributary towns under the various kings, inconsistencies inevitably arise. I have considered these, but the vast bulk of this material has been put in the notes rather than in the body of the text. Since most readers probably lack interest in these sometimes arcane debates, I have presented the historical sequence as a straightforward account, relegating full consideration of the various source inconsistencies and debates to notes, along with my reconstructions of the various march routes. While this may render the body of the text somewhat less immediately useful to the scholar, the advantages to most readers, in my estimation, more than offset this slight inconvenience.

In reconstructing Aztec conquests, I have placed the conquered towns in a temporal framework—by specific year where possible, in the proper sequence where specific dating is unavailable, and by kingly reign at a minimum. Problems of interpretation necessarily arose, since the historical sources sometimes contradict one another or list towns that are highly improbable at the time mentioned. My reconstruction, then, is a reasoned account, not a verbatim one, and seeks to list the sequence of conquests so that some sense can be made of the various imperial military strategies. The total number of towns I discuss is far below the total actually dominated by the Aztecs when the Spaniards arrived. Even the expansive *Codex Mendoza*, which does not list all of the towns known to have paid tribute to the Aztecs, presents a listing at the time of the Spanish conquest that is almost twice as extensive as the total number of towns recorded in chronicle sources as having been conquered by all the Aztec kings. Thus the reconstruction is necessarily incomplete, and, given the way the empire expanded, there is no reliable way to reinsert all of the tributaries into the historical sequence.

Because the lists of Aztec conquests are incomplete, so, too, are the maps. I have included all the conquered towns that could be located. Towns for which only approximate locations could be established are also included and are so designated; towns that could not be located at all are not included. I have included an initial map showing the basic tripartite land division (tropical lowlands from 0 to 1,000 meters [0–3,280 feet], temperate regions from 1,000 to 2,000 meters [3,280–6,560 feet], and cold lands above 2,000 meters [6,560+ feet]) of central Mexico to orient readers. Contour maps, however, have not proven useful: terrain type, not altitude per se, is the main determinant of military routes, and my maps reflect this. As a result, the landforms will appear strange even to those familiar with Mesoamerica, but the resultant maps offer a superior, though necessarily simplified, display of march information. Thus, although some marches appear to violate the principle that the easiest route (considering terrain and distance together) was the route followed, a more detailed map would reveal topographical features making the proposed routes logical. I deleted that detail, however, in the interest of readability.

Acknowledgments

Many thanks are owed to various people for assistance rendered throughout my work on this book. First and foremost, I am deeply indebted to J. Richard Andrews for reading numerous drafts and offering suggested revisions. He also provided translations of Nahuatl passages as needed and provided the orthographic format I have adopted in dealing with the names of towns and peoples, as explained at greater length below. While I have not always followed his advice, I cannot overstate my indebtedness to him.

Although I had already conceived the basic ideas embodied in this work before I met Neil Goldberg, the shape of the book has been greatly altered by my conversations with him, his advice, and his considerable knowledge of military matters. I also owe thanks to Claudio Lomnitz-Adler for clarifying several aspects of this work that I had not thought through clearly, and to William Macdonald for help in dealing with roads. I am also indebted to Woodrow Borah and Edward N. Luttwak for pointing out several areas that needed clarification and elaboration and for providing guidance on a number of significant issues in the later stages of this work. I would also like to thank Debran Rowland for drawing the maps. And finally, I owe my wife, Debi, many thanks for reading drafts of the volume and offering editorial suggestions, as well as for putting up with considerable inconvenience during the writing of this book.

New York City ROSS HASSIG

Note on Orthography

I have attempted to conform to a standardized Nahuatl orthography as far as possible, but I have made some exceptions for clarity and brevity; these are noted below. The Nahuatl orthography generally follows J. Richard Andrews's *Introduction to Classical Nahuatl*. Because no length marks have been used in the text, vowel length is not displayed; except as noted below, however, the glottal stop (*h*) has been added as appropriate.

Pronunciation Guide

Letter	*Pronunciation*
c + a/o	as in *can*
qu + e/i	like *k* in *kit*
c + e/i	as in *cease*
z + a/o	like *s* in *sod*
ch	as in *church*
chu	like *ckw* in *backward*
cu/uc	like *qu* in *quick*
h	as in *hill* (but, strictly, a glottal stop)
hu	like *w* in *wake*
uh	like *wh* in *wheel*
tl	similar to *tl* in *settler*, but a single sound
tz	like *ts* in *hats*
x	like *sh* in *ship*

All other letters are pronounced with standard Latin values.

In general I have not tampered with the form of the Nahuatl

words. For example, in Nahuatl a word that refers to an entity not considered to be animate lacks marked pluralization; thus one sandal is a *cactli,* and two sandals are two *cactli.* (Contrast this with animate nouns; for example, one noble is a *pilli,* while two nobles are two *pipiltin.*) A *-tl* or *-tli* on the end of a noun is a singular-number suffix (or a common-number suffix), and I have not attached an English pluralizing *-s* to make a word fit the English reader's expectations. However, some Nahuatl words have entered the English language and therefore conform to English spelling, pronunciation, and pluralization; for example, *ahtlatl* has become *atlatl,* pluralized *atlatls.* In such instances I have used the anglicized word, after first noting the source form in its standardized spelling. Nahuatl words that are marked for plural are, of course, left with their plural endings; the plural suffixes for nouns are *-tin, -meh,* and *-h;* the plural suffixes for verbs and derivative nouns are *-h* and *-queh.*

I have chosen not to use the plural form of gentile names (i.e., names designating a group or a people). I have anglicized them to a certain extent. A large number of such names end in *-catl* for the singular and *-cah* for the plural; for example, *Aztecatl/Aztecah* and *Chalcatl/Chalcah.* In Spanish all such words are easily hispanized by dropping the suffix *-tl* for the singular (*Aztecatl* becomes *Azteca; Chalcatl* becomes *Chalca*) and replacing *-h* with the Spanish plural *-s* (*Aztecah* becomes *Aztecas; Chalcah* becomes *Chalcas*). This procedure would work as easily for English, except that by tradition we have forms such as *Aztec/Aztecs* and *Toltec/Toltecs;* that is, whenever the *-catl* and *-cah* are preceded by a vowel, one deletes not only the number suffix but the preceding *-a-* as well. A problem arises, however, when either the *-catl* or the *-cah* is preceded by a consonant, as in the case of *Chalcatl/Chalcah* or *Tetzcocatl/Tetzcocah.* For these I have chosen to drop the Nahuatl singular suffix *-tl* for the anglicized singular and to replace the Nahuatl plural suffix *-h* with the English plural suffix *-s*: *Chalca/Chalcas* and *Tetzcoca/Tetzcocas.* The only problem with my proposed usage is that my singular form has frequently been used as the plural form in the scholarly literature. My solution, however, permits the singular form to serve as an adjective with both types of formations: "Aztec banner," "Chalca banner." There is one other situation in which the second technique for anglicizing is used—when the first technique would produce a place name. For example, any gentile noun ending in

-tepecatl/-tepecah would yield *-tepec* (. . . hill-place or . . . mountain-place) in the singular. For this reason *Xaltepecatl/Xaltepecah* is anglicized as *Xaltepeca/Xaltepecas* (not *Xaltepec/Xaltepecs*); and for the same purpose of avoiding a place name, *Cuauhnahuacatl/Cuauhnahuacah* is anglicized as *Cuauhnahuaca/Cuauhnahuacas*, and so forth. In most instances, I have not used gentile names that do not conform to the generalities noted above. But where unavoidable (e.g., *Mazahuaque* [*Mazahuahqueh*], sing. *Mazahua* [*Mazahuah*]), to form the plural I have added *-s* to the singular (e.g., *Mazahua*, pl. *Mazahuas*).

One word in particular requires attention. *Pochteca*, the term commonly used to designate the traditional Aztec merchants, is a gentile noun derived from Pochtlan, the name of a ward of Tenochtitlan-Tlatelolco. Originally *pochtecatl* (pl. *pochtecah*) referred only to a person(s) from that ward. According to the first technique for anglicization described above, the anglicized singular would be *pochtec* and the plural would be *pochtecs*. However, the original gentile meaning of the word was superseded by its professional meaning. These people were significant not as residents of a particular ward but as merchants, regardless of their residence. For that reason, and to conform to tradition in the Mesoamerican literature, I have retained the proper Nahuatl forms of their name: *pochtecah* (sing. *pochtecatl*).

All town names found in the sources have been altered to what they should be if standardly rendered. But in order to ease the readers' task, I have not included the glottalized *h* in town names, or in their derivative gentile names. Thus, for example, Mexihco becomes Mexico, and Tetzcohco becomes Tetzcoco. The complete spellings are included with the town names in the index. Generally this presents few difficulties. Tenochtitlan, Xochimilco, Chalco Atenco, Tlatelolco, Tlacopan, and many others remain unaltered. Others have been changed somewhat. I have standardized the names of towns of little note, because their nonstandard spellings have had no opportunity to take hold. In addition I have altered the names of a few noted cities, among them Texcoco (to Tetzcoco), Toluca (to Tolocan), Tula (to Tollan), and Tlaxcala (to Tlaxcallan). To orient the reader, when the town is first introduced, the conventional spelling follows the standard one. While this may cause some initial discomfiture, the value of the standardized orthography far outweighs any advantage to be gained by perpetuating an erroneous traditional spelling.

I have attempted to use pre-Hispanic designations for regions and topographical features. When this was not possible, I have used modern political designations, preceding the word with "present-day" and spelling it according to contemporary usage: thus, "present-day Tlaxcala," as opposed to pre-Hispanic Tlaxcallan. Also, in discussing the specific identification and location of some towns, I have retained modern spellings, even when they are orthographically nonstandard in Nahuatl, in order to clearly distinguish between various settlements. However, except for the parenthetical material following the initial introduction of a town, this occurs only in the notes following the text.

To clarify the names of kings and nobles in this work, I have omitted the honorific suffix *-tzin*. Sometimes the omission is unnecessary, because the names are commonly offered in both forms, such as Ahuitzotl and Ahuitzotzin. Other names, almost never given without the honorific, I have shortened. Thus Moteuczomah Xocoyotzin appears as Moteuczomah Xocoyotl.

Aztec Warfare

Montezuma had two houses full of every sort of arms, many of them richly adorned with gold and precious stones. There were shields great and small, and a sort of broadswords, and others like two-handed swords set with stone knives which cut much better than our swords, and lances longer than ours are, with a fathom of blade with many knives set in it, which even when they are driven into a buckler or shield do not come out, in fact they cut like razors so that they can shave their heads with them. There were very good bows and arrows and double-pointed lances and others with one point, as well as their throwing sticks, and many slings and round stones shaped by hand, and some sort of artful shields which are so made that they can be rolled up, so as not to be in the way when they are not fighting, and when they are needed for fighting they let them fall down, and they cover the body from top to toe. There was also much quilted cotton armour, richly ornamented on the outside with many coloured feathers, used as devices and distinguishing marks, and there were casques or helmets made of wood and bone, also highly decorated with feathers on the outside, and there were other arms of other makes which, so as to avoid prolixity, I will not describe, and there were artisans who were skilled in such things and worked with them, and stewards who had charge of the arms.

BERNAL DÍAZ DEL CASTILLO

CHAPTER 1

Introduction

THE name Aztec conjures up many images, such as captives having their hearts torn from their chests to satisfy the gods. Without these sacrifices, the Aztecs believed, the gods would die, and the world would end; hence the stories of sacred rites in which each year thousands of people captured in war were led up temple pyramids in the Aztec capital of Tenochtitlan, where their hearts were used to feed the gods. This insatiable demand of the gods drove the Aztecs toward war, and the very fate of the world depended on their success. But probably the most striking popular image is that of the confrontation between the Spanish conquistador Hernán Cortés and the Aztec king Moteuczomah Xocoyotl (popularly known as Montezuma). These men embodied the clash of two cultures that were different in customs, practices, beliefs, and technologies, and the resulting conquest was unquestionably one of history's great military exploits. A few hundred Spaniards, helped by Indian allies, succeeded in reducing the imperial city of Tenochtitlan to rubble, destroying its rulers and elites and subjecting its people to forced labor, social and political subordination, and economic peonage.

The Spanish conquest of Mexico was indeed a feat of incredible daring, military prowess, and political skill. And though what most of us know of Aztec culture is what the conquistadors saw, it was only the tip of the historical iceberg. When Cortés arrived, the Aztecs had lived in central Mexico for only a few hundred years and had been its dominant power for only a century. Yet their vast armies had marched on campaigns stretching hundreds of miles to meet, fight, and subdue competing states and cultures, and they had performed feats of daring in battle and exercised astute political control over an expanding imperial domain. But in the popular mind, no kings dominate the Aztec ascendancy as Genghis Khan dominated the Mongols, the Caesars, Rome, or Charlemagne, the Franks. All too often Aztec history is viewed as the product of an almost mechanistic need to expand, to fight for the sake of their gods.

Beneath this stereotyped perspective on Aztec warfare, however, there were commoners who fought the wars for reasons as rational and justifiable as our own, nobles who rose to prominence as warriors, and kings and councillors who plotted the course of the Aztec rise, often through their own feats of military daring and political savoir faire.

But what is known of the earlier Aztec kings? Who were they, what did they accomplish, and why? It is a historical accident that Moteuczomah Xocoyotl is the most famous of the Aztec kings: widely known as the king who was defeated by the Spanish conquistadors, he would not have wanted this fame. Earlier kings are largely relegated to obscurity, not so much lost to Western scholarship as overlooked. Their feats and exploits are all but forgotten, yet many of them were giants. They took a small, backward people and raised them to dominate their world. Thus, although it is difficult to capture the popular imagination with references to such relatively unfamiliar figures as Kings Itzcoatl and Ahuitzotl, their exploits were the reality behind the Aztec expansion. And their deeds rank with those of the better-known kings and generals of Old World fame.

A dispassionate analysis is required to achieve a better understanding of actual events—their sequence, rationale, and purpose. The Aztec Empire must be considered in the same light as Caesar's Rome, Shang China, or any other imperial system. And the people must be considered in the same way, as men and women with real motivations, real goals and purposes, and real constraints.

THE HISTORICAL RECORD

The Aztecs were the latest in a series of groups to dominate central Mexico. The region had seen the emergence of many powerful political systems, major urban centers, widespread economic ties, and a shared cultural tradition with many local artistic and intellectual variations. The main outlines of the Aztecs' culture were neither original nor unique to them. To appreciate the Aztecs' position in the overall scheme of Mesoamerican development, some consideration—however brief—must be be given to their cultural forebears in central Mexico (see map 1).

The Aztecs arrived comparatively late, reaching the basin of Mexico in the thirteenth century A.D., and they did so as Chichimecs—the Mesoamerican version of barbarians, uncultured in the great traditions of central Mexico. They ultimately settled at the site of what became Tenochtitlan in 1345 and emerged as a fledgling empire less than a century later.

Much of the Aztecs' military technology and organization was an elaboration on that of the earlier Toltecs, centered at Tollan (present-day Tula, Hidalgo). The Toltecs dominated central Mexico from about A.D. 900 to 1200, the period during which political rule shifted from the hands of a theocratic priesthood to those of more secular warrior classes, a pattern carried forward by the Aztecs. But even the Toltecs were not the most important cultural innovators in central Mexico. They, too, perpetuated many of the traditions bequeathed to them by earlier civilizations.

Monte Albán, El Tajín, Xochicalco, and Chalollan (Cholula) were among the most important city-states before the Toltecs. Yet none achieved more than regional significance, creating few new social patterns and technologies. Rather, they served as conservators of the cultural traditions to which they were heirs. It was from these cities and peoples that the Toltecs picked up the major threads of the Mesoamerican social fabric.

The main outlines of Mesoamerican civilization date from the Classic period (roughly the first two centuries A.D. to about 900).[1] Teotihuacan, situated in the northeastern portion of the basin of Mexico, was the first major Mesoamerican empire, dominating all of central Mexico and extending its influence as far as present-day southern Guatemala. The nature of Teotihuacan's domination is not entirely clear: the city is usually considered to have been under theocratic rule, and there is little evidence of extensive military activity. Nevertheless, most of the basic Mesoamerican armaments were in existence at this time—atlatls, darts, and spears, as well as clubs (bladed and unbladed), shields, cotton body armor, and unit standards—and elite military orders had apparently arisen. This military organization and technology was carried forward and elaborated on first by the Toltecs and then by the Aztecs.

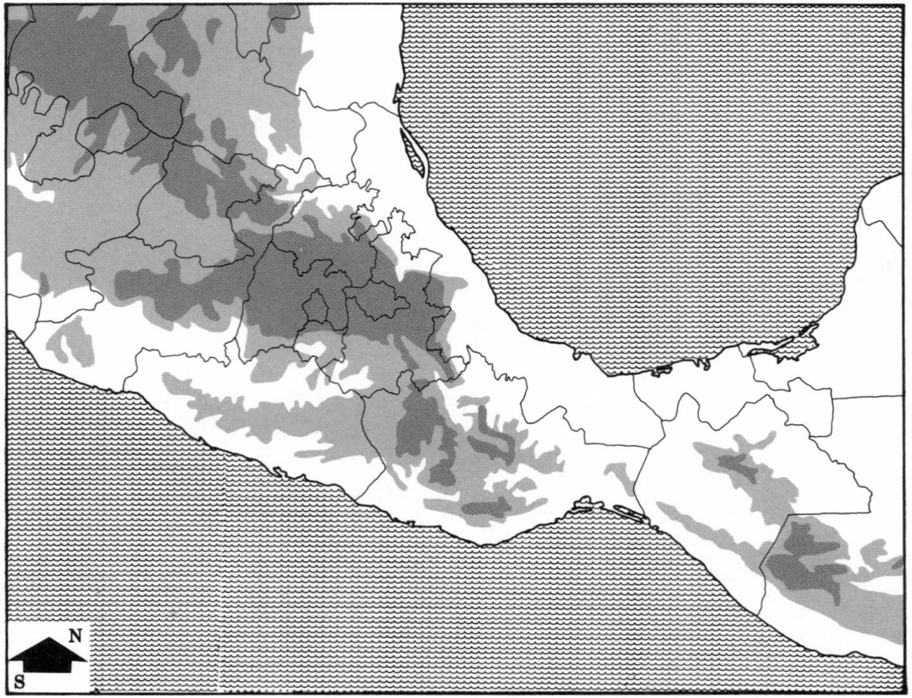

Map 1. Topography of central and southern Mexico and western Guatemala (unshaded areas = 0–1,000 meters [0–3,280 feet], light shaded areas = 1,000–2,000 meters [3,280–6,560 feet]; dark shaded areas = 2,000+ meters [6,560+ feet]) and present-day political boundaries.

Though the people of Teotihuacan established the first truly sophisticated military organization and technology in Mesoamerica, many of their general patterns derived from the Olmecs (1200–400 B.C.). Although there is little persuasive evidence of an empire or other widespread political integration,[2] the Olmecs oversaw the emergence of elites and a class-based society; the development of increasingly sophisticated political systems; new and more complex religions, writing, astronomy, numerical systems, and calendars; and the growth of urbanization and interregional exchange.

TRADITIONAL PERSPECTIVES

It is easy to place the Aztecs in the general sequence of Mesoamerican cultural development, but assessing precisely what occurred in Aztec society and why is more difficult. This difficulty arises both from the information available and from the theories employed by writers to interpret them.

Data

The information available to us was recorded long after the events in question and consists of generalized accounts that do not deal adequately with specific sequences of events. Frequently these accounts were attempts to place Aztec behavior in a favorable light from the European perspective, often comparing Aztec actions to those of peoples of the classical or biblical worlds. Thus general discussions of Aztec concepts of war all too often present a sanitized view of wars and their causes in Aztec society. Some sixteenth-century writers even went so far as to claim that the Aztecs had never waged unprovoked war.[3] Three different but interwoven perspectives on Aztec war arise from emphasizing, or drawing on, (1) the idealized views presented by many of the chroniclers; (2) the religious aspects of Aztec warfare, on which many modern writers have focused; and (3) the descriptions of the *xochiyaoyotl*, or "flower war."

The first approach—the idealized view—is based on one Aztec rationalization for war, which was often belied by actual practice. In this view the entire sequence of warmaking events—initial provocation, intelligence gathering, decision making, negotiations, and combat—had a standardized format. A just war could be waged against an independent city or state if Aztec or allied merchants were killed there.[4] If a town was already an Aztec tributary, further war was just only if that town had rebelled,[5] and the action taken depended on whether the rebellion had been caused by all the people or just by their political leaders—the lords. If a rebellion occurred, spies were sent to determine who caused it.[6] If the town's lords were at fault, the army and judges were dispatched to capture and publicly try them. But if it was a general uprising by all the people, the residents were first asked several times to resume paying their tribute. If their lords came humbly to Tenochtitlan and paid, they were pardoned, but if they did not, war was declared.[7]

Other Aztec actions were also provocative, among these, requests to other city-states to accept the Aztec gods and to revere the Aztec king and pay tribute to him. Failure to do either was regarded as a *casus belli*,[8] especially if the ambassadors who took the request were slain.[9] These officials (*tititlantin*; sing. *titlantli*)[10] were often sent to foreign cities carrying seemingly minor requests,[11] but their overt purpose cannot disguise their covert political intent.

After the Aztecs decided to go to war, ambassadors were sent to the city in question to announce that it had wronged the Aztecs and to ask for satisfaction. Three different embassies were sent; the first to the rulers, the second to the nobles, and the third to the people. If the enemy city still failed to provide redress, war followed.[12]

The Aztecs also had certain expectations concerning what constituted normal relations among nations. These expectations, which may have been common throughout much of Mesoamerica, included free passage of nonhostile people and even of armies. Blocking a road would not have been effective in completely barring traffic in a civilization whose transportation was based on foot travel. Instead, such a blockade was significant for political purposes, signaling the intention of cutting relations, resisting hostile passage or entry, and initiating war. When taken by tributaries, such actions signaled rebellion. And, since they constituted a breach of international etiquette, they were similarly regarded as acts of rebellion when taken by independent cities. But actual Aztec war practice differed markedly from the foregoing (see chaps. 9–15).

The second approach—the religious view—is based on the role in warfare that the Aztecs attributed to the supernatural. The gods were often viewed as dictating when war was auspicious, when it was to begin, what the outcome would be, and what the Aztecs needed to do to appease the gods. Before going into combat, the Aztecs prayed to their gods for victory,[13] and the priests played a major role in communicating with the gods about matters of war.[14] Also, after human sacrifices were made, the gods were said to have promised the Aztecs victory.[15] Supernatural aid was also sought in defensive actions. When a city was besieged, the Aztecs performed human sacrifices in hopes of eliciting supernatural assistance.[16]

Before leaving for war, the soldiers went to the main temples. There they received weapons and performed autosacrifices, cutting their flesh—ears, tongues, and limbs—to offer blood to the gods in return for their blessings.[17] Soothsayers predicted the war's outcome.[18] During the campaign against Tlaxcallan (Tlaxcala), Huexotzinco (Huejotzingo), and Atlixco, astrologers for the Triple Alliance of Tenochtitlan, Tetzcoco, and Tlacopan advised the kings to stop advancing, and they did.[19] The Aztecs also tried magic to help defeat the enemy if necessary.[20] After one successful war, the king enlarged the temple to Huitzilopochtli and adorned the god's image with war spoils, a practice followed since the reign of Tizoc in the 1480s and probably earlier.[21] Astrology also played a prominent role in martial matters as it did in Aztec life generally;[22] the calendar dictated other ritual events dealing with war as well.[23] While the army was away at war, the priests in Tenochtitlan kept a vigil throughout each night and performed penances.[24] But priests did not play an exclusively passive or supporting role; senior priests also went to war, fighting in battle and being awarded clothing and insignia just as the warriors were.[25] Priests bearing images of the gods accompanied the army on wars of conquest and encouraged the soldiers through appropriate rituals[26] (see fig. 3).

Thus the supernatural was interwoven with Aztec warfare, but this was just as true of other civilizations. Yet the religious elements, which were of such interest to the Christianizing Spaniards and which occupied a large portion of the clerical chroniclers' attention, have assumed enormous proportions in some modern analyses of Aztec warfare, many writers seeing Aztec warfare as inextricably tied to religion.[27] Much of this orientation derives from the often repeated Aztec view that the gods required the nourishment of human blood and that this blood was best obtained from captives taken in battle. Without such nourishment the gods would die, and the world would end. Thus a failure to engage in warfare was a threat to the continuation of the world. While this belief may have underlain some warfare, it cannot explain the extent, direction, and execution of the Aztec expansion. Moreover, much of this perspective comes from an unwarranted intermingling by modern writers of data from ordinary wars of conquest with data from the flower wars (*xochiyaoyotl*).

The third approach—based on the flower wars—derives from overemphasizing the practices in, and the role of, these wars. In its classic manifestation, the xochiyaoyotl was a ritual war allegedly undertaken for several purposes; most prominently mentioned are combat training and securing captives for religious sacrifices.[28] However, this explanation is not universally accepted,[29] and sacrificial captives were not taken exclusively in flower wars.

The xochiyaoyotl was characterized by the formality of the battles and the conventions that surrounded them. A day was set for the battle, which was to be held in a space purposely left as common ground between the lands of the two enemies. This space, the *cuauhtlalli* or *yaotlalli*, was sacred[30] and took on special significance.[31] The fighting was formally initiated by burning a large pyre of paper and incense between the two armies.[32] Death in the flower wars, as opposed to death in an ordinary war, was called *xochimiquiztli*—flowery death, blissful death, fortunate death.[33]

The xochiyaoyotl was unquestionably one of the most unusual and spectacular aspects of Aztec warfare, prompting analogy with the medieval melée.[34] However, both early and modern analyses have generalized the ritual elements of flower wars, projecting them onto ordinary warfare and perpetuating the idea that the "classic xochiyaoyotl" was a distinct type of warfare. While it is true that the flower wars were conceptually distinct from "ordinary" wars, their functional distinction is less clear. To assess the role and purpose of the xochiyaoyotl properly, we cannot extract its stereotypical characteristics. Rather, we must reinsert it into the historical sequence as an integral part of the Aztec military repertoire.

The three foregoing perspectives present Aztec war as a matter of principle, undertaken only after grievous provocation and after all peaceful options had been presented to the enemy; as a religious and ideological imperative; and as a formal and ritualistic endeavor. These views also present battle as a matter of demonstrating superior ability and, perhaps, divine favor, rather than as a matter to be concluded by whatever means were effective. In fact, Aztec practices were shaped by political realities and practical necessities. And many of the religious explanations were ex post facto rationalizations for warfare—ideological overlays to justify actions they were determined to take. In short, religion and ideology were manipulated in the service of the state, rather than the reverse.[35] Consequently, relying on idealized descriptions or religious and ritual imperatives to present a portrait of Aztec warfare as it was initiated and executed is largely unjustified. To the Aztecs, warfare was a practical matter and was pursued in that fashion.

Theory

Understanding the Aztecs and comparing them with earlier Mesoamerican cultures (as well as with Western cultures) depends on the theories and models used to make sense of the information available and to indicate which data are pivotal and which are peripheral. Theories channel observation and explanation, and what is anomalous when seen from the perspective of one theoretical approach may be intelligible when seen from another.

The theoretical approaches of various academic disciplines over many years have resulted in so many different perspectives on the Aztec Empire that it is difficult to present a consensual view of the way it has been conceived.[36] Nevertheless, there has been considerable unanimity about the political structure of the empire, the towns and provinces conquered by each king have been noted, and there is essential agreement on the sequence, shape, and size of the evolving Aztec system.[37] Whether the Aztecs had a true empire has been vigorously debated, largely because of the implicit use of Karl von Clausewitz's theoretical perspective. He asserts that the main concerns of empires are territorial expansion, internal control of conquered areas, and the maintenance of secure borders, all of which require a standing army, control of the enemy's will (most easily accomplished by control of its territory and leadership), and fortifications to guarantee territorial defense.[38] When viewed from this perspective, several Aztec practices have been found wanting, throwing doubt on the imperial status of their polity. Aztec warriors have not always been considered professional soldiers (despite the existence of military orders), because membership in the army was not a full-time occupation.[39] Rather, the military was constituted from the populace as needed. But because no permanent standing army existed to impose the Aztecs' will on conquered territories, political centralization was impossible. As for fortifications and troops to man them, the absence of a standing army has been taken as proof that they did not really exist.[40] The numerous reports of fortified sites throughout Mesoamerica[41] have been dismissed with the explanation that, in the absence of a professional army, mere walls do not imply actual fortifications. Such strongholds were simply matters of expediency, in this view, not permanent military installations. Also explained away are the Aztec garrisons reported in both Spanish and native accounts.[42]

On the basis of this approach the Aztec Empire has been criticized as being politically inadequate, lacking internal cohesion, and displaying a deficient military organization. And since the Aztecs did not possess the attributes considered necessary to pursue imperial goals successfully, ipso facto they could not have effectively controlled vanquished territories. This conclusion, which seems logical because it is based on the European experience of territorial expansion, underlies much of the modern writing on Mesoamerica.[43] However, this position assumes an essential similarity between Western and Aztec polities, differing only in the strong ritual overtones in Aztec warfare. Thus recurring revolts throughout the empire and the Aztecs' failure to replace vanquished rulers are taken as indications of poor political control. Moreover, as noted above, the Aztecs apparently did not maintain either a year-round standing army to put down revolts or garrisons of troops in occupied territories. Nor were fortifications distributed equally throughout the empire, or in a spatially systematic way.[44] In short, the Aztec Empire presents a series of phenomena that, when viewed from the traditional perspective, indicates a deficient political system.

MY PERSPECTIVE

My approach, by contrast, applies perspectives that are more congruent with the Aztec Empire as it functioned. Although my focus is largely political and economic, I do not rule out the role of religion and ideology. People today fight for ideological reasons, and there is no justification for eliminating such reasons from any analysis of Aztec practices. However, people today also fight for economic and political reasons; thus one cannot simply assume a rationale for war and thereby avoid the need to demonstrate its accuracy. In my assessment of the mechanics of Aztec warfare—its role in everyday life, its practice, and its internal and external political significance—I have proceeded on the assumption that Aztec practices were as rational as those of any other society, albeit tailored to the social and technological realities of Mesoamerica.

In attempting to explain the pattern of Aztec history, I will stress the decision to go to war and the execution of that decision once reached. External political factors were of great importance in the decision when and where to fight, but so, too, were political factors within the ruling elite. The nature of Mesoamerican political integration determined not only which polities might be suitable targets, but also how and to what extent such polities might be integrated into the Aztec imperial system once they were conquered. Technological and organizational constraints placed limits on how far armies could march and on how they functioned in combat; both sets of constraints, in turn, affected the decision to engage in, or refrain from, war. By examining the Aztec Empire in terms of its own goals and objectives (rather than in terms of a theory of empire of questionable appropriateness), we can come to a new understanding of its achievements.

PART ONE

War in Aztec Life

Most of their Weapons were Bows and Arrows: The Bow-Strings were made of the Sinews of Beasts, or of Thongs of Deer-Skin twisted; and their Arrows, for want of Iron, were headed with Bones ground sharp, or Fish-Bones. They used also a kind of Darts, which sometimes they threw; and at others they managed like a Pike, as Occasion required. They had likewise long Swords, which they used with both Hands, as we do our Scimitars or Falchions, made of Wood, in which they fixed sharp Flints. The strongest of them had Clubs, pointed with Flints. And there were Slingers, who threw Stones with great Force and Skill. The defensive Arms, which were only used by Commanders and Persons of Distinction, were Coats of quilted Cotton, ill-fitted Breast-Plates, and Shields of Wood or Tortoise-Shell, adorned with Plates of such Metal as they could get; and some made use of Gold as we do of Iron. The rest were naked; and all of them deformed with various Dies and Colours with which they painted their Faces and Bodies; a Martial Sort of Ornament, which they made use of to strike a Terror into their Enemies, believing that Ugliness made them appear dreadful; as Tacitus *relates of the* Arii, *a People in* Germany, *and remarks that an Impression on the Eye is the first Step to Victory. Their Heads were covered with divers Plumes of Feathers, like Crowns, raised high to make them appear taller. They had also warlike Instruments, and Musick, with which they animated their Soldiers, and gave Signals; as Flutes made of great Canes; Sea-Shells; and a Sort of Drums, made of the Trunk of a Tree, so hollowed, and made thin, that they answered to the Stroke of the Stick a very displeasing Sound, but seemed well suited to the Ears of those People. They formed their Battalions of great Numbers, without any Order; but had Troops of Reserve to relieve where there was Occasion. They made their Attacks with great Fury, and terrible Outcries, with which they thought to intimidate their Enemies; a Custom which some accounted among the Brutalities of those* Indians, *without observing that it has been used by many antient Nations, and not despised even by the* Romans*: For* Caesar *in his* Commentaries *commends the Cries of his own Soldiers, and blames the Silence of those of* Pompey*; and* Cato *the Elder was wont to say, that he had obtained more Victories by the Cries of the Soldiers, than by their Swords; both of them being of Opinion, that the Cries of the Soldiers proceeded from the Courage that was in the Heart. We do not argue whether this is a commendable Custom or not; but only say, it was not so barbarous in the* Indians, *as to be without Example in other Nations. Their Armies were compos'd of Natives, and several Troops of Auxiliaries from the neighbouring Provinces, who came to the Assistance of their Confederates, being led by their Caziques, or some Prime* Indian *of their Family. They were divided into Companies, whose Captains led, but could scarce govern their Men; for, when they came to engage, they were directed either by Fear or Rage, as is usual among such Multitudes, being equally eager to attack, and to run away.*

ANTONIO DE SOLÍS Y RIVADENEYRA

CHAPTER 2

The Political Bases of Aztec Warfare

THE Aztecs conquered and incorporated other polities into an overarching political system. But it was a political system based on pervasive and dominating influence rather than on territorial control.

Why the Aztecs developed this form of imperial system can be understood largely in terms of technology. Mesoamerican civilization lacked efficient transportation, having neither wheeled vehicles nor draft animals. This limited the area from which goods could be drawn efficiently and correspondingly reduced the economic benefits of politically incorporating vast regions.[1] Thus economic benefits depended on exercising political control and extracting goods at local expense, by requiring tributaries to both produce and transport goods without recompense. In doing this, the Aztecs were faced with two basic options as they expanded their empire. On the one hand they could have conquered areas and consolidated their political hold by replacing local leaders and conquered troops with Aztec governors and garrisons. By exercising this much political control, the Aztecs could have extracted large quantities of goods from the conquered areas, but the cost in terms of administration, security, and the threat of rebellion would have been very high. On the other hand the Aztecs could have left the government of conquered areas in local hands. This approach would not have permitted so much economic extraction from the conquered area, but its administrative costs were relatively low. These two alternatives offered distinctly different advantages for empires. The former provides greater depth of political control but because of high manpower requirements it can be employed only in limited areas. The latter offers less control but frees more men for further imperial expansion.[2] The Aztecs employed the latter approach—a hegemonic one—and by analyzing it as such, we can explain many seemingly anomalous features of their empire.

IMPERIAL ORGANIZATION

My analysis of the Aztec Empire is based on the work of Edward N. Luttwak,[3] who analyzes political relations in terms of the degree to which they rely on force and power. Force is defined as direct physical action, which can be exercised only in proportion to its availability and is consumed as it is used. Power (in which force is a component) operates indirectly and, unlike force, is not consumed in use. Rather than being primarily physical, power is psychological—the perception of the possessor's ability to achieve its ends.

The more a political system can rely on power rather than force, the more efficient it is, because the effort required to implement its goals comes from its subordinates; that is, the subordinates police themselves, allowing the dominant polity to conserve its own force. Such a political system is more than an elaborate game of deception and bluff; the ability to wield force is a necessary requirement of power, although its actual use is not always required. A single strong example by a polity of its ability to compel compliance may render repeated demonstrations unnecessary.

The effectiveness of a political system also depends on its goals: the perceived costs of compliance must not outweigh the perceived benefits unless the dominant polity is, in fact, prepared to exercise force on its own behalf. For example, if the dominant polity has a goal of keeping the populace of the subordinate polity from rebelling, it may exert power by demanding that the people be repressed by their own leaders. Regardless of their own sentiments, the leaders will do so (using their own force) if they perceive that such repression will forestall the dominant polity's use of force, perhaps in the form of a punitive invasion. In short, as long as the subordinate polity perceives the benefits as greater than the costs, it will generally comply with the desires of the dominant polity. The very real limitations of such a political system arise from different perceptions of the power of the dominant polity. As the costs to the subordinates rise, the benefits decline, and compliance becomes increasingly unreliable. Consequently, the more exploitative a political system is perceived to be, the more it must rely on force rather than on power.

While both territorial (i.e., Clausewitzian) and hegemonic systems use force and power to dominate and control, the territorial system emphasizes the former, whereas the hegemonic system emphasizes the latter, with markedly different consequences for control, extraction, integration, and expansion. The object of a territorial empire is to conquer and directly control an area, using the minimum force necessary to conquer and then to administer it. The object of a hegemonic empire is to conquer and indirectly control an area, but economy of force does not have the same meaning. Since no imperial troops remain in the conquered areas, overwhelming force and extraordinary measures may be used in the initial conquest to intimidate the local leadership into continued compliance after the conquering army leaves. Thus what may appear as excessive force from the perspective of territorial objectives is not excessive from the perspective of hegemonic objectives. Territorial conquest may require less force than hegemonic conquest, but territorial control requires a constant level of force in the area thereafter, whereas hegemonic control does not.

The salient features of the Aztec Empire were (1) achieving political expansion without direct territorial control, (2) maintaining internal security by exercising influence over a limited range of the subordinate states' activities (usually political and economic matters), and (3) achieving the latter by generally retaining rather than replacing local officials. Because the Aztecs' imperial concerns were limited, they maintained the empire with great economy of force by relying on local resources for local security and order. The Aztec army did not have to maintain a presence but was mobilized only for further conquests or to deal with rebellions and other major disruptions. For lesser matters the threat of its return was sufficient to ensure compliance by the subordinates.

POLITICAL INTEGRATION

In Mesoamerica the basic political unit was the city and its dependencies, legitimately governed by the local ruler (*tlahtoani*, pl. *tlahtohqueh*) and his successors. Such polities were generally small, usually having a radius of about ten kilometers (6.2 miles). Though larger political organizations occasionally arose, there were few stable long-term means of integrating them. Sometimes ethnicity offered a basis for larger polities, but because each city's tlahtoani was theoretically autonomous, any political integration above the level of the city involved his relinquishment of his autonomy. The surrender of the various tlahtohqueh's authority, even if only partial, was not entirely voluntary. Rather, they subordinated themselves to a greater tlahtoani for reasons ranging from voluntary alliance to outright conquest. The result was larger polities that were built on a system of alliances in which obedience and tribute were owed to the higher tlahtoani. And although a common ethnic identity may have eased some of these hierarchical relationships, they were ultimately based on the perceived power of the dominant tlahtoani.

The surest way for a particular city to increase its perceived power was to demonstrate it through the exercise of force, which was most readily accomplished by war. To the Aztecs war was not simply the fulfillment of some religious imperative or the defense of what they perceived as vital interests. War *was* the empire. Halting war for too long diminished perceived Aztec power, undermined imperial ties, encouraged resistance to further expansion, and fostered disaffection and rebellion.

Because the Aztecs needed to maintain the perception of power to keep local rulers compliant, affronts or challenges to Aztec authority were often met with seemingly disproportionate harshness. Such exercises punished rebellious cities and emphasized the consequences of rebellion for all other tributary cities in the empire. The Aztecs' willingness to exact a harsh retribution raised the stakes for any city contemplating rebellion and played a key role in the perceived balance of costs and benefits of being in the Aztec Empire.

The threat of harsh reprisals did not entirely forestall rebellion, however, because political relations do not always conform to such logical expectations or to economic rationalities. Hopeless battles are fought and matters of principle are supported. But most important, political relationships based on power are in constant flux because perceptions of power change through time. Time, distance, new successes and allegiances, and organizational changes alter the perceptions of relative power—hence the Aztecs' emphasis on driving home the consequences of rebellion when a favorable opportunity to do so arose.

Although power was at the heart of Mesoamerican political relations, logistics played a key role in shaping empires. Spatial contiguity was not of primary importance in the integration of a hegemonic empire, but logistical constraints did foster the creation of efficient spatial arrangements, and areas otherwise of little interest to the Aztecs were conquered when they formed vital links in the supply chain.

Cities were often attacked sequentially, with the resources, intelligence, and, sometimes, the soldiers of the latest conquest aided in the next one. The army attacked targets until it exhausted its resources, attained its objectives, reached some boundary (physical or cultural), or was defeated. The Aztecs' unprecedented expansion took them to regions where they had no traditional enemies but where they were sometimes able to exploit local antagonisms by siding opportunistically with one adversary against another. They also waged campaigns of intimidation against cities they did not attack directly. Emissaries were sent to such cities to ask that they become subjects of the Aztec king—usually on reasonably favorable terms. Both the proximity of a large, trained, and obviously successful army and the object lessons burning around them led many cities to capitulate peacefully.

Because the Aztecs integrated their empire through indirect control enforced through their opponents' perception of their power, victory and defeat were conceived of differently than in a more territorial system. Victory did not involve the destruction of the target polity's army but their acquiescence in becoming tributaries of the Aztecs. Thus unconquered city-states or empires were not necessarily those that remained unbeaten on the battlefield but those that refused to acknowledge their tributary status after the withdrawal of Aztec forces. And one reason that potential tributaries sometimes resisted the Aztecs so fiercely was that they feared an alteration in their own internal hierarchy of power after conquest. This threat came not from the Aztecs, who usually retained existing arrangements, but from subordinate groups within a polity, which sometimes shifted their allegiance directly to the Aztecs, bypassing and undermining the power of the local tlahtoani.

Governance of these conquered areas was tailored to the hegemonic imperial system: the Aztecs were unconcerned about many local activities. They allowed local laws, customs, and beliefs that did not obstruct imperial aims to be retained, even when they differed from those of the Aztecs. Thus incorporation into the Aztec Empire did not necessarily mean that tributaries altered their behavior vis-à-vis other subgroups. In effect, there was no imperial foreign policy, just an Aztec foreign policy coexisting with the policies of individual tributaries as long as the latter did not conflict with the former. This limited interference in local affairs made submission more palatable to the tributary cities, and often they did not vigorously contest domination. Conquest was not a matter of total intimidation and destruction of the tributaries. Although incorporation into the empire had liabilities—notably, the imposition of annual tribute payments, logistical support for the Aztec armies, and, sometimes, troop support—there were also benefits, such as participation in the Aztec trading network.

As long as the core of the coalition remained strong, it was in the allied cities' best interests to adhere to it. But because each city retained its own leadership with its own goals and ambitions, the system was unstable. Any weakness in the core alliance reduced its ability to enforce adherence and offered an opportunity for cities to withdraw. As a result, the system possessed considerable elasticity, allowing rapid shifts in power.[4]

To avoid any perception of weakness, information about conquests was disseminated, which was as significant to the Aztecs as the actual victories. Thus, when they won a victory, they dispatched messengers with the news. Often these messengers were not merely runners but formal emissaries of some status. They disseminated information, but their primary function was to elicit new signs of loyalty from tributaries potentially disaffected from the empire. The Aztecs also sent emissaries to potential tributaries with gifts (and implicit threats) to seek peaceful submission. The most fruitful time for such missions was immediately after a successful campaign.

When a war was lost, that also was learned, at least along the army's line of march. Enemy spies and wide-ranging merchants quickly spread such information throughout Mesoamerica. Unlike victories, which were formally communicated both throughout the empire and to enemies and nonallied polities, formal news of defeat was largely confined to the empire, usually as a prelude to recruitment of troops and arms for another campaign.

POLITICAL OPPOSITION

Conquest and internal control were only two of the problems the Aztecs faced. Another was the presence of independent and hostile polities. Individual city-states posed little threat because of their relatively small size, but complex polities such as multicity states, multicity alliances, and empires, posed greater problems.

Multicity states composed of several major cities and their dependencies, varied considerably in their internal power structures, but their member cities possessed relatively autonomous leadership, offering a range of centralized control. Those states reinforced by ethnic ties, however, were relatively stable and unlikely to fragment under external pressure.

Multicity alliances were composed of allied city-states or multicity states drawn together by mutually perceived interests, including security from external military threats, and they could thus be of considerable size. Although they lacked the coordinated and disciplined control of a centralized government and persistent stabilizing ties, such as a common ethnic identity, they were less bound by geographical limitations. These alliances were essentially special-purpose institutions, arising from perceived needs and persisting as long as the needs were satisfied. But over time if there were no changes in the way an alliance was structured, it disintegrated when its members' interests diverged.

Empires were the most complex Mesoamerican polities, reaching considerable size and having a relatively centralized and hierarchical political organization. Being multiethnic, empires suffered some internal divergence of interests, but because they were centralized (at least for imperial matters), they could ward off some of the centrifugal forces that pried alliances apart. Thus, although the various political subunits were not free to leave the empire, they might nevertheless lack a major commitment to it. Because these complex polities had larger populations and greater military potential than individual city-states, the Aztecs used different tactics in dealing with them.

City-states generally controlled relatively modest areas, so they confronted attacking armies at the outskirts of the city, and the defenders' defeat in battle meant defeat of the city-state. The attackers could immediately follow up such a victory by sacking the city. Empires and multicity groupings, by contrast, controlled relatively large areas and intercepted attacking armies at their borders, where the loss of a battle meant only a tactical defeat rather than the loss of the entire polity. The defenders could simply fall back, regroup in friendly territory, and renew the fight. Thus complex polities could not be easily conquered in their entirety; the attackers could only chip away at the borders, since each side's main centers remained far from the battle, and transport and logistical constraints made deep penetration of hostile territory very difficult. Nevertheless, the advantage lay with the aggressor: defenders risked their armies and their polities (entirely, if they were city-states; partially, if they were larger), while the attackers risked only their armies.

Alliances could be formed en route to the battle to offset the strength in depth of larger polities, but the effectiveness of this strategy depended on the degree of internal disaffection in the defender's system. Generally, this strategy was most feasible for alliances, less so for an empire, and least for a multicity state.

The presence of moderately disaffected elements was not too significant as long as the defenders kept the attackers at a distance so that they could not challenge the polity's internal control. But once the defender's area of dominance was penetrated, its internal control was demonstrably challenged, and the dissidents could ally with the invader. These considerations of internal control further prompted larger polities to meet the enemy at the borders, not for territorial purposes but for hegemonic ones; the defending polity needed to ensure that its internal support remained intact and, inter alia, this was achieved by marching to the borders.

The defense-in-depth strategy was an effective one, and the more area a state dominated, the safer it was from external conquest, all other things being equal. This safety, together with the vulnerability of individual city-states, led to their general absorption into one of the complex polities.

Cities between more powerful polities were in a difficult position. As polities expanded, nearby city-states could not remain neutral; only alliances offered any security. Conquest left no choice of allies, so many precariously situated towns selected allies on the basis of military considerations, frequently favoring whichever polity could and would project force into the area. A city-state located where several polities exercised influence, might consider factors such as ethnic ties, trade, and access to markets.

Whatever the choice, city-states situated between power blocs allied with one or the other and thereby formed the imperial perimeter. This realignment of perimeter cities altered the relationship of the competing power blocs, since the successful empire gained additional military and logistical capacity from these city-states. Similarly, the newly-incorporated city-states gained by being tied into the empire's trading network (which was exceptionally far-flung and prosperous) and by falling under its protection. Conversely, however, the city-states were then vulnerable to attack by an enemy over matters previously of concern only to the empire, and they were dependent on that empire for protection.

The existence of various power blocs altered the political environment in Mesoamerica but did not lead to the ultimate emergence of only two competing coalitions, largely because of the limits on projecting force. Logistical constraints meant that areas had to be relatively contiguous to be incorporated or to form an effective coalition, because widely dispersed areas could not readily reinforce one another. Moreover, this type of empire was effective only when the conquered groups were settled, civilized peoples. The Aztecs' method of extracting goods through an existing power structure was unsuited to seminomadic peoples such as the Chichimecs who lacked formally recognized political hierarchies and offices.[5]

REBELLION

Empire building also caused internal opposition, the most serious manifestation of which was rebellion. Rebellions ranged from the failure of a region to grant the Aztecs certain presumed rights, such as unobstructed transit, to defaulting on tribute payments, to killing Aztecs and their subjects. Few or no imperial forces were necessary or available at any given location in the empire; only the local leadership kept tributary provinces loyal. But because the hegemonic system depended on the perception of Aztec power, this situation could change with any alteration in the status quo; thus one of the expected results of a hegemonic system was the occurrence of intermittent rebellions.

Rebellions were likeliest to succeed when the empire was temporarily weakened (e.g., after a disastrous campaign or the death of a king), especially if the rebellious polity could form an alliance with another power nearby. Thus cities near Tenochtitlan were less likely to revolt, even under oppressive conditions, than were more distant cities and those near independent regional powers.[6] Moreover, many of the tributaries that had been "voluntarily" incorporated into the empire—particularly those at some distance from Tenochtitlan—were less reliable allies and more likely to rebel than those that had been militarily subdued, because they had never experienced the full might of the empire.

Although they were expected, rebellions were not taken lightly, and the Aztecs monitored the level of disaffection among tributaries at least intermittently. When rebellions broke out, vigorous action was crucial to prevent their spread. When the empire was weak, less direct challenges and affronts were ignored, but they were not forgotten.

The Aztecs could have reduced the threat of rebellion within the empire by fragmenting large tributaries to increase the power disparity between ruler and subject, but they rarely did so. They generally retained large tributaries intact because larger client states could more effectively maintain internal order. This arrangement also lessened Aztec military cost, and the benefits of greater internal order apparently outweighed the threat to imperial stability.

SUMMARY

In summary, the Aztecs' reliance on hegemonic rather than territorial control produced an empire of distinctive character and vast expanse but loose control. Mesoamerican technological contraints limited the size, strength, and duration of forays outside the empire, and such engagements took on strategic characteristics that varied with the political nature of the target. Furthermore, the Aztec Empire was essentially an alliance, and was expectedly fraught with rebellion. Nevertheless, the system functioned admirably within its cultural context, and through it the Aztecs expanded their domain to a size unprecedented in Mesoamerica.

CHAPTER 3

The Military Life Cycle

CONQUEST and warfare in the Aztec Empire were tied directly to the army and its organization. This organization is not clearly understood: however, the interpretations of many modern writers often conflict.[1] Unfortunately, there is no extant account of the complete ranking system and organization of the Aztec army. Thus, any description of the army system must necessarily be a reconstruction.

There were army ranks similar to the modern "general," "major," and so forth, and there were likewise general groupings of warriors much like our "enlisted men" and "officers."[2] However, the members of the Aztec army had many different and cross-cutting loyalties—to the city, the *calpolli* (ward), the king, the calpolli headman, and so forth—and their rank did not depend merely on their position in a monolithic, centralized military hierarchy. Thus, an exact classification of ranks and statuses, in the modern Western military sense, is falsely precise and distorts the way the Aztecs conceived of their military system. There are parallels between the Aztec and Western systems, born of similar organizational and operational necessities, but these similarities should not blind us to the differences.

The historical development of the Aztec military system creates another problem in interpretation. The writings of the conquistadors and other chroniclers offer the impression that the Aztec military system as encountered by the first Spaniards reflected an unchanging norm. In fact, Aztec developments were not always simply an elaboration on common Mesoamerican themes. Both the political and military organizations of other central Mexican polities varied considerably.[3] Furthermore, the Aztec military system had been evolving rapidly. The army created new offices and it promulgated

890433

new requirements for holding existing offices. My discussion of the system reflects the situation in the last years of the Aztec Empire; changes in this system are discussed in chapters 9–15.

MILITARY RANK

Along with commerce and the priesthood, a distinguished military career was the most widely accessible of the three major avenues for social advancement in Aztec society. Social advancement was usually attained through feats of military prowess, which were generally measured by the number of captives taken in battle. This does not mean that slaying the enemy was not important—it was—but success that led to advancement lay in taking the enemy captive. Furthermore, some enemies were regarded as notoriously more difficult to capture than others, so achieving rank depended on the quality as well as the quantity of one's captives.[4]

Historical accounts place the greatest emphasis on the elite warriors, but most of the army was composed of commoners without military distinction—*yaoquizqueh* (sing. *yaoquizqui*). It was possible to rise from this status by virtue of one's deeds and ability, but social class did influence one's military career, despite the emphasis on advancement by merit. To appreciate what the system of achievements and class distinction entailed requires some consideration of both the context of Aztec social classes and the individual's military life cycle.

SOCIAL ORGANIZATION

Military ranking was intimately tied to the overall social structure of Aztec society, and social ranking was intimately tied to political offices, the latter defining rights and requiring the holder to have specified a status.[5] At the apex of Aztec society were the ruling nobles who were subdivided into several categories. The tlahtoani was the ruler of a province or town—the king. A tlahtoani who was subordinate to a higher tlahtoani was called a *teuctlahtoh* (pl. *teuctlahtohqueh*). The occupants of these positions were nobles who received their offices through some form of hereditary succession, although the process was not uniform throughout central Mexico. The tlahtohqueh were supported by tribute from commoners and subject towns, as well as by the income from lands (*tlahtohcamilli*) belonging to the office of the ruler.

Below the tlahtohqueh were the *teteuctin* (sing. *teuctli*), or lords, who held positions of varying status and authority. (The tlahtohqueh were also teteuctin.) The teuctli was head of the *teuccalli* (lord's house), to which some tribute-paying commoners were attached. He could also possess patrimonial lands received through inheritance. The position of teuctli was hereditary for life, with his successor nominally appointed by the tlahtoani and the teteuctin often served in the capacity of judges, meeting in the tlahtoani's palace and ruling on the affairs of commoners.

Below the ruling class were the *pipiltin* (sing. *pilli*), hereditary nobles who were the offspring of tlahtohqueh and teteuctin. They held many governmental positions, such as ambassador or minister of justice and were supported by the tlahtoani. They were allocated lands (*pillalli*) worked by *mayehqueh* (sing. *mayeh*), but these lands were considered part of the holdings of the teuccalli. There were several ranks within the pipiltin class: *tlahtohcapilli* (a tlahtoani's son), *tecpilli* or *teucpilli* (a teuctli's son), *tlazohpilli* (son of a legitimate wife), and *calpanpilli* (son of a concubine).

Below the pipiltin were the *cuauhpipiltin*, commoners who had achieved noble status by virtue of their deeds in war. They were freed from their tribute obligations, received lands, and took part in the deliberations of the war council with the distinguished warriors of noble rank. But the cuauhpipiltin did not enjoy full noble rights: they could have no tenants on their lands, nor could they sell their lands to commoners, they could join the knightly orders, but, although their sons became pipiltin, their humble heritage was remembered. The position of *achcacauhtin* (executioners, keepers of the arms, and military trainers; sing. *achcauhtli*) was apparently held by members of the cuauhpipiltin.

Below the nobility were the *calpolehqueh* (sing. *calpoleh*), the calpolli (or ward) headmen, who were responsible for watching after the interests of the members of their calpolli and representing them before the government. The position was nominally an elected one but tended to be hereditary in practice, and Zorita's sixteenth-century account indicates that they were commoners (but see the discussion in chap. 13).

Below the nobility were the commoners, the *macehualtin* (sing.

macehualli), who formed the bulk of Aztec society. They were organized by calpolli, worked with their hands, and paid tribute in goods and labor until the age of fifty-two. However, some particularly important commoner groups, such as the merchants and artisans, were exempt from some types of labor obligations and paid tribute in their wares.

Another group of commoners, the mayehqueh or *tlalmaitin* (sing. *tlalmaitl*), were permanent laborers on the patrimonial lands of the nobility. This was a hereditary position, and except for war service the mayehqueh were exempt from tribute obligations.

Below both the macehualtin and the mayehqueh were the slaves (*tlatlacohtin*; sing. *tlacohtli*). These slaves had usually sold themselves into service, although some had been enslaved as punishment for criminal acts. The rights of their owners were limited, and except for labor, slaves were free, could marry, and could own property, including other slaves. Not all of these social groups were eligible for military service, nor did everyone who was eligible aspire to it. But those who did received lengthy and professional training.

MILITARY TRAINING

Warfare no doubt emphasizes people's aggressive behavior. Certainly the Spanish conquistadors saw it thus in the Aztecs. The Anonymous Conqueror[6] described them as very warlike and fearless, facing death with absolute determination, and Cortés[7] reported that they were courageous men. The ability to face death on the battlefield was a valued trait, one that was not innate but was learned from an early age.

Two separate types of schools offered military training; the *telpochcalli* and the *calmecac*. Which school one entered depended largely on heritage. The following account presents the idealized sequence of events.

Four days after a male child was born, he was given the symbols of his father's profession. If the father was a soldier, these were a shield and arrows, and the child's umbilical cord was then buried with the weapons in the direction from which the enemy was expected. If the parents wished the child to serve in the army, when he was twenty days old he was taken to a school—the telpochcalli—and presented to the master of youths (*tiachcauh*; pl. *tiachcahuan*) or instructor of youths (*telpochtlahtoh*; pl. *telpochtlahtohqueh*), with the appropriate gifts so he would be accepted when he came of age.[8] Each calpolli in the city possessed its own telpochcalli;[9] most of the students were commoners, but sons of nobles also attended—probably the traditional nobility directly associated with the leadership of each calpolli rather than those more directly dependent on the king.[10]

When the boy was still small, the hair on his head was shorn. But at the age of ten a tuft of hair was allowed to grow on the back of his head, and by the age of fifteen, it was long, signifying that he had not yet taken captives in war.[11] The father relinquished responsibility to the telpochcalli to train the youth to become a warrior.[12] The telpochcalli was apparently responsible for educating all the youths of their respective calpolli (an average of 419 to 559 youths between fifteen and twenty years old for each of the twenty telpochcalli in Tenochtitlan in 1519),[13] but not everyone who entered became a warrior or was intended to. Youths destined for the telpochcalli entered at the age of fifteen and were dedicated to the patron god, Tezcatl-Ihpoca (also called Yaotzin or Titlacahuan).[14] The parents entreated the school priests to accept the responsibility of training the child, as follows:

> Our Lord, the Ever-present, places you [priests] here. And we have come to tell you [lit., and now you hear and understand] that our Lord has given us a child [lit., has dropped a jewel, a quetzal-plume]. A son has arrived, and here he in truth now wishes to stay [lit., He wants to become substantial]. He is a glittering jewel. But we confess we do not know how to raise him [lit., Shall we put a spindle and a weaver's reed in his hand?]. Therefore, he is yours; he is your child, your son. We place him in your charge [lit., into your laps and on your carrying devices]. You are skilled in training children to be men [lit., You have children. You raise men, you bring up men. You create eagles, you create jaguars. You bring up men for our Mother and our Father, Tlalteuctli (Earthlady) and Tonatiuh (Sun)].
>
> And now we dedicate him to the war god [lit., to Night-and-Wind, the Lord, the Youth, Honored Enemy, He-whose-slaves-we-are, Tezcatl-Ihpoca]. We hope he will have a long life [lit., Perhaps our Lord will support him for a little while]. We leave him to become a warrior [lit., a youth]. There he will live at the place that is the house of penance, the house of lamentation, the house of tears, the house for youths, where warriors [lit., the eagles and jaguars] live and become men. There people serve our lord [lit., All use their hands upon our Lord's belly and throat], and there he recognizes people, there he continually rewards [lit., continually gives things to] people, there he looks at people with compassion, and he gives power [lit., the eagle mat and the jaguar mat] to those who are worthy [lit., whose who weep and those who are sad], from there he who is our Lord sends them forth, from there our

Lord's acquaintances ascend to power [lit., press down on and guard the mat and chair].

But with regard to this [child], are we worthy [lit., Are we weepers? Are we sad ones?] Will we succeed? [lit., Will we have a reward and a recompense?]? Will he become perceptive? Will he become sensible? Perhaps this will not have happened. [And in that case,] oh how unfortunate will we old men and old women be! Would that you truly accept him! Would that you take him! May he follow the sons who have been reared and trained and those who are worthy sons, the worthy warriors [lit., the worthy eagles, the worthy jaguars].[15]

The priests, in granting the petition and accepting the responsiblity for the child, answered:

You do us honor [lit., Your hearts have granted things]. Indeed we listen here for the war god [lit., our Lord, the Lord, the Youth, Night-and-Wind, Honored Enemy]. But, in fact, he is the one whom you entreat, whom you call to. Verily, he is the one to whom you give your son [lit., your jewel, your quetzal-plume], your engendered one. We do no more than accept him, we take the one whom you give to our Lord. We are only his representatives [lit., We only hear things for him]. But we do not know what the god wants of your son [lit., How is he wanting him?]. We do not know what plans he has for him [lit., How is he who is our Lord desiring it for your son (lit., your jewel, your quetzal-plume)?]. We are ignorant of such things [lit., Truly people say that we humans (lit., we who are commoners) are unhappy. It is in the darkness that we speak]. What endowments does the child have [lit., How and with what is our Lord, the Ever-present, distributing it to the child? How was he adorned?]? What program of life was assigned to him [lit., How was he commanded in the darkness?]? What role will he play in life [lit., With what was he dressed? What did he come carrying when he was born?]? And what will his fate be [lit., What is his day-sign? And, furthermore, on which one was he washed?]? How will he fare [lit., What is the child's recompense? What is his reward?]? Truly people say that we humans [lit., we who are commoners] ponder such things uselessly [lit., uselessly invent it]. But will they not from somewhere later on earth be fulfilled? From the first we come carrying our apportioned lot [lit., our property]. Right off from the darkness it goes along with us.

And as for this one, may he enter into the service of the god [lit., enter into sweeping, tidying things up, setting things in order out of the way, and laying fires]. Would that he serve [lit., use hands upon the belly and upon the throat of] our Lord, Night-and-Wind. We hope his potential will be realized [lit., Would that his gift be placed there above in the place of light, (his gift) with which he comes clothed, how he arose, wherewith he was adorned in the darkness]. But perhaps he will die young [lit., he will lose everything]; perhaps it is our reward; perhaps it is our recompense. Or perhaps he will live a long life [lit., Perhaps Tonatiuh will pursue him in common]. Or perhaps Tonatiuh will reject him [lit., will throw him thither, will thrust him thither into hands].

But now what can we say to comfort you [lit., How can we say whether we will comfort you?]? We are ignorant of what will happen in the future [lit., Shall we say that this one will be thus, that he will be this one, that he will do this, that our Lord will change this one, that this one will be fulfilled, that he will become something, that he will succeed, that he will live upon the land?]. But perhaps it will be our reward, our recompense, that he will perhaps act shamefully [lit., that he will perhaps continually wallow in dust and filth upon the land]. Perhaps he will be a thief [lit., will use his hands in someone's pot, in someone's bowl]. Perhaps he will be an adulterer [lit., will seize a skirt and a blouse from someone, and he will amuse them]. Or perhaps he will continually see misery and difficulties.

May we be educators, may we be trainers. May he accept us as his parents [lit., Would that one word or one phrase, motherhood and fatherhood, issue forth]. We hope we will inspire him [lit., Will we enter within him to set down our heart for him?].

And now you should [lit. would that you] still continue with prayers and weeping and tears. Beware lest you become negligent because of sleep. Continually call on the Ever-present with piety, for we do not know God's will with regard to the boy [lit., How does he want him for us? How does he say it for him?].[16]

While he was in the telpochcalli, the youth was given duties, such as sweeping the house and laying the fires, and he began his penances. The leaders, the *yaotequihuahqueh* (sing. *yaotequihuah*), tested the youth to see if he would fare well in war and took him on campaigns as a shield-bearer. The youth ate in his own home but was required to sleep at the school and work and associate with other telpochcalli youths during the day. At sunset the youths bathed and painted their bodies black, but not their faces, and donned netted capes and neck bands. When the sun had set, they started the fires and sang and danced until after midnight, when they retired to the telpochcalli to sleep.[17]

Training in matters of war was primarily entrusted to the war captains (yaotequihuahqueh) and the trainers (achcacauhtin), although noble veteran warriors (pipiltin) also played a rôle in the education of the youths.[18] Veteran warriors taught the youths to handle weapons—how to shoot arrows from a bow, how to throw darts with an atlatl, how to hold a shield, and how to hold a sword. When an instructing warrior went to war, he took a youth as an apprentice to carry his supplies and arms.[19] Many youths sought to became warriors,[20] though life in the telpochcalli was spartan.[21]

The telpochcalli youths were prohibited from drinking *octli* (pulque) on pain of death by public beating or by hanging. These penalties applied to the attending sons of the nobility, but the punishments were carried out in private. The youths could not marry, but they were permitted mistresses.[22]

Many who entered the calmecac were trained to become priests, but the political and military leaders of the Aztecs were also trained there.[23] Those trained in the calmecac were overwhelmingly noble—the sons of the tlahtohqueh and the sons of some of the pipiltin (apparently those less dependent on the calpolli, although some commoners also attended).[24] Apparently the commoners who entered the calmecac did so to become priests, while the nobles could also become priests or, as many seemingly did, warriors.[25] Attached to temples, the calmecac were dedicated to patron gods—the calmecac in Tenochtitlan was located in the main ceremonial complex[26] and was dedicated to the god Quetzalcoatl—and there the noble youths were trained more privately and individually in the ways of war.[27] When he vowed to raise his son in the calmecac, the king, noble, or lord prepared food and drink and summoned the priests and besought them:

Our lords, priests, welcome [lit., Here you came bringing yourselves. You have brought your feet]. We hope your coming here has not inconvenienced you [lit., Perhaps somewhere you have stumbled against sticks or straw; perhaps somewhere you have twisted a foot or hit it on something]. Indeed our Lord places you here. You pick up, you hear—and it is true—that now we have a son [lit., The Lord, the Ever-present, has released from his hand a jewel, a quetzal-plume]. We dream, we wake up, and it is true now that what he is is a little child, a little son. But we do not know how to raise him [lit., Shall we not give him a spindle and a weaver's reed?]. Therefore, he is yours, your property. Now we dedicate him to the Lord, our Prince, Quetzalcoatl, the One-befeathered-in-black. He will enter the *calmecac*, the house of lamentation, the house of tears, the house of piety, where our nobles, the children, are reared and are trained. And there the Ever-present is prayed to [lit., is asked for things], there people serve our Lord [lit., people use hands upon our Lord's belly and throat]. There he is importuned for things with weeping, with tears, and with sighing. And there he continually rewards people, there he chooses people. Indeed there we dedicate him into his house, where conch-shells are blown and fires are lit, where our nobles, the children, are reared. There he will do the sweeping, the cleaning up, the setting of things off to one side for our Lord. We place him in your charge [lit., in your laps, upon your backs, on your carrying devices]. May you do us this honor [lit.,May your hearts grant things]. We give a child to you. May you consent to this. May you take him. May he follow and mingle with those who are being reared, those who are being trained, the ones who perform penance day and night, those who go around walking on their elbows and knees, those who call and shout to our Lord, those who are worthy [lit., those who weep, those who are sad, those who sigh].

Our speech is finished [lit., This is all]. You are informed of it, you hear it, O priests.[28]

The priests answered:

Here we have heard your utterance [lit., We get and take your breath and your words]. May we be worthy, may we be worthy of the favor, may we deserve it. Here your utterance [lit., your breath and your words] comes forth because you are concerned for your son [lit., your jewel, your quetzal-plume]. But we only represent the god [lit., only hear things for our Lord, our Prince, Quetzalcoatl, the One-befeathered-in-black]. We do not know his will with regard to your son [lit., How does he desire things for your jewel, your quetzal-plume?]. And we do not know his will with regard to you [lit., How does he desire things for you yourselves?]. We do not know how your son will fare [lit., How will the jewel, the quetzal-plume, be?]. We certainly pray to him [i.e., to God] that this one be fulfilled, that this one prosper. Let us have full confidence in our Lord, the Ever-present, regarding what he desires for us. Let us have full confidence.[29]

The priests then took the youth to the temple, and the parents gave them gifts—rich gifts if the parents were rich and poor ones if they were poor. The child was then anointed in black, including his face, and given neck bands of birthwort roots if his parents were rich and of loose cotton if his parents were poor. The priests cut his ears to draw blood for a sacrifice to Quetzalcoatl. If the child was still young, he was then taken home, unless he was the son of the king.[30]

The age at which youths entered the calmecac is uncertain: several are recorded, which may reflect status differences or various permissible ages for entry. The king's sons apparently entered the temple at the age of five and were raised there until they were old enough to go to war.[31] The sons of the other nobles entered the calmecac at ages recorded as ranging from six to thirteen.[32] In any case, training in the calmecac began earlier than that in the telpochcalli.

Training in the calmecac was rigorous, covering the intellectual aspects of Aztec life plus all that was taught in the telpochcalli. The youths were taught discourse, songs, reading and writing, the calendar, the book of dreams, and the book of years. The youths prepared their own food, and at midnight everyone arose and prayed to the goods. Among their duties were sweeping before dawn, and gathering wood to tend the fire.[33] At the age of fifteen they began their formal instruction in the use of weapons.[34]

The sons of nobles and warriors were held to be more inclined to the warrior's life than were others.[35] They probably did excel, since the sons of nobles, whether trained in the telpochcalli or the calmecac, received military instruction in the houses of the eagle and jaguar military orders—the *cuauhcalli* (eagle house)—from the members of the order that each had vowed to join (see fig. 1).[36] Thus the military training of noble youths was better than that of commoner youths.

While accompanying the warriors on campaigns, the youths learned about military life and lost their fear of battle. At the age of twenty those youths who wanted to become warriors went to war. But first the youth's parents approached the veteran warriors with food, drink, and gifts, to seek a sponsor to take their son to war. The nobles' greater ability to pay doubtless resulted in their sons' being watched over by better and more experienced warriors than were the sons of poorer parents, and the success rate in battle was predictably higher for the noble youths. The warriors took great care of the youths in the wars, and they showed the youths how to take captives once the tide turned in the Aztecs' favor.[37]

If he was fortunate, the youth took a captive unaided. If he had assistance (from up to five others), a decision was made about who had actually made the capture, and the captive was apportioned among those helping, in the following manner: the actual captor took the body and the right thigh; the second who had helped him received the left thigh; the third took the right upper arm; the fourth took the left upper arm; the fifth took the right forearm; and the sixth took the left forearm. A captor's tuft of hair was cut. If the capture had required the help of others, however, the hair was shorn on the left side of his head, but the right side was left long, reaching the bottom of his ear. Thus the youth was honored, but he was also told to take another captive unassisted to prove that he was a man.[38]

A youth who had failed to take a captive after going to war three or four times was called a *cuexpalchicacpol*, or "youth with a baby's lock." Thus shamed, he redoubled his efforts to take a captive, but if he failed to take one unassisted, his head was pasted with feathers. One who took no captives at all, even with asistance, had the crown of his head shaved, and he would never achieve martial fame.[39] This was a consideration only for youths aspiring to a military career. The

Fig. 1. Detail from bench in the House of the Eagle Warriors, Templo Mayor. (Courtesy of the Instituto Nacional de Antropología e Historia, Mexico)

bulk of the army was made up of commoners who were sent into battle as auxiliaries and had little hope of achieving martial fame in any case.

MILITARY LIFE

If a youth showed courage on the battlefield, he might be admitted to the company of the warriors.[40] Rank was achieved primarily by the taking of captives, and it was reflected in one's dress (see fig. 2). For valiant deeds in battle, warriors—both nobles and commoners—were given great honors, rewards, arms, and insignia, as merited.[41]

When a youth took a captive without any assistance, he became a leading youth (*telpochyahqui*) and a captor (*tlamani*), and was taken before the king. There his face was painted with red ochre, the king's *calpixqueh* (tribute collectors; sing. *calpixqui*) anointed his temples with yellow ochre, and the king gave him warrior's garb to be worn in peacetime.[42] Accounts of this clothing differ. Sahagún[43] reports that the young warrior was given an orange cape with a striped border and scorpion design and two breech clouts, one carmine-colored with long ends, and the other of many colors. The *Codex Mendoza*[44] reports the clothing as consisting of a mantle with a flower design, called a *tiyahcauhtlatquitl*, or "brave man's equipment." In either

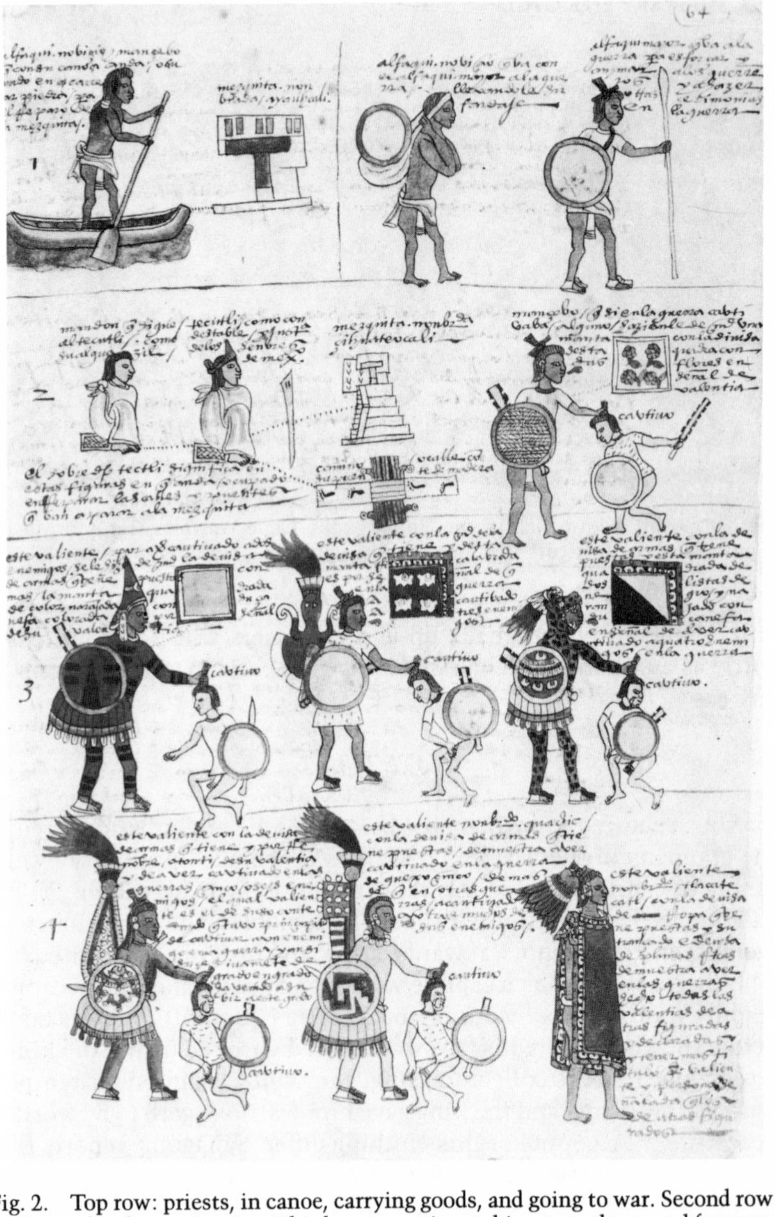

Fig. 2. Top row: priests, in canoe, carrying goods, and going to war. Second row: lord; youth taking a captive. Third row: warriors taking two, three, and four captives, and the attire achieved by these levels of attainment. Fourth row: an *otomitl* warrior, a *cuahchic* warrior, and a *tlacateccatl*. (*Codex Mendoza*, MS Arch. Seld. A 1, fol. 65; courtesy of the Bodleian Library, Oxford)

case, the simple clothing of the undistinguished warrior was abandoned in favor of a costume denoting accomplishment.

Soldiers were also rewarded for their actions in direct material recompense. According to the available documents, most of the rewards went to nobles. This is to be expected, for at least two reasons. First, the most spectacular rewards were given to nobles, rather than to commoners, and were thus more often reflected in the records. And second, nobles, by virtue of their superior training and opportunities were likelier to perform the deeds that would be rewarded. However, commoners were also rewarded when suitable acts were performed. Thus youths often went to war as novices to carry loads and returned warriors. The youths who were still not accomplished warriors continued to live together in the telpochcalli.[45]

For taking two captives the warrior was again taken to the king's palace and was given a mantle with red trim.[46] For taking three captives he was given a richly worked garment, called an *ehehcailacatzcozcatl*, or "wind twisted jewel" mantle, and a *tlepapalotlahuiztli*, or "fire butterfly device," which had an accompanying red-and-white feather tunic.[47] He became a tiachcauh, a leader of youths, and resided in the telpochcalli to instruct the young men about war.[48] For taking four captives a warrior was given a device of arms and the *ocelototec* war garment, a mantle of two stripes of black and orange with a border.[49] The king allowed the warrior's hair to be cut like that of a *tequihuah*, a veteran warrior, and he assumed the titles of the veteran warrior—*mexihcatl tequihuah, tolnahuacatl tequihuah*, or *cihuatecpanecatl tequihuah*.[50] The tequihuahqueh were those who had been presented honors, weapons, and special insignia by the king to distinguish them from the rest of the soldiers.[51]

How a warrior was treated after he took more than four captives varied, depending on the reputed ferocity of the enemies he had captured. Which enemies were considered particularly ferocious changed throughout the history of the Aztec conquests as different groups were encountered and varying resistence was met. At the time of the Spanish conquest Huaxtecs and the other coastal groups were held in low esteem, so for capturing even ten of these a warrior received no further fame but was simply known as yaotequihuah, (veteran warrior and leader of the youths). If his fifth captive was from Atlixco, Huexotzinco, or Tliliuhqui-Tepec (Tliliuhquitepec), however, he gained great honor and was named *cuauhyahcatl* (great captain). The king gave him many gifts: a blue labret; a headband with two tufts of eagle feathers and ornamented with silver flint knives; leather earplugs; a bright-red, rich, netting cape; a diagonally divided two-colored cape; and a leather cape.[52]

Taking another captive from Atlixco or Huexotzinco was considered an awesome accomplishment, and the captor was given further gifts: a long yellow labret (he could alternately use the yellow one and the blue one); a headband with two tufts of eagle feathers and ornamented with gold flint knives; a cape with several possible designs—serpent mask, earthen vessel—or a jaguar cape with a red border; a breech clout with long ends and having either the eagle claw or marketplace design; and black sandals with red or orange leather thongs. For his deeds the warrior received the title of *tlacochcalcatl* (commanding general) or *tlacateccatl* (general).[53]

The awards to the warriors for their exploits were made at the feast of *Tlacaxipehualiztli* (Flaying of Men), held during the second of the eighteen months of the solar calendar. Then each veteran warrior was given four pieces of black cloth, and the telpochyahqui, or leading youths, were given capes.[54] Thus, clothing was not merely a necessary or vanity item among the Aztecs but also a marker of martial and social status.

Commoner warriors were not entitled to wear the garb of the accomplished warriors but instead wore only a maguey-fiber mantle without special designs or fine embroidery and did not use sandals. Their mantle could not reach below the knee, on pain of death, unless it was concealing war wounds on the legs.[55] Nor could insignia awarded for valorous deeds be worn by novices entering battle for the first time, whether commoners or nobles.[56] For their first battle novices wore clothing of maguey fiber,[57] and undistinguished warriors wore only a breechcloth (*maxtlatl*) and body paint.[58] Only the military leaders wore body armor (*ichcahuipilli*).[59] Valiant warriors and war leaders wore neck bands of shells or gold, netted capes of twisted maguey fiber and leather corselets, and turquoise earplugs, and they painted their faces with black stripes.[60] Only nobles could wear lip plugs, earplugs, and noseplugs of gold and precious stones. Valiant warriors and military leaders could also wear plugs, but only of such common materials as wood or bone.[61] Only the king and great lords could wear armbands, anklets, and headbands of gold.[62] In peacetime the king wore a blue and white mantle, called a *xiuhtilmahtli*, which no one else could wear, on pain of death. In war he wore many jeweled ornaments as well as a helmet and an insignia called a *cuah*-

chiahtli, used only by kings. Since he was also an emperor, he wore two plume tassels, called *ananacaztli*, on the side of the royal insignia crest[63] (see fig. 13). But this distinction between wartime and peacetime was not absolute. Some parts of the uniforms were principally status markers without significant protective function, such as greaves and armbands, yet major leaders occasionally wore them in battle.

Thus, status achieved in war was marked by the honors one received, the way one's hair was worn, the jewelry one was entitled to wear, the clothing one wore in peace, and the arms, armor, and insignia one wore in war. Status was indicated for both commoners and nobles, although in different ways. But what could be worn and by whom changed during the course of Aztec history.

The use of body paint in warfare extended throughout Mesoamerica and was practiced, inter alia, by Mayas, Tlaxcaltecs, Huaxtecs,[64] and Aztecs.[65] Among the Aztecs, the use of specific face paint was a sign of martial accomplishment. Thus, when a warrior took a captive, his face was stained red and yellow.[66] The valiant soldiers and *tiyahcahuan* painted their body black and painted their face with black stripes on which they sprinkled iron pyrite (*apetztli*).[67] The members of the military orders painted themselves as well. The "shorn ones" (see below) had half their heads painted blue and the other half red or yellow.[68] Thus, face and body paint were used in much the same fashion as insignia presented for valorous deeds.

Individual markings were given to warriors in recognition of martial feats.[69] These markings, often in the form of helmets and crests of various sorts, shields, and other attire, indicated the general rank one held in the military, such as tequihuah, but could also be highly individualistic. Like other aspects of military ranking among the Aztecs, individual markings could reflect social class, but nobility alone was insufficient to merit such distinctions, and even a king who had not performed certain deeds lacked some of the distinguishing insignia.[70]

The insignia and other devices were kept with the royal tribute and brought out when the occasion warranted.[71] They were awarded by the king in Tenochtitlan on special and auspicious days and during special feasts.[72] But insignia were also awarded to brave warriors and nobles before a campaign, and additional insignia were taken on campaigns to be awarded to other kings and their brave and noble warriors just before a major battle.[73]

The insignia depicted many things—weapons, scenes of great deeds in the past, gods, and previous kings[74]—as well as more abstract designs.[75] While some of these insignia were received in tribute and others were made by the feather workers of Tenochtitlan,[76] many were also captured in war.[77] Captured devices were given to the king, who then awarded them to the deserving, and many indicated participation in a specific battle.[78] It was in this manner that the *quetzalpatzactli* feather crest was first introduced among the Aztecs. It was captured in Ayotlan, and King Ahuitzotl adopted it as his own, although he had apparently remained in Tenochtitlan, and the army was commanded in the field by Moteuczomah Xocoyotl.[79]

The shield designs and insignia of the Aztec tlahtoani seem to have been adopted as symbols of major events, such as great victories. Thus, the dress resembled medieval heraldry depicting an individual's great accomplishments.[80] For example, King Moquihuix of Tlatelolco had a *quetzalhuehxolotl* for his standard, while King Axayacatl's standard was a human skin.[81] King Ahuitzotl's insignia was a *cuauhxolotl* of gold on top of a straw dwelling (a *xahcalli*, used for shelter during military campaigns), while that of Moteuczomah Xocoyotl was a bird called a *tlauhquechol*.[82] The penalty for using insignia and colors to which one was not entitled was death.[83]

Wearing such distinctive insignia also meant that great warriors could be identified and targeted by the enemy. For example, in the campaign by Tetzcoco against Huexotzinco, the king of Huexotzinco inquired about the insignia carried by King Nezahualcoyotl so that he could direct the whole of his army against him and kill him. Nezahualcoyotl learned of this scheme and exchanged arms with a captain in his army, saying that he wanted to honor him by allowing him to wear the king's arms. Thus Nezahualcoyotl survived the battle; the captain did not.[84]

The king could deprive the warriors of some of the insignia honoring their military accomplishments if they subsequently performed poorly.[85] Because insignia were earned by individual achievements, they did not pass from father to son. When a warrior died, his insignia were cremated or buried with him.[86]

In addition to the ranks and offices set forth above, there were others dealing with war.[87] Once the telpochcalli youth had been tested in battle, if he was brave he was named the tiachcauh, the master of youths, and if he became valiant and reached manhood, he was named the telpochtlahtoh, the ruler who governed, judged, sentenced, and corrected the telpochcalli youths. Each calpolli had a telpochtlahtoh, tiachcauh, or telpochtequihuah.[88] If he further excelled and took four captives, he could become a tlacochcalcatl (commanding general), a tlacateccatl (general), a *cuauhtlahtoh* (chief), or perhaps a *topileh* (literally, one who has owned a staff; a constable; posthispanically, an *alguacil*).[89]

The king was the commander in chief and often led the army in battle himself. The *cihuacoatl* (woman snake) was reportedly the king's most trusted adviser, but may have been just one among many advisers.[90] Below the king and the cihuacoatl came the supreme council, composed of four main officers: 1) the tlacochcalcatl (person from Tlacochcalco [place of the house of darts]), 2) the tlacateccatl (person from Tlacatecco [place where people are cut up]), 3) the *ezhuahuancatl* (person from Ezhuahuanco [place where one has scratched with blood]), and 4) the *tlillancalqui* (dweller in Tlillan [beside the black paint]).[91] These four offices were held by the highest nobility, usually by the king's brothers or near relatives,[92] with the highest held by the king's heir apparent (see fig. 3).[93]

Additional offices, held by valiant warriors and part of the king's council, were: the *tezcacoacatl* (person from Tezcacoac), the *tocuiltecatl* (person from Tocuillan), the *ahcolnahuacatl* (person from Acolnahuac), the *huei teuctli* (great lord), the *temillohtli* (honored owner of stone fields), the *atempanecatl* (person from Atempan), the *calmimilolcatl* (person from Calmimilolco), the *mexihcateuctli* (Mexica lord), the *huitznahuacatl* (person from Huitznahuac), the *atemanecatl* (person from Ateman), the *quetzaltoncatl* (person from Quetzaltonco), the *teuctlamacazqui* (lord priest), the *tlapaltecatl* (person from Tlapallan), the *cuauhquiahuacatl* (person from Cuauhquiahuac), the *coatecatl* (person from Coatlan), the *pantecatl* (person from Pantlan), and the *huehcamecatl* (person from Huecaman).[94] All were tiyahcahuan, and each could also be a general and command armies as circumstances demanded.[95]

These titles bestowed on valiant warriors did not strictly designate rank but were honors for the performance of great deeds in war. Moreover, they could also be bestowed on commoners and non-Aztecs. When the Aztecs conquered Coyohuacan (Coyoacan), for example, two Aztec warriors were awarded the honored titles of *cuauhnochteuctli* (eagle prickly-pear lord) and *cuauhquiahuacatl* (person from Cuauhquiahuac), and three allies from Colhuacan (Culhuacan) were honored with the titles of *yopihcateuctli* (Yopihca

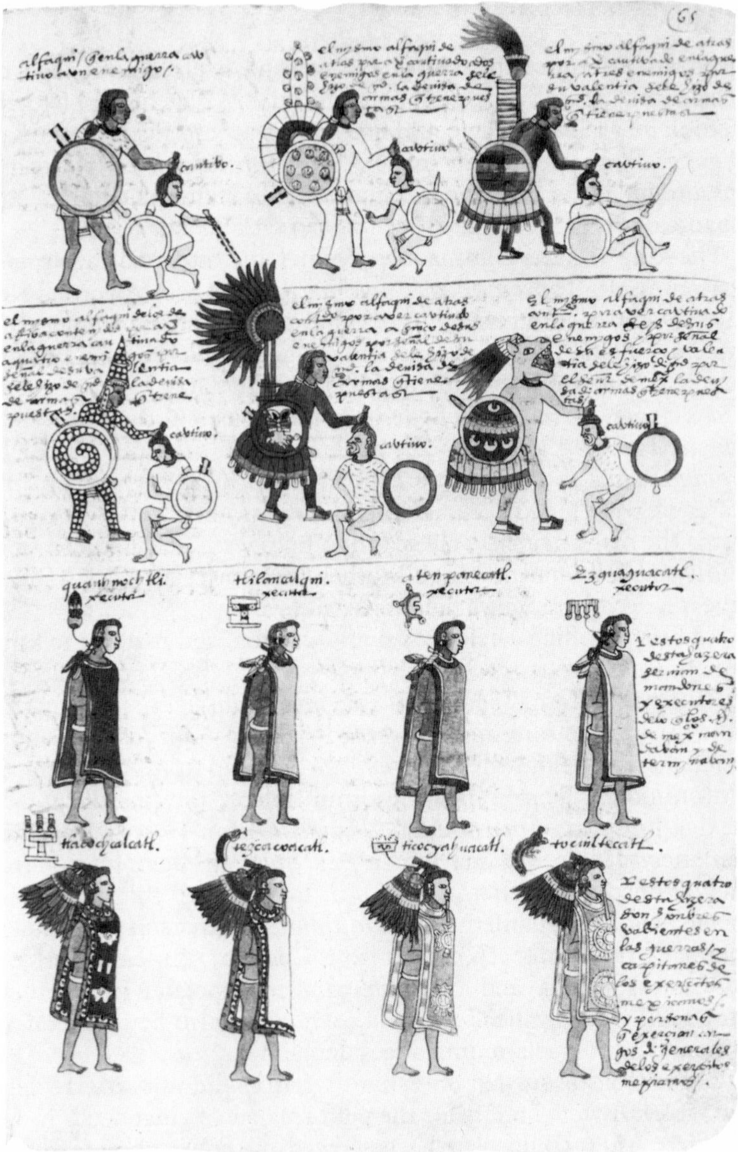

Fig. 3. Top row: priest taking one, two, and three captives, and the attire achieved by these levels of attainment. Second row: priest taking four, five, and six captives, and the attire achieved by these levels of attainment. Third row: cuauhnochteuctli, tlillancalqui, atempanecatl, and ezhuahuancatl. Fourth row: tlacochcalcatl, tezcacoacatl, ticociahuahcatl, and tocuiltecatl. (*Codex Mendoza*, MS Arch. Seld. A 1, fol. 66; courtesy of the Bodleian Library, Oxford)

lord), *huitznahuacatl* (person from Huitznahuac), and *itzcoatecatl* (person from Itzcoatlan).[96]

There were also military orders composed of seasoned warriors. These orders are conventionally referred to as eagles (*cuacuauhtin*) and jaguars (*ocelomeh*).[97] Conceptually, there appears to be no distinction between these types of warriors, and, indeed, other, less common terms were used to denote them, including *cuauhtlocelotl* (eagle-jaguar).[98] These variant terms probably signified differences in the attire of the individual warriors rather than internal distinctions drawn by the orders themseles. Only noble tequihuahqueh could be admitted to the military orders, but they did not have to come exclusively from the calmecac; telpochcalli-trained warriors were also admitted to the military orders.[99]

The military orders were not an officer corps, although they were composed largely of members of the nobility. However, noble background alone was insufficient to qualify a man; entry depended upon military prowess and demonstrated ability in the form of captives taken in battle—more than four. Because of the emphasis on military skill, common warriors could gain admittance by being elevated to the cuauhpipiltin. But given the superior training available to noble youths, the positions of their fathers, and their attachment to veteran warriors, success in battle and entry into the military orders was heavily skewed in favor of hereditary nobles.

Meritocratic nobles were admitted to the eagle and jaguar orders, and the king granted them the rights owed to members. These included the right to wear otherwise proscribed jewelry and daily military attire, dress in cotton and wear sandals in the royal palace, eat human flesh and drink octli in public, keep concubines, and dine in the royal palaces. Nevertheless, they were held in less esteem than the hereditary noble members.[100] And their war suit (*tlahuiztli* suit) was made of animal skins, not of feathers, as was that worn by the pipiltin.[101] Nevertheless, once a commoner became a cuauhpilli, his sons were eligible for noble treatment, including warrior training in the calmecac.

Above the eagle and jaguar military orders were two other orders or societies—the *otontin* (otomies; sing. *otomitl*) and the *cuahchicqueh* (shorn ones; sing. *cuahchic* or *cuahchiqui*). For taking five or six captives a valiant warrior might be named an otomitl warrior and given a *tlahuizmatlatopilli*, or "net device staff." In addition to his *macuahuitl* (sword), the otomitl carried a shield with the four "nose-moons" device,[102] and wore his hair bound in a tassel with a red ribbon.[103]

Soldiers were honored by being made cuahchic warriors for taking many captives in battle[104] and performing more than twenty brave deeds.[105] This military order had higher status than the otontin, and several high-ranking military commanders—the *cuauhnochteuctli*, the tlacateccatl, and the tlacochcalcatl—were members.[106] Their heads were entirely shorn except for a shock of hair above the left ear braided with a red ribbon. Half of the head was painted blue and the other half either red or yellow, and members wore a loincloth and an open-weave mantle of maguey fiber.

It has been suggested that the otontin were commoners, an interpretation supported by their lower status in relation to the cuahchicqueh, but other evidence argues against this view.[107] In the Spanish conquest of Tenochtitlan, for example, an otomitl warrior named Tzilacatzin played a prominent role in the defense. The use of the honorific *-tzin* and his attire, which included gold armbands, both strongly indicate a noble status.[108] Moreover, the depictions of otomitl costumes do not seem to indicate skin suits but the feather ones typical of the noble tlahuiztli suits. Although particularly accomplished cuauhpipiltin may have been admitted to otomitl and cuahchic ranks, there is little evidence in support of this possibility.

All of the military orders had separate houses in the king's palace, including one for commoners who had achieved the status of military orders. These groups provided the nucleus for action, even when Tenochtitlan was quiescent. The house of the eagle and jaguar military orders, the cuauhcalli, also served as the meeting place of the war council where military matters were discussed and decided,[109] presided over by the king.[110] Similarly, in Tetzcoco the council rooms were in the king's palace, as were the rooms of his bravest captains and soldiers and the armory.[111] The cuahchic (but apparently not the otomitl) warriors also met in the cuauhcalli, but they did not form a cohesive organization that played a role in decisions of state. Their roles were more individual and more strictly martial in nature.[112] That the cuahchic warriors met in the cuauhcalli suggests they were also eagle and jaguar warriors, the latter being a prerequisite for the former. The same was probably true of the otontin warriors, but this is unclear. In any case they, like the cuahchicqueh and the tiachcahuan, were supported from state revenues.[113] Given the evidence that the otontin were nobles, the slight disparity in treatment between the otontin and cuahchicqueh may simply reflect the differences in status that were tied to the differences in achievements needed for each. The highest of the four warrior houses was that of the nobles, followed by the eagle warriors, the jaguar warriors, and, last, the commoners who had achieved military order status.[114]

The achcacauhtin were warriors in charge of declaring war or subduing rebelling provinces.[115] The achcauhtli position was usually held by a valiant warrior, but rather than being warriors per se the achcacauhtin were a type of judicial officer[116] and oversaw arms, doctrine, and training.[117]

Old warriors, the *cuauhhuehuetqueh* (eagle elders; sing. *cuauhhuehueh*), who were no longer permitted to go into combat, nevertheless played a major role in the campaigns. They were in charge of organizing the men and were given responsibility for the camps.[118] They were also responsible for informing the wives of warriors slain in battle.[119]

The issue of professionalism in the Aztec army is largely a semantic one, varying according to what is meant by "professional." But clearly the Aztec army was complexly organized, reflecting the ascribed structure of Aztec society as well as the achieved ranking of sophisticated military organizations.

CHAPTER 4

Declaration, Preparation, and Mobilization

IN theory, not all provocations were serious enough to prompt an Aztec declaration of war. The king might call for a war for minor offenses (such as the killing of an emissary), but the basic decision rested with his councilors and the people, who required a just cause if they were to accept going to war.[1] They could counsel against war, but if the king persisted, calling them back two or three times to ask for war, they relented, and war was declared; but it was not considered a just war, and the responsibility was the king's alone. When merchants were killed, however, there was no question of sufficient cause, and the appeal to the councilors and to the people was unnecessary.[2]

The ideal was to announce the declaration of war both to the Aztec people and to the new enemies, but this was not always done.[3] The Aztecs rarely initiated war against a major opponent without cause (from their perspective), but they rarely provided formal advance warning, although targets usually knew the Aztecs were coming.

A high official announced the decision to wage war to the people. During the reign of Moteuczomah Ilhuicamina the cihuacoatl performed this act, notifying all the wards (calpolli) and the telpochcalli schools, where many warriors were trained.[4] At other times war leaders alerted the people and told them to begin preparing supplies.[5] And at still other times the four main war leaders—the tlacateccatl, the tlacochcalcatl, the cuauhnochteuctli, and the *tlillancalqui*—told the captains and valiant warriors of the decision.[6] The declaration of war was announced in the plaza, usually for five days.[7]

INTELLIGENCE

Many basic operations had to be performed to put the armies in the field. Among these were gathering and assessing intelligence, securing moral and material support on the home front, mobilizing and arming the troops, and supplying them en route. Because of the hegemonic nature of the Aztec system, security did not lie in the static defense of fortified sites or in the questionable loyalties of subjugated tributaries. Security lay in the offensive, so of all martial preparations none was more important than intelligence.

Intelligence and communications were two of the most crucial aspects of Mesoamerican warfare: the former kept leaders apprised of political and military events, and the latter allowed them to establish and maintain political initiatives and ties and to direct armies in the field. Because the empire was held together by Aztec action or threat of action rather than by structural reorganization, communications and intelligence concerning both foreign and internal areas were vital. To gather information and convey messages, both formal and informal, four institutions were used: merchants traveling throughout Mesoamerica, formal ambassadors, messengers, and spies.

Merchants

General information could be gleaned from many sources, including returning troops and travelers, but perhaps the most useful and organized conduits of general intelligence were the merchants.

The *pochtecah* (merchants; sing. *pochtecatl*)[8] traded in a wide range of commodities throughout a vast geographical expanse. Not only did they travel throughout the Aztec Empire, they also went beyond it to trade with independent groups owing no allegiance to Tenochtitlan. In both areas the merchants brought back specific information for the state as well as general assessments of the local political climate, based on the way they had been received.[9]

Much of the merchants' intelligence gathering was incidental to their primary trading functions, but they were sometimes given intelligence duties to perform for the state. King Ahuitzotl ordered merchants to penetrate the lands of Anahuac, ostensibly to trade but actually to reconnoiter.[10] On at least some occasions when entering hostile areas beyond the Aztec Empire, the merchants disguised themselves as natives of other areas, cutting their hair in the local manner and learning the language, because if they had been discovered, they would have been killed.[11]

As noted, killing a merchant was a just cause of war in Mesoamerica,[12] and such incidents initiated many wars.[13] The merchants often acted as provocateurs. By demanding to trade or requesting materials for some domestic or religious purpose, they left independent cities little alternative but to expel or kill them or to become subjects of the Aztecs.

On other occasions the merchants passed through enemy lands armed with shields and swords, as if prepared for war.[14] They met with some success when battle was thrust upon them[15] and were rewarded by the king in the same manner as valiant warriors.[16] If the merchants were openly attacked or were besieged, the king sent warriors to their aid.[17] Although flight was not honored among warriors, it was rewarded among merchants because of the emphasis on obtaining their information.

The importance of the merchants' intelligence functions increased as the empire expanded, because the time required to learn of an offense and for the army to respond increased. Consequently, rebellions and, more importantly, invasions or hostile actions by other polities could not be met in a timely manner without advance knowledge. An unanticipated attack might attain its objective before the Aztecs could muster their army and march to the defense. Though small rebellions and enemy intrusions were expected in a hegemonic system, large thrusts or massive rebellions could not be tolerated or allowed to gain momentum. Only warnings could stem such a tide, and providing them was perhaps the merchants' most significant role in state activities. Thus the immediacy and force with which the Aztecs retaliated for the killing of their merchants had less to do with the value placed on their persons than on the need for their information. Moreover, a region where merchants were killed or excluded was a blind spot and a danger to the empire.

Ambassadors

A more formal means of contact and intelligence was official ambassadors, who were received in peace even by enemy cities[18] and who enjoyed certain immunities when traveling, as long as they stayed on the main roads.[19] The Aztecs often sent an ambassador to a foreign group to ask that it submit to Tenochtitlan and become a tributary of the Aztec state. If it refused, the area was a candidate for conquest, and the killing of an ambassador definitively meant war.[20]

Messengers

The Aztecs used a system of messengers to transmit information within the empire and maintain contact with distant cities and armies in the field. Messengers existed elsewhere in Mesoamerica (for instance, in Tlaxcallan),[21] but the system was apparently developed to its greatest extent by the Aztecs.[22]

Messages were carried by relays of men stationed about two leagues (1 league = 4.2 kilometers or 2.6 miles) apart along the main roads. Like the ambassadors, the runners were nominally free from abuse as long as they remained on the main roads.[23] General intelligence from all over Mesoamerica reached Tenochtitlan via the messengers,[24] and information was dispatched from the capital in the same way, as, for instance, when a king died.[25] But the runners' primary function was to relay political messages to and from the king, and these often involved war. For example, the king dispatched runners to inform allied kings about rebelling provinces,[26] to instruct allies to mobilize men for a war,[27] to order the gathering of arms and foodstuffs for the impending war,[28] and to advise tributary towns along the army's line of march of its imminent arrival and of its food needs.[29] Before a battle runners also took messages between the opposing armies.[30] And during the war, if necessary, messengers were sent to Tenochtitlan for more assistance.[31]

On the return from war, runners were again sent to towns en route to indicate the needs of the passing army,[32] and news of the war's outcome was sent back to Tenochtitlan by messenger.[33]

Spies

For tactical intelligence formal spies were employed. Once war had been decided on but before mobilization, spies (*quimichtin*, literally, mice; sing. *quimichin*) were sent into enemy territory dressed like the foes and speaking their language, but they traveled at night and tried to remain hidden. Their job was to observe the enemy's fortifications, army, preparations, and so forth. They also sought out the dissidents present in virtually every land and paid them for information. Maps were then drawn of the territory to be crossed, and obstacles such as rivers were marked.[34]

The use of spies was a two-edged sword, however, and Tenochtitlan was also penetrated by disguised enemies, foreign merchants, disgruntled "allies," and domestic traitors. If enemy spies or local informers were discovered, they were torn apart, and their families were enslaved. The same fate awaited Aztec spies who fell into enemy hands, so spies were well compensated (usually with land) for the danger of their work.[35] But plans could not be kept secret forever, particularly once mobilization had begun.

HOME FRONT

The home front played an important role in Aztec warfare. Tenochtitlan provided a resting place for the warriors in times of peace and was a source of soldiers, arms, and supplies in times of war.

Tenochtitlan was not fortified, in contrast to some Mesoamerican towns, but it was defensible.[36] Many public buildings had a fortress-like aspect, and the city's position on an island the lakes connected to the mainland by only a few causeways greatly reduced the need for specialized fortifications.

As the Spaniards discovered, Aztec warriors made effective use of the parapeted, flat-roofed buildings throughout the city.[37] The conquistador Francisco de Aguilar complained that when the Spaniards came out to fight, the Aztecs remained on the rooftops of houses and showered them with projectiles in relative safety.[38] However, the city did have a few specialized defensive structures, such as a two-towered fortification ringed by a crenellated wall twelve feet wide, which was at the juncture of two causeways. This structure, which could be entered by only one gate and exited by another, commanded both entries, and there were removable bridges farther along on the causeway.[39] More important to Tenochtitlan's defense than these edifices were the strategic intelligence discussed above and the tactical intelligence supplied by the city's guards.

Many cities used lookouts to spot approaching danger during troubled times.[40] But even when the city was not actively at war, Tenochtitlan's vigilance was constant, since the danger of a sneak attack was ever-present. Thus, the king ordered that watch be kept day and night. Youths in all the telpochcalli were ordered to sing and dance throughout the night so that all the surrounding towns could hear that Tenochtitlan was awake. And the priests of the city blew conch shell trumpets (*teucciztli*) and beat on the two-tone drum (*teponaztli*) during the night. Watch was also kept in the king's palace, in the houses of all the military orders, in the nobles' houses throughout the city, and in the temples.[41] In addition, scouts were dispatched to observe the advance of the enemy. If they were not alert or if they were thwarted, the city was at the enemy's mercy.[42]

MOBILIZATION

Political provocations could occur at any time, but Mesoamerican city-states did not always react to them immediately, because they could not mount effective military campaigns year round. Two factors influenced the timing of campaigns: the agricultural cycle and the rain cycle.

Since the army was largely composed of commoners who were agriculturalists, the availability of soldiers was determined by cultivation and harvest schedules. In the central highlands planting was done in the spring (usually beginning in late April or May), and harvesting, in the late summer or fall (as late as October or early November). Thus throughout the summer and early autumn the men needed for a major campaign were occupied in activities vital both to themselves and to the society as a whole. Moreover, this seasonal cycle also affected the supplies needed to mount a campaign. Grain was stored for use throughout the year, but the greatest surplus was available in the autumn just after harvest.[43] As a result an army was best able to gather supplies for a campaign in the late autumn and winter.

The second event affecting the Aztec campaigns was the rainy season. Central Mexico's climatic cycle involves a dry season, stretching from around late September through mid May, followed by a rainy season through the summer. This pattern not only regulated the agricultural season but also affected the feasibility of moving large numbers of men and supplies.[44] Such movements were significantly easier during the dry season, in terms of both the soldiers' physical comfort and the quality of the roads. Dirt roads used by large numbers of men during the rainy season (and for some time thereafter) quickly turned into quagmires. And streams that could be forded during the dry season often became swollen, impassable rivers during the rains.

Thus, the availability of men and supplies, as well as the absence of rain, meant that major wars were normally fought from late autumn through spring of the following year. The festival of *Panquetzaliztli* marked the end of the harvest and signaled the usual beginning of the year's wars.[45] But this was a practical restriction, not a ritual one, and there were exceptions. Small armies requiring fewer men and less logistical support could still be dispatched during the agricultural season. The campaigns probably involved elite warriors—largely the nobles—who were not tied so rigorously to the agricultural cycle. But the objectives of such campaigns were necessarily quite limited.

And flower wars could still be fought, largely for the same reasons that small armies could be sent: they normally involved fewer warriors, and these were drawn disproportionately from the nobility.

Once the decision to fight had been made, troops had to be marshaled, the conduct of the war planned, the city alerted, and supplies prepared and gathered. Someone had to decide how much military action was warranted. And decisions about troops and supplies were pivotal to the success of the venture.

Decisions about the appropriate response for a given incident were made by the king and his war council. In the case of an alarm or revolt in Tenochtitlan or the surrounding region, the military orders residing in the royal palace took action. These orders were not a pretorian guard, but by the time of the Spanish conquest the Aztec king was surrounded by a body of soldiers estimated in one account at six hundred nobles, each accompanied by three or four armed men, totaling approximately three thousand men;[46] a second account put the figure at ten thousand men.[47]

War and the marshaling of troops did not involve everyone subject to the Aztec Empire. Rather, responses were geared to the Aztecs' perception of the threat. The first action was taken by these military societies. If the threat was larger than their limited numbers could handle, additional men were marshaled, first from Tenochtitlan, next from Tetzcoco, and then followed by Tlacopan, the third member of the Triple Alliance.[48] Troops could also be mobilized from wider areas in accordance with the seriousness of the threat,[49] beginning with the cities in the basin of Mexico, and then tributaries from elsewhere in the empire.[50] The army's size was manipulated by altering both the depth and the breadth of the call-up of forces. The depth of the call-up determined how intensive it was in a given city; for example, many youths and older men remained behind when only a small army was needed.[51] The job of marshaling the troops presumably fell to some high official, as it had during the Aztec rebellion against the Tepanec Empire, or to the commanding generals,[52] but it doubtless followed the existing political hierarchy down through the calpolli level.

Army Organization

Armies in Mesoamerica varied in size. "Army" referred to the largest aggregation of warriors marshaled by the polity in a particular instance and was applied to units as small as 7,000 or 8,000[53] and as large as a combined force of the Tetzcocas, Aztecs, and Chichimecs reportedly numbering 700,000 men.[54] Whatever the size, it was this unit that the king or, in his absence, the tlacochcalcatl or tlacateccatl led when he went to war.

The Aztec army did not always march or fight as a single unit under an overall commander. On numerous occasions the Aztecs divided their army—for example, into two units for purposes of establishing camp, into three for purposes of multiple simultaneous attacks, and into four for marching.[55] However, these segments were complete command units.

There were, of course, internal divisions in the Aztec army, but the available descriptions are inadequate to reconstruct them fully. Many generalizations about the sizes of armies and their subunits have been made by modern scholars, sixteenth-century conquistadors, and other writers. Too often figures cited for troops in battle conform closely to round numbers—10,000, 100,000, and so on—suggesting that general magnitudes were being indicated rather than precise numbers. And even where the figures do not appear to be round, they are often from the perspective of the Aztec vigesimal (base-20) numerical system (which had place values of 1, 20, 400, 8,000, and so on), resulting in typical troop numbers of 200, 400, 8,000, and so forth. Consequently, the data about the internal structure of the Aztec army are both scant and, quite probably, flawed. Nevertheless, some clarification is possible.

The basic Mesoamerican army units (called squadrons in the Spanish chronicles)[56] were probably town or calpolli commands. Each town marched under its own banner with its own leaders,[57] and if it was large enough to have more than one calpolli, it had one overall leader, or tlahtoani, and subordinate leaders for each of the several calpolli units. These calpolli units were often dispersed among and incorporated into the larger armies of a major campaign, but they apparently were not divided. They were the basic command, logistical, and tactical units, and violating their integrity would have caused too many supply and control problems.

In theory the army was organized by *xiquipilli* (units of 8,000 men). In the war with Coaixtlahuacan, the army reached twenty-five xiquipilli, or 200,000 warriors.[58] But Aztec military requirements often dictated smaller armies than could be created if whole xiquipilli were used. And since the responsiblity for supplying men was dispersed throughout the allied cities and their basic units were not divided, towns and calpolli each apparently contributed fewer men than a xiquipilli.

If each calpolli in Tenochtitlan had been responsible for a xiquipilli, the result would have been 160,000 soldiers, a number in excess of the city's male population. Instead, an equal manpower assessment was spread over the twenty calpolli in Tenochtitlan, requiring each to supply 400 men.[59] This interpretation is supported by two widely reported facts: each calpolli marched under its own leadership, and there were leaders of 400-man units. It is apparent that the twenty calpolli taken together with the xiquipilli derived from the base-20 numerical system generate de facto leaders of 400-man units. There are also reports of 200-man units (and possibly of 100-man units if a Tlaxcaltec analogy is correct),[60] which would have resulted either from unit subdivisions or from smaller mobilizations by half a xiquipilli; each unit had its own leader.[61] The existence of a 20-man unit has been suggested,[62] a logical assumption given the Mesoamerican counting system, but the existence of such units derive from Bandelier. He suggested them because paintings designated each unit by a banner and the Nahuatl word for flag or banner (though not the Nahuatl term for a war banner) was *pantli*, which is also the pictographic element indicating 20.[63] There is no direct evidence of a unit of this size, but the army was divided below the level of 100 or 200 men, probably into squads of some type and certainly into tactical units.

In each squad veteran warriors—cuahchicqueh, otontin, achcacuauhtin, or tequihuahqueh—were placed between every four or five youths. They watched over these fledgling soldiers but did not fight unless some experienced enemy warrior advanced on the youths.[64]

However, these small tactical units of five or six soldiers, led by an experienced warrior, may not have been as permanent as those of the calpolli or served as building blocks of the larger units.

The units into which the army was divided for marching were probably quite large—some multiple of the xiquipilli—and differed substantially from combat units, which could be quite small. This meant that multiple combat units probably marched together and were subordinated to the army's more comprehensive command structure, led by the tlacochcalcatl and the tlacateccatl.[65]

As was common throughout central Mexico,[66] each unit was designated by a standard (*cuachpantli*), the banner carried on marches and into battle (see figs. 2–4, 7, and 33). The *Codex Mendoza*[67] lists four types of standard used by the Aztec army: (1) *tlahuizmatlacopilli*, or "reticulated crown device" (2) *itzpapalotl*, or "obsidian butterfly" (3) *xolotl*, or "double" and (4) *cuachichiquilli*, or "crest." These may have represented the four great quarters into which Te-

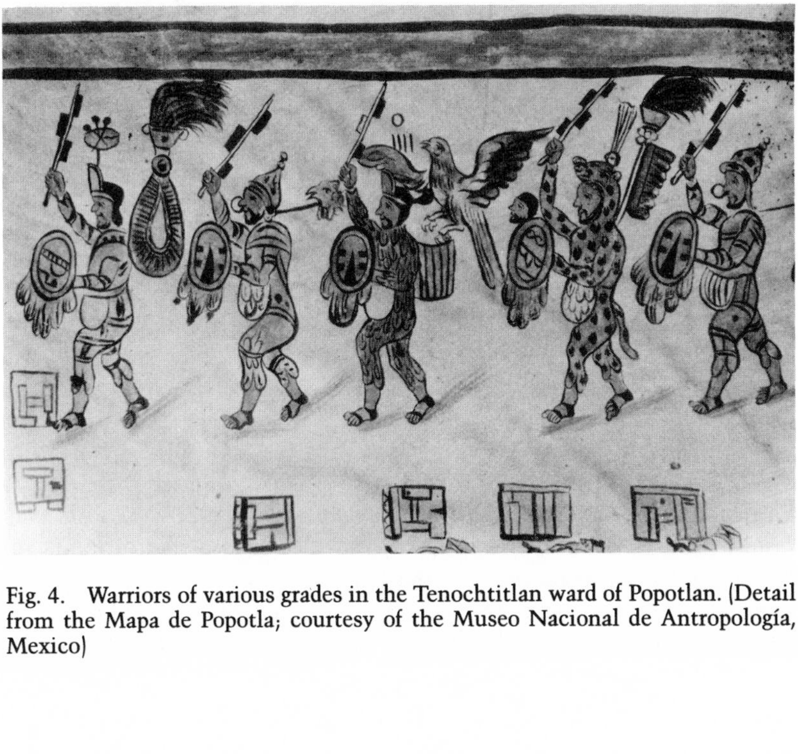

Fig. 4. Warriors of various grades in the Tenochtitlan ward of Popotlan. (Detail from the Mapa de Popotla; courtesy of the Museo Nacional de Antropología, Mexico)

nochtitlan was divided. Additional standards reflected lesser divisions and were normally worn by the commanders of the army, town, or calpolli and of 400-, 200-, and 100-man units. The standards were mounted on light bamboo frames strapped to the wearer's back[68] so as not to hinder his fighting. The binding was so tight that it was virtually impossible to take the banner from him without killing him first.[69]

Individuals in the various units—usually at the town or calpolli level—also wore insignia designating their membership. For example, the men in the unit of Tlaxcallan's commanding general, Xicohtencatl, all wore mantles that were half red and half white.[70] A similar practice was followed in the Aztec army.[71] Unit markings were also employed by each of the military orders and by the commoners elevated to membership in the orders.[72] In the Aztec army the standard was placed in the center of the unit in battle, and great attention was paid to its defense. When a unit standard was taken, the entire unit fled, and if it was the standard of a general or of the king, the entire army retreated.[73]

When the army left on a campaign, two supreme chiefs remained in Tenochtitlan to send supplies and reinforcements if necessary. Two others led the soldiers, and two deputies were designated by the king to replace the two leaders if they should be killed or captured or prove to be incompetent. These latter four leaders had command over the entire army when it was en route and exercised supreme powers in matters regarding war and justice far in excess of their peacetime powers.[74] In battle the tlacochcalcatl led the strongest and most noted army, and he directed the battle from the midst of his nobles.[75] But strategic considerations, such as when the army would leave home, where it was to march, for how many days, and how the battle was to be fought, were decided in advance by the king.[76]

Army Size

For the king to assess Tenochtitlan's military potential accurately and to predict the needed training, arms, and supplies in the event of war, he had to make a count of the available manpower. This was done through the calpolli organization. Each ward had officials responsible for a designated number of houses, who ensured that citizens paid their tribute and contributed their share to the public works. If the official had a hundred houses, he, in turn, delegated these among five or six of his subjects. When a male child was born in a calpolli, he was reported to the heads of the ward,[77] so the Aztec leaders knew their potential strength even though they rarely used it to the maximum.

The sizes of the armies mustered for specific campaigns are occasionally given in historical sources, but these figures are doubtless approximations. Their reliability can be assessed by examining the total population of the region and then estimating the soldier population. Unfortunately, there is no general consensus on the population of central Mexico, or even of the basin of Mexico. For the basin, Sanders' low estimate of 1,000,000 to 1,200,000[78] and Cook and Borah's high estimate of 2,200,000 to 2,650,000[79] offer the most reasonable range. Tenochtitlan's population in 1519 is estimated at 150,000 to 200,000.[80]

It is widely agreed that in preindustrial populations virtually the entire male population capable of bearing arms took part in military affairs and that no one was exempt from war service among the Aztecs.[81] The makeup of the Aztec army, moreover, has been estimated at 90 percent of the male population.[82] Nonetheless, while virtually all males were mobilized in nonstate societies, in states, this was likely to be true only in emergencies or defensive actions. Estimates of 90 percent participation are instructive for the cities attacked by the Aztecs, but they reveal little about the Aztecs' offensive actions. Distinguishing between offensive and defensive armies highlights the differences between imperial battles, in which professional armies fight each other, and wars of conquest, in which a defending city-state is placed in the position of fighting for its life. In the former situation trained soldiers are used exclusively, although some of the combatants may be commoners, and others, inexperienced. In the latter situation the 90 percent figure is closer to reality, with virtually every able-bodied man participating. Consequently, victories are more difficult in the former situation than in the latter, and more captives are taken in the latter situation.

The Aztecs used a selected portion of the available manpower for offensive actions, calling up only the number of men actually needed for a specific campaign. Nevertheless, how many could be summoned from any city depended on the demographic structure of the population. I have adopted the population model that is most likely to reflect the indigenous demographic structure,[83] with the result that only 32 percent of the males (not of the total population) were between the ages of 20 and 40, and 43 percent were between 20 and 50.[84] Thus in an ordinary offensive war a city with a population of 200,000 could muster 43,000 warriors, if every male between 20 and 50 was called up. Since the nobility constituted 10 percent of the population,[85] the 43,000 figure represented the total potential manpower and not that available through all the calpolli (which would be 38,700). Moreover, the number of nobles recorded in the "palace guard," and hence in military orders (600 to 2,000 at the 1-to-4 ratio suggested by the historical accounts), virtually equaled the total noble population of Tenochtitlan (1,612 to 2,150 noble males from the ages of 20 to 50).

On the basis of these ratios a basinwide population of 1,200,000 to 2,650,000 could generate an offensive army of 258,000 to 569,750, far exceeding the military forces in cities elsewhere in central Mexico. However, there are no records of an army that large ever having been raised, and when large armies were mustered, they were drawn from an area much greater than the basin of Mexico. Even an army composed of men age 20 to 25 would generate a minimum of 54,000 men in the basin, and one composed of those 20 to 30 would generate 105,000. So it is apparent that the full military force of the basin of Mexico was not used in an offensive war (and a sizable defensive contingent always remained in Tenochtitlan to protect the city from an opportunistic sneak attack).

But as the Aztec Empire expanded and wars required more soldiers, there was a net increase in the number of commoner soldiers, because the elites participated in virtually all of the wars.

Arms and Armories

Recognizing a threat and then ordering a response were only the first steps in warfare. Actually gathering, arming, training, and provisioning troops and then directing them to war required more than legislative fiat. Most of the men needed some retraining, which they underwent daily in each ward before departing.[86] Arms also had to be prepared and supplies gathered, and these tasks were placed under the direction of the cuauhhuehuetqueh, the old captains.[87]

The men in Tenochtitlan did not wear arms in peacetime.[88] Weapons were kept in the numerous armories of the city.[89] At each of the four entrances to the main ceremonial precinct of Tenochtitlan was a large armory, called the *tlacochcalco*. It was filled with weapons made and deposited there each year:[90] conquistador Andrés de Tápia estimated the armory's capacity at five hundred cartloads.[91] The symbol of an armory was any of several weapons secured above each door.[92]

There were also two armories in the king's palace in which skilled craftsmen and armorers produced the weapons, with royal stewards overseeing them.[93] Apparently, one building was a factory in which specialized production was carried out by a range of craftsmen, while the other was a repository.[94]

The distinction between the two types of armories—those in the royal palace and those associated with the temples—apparently reflects the way different grades of warriors were equipped. Since each town or calpolli was responsible for its own armaments, there were doubtless as many armories dispersed throughout the city and countryside as there were towns and calpolli, and it was to these that the commoners flocked for arms in the event of war. The armories located in the king's palace, on the other hand, apparently supplied the nobility and the military orders, since these groups were housed in the palace and owed primary allegiance to the king rather than to the calpolli.

Arms were also available in Tenochtitlan's marketplace,[95] although the demand for such goods must have been small. The military items available there were elaborate and highly decorated,[96] as the marketplace largely served the elite warriors, including the nobles, who sought sumptuous goods for status rather than functional purposes.

War Supplies

Some lands (*milchimalli* or *cacalomilli*) in all the towns were set aside to produce war supplies.[97] The Aztec king summoned these supplies from all over the empire, though usually from areas adjacent to Tenochtitlan. Arms and food were gathered for the journey, as well as all the other supplies needed by an army in the field.[98] The king ordered the people to prepare food, supplies, and arms. Each calpolli and subject town provided food—maize cakes, maize flour, toasted maize, beans, salt, chili, pumpkin seeds, and *pinolli*—as well as equipment for the journey.[99] In Tenochtitlan preparing the foodstuffs was an obligation of the marketplace vendors.[100] Elsewhere this was a general tribute obligation,[101] and towns along the army's route were ordered to have food prepared for their arrival.[102]

Contacting potential allies was often difficult and invariably time-consuming. Allies were called to arms by runners, so the time required varied with the geographical breadth of the call-up. How much time passed between the declaration of war and the departure of battle-ready troops also varied, five days was usual for relatively nearby conflicts[103] and eight for distant campaigns.[104]

CHAPTER 5

The March and the Encampment

ENSURING the efficient passage of the marshaled troops to their target and providing them with logistical support required considerable planning and organization by the Aztecs.

LOGISTICS EN ROUTE

The army units left their respective cities with a variable amount of foodstuffs. In some cases supplies for long journeys are specified, including double rations.[1] One indication of the amount carried was Moteuczomah Xocoyotl's demand that Tlatelolco prepare a three-day supply of cacao as part of its obligatory war supplies.[2] In addition to their weapons, the soldiers probably carried light condiments rather than heavy staples, although each soldier carried as much of his own food as he could to supplement the amounts he received from the army's supplies.[3]

Nobles had more equipment, apparently ate better food, and were better housed than common soldiers, so they had more goods. Adding to the problem of portage was the nobles' practice of marching to war clad in fine mantles, which meant that their arms, armor, and insignia had to be carried. Youths from the telpochcalli who were still too young to fight accompanied the army and carried a limited amount of the supplies and arms,[4] but the most important logistical functionaries of the army were the porters (*tlamemehqueh*; sing. *tlamemeh*) who accompanied them.[5]

Weapons, armor, and shelter were necessary for a major campaign, but food (*yaoihtacatl*, war victuals) was the greatest logistical barrier on distant and lengthy campaigns. The records are silent on the actual quantities of food consumed on a campaign, but reasonable conjecture can shed light on the matter. Sixteenth-century records of Indian food consumption place daily adult male rates at around 3,800 calories[6] (approximately .95 kg. or 2.1 lb. of maize).[7]

Under normal transport conditions, each porter carried an average load of two *arrobas* (23 kg. or 50 lb.) per day.[8] And while war would demand that loads be heavier, military conditions limited their size. Because the porters had to carry their burden day after day for the duration of the campaign, the size of their load was limited. They nevertheless provided the army with considerable logistical support through sheer numbers. In the war against Coaixtlahuacan, for example, the Aztec army numbered 200,000 warriors and 100,000 porters, an average of 1 porter for every 2 warriors, or an additional fifty pounds of supplies for every 3 men (2 warriors and 1 porter). Nevertheless, this porter-to-warrior ratio and the above consumption rates meant that the army could travel only eight days if all the porters' loads were dedicated to food (which they were not).

However, the Aztec army was not dependent solely on its own resources for the journey. Many war supplies flowed into Tenochtitlan as part of subject towns' tributary obligations,[9] part of which often included providing porters to carry the supplies.[10] But more important was the assistance supplied by towns en route.

Two days before the march messengers were sent to all tributary towns along the designated route to notify them of the army's coming.[11] From lands set aside to supply goods in war,[12] each town gathered its tribute obligations to support the passing troops,[13] and major towns en route served as focal points for the supplies drawn from other towns within a twenty-league radius.[14] Thus tributaries not only provided supplies but also transported them from the outlying areas. Supplies to feed even a single xiquipilli (8,000 men) for one day amounted to 7,600 kilograms (16,755 lbs.) of maize—330 porter loads—and at a minimum, enough was required to feed the army (warriors and porters) until it reached the next major town. If that town was only twelve miles distant, a single day's supplies would have been adequate, but if it was twenty-four miles away, the local town's tribute responsibilities doubled, at least. Consequently, both the actual foodstuffs supplied and the labor transporting it to the transit town were a considerable expense to be absorbed by the local lord.

The obligation to provide goods for the passing army was well understood, even if not always happily undertaken,[15] and several towns also supplied porters to transport the goods and, occasionally, guides.[16] Failure to meet these these tributary obligations was considered an act of rebellion and could prompt the sacking of the town,[17] as could abandonment of the town in the face of the Aztec arrival.[18] As they waged their campaigns, the Aztecs simultaneously appraised and consolidated their empire. Their army's march through existing tributary areas forced the local rulers to declare their loyalties: they could either render aid, as demanded, or revolt. But the brief time for preparations made rebellion unlikely in the face of a large, well-trained and well-equipped army, and thus the periodic demand of proof of obedience emphasized the weakness of the local tlahtohqueh vis-à-vis the empire.

Another major logistical problem was securing the necessary two quarts of water per man per day.[19] While providing water was easier than supplying food, the need for water could affect the route selected, and using available sources such as rivers involved considerable time.

Thus the Aztecs' logistical capacity depended on imperial expansion and was unmatched by groups without extensive tributary relationships. The Tlaxcaltec army, for example, reportedly stole food en route but the amount was inadequate and did not compensate for the lack of a more sophisticated system of supply.[20] If the inhabitants of a town fled an approaching army, the army could pillage it in retaliation. But such an action greatly lengthened the march, yielded only the amount of supplies available in the pillaged town itself, and made a return passage even more difficult.[21]

In contrast, the Aztec system not only alerted the transit town but also funneled goods from a large area to the march route. The Aztecs also built on their conquests, using towns they had just defeated to supply them for further expansion.[22] Because they relied on tributary obligations rather than on plundering, the Aztec army was similarly supplied by transit towns on their return from war.[23] Thus it was considerably more mobile than were nonimperial troops.

MARCHES

Assembling and coordinating a march of the large Aztec army was a complicated undertaking. Overall control was the responsibility of the king, who determined the route the army was to take, how many days it would march, and the battle plan once the enemy cities were reached.[24] The king did not always accompany the army. But when he did two generals remained in Tenochtitlan, as noted earlier, responsible for sending reinforcements, food, and supplies to the combatants.[25]

The time of day the Aztec army left Tenochtitlan was largely determined by the distance to be traveled. In the battle against nearby Chalco the Aztecs left at midnight, reaching the target in time for a dawn attack.[26] When great distances were involved and the starting time did not seriously affect their arrival time, the march began in the morning.[27] If necessary the army could travel day and night until it reached the objective,[28] but the rate of march was usually slower.[29]

Except for a few accounts of towns visited en route, the records are silent on how far the Aztecs marched per day. However, the march rates of other preindustrial armies shed light on the situation. In the invasion of ancient Greece, Xerxes's army required at least nineteen days to cover 280 miles; resting one day in seven, the army marched at a maximum rate of 16.5 miles per march day, or slightly less than 15 miles per campaign day.[30] Alexander the Great's army achieved a maximum march rate of 19.5 miles per day,[31] Hannibal's rate was 10 miles a day, and in the time of Queen Elizabeth I, the average was 15.[32] In 1760, General Lascy marched on a road for ten days, averaging 22 miles per day, while in the early nineteenth century, Napoleon, Marshall Blücher, and Frederick the Great all averaged 15 miles per day for ten days[33]—the standard distance for the time.[34] Premodern infantry rates of march generally varied from 5 to 20 miles per day.[35]

United States Army march rates are 4 kilometers (2.5 miles) per hour on roads, or 20 to 32 kilometers (12.5 to 20 miles) in a normal 5–8 hour march per 24-hour period. The actual speed of march is 4.8 kilometers (3 miles) per hour—calculated at a pace of 76 centimeters (30 inches) and a cadence of 106 steps per minute, with a 10-minute rest halt per hour included—under relatively ideal conditions. When marching uphill or on steep downhill slopes, the pace decreases, slowing to 2.4 kilometers (1.5 miles) per hour cross-country, rests included; marching in mountainous country requires approximately 20 percent more time than marching on level terrain.[36] Nor are night marches very efficient, averaging 3.2 kilometers (2 miles) per hour on roads and 1.6 kilometers (1 mile) cross-country.[37]

The above figures are for a normal march. A forced march covers greater distance by marching more hours, not by going faster, but it is avoided if possible because it impairs the fighting efficiency of the army.[38] Any march in excess of 32 kilometers (20 miles) per 24-hour period is considered a forced march, and the U. S. Army's maximum recommended distances are 56 kilometers (35 miles) in 24 hours, 96 kilometers (60 miles) in 48 hours, and 128 kilometers (80 miles) in 72 hours.[39] Based on these examples, and considering the rudimentary nature of most Mesoamerican roads, the Aztec rate of march was probably closer to the modern cross-country rate of 2.4 kilometers per hour than to the faster rate for roads. In subsequent calculations, however, I will present a range, using 2.4 kilometers per hour as the low and 4 kilometers per hour as the high, yielding a day's march of 19 to 32 kilometers (12–20 miles). The effect of these rates of march is to produce a long column.

Premodern armies usually did not formally march, but some discipline had to be observed to keep the army from fragmenting. The U.S. Army normally calculates a distance of 2 meters (6.6 feet) between men,[40] the same distance recorded for the Roman imperial army.[41] Furthermore, each soldier is calculated to occupy a square meter.[42] Thus, a single-file column for an army as small as 8,000 men (a xiquipilli) would stretch 24,000 meters (15 miles), calculated without considering the accordion effect that normally occurs on a march. This means that the end of the column would not begin the march until 6 to 10 hours after the head had begun, depending on the march rate. This difficulty with stretching out the columns can be reduced by increasing the number of files in the column. In the Aztec case there is no good evidence for the width of the column, though some light may be shed on the question by examining road widths. Armies can march where there are no roads, including on the sides of existing roads, terrain permitting, but doing so drastically reduces their speed, lengthens the campaign, and significantly increases the logistical costs. Staying on roads is much preferred, being faster, safer, and less costly.

Mesoamerican roads were locally maintained and were swept and cleared of debris for the advancing army by inhabitants of the towns en route, but they were simply dirt routes, not paved highways. There are few indications of deliberate road construction for military purposes and none outside the basin of Mexico. Rather, roads were built primarily for local trade purposes, to connect a maximum number of towns,[43] so they were only wide enough to allow single-file or, possibly, double-file two-way traffic. Anything larger was an extraneous expense. Thus, while local topography may have dictated maximum road size, usage defined the minimum. Only in the case of armies did wider roads become more significant.

Two records of formal road widths—the 7-meter (23-foot) wide causeways leading out of Tenochtitlan[44] and the 4- to 6-meter (13.1- to 19.7-foot) stone roads built by the classic Maya[45]—offer some help in evaluating how many columns there were. The imperial Roman army calculated approximately a meter between columns,[46] and given the equipment carried by the Aztecs, such a figure seems appropriate in their case as well. Thus normal Aztec roads indicate a column of twos as the likely minimum width (see fig. 4),[47] while Tenochtitlan's 7-meter causeways permit a column of fours as the likely maximum width. This range yields a minimum column length of 6,000 meters (3.7 miles) and a maximum of 12,000 meters (7.5 miles); at 2.4 kilometers per hour the end of the column would begin marching 2.5 to 5 hours after the head began (or 1.5 to 3 hours later at 4 km/hr).

There are also tactical reasons to reduce the column length. Sudden small attacks followed by quick withdrawals could be directed at any part of the army.[48] Thus the more compact the column, the safer it was because any element of the line could be more quickly reinforced in the event of attack. Moreover, the thicker the column, the more difficult it was to cut. However, there were disadvantages to this formation as well. The wider the column, the greater the impact of any bottleneck in the march, so hindrances, such as narrow passes, unfordable rivers,[49] and so on, slowed the march, backed up the troops, and rendered them more vulnerable to attack at a time when the soldiers on either side of the obstacle could not be reinforced quickly.[50]

On the march the army went by units and in silence, with the Aztecs leading.[51] The priests went first, bearing the gods on their backs, marching one day ahead of the warriors of each city (see fig. 5). Second came the military orders and veteran warriors with the generals—the tlacochcalcatl and the tlacateccatl. They, too, went one day ahead of the next group, which was composed of the rest of the warriors from Tenochtitlan, all marching in their respective units. Then, also separated by one day, came the warriors of Tlatelolco and of Tetzcoco, then the Tepanecs, Xilotepecas, Matlatzincas, and all the rest of the cities.[52] Subject towns marched separately; each was obligated to heed the Aztecs' call to war once a year.[53]

Fig. 5. Priests en route to war bearing images of the gods on their backs, followed by various grades of warriors and various grades of warriors in battle. (Med. Palat. 219, c. 284; courtesy of the Biblioteca Medicea Laurenziana, Florence)

The one day separation between armies was neither ritual nor a matter of individual cities' martial integrity and pride but a function of march dynamics. By the time the end of the previous army's column had begun marching, starting another army that day was impractical, since it entailed an 8 hour march plus the minimum lag 2.5 to 5 (or 1.5 to 3) hours for the entire army to get under way. In addition to making the march more efficient, starting on different days also spread out the logistical burden of towns on the route. Rather than providing the entire amount of tribute goods at one time, the goods each town was obligated to furnish were spread out over several days, allowing more goods to be called in from outlying areas. This arrangement also allowed limited campsites and drinking water to be used by the greatest number of men.

The Aztecs were faced with two options in dispatching their armies: they could march as a single unit or as several. Marching en masse was feasible only when the distance was short or the army was small. Marching in dispersed formation took two forms: armies could march in sequence along the same route but one day apart, or they could march by entirely different routes. When the army marched along the same route, scouts (*yaotlapixqueh*; sing. *yaotlapixqui*) provided intelligence about conditions, terrain, and enemy activity[54] that could be shared by all. Moreover, in the event of an attack the following unit could reinforce the preceding one. Marching by different routes had other advantages and disadvantages. Depending on the size, number, and proximity of the participating towns, the various armies would march separately to a predetermined location and there join to form the larger body.[55] But each large unit retained its own integrity as a complete fighting unit and carried its own baggage and supplies. However, using different routes compounded the problem of safety. Each route required the gathering of intelligence, and in the event of attack, and other units would not be in a position to assist. But using separate routes spread the burden of supply to more towns.

There were also tactical reasons for marching by separate routes, but surprise was not among them. Given the slow rate of army march and the rapid pace at which messengers traveled, warnings of the army's coming could easily be sent ahead by scouts or by towns en route, even if more sophisticated intelligence was lacking. Moreover, the separately marching armies usually regrouped for battle.

The tactical advantages of marching separately were three. First, by marching along different routes it was possible to keep the enemy from knowing the size of the entire army, at least long enough that it might not seek assistance from allies elsewhere or might lack the time to assemble. Second, the larger the army, the longer it took for everyone to reach the battle site if only one route was followed. For example, an army composed of twelve xiquipilli would stretch out over twelve days, leaving the advance troops outnumbered during the time the main forces required to catch up. But dividing the army substantially reduced the total march time, allowing the entire army to assemble more rapidly. Third, proceeding along separate routes removed one defensive tactic from the enemy. The attacking Aztec army was almost always larger than the defending city's army, and the one way the target city could offset this advantage was by attacking the Aztecs as they approached. Regardless of how many men the army had, only those at the front could actually fight. Therefore, if the defenders attacked the Aztecs in a pass or other constricted terrain, they could neutralize the advantage of numbers. With a restricted front, the two armies were tactically equal, and the longer the Aztecs were stalled, the more their logistical support eroded. But if the Aztecs sent their armies along several routes, the defending army usually lacked the manpower to fight all of the advancing armies simultaneously and so withdrew to its city. The primacy of the tactical reasons for separate routes over the logistical ones is evidenced by the fact that the Aztec army did not divide for the return trip.

Defense of the road or its destruction were primary aims in Mesoamerican warfare.[56] If roads could be controlled, access could be denied, or enemy troops could be funneled along less advantageous routes.[57] Thus the closing of roads was one of the first defenses in the event of war.[58] Trees and large cacti were felled to block roads,[59] grass ropes were employed as barriers,[60] bridges and causeways were often destroyed,[61] and roads were rendered generally impassable.[62]

But closing a road was not intended to prevent all passage, and in a world based on foot traffic it could not do so. It did, however, hinder the progress of an invading army. Such a bottleneck slowed the army and caused logistical problems. The greater the delay, the less time the army could afford to spend fighting an enemy. Furthermore, marching armies were usually attacked in the rear, where the baggage was located, in an effort to destroy the supplies.[63] Thus the

Aztec army might remain militarily undefeated but be vanquished logistically.

Some of these problems lessened during the course of a campaign as the number of men involved declined. Combat casualties aside, large numbers of men are normally lost on marches; although there are no direct data on this point for the Aztecs, comparative data are instructive. In 1812 Napoleon lost one-third of his forces to sickness and straggling on a 52-day march of 350 miles (an average of less than 7 miles per day), and Blücher lost 40 percent in eight weeks.[64] The Aztec attrition rate was probably highest among auxiliary troops and those from cities beyond the basin of Mexico, where the motivation to fight was presumably lowest.

CAMP

Camps resupplied, fed, and reinforced the combatants and offered a sanctuary to which they could retire after the battle. Thus, they were set up even when the battle was near Tenochtitlan, since they performed functions that had to be carried out closer at hand than was possible from the home city if the battle was expected to be of any duration.[65]

The armies were strung out on the trail, so not everyone arrived at once. The military orders arrived first and formed a guard to protect the others against attack. On reaching the target area, the Aztecs and their allies set up camp. The camps of the allied towns were located to each side of the Aztec contingent.[66] However, the structure of the Aztec camp was not consistent. In most cases the Aztec army and allies encamped as a single entity, but on other occasions, they were divided.[67] As the troops continued to arrive over several days, the camps grew.[68]

Immediately upon arrival the king's residence was constructed, and his insignia was placed atop it. Around the king's residence were placed those of the other nobles, so they could reinforce him in the event of a surprise attack.[69] Among the first structures to go up after the king's were the fortifications and the great tent where the nobles' arms and war supplies were stored.[70]

The cuahchic and otomitl military orders camped in front of everyone else,[71] followed by camps of the army leaders.[72] Each encamped unit was responsible for organizing its own people, campsite, bulwarks, arms, firewood, water, and other necessities and was under the immediate control of its own military leaders.[73]

The camp itself was constructed of tents and huts (xahcalli) made of woven grass mats. These mats were usually carried as baggage from the home cities, but some tribute labor gathered en route was also allocated to carry them to the battlefield and set up the camp.[74]

Arms were generally brought by the soldiers and the accompanying youths and porters, while other supplies, especially foodstuffs, came from towns along the route and tributary towns near the enemy. The food was divided among the army units and stored in huts, each unit being responsible for the storage and maintenance of its own.[75] Individuals may have supplemented their supplies, but the troops were generally fed from the general stores. During combat each warrior was given a quantity of toasted tortillas (*tlaxcaltotopochtli*) and a handful of toasted maize flour, which was mixed in water to form a beverage (pinolli).[76] The usual Mesoamerican provender of fresh tortillas and maize flour did not travel well and would have required daily preparation—normally a woman's function. Because women did not accompany Aztec armies, the troops relied on these two toasted-maize products, which would keep for several days.[77] Drinking water was provided from artificial reservoirs.[78]

When the camp had been set up and the area fortified to the extent feasible, lookouts were placed,[79] and messengers were sent to the enemy if appropriate—for instance, if it was a rebel town.[80]

Posting lookouts was an integral part of Aztec camp procedures.[81] How lookouts behaved and how often they were changed were recorded by a conquistador during the Spanish conquest of Tenochtitlan. The lookouts lighted great fires that burned throughout the night, but they took care to stand away from the fire so they could not be seen from a distance. Each time the watch changed, the lookouts fed the fires, and if rain put them out, they rekindled them without speaking, using whistles to signal between themselves.[82]

Scouts (yaotlapixqueh; not the quimichtin, or spies) were sent to reconnoiter the enemy town's fortifications.[83] These scouts were veteran warriors, and at dawn they reported to the king and the commanding generals.[84] Often they gathered valuable information, even to the point of bringing enemy captives for interrogation,[85] although they were not always successful.[86]

Scouts were also sent to gather intelligence concerning mobile forces, such as enemy armies. When the Aztecs tried to conquer the Tarascans, their army reached a point within the Tarascan-dominated area and set up camp. Scouts were sent out and soon reported the Tarascan army nearby. To discover how many warriors there were and how they were organized, the scouts were sent again. When they neared the Tarascan camp, the scouts tunneled toward the enemy tents and listened to what was being said before reporting back to the king.[87]

CHAPTER 6

Arms and Armor

OUR knowledge of Mesoamerican arms is incomplete, but information is available from a wide range of sources. Sixteenth- and seventeenth-century accounts contain considerable discussion of Aztec weapons, there are numerous depictions in various codices, in sculpture, and in paintings, and a few examples have been preserved in museums. Although the most important weapons are repeatedly mentioned in the historical sources, others receive only few references in scattered documents, which suggests that additional, less common arms are no longer known. Therefore, the likelihood of achieving a comprehensive listing of Aztec arms is small.

OFFENSIVE WEAPONS

The most general division of arms, for our purposes, is into offensive and defensive weapons. Offensive weapons are used to take an objective by projecting force, and they include bows and arrows, darts and atlatls, spears, slings, swords, and clubs. Defensive weapons more or less passively protect the user, and they include body armor, helmets, and shields. The Aztecs' main offensive arms were projectile weapons and shock weapons such as spears and clubs.[1]

Projectile Weapons

Projectile weapons enable the user to strike at the enemy at a distance and, among the Aztecs, included atlatls, bows, and slings.

The atlatl (*ahtlatl*), or spear-thrower, was used to throw "darts"

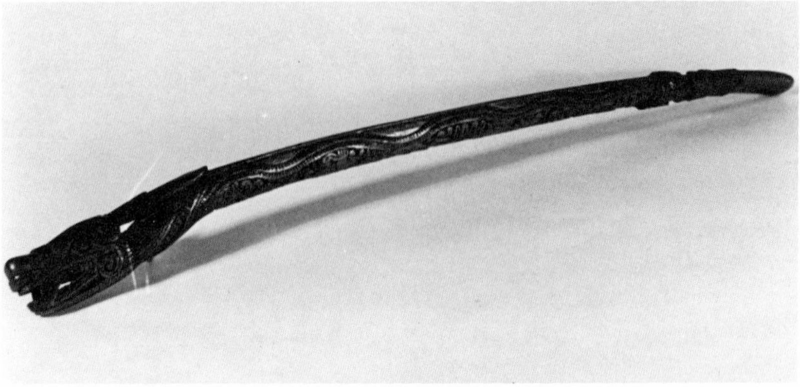

Fig. 6. Aztec atlatl. (Courtesy of the Museo Nacional de Antropología, Mexico)

with greater force and for longer distances than spears could be hand thrown (see figs. 6–8). By one account the god Opochtli created the atlatl,[2] while another credits the Aztecs with inventing it during their early years in the basin of Mexico.[3] But actually the weapon greatly predates the Aztecs and is depicted in murals at Teotihuacan[4] and at the classic site of El Tajín,[5] and atlatls have been recovered archaeologically from the classic period.[6] More than any other Mesoamerican weapon, the atlatl was associated with the gods, who are often depicted carrying it.[7] Many of these spear-throwers were ornately and artistically crafted, such as the one with a turquoise head in the shape of a serpent that Moteuczomah Xocoyotl sent to Cortés.[8]

The few examples extant are finely carved specimens depicting human figures and symbols in low relief.[9] One is also covered with gold. These elaborately decorated examples were probably used only on ritual or ceremonial occasions. The existing examples of the atlatl are approximately 0.6 meters (2 feet) in length and 35–37 millimeters (1.5 inches) in width at the upper end, tapering to 19–25 millimeters (0.7–1 inch) at the lower. They have a hook at the upper end against which the dart is placed, and a 5–10-millimeter (0.2–0.4-inch) groove for its bed. Another specimen has two grooves, suggesting that it was intended for throwing two darts simultaneously. Finger grips were provided by loops attached to the sides of the atlatl, holes in the device, or pegs extending from the sides, and they were

Fig. 7. *Cuahchicqueh* land from canoes; Spaniards attacked from both sides; Aztec warriors throw a captured Spanish cannon into the water at Tetamazolco, a deep-water spot near the hill of Tepetzinco. (Med. Palat. 220, c. 465; courtesy of the Biblioteca Medicea Laurenziana, Florence)

Fig. 8. Warrior with atlatl, darts, and shield, from the Stone of the Warriors in Tenochtitlan. (Courtesy of the Museo Nacional de Antropología, Mexico)

usually positioned about a third of the way up from the lower end.[10] However, several examples show no indication of finger grips.[11]

The "darts" used with the atlatl, made of oak and with feathered butts, were of several varieties.[12] Most were single-pointed, many were fire-hardened, and others had obsidian, fishbone, copper, or flint points. Some darts were barbed, others were two-pronged, and still others were three-pronged.[13] The fire-hardened darts were called *tlacochtli*, or *tlatzontectli*, while three-pronged ones were called *minacachalli* and were also commonly used to hunt aquatic birds.[14] According to Sahagún,[15] the darts were made during the feast of *Quecholli*, but this account probably refers only to the normal resupply of darts for the armory. Claims that atlatl darts were carried in a quiver[16] appear to be erroneous, and the way they were used in battle argues against it (see below).

Spanish sources attest to the effectiveness of these weapons, asserting that darts thrown with the atlatl could pierce any armor and still inflict a fatal wound.[17] The barbed darts were particularly dangerous, since the point had to be cut out rather then simply being pulled out.[18]

Few quantitative data are available about the effectiveness of the prehispanic Mesoamerican atlatl, but examples from elsewhere in the world indicate remarkable accuracy and force for up to 46 meters (150 feet);[19] experimental tests put the range at over 55 meters (180 feet),[20] with an extreme in one test of 74 meters (243 feet) with an inexperienced thrower.[21] The atlatl provides almost 60 percent more thrust and, hence, greater range and accuracy than the unaided spear.[22] Atlatl-propelled darts have greater penetrating power than arrows at the same distance.[23]

Bows (*tlahuitolli*) up to 1.5 meters (5 feet) long, with animal-sinew or deerskin-thong bowstrings,[24] were also major weapons in prehispanic Mesoamerica (see fig. 33), but they were apparently simple rather than compound bows.[25] War arrows (*yaomitl*) had a variety of points—barbed, blunt, and single pointed of obsidian, flint, or fishbone.[26] During battle, archers kept their arrows in quivers (*micomitl* or *mixiquipilli*)[27] (see fig. 3). How many arrows they had is uncertain, but data from elsewhere suggest around twenty per quiver,[28] and archers are invariably depicted with a single quiver.[29] Unlike arrows of Indian groups elsewhere,[30] those in Mesoamerica were not poisoned (despite Huaxtec claims to the contrary),[31] but fire arrows (*tlemitl*) were used against buildings.[32]

The Aztecs received many bows and arrows as tribute.[33] But like atlatl darts, arrows were made during the feast of Quecholli (at least this was the time the normal war supply was made). Reeds gathered for shafts were straightened over fires and smoothed. Then they were cut to equal size, just as the arrow points were standardized. The ends were bound with maguey fiber so they would not split, the points were glued to the shafts with pine pitch, and the arrows were fletched.[34] Making the arrows uniform meant greater accuracy for the archers, as the effects of given bow pulls would be similar and predictable.

The conquistador Bernal Díaz del Castillo mentioned the deadly effect of the Indians' archery and reported that the people of Cimatlan could shoot an arrow through a double thickness of well quilted cotton armor.[35] The archers of Teohuacan (Tehuacan) were reputedly so skilled that they could shoot two or three arrows at a time as skillfully as most could shoot one.[36]

Quantitative data are lacking for the Aztecs, but tests with North American Indian bows indicate ranges of about 90 to 180 meters (300–600 feet),[37] varying with the size and pull of the bow and the weight of the arrows. The stone points normally used on Aztec arrows were the equal to steel points. Obsidian points are markedly superior in penetrating animal tissue, by approximately threefold,[38] the result of the superior cutting edges of the glasslike obsidian, the serrated edges of the points, and their conoidal shape.[39] The Spaniards felt the stone arrow points to be particularly damaging.[40]

Completing the projectile triad were maguey-fiber slings (*tematlatl*) used to hurl stones at the enemy.[41] The stones thrown by the slings were not casually collected at the battle site but were hand-shaped rounded stones stockpiled in advance, and these also were sent to Tenochtitlan as tribute[42] (see fig. 9).

Comparative data indicate that slings have a range in excess of 200 meters (660 feet) with randomly selected stones, exceeded 400 meters (1320 feet) with lead pellets in ancient Greece;[43] slingers in the imperial Roman army could pierce chain mail at 500 paces.[44] As with arrows, standardizing the pellet shape and size increases velocity, distance, and accuracy, and such pellets could be lethal against even armored targets.[45] Díaz del Castillo admired the Indians' use of bows, lances, and swords, but he commented that the sling stones were even more damaging,[46] the hail of stones being so furious that even well-armored Spanish soldiers were wounded.[47] Slings were suf-

manera, que quiere dezir:
hombre de cabeça de piedra.
Estos dichos Quaquatas, co
mo en su tierra dellos, que es en

Fig. 9. Matlatzinca slingers. (Med. Palat. 220, c. 133; courtesy of the Biblioteca Medicea Laurenziana, Florence)

ficiently effective that the slinger and the archer were essentially equals;[48] when both were used, they were complementary and usually served close together.[49]

Shock Weapons

Shock weapons cut, crush, and puncture in hand-to-hand combat, and it is these that determine the outcome of battles. Among the Aztecs, these weapons included thrusting spears, swords, and clubs.

Aztec thrusting spears (*tepoztopilli*) were described as longer than those of the Spaniards and as having a *braza* (1.67 meters or 5.5 feet)[50] of stone blades that cut better than the Spanish knives, well enough, in fact, for the Indians to use them to shave their heads.[51] Terming this implement a lance or spear distorts its actual function in combat: the length of the blade indicates that it was used to slash and not simply to thrust, which would have been as easily achieved

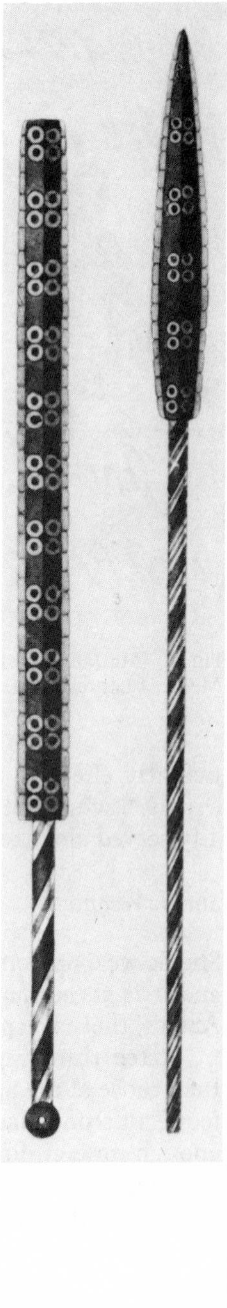

Fig. 10. *Macuahuitl* (sword) and *tepoztopilli* (thrusting spear), from an engraving of the Armería Real collection in Madrid. The *macuahuitl* is 0.84 meter (2 feet, 9 inches) long; the cutting surface is 0.57 meter (1 foot, 10 inches), and the handle is 0.27 meter (11 inches). The *tepoztopilli* is 0.91 meter (3 feet) long; the cutting surface is 0.31 meter (1 foot), and the handle is 0.60 meter (2 feet). To judge by sixteenth-century pictures, the tepoztopilli was usually longer than this example, which may have been truncated, possibly for shipment to Spain. These examples were destroyed in a fire in the nineteenth century. (Jubinal 1846: plate 9)

with a simple point. Thus, Nickel[52] classes these implements as "halberds." The tepoztopilli is effective for thrusting and slashing as well as for parrying at a distance, but it is less effective if the enemy closes, although the blades on the rearward portion of the head permit an effective backward pull. In one engagement a spear pierced Díaz del Castillo's metal armor and was stopped only by the thick underpadding of cotton.[53] They were not intended for throwing, but could be if necessary.[54]

There are no known surviving examples of the Aztec thrusting spears,[55] but there are numerous illustrations in various sixteenth-century drawings and one example did survive in the Real Armería in Madrid until it was destroyed in the great fire of 1884. There is a print of the weapon, although the implement is mislabeled (see fig. 10).[56] The tepoztopilli was usually about the length of a man, from around 1.8 to 2.2 meters (5.9–7.2 feet) long, with a triangular, ovoid, or diamond-shaped head with closely set stone blades forming a nearly continuous cutting edge.[57] The use of thrusting lances and other thrusting spears greatly predates the Aztecs in Mesoamerica. The weapons were present among the formative-era Olmecs,[58] at Teotihuacan,[59] and among the classic Maya.[60]

The Aztec swords (macuahuitl), which the Spaniards quickly labeled with the Taino word *macana*, seem to have been of at least two varieties—one-handed and two-handed[61] (see figs. 4, 5, 7, 11, 13, 31–33). These were made of wood, usually oak, 76 to 102 millimeters (3–4 inches) wide and a little over a meter (3.5 feet) long.[62] They had obsidian or flint blades fitted and glued into grooves along the edge. Drawings indicate rectangular, ovoid, and pointed designs.

The adhesive employed varied, with both bitumen and "turtle dung glue" being cited for the task.[63] Some swords had thongs through which the user could put his hand to secure the weapon in battle. The two-handed variety is described as being about four inches wide and as tall as a man.[64] Macuahuitl wielders are regularly depicted with the sword in one hand and a shield in the other, but using a two-handed sword obviously precludes that.[65]

The macuahuitl is bladed on both sides and can be used in a powerful downward slash, but it can also inflict a sharp backhand cut. One of the persistent observations of the conquistadors was the ability of these swords to cut the head from a horse with a single blow.[66] Furthermore, the Aztec swords were described by the con-

Fig. 11. Two Tlaxcallan nobles with swords (*macuahuitl*). Note their different construction. (Courtesy of the Archivo General de la Nación, Mexico. Tierras Vol. 914, exp. 2, fol. 60)

quistadors as cutting better than the Spanish swords and being so cleverly constructed that the blades could be neither pulled out nor broken.[67]

There are no known surviving examples of the macuahuitl.[68] However, there are numerous illustrations in various sixteenth-century drawings, and, as with the lance, one example did survive in the Real Armería in Madrid until it was destroyed in 1884. A print remains, but it is also mislabeled (see fig. 10).[69] As with the thrusting spear, the stone blades of the macuahuitl in the print are closely set, forming a virtually continuous cutting edge. Other drawings indicate that they were sometimes discontinuous, forming a gapped, possibly serrated, edge.[70] I can find no depictions of the typical Aztec macuahuitl predating the postclassic. In several early postclassic carvings at Chichen Itza, however, single warriors are holding clubs with two separated blades protruding from each side,[71] these may have been early variants of the macuahuitl. Another example comes from a mural from the eighth-century Maya site of Bonampak, in which one warrior is wielding a club with blades on one side and a single point or blade on the other.[72]

Clubs of various types were also used in Mesoamerican warfare.[73] Some were made of wood alone, but others (*huitzauhqui*) had stone blades.[74] Another type of club was the *cuauhololli* (see fig. 33), a simple wooden club with a spherical ball at the end.[75] The cuauhololli is a crusher and is thus effective in the downward blow but notably less so on the upward. Moreover, its lateral blows are probably less effective in absolute terms and impractical in combat. Yet another type of club was the *macuahuitzoctli*, which had a knob of wood protruding from each of its four sides and a pointed tip,[76] which Seler[77] likens to the medieval "morning star" club. These relatively unspecialized clubs were fairly widespread.[78]

DEFENSIVE WEAPONS

Aztec defensive weapons included shields, helmets, and various types of body armor. Aztec military shields (*yaochimalli*) were of a variety of designs and materials, with many being made of hide or plaited palm leaves[79] (see Figs. 4, 5, 7, 13, 15, 31–33). One conquistador described shields, called *otlachimalli*, made of strong woven cane with heavy double cotton backing.[80] An early account describes shields of split bamboo woven together with maguey fiber, reinforced with bamboo as thick as a man's arm, and then covered with feathers. Other shields called *cuauhchimalli*, were made of wood.[81] Some shields were made with a feather facing over which was laid beaten copper.[82] One type of shield was constructed so that it rolled up when it was not needed in fighting and was unrolled to cover the body from head to toe.[83] Shields were covered with painted hide, feathers, and gold and silver foil ornamentation.[84] The feather ornamentation varied by color, type, and design, according to the owner's status, merit, and so forth.[85] The Aztecs used round shields,[86] although square or rectangular examples are found throughout the classic and early postclassic in the Maya area, Gulf coast, and at Cacaxtlan (present-day Cacaxtla, Tlaxcala).[87]

As part of the royal fifth, Cortés sent the king a shield of wood and leather with brass bells on the rim and a gold boss with the figure of Huitzilopochtli on it. The handle had carvings of four heads—a puma, a jaguar, an eagle, and a vulture.[88] As the Anonymous Conqueror cautioned of the Aztec shields sent to Spain, many were of the type used in dances and ceremonies (*mahuizzoh chimalli*) and not the sturdy war shields (see fig. 12).[89] One shield examined by Peter Martyr d'Anghera in Spain was made of stout reeds covered with gold, and the back was lined with a jaguar skin. The lower part of the shield was decorated with a feather fringe that hung down more than a *palma* (0.209 meters or 8.2 inches).[90] The hanging border of feathers was a common feature, and, though appearing fragile, it afforded additional protection to the user's legs.[91] Such feather fringes could easily stop a spent projectile and deflect others, and the feature predates the Aztecs, being depicted in murals at the classic site of Cacaxtlan, at Teotihuacan,[92] and among the classic Maya.[93] They were probably intended primarily for protection against projectiles and not against clubs or swords.[94]

The feather workers of Tenochtitlan made shields,[95] and as part of their tribute the Aztecs received shields covered with fine, many-colored feather work and gold, depicting weapons, gods, kings, and scenes of great deeds in the past.[96] These were made of fire-hardened sticks so strong and heavy that, reportedly, not even a sword could damage them. According to the conquistadors, a crossbow could shoot through them but not a bow.[97]

The two feather shields in the Württembergisches Landesmuseum in Stuttgart are 0.71 and 0.75 meters (28 and 30 inches) in

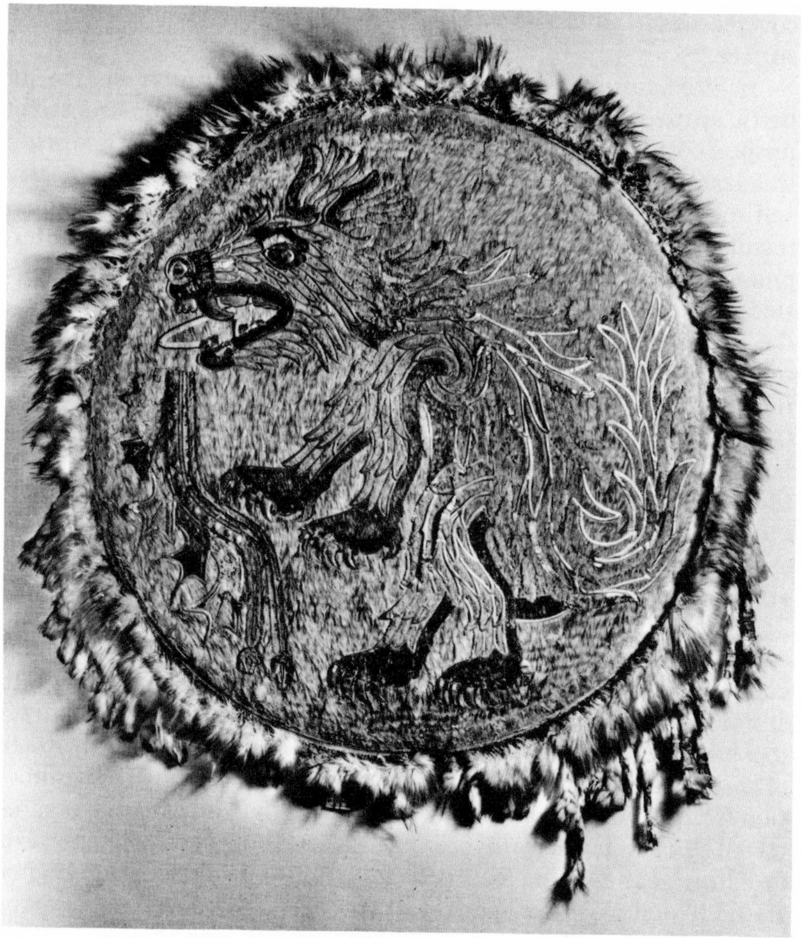

Fig. 12. Aztec feathered shield. This is an ornamental shield (*mahuizzoh chimalli*), not a functional war shield (*yaochimalli*). (Courtesy of the Museum für Völkerkunde, Vienna)

diameter, respectively, and have 3-millimeter (0.12-inch) foundations of wood strips bound together by fine interwoven cords. Four round sticks, 12 millimeters (0.47 inches) in diameter, cross the shields horizontally, and to these sticks and the leather patch on each shield are attached two leather handles. The outer surfaces of the shields are covered with thick parchment, covered with feathers glued to the surface.[98]

Quilted cotton armor (ichcahuipilli) was a common element of battle attire in Mesoamerica[99] (see figs. 31–33). It was constructed of unspun cotton tightly stitched between two layers of cloth and sewn to a leather border. The belief that the cotton was soaked in coarse salt to strengthen it[100] derives from de Landa;[101] but this account is unsubstantiated elsewhere, and Gates[102] thinks this is a misinterpretation of *taab*, "to tie," for *tab*, "salt," and that the cotton was tied or quilted, not salted.

The ichcahuipilli was so thick (one and a half to two fingers) that neither an arrow nor an atlatl dart could penetrate it.[103] It was made in several styles: a type of jacket that tied at the back, a sleeveless jacket that tied in the front, a sleeveless pullover that hugged the body and reached to the top of the thigh, and a sleeveless pullover that flared and reached the midthigh.[104] As with their other weaponry, the Aztecs received some cotton armor in tribute.

The war suit (tlahuiztli suit) encased not only the torso but the arms and legs as well in long sleeves and leggings (see figs. 4, 5, 7, 15, 31, and 32). These suits were not padded but were worn over the cotton armor.[105] They existed in many different types; twelve are recorded as having been received as tribute.[106] Despite appearing like animal skins, the suits of noble warriors were made of feathers sewn to a backing fabric.[107] Only meritocratic nobles wore tlahuiztli suits of animal skins.[108] Both types of tlahuiztli suit afforded some protection from projectiles, especially the body if the wearer was also protected by the ichcahuipilli, but the limbs were also protected, though to a lesser extent. The feathered garments were finer and of higher status. The slick surface of the feathers may have offered greater protection than would skins, especially against glancing blows, and depending on the backing, these suits were probably lighter and cooler.

In addition to the jacketlike top, leggings were worn.[109] They offered the same protection provided to the upper limbs, since there was no cotton armor below the torso proper. But the legs were not major targets with the weapons in use, and the arms were most endangered by the force of blows rather than by the cutting power of the weapons used. Tlahuiztli suits apparently predated the Aztecs; a jaguar suit worn by a warrior is depicted at classic El Tajín.[110]

Over their cotton armor some warriors—apparently the war leaders—wore feather tunics (*ehuatl*) (see fig. 13).[111] Not as common as

Fig. 13. Nezahualcoyotl, king of Tetzcoco, dressed in war attire: a feather tunic and kilt (*ehuatl*) usually worn over padded cotton armor (*ichcahuipilli*), greaves (*cozehuatl*), armbands (*matemecatl*), wristlets (*matzopetztli*), sandals (*cactli*), a helmet, and a gold lip plug. He is armed with a feather-fringed shield (*yaochimalli*) and a sword (*macuahuitl*) and carries a small upright drum (*huehuetl*) on his back to signal the attack. (*Codex Ixtlilxochitl* 106r; courtesy of the Bibliothèque Nationale, Paris)

the tlahuiztli suit, the ehuatl was used primarily in the areas to the east of Tenochtitlan, stretching from Tetzcoco to Tlaxcallan.[112] The tunic was fashioned of cloth over which feathers were set in rows. It had a hanging border of feathers,[113] and it resisted lances, arrows, and even swords.[114] Because it lacked sleeves and leggings, however, the ehuatl appears functionally inferior to the tlahuiztli suits,[115] and its continued use may have been due to its divine associations, as many gods bearing arms are depicted thus clad. Examples are shown in murals at Teotihuacan[116] and in carvings at early postclassic Chichen Itza.[117]

Some warriors (mostly higher nobles) also wore other body armor. Among these were armbands (*matemecatl*) and greaves (*cotzehuatl*) of wood, bark, or very thin gold; both were covered with leather and feathers. There were also wristlets (*matzopetztli*)[118] (see fig. 13). These pieces were worn with the ehuatl but were of little protective value.

Some helmets made of wood and bone were highly decorated with feathers,[119] while others were made of the heads of wild animals—wolves, jaguars, and pumas—over a frame of wood or over quilted cotton, with the wearer gazing out from the animal's opened jaw.[120]

Some warriors wore a wide breechcloth (maxtlatl) that covered their thighs.[121] Over this was often worn a hip-cloth.[122] Sandals (*cactli*) were also worn by some of the warriors.[123]

NONMARTIAL WEAPONS

Several other weapons served little or no martial functions in postclassic central Mexico—blowguns, axes, and knives.

The blowgun (*tlacalhuazcuahuitl*) was used primarily for hunting birds and was not a military weapon.[124] It was a hollow tube[125] through which molded clay pellets were propelled by blowing.[126] Pellets ranging from 8.5 to 34 millimeters (averaging 14.7 millimeters, or 0.3–1.3 inch, averaging 0.6 inch) were found at the classic site of Teotihuacan, indicating a blowgun of 1.5 to 1.7 meters (5–5.5 feet) in length.[127]

The ax (*tlateconi*) is frequently depicted in codices in martial contexts,[128] but it is not mentioned in the chronicle accounts.[129]

Fig. 14. Left: Aztec stone knife. (Courtesy of the Museo Nacional de Antropología, Mexico). Right: Aztec knife with wooden handle in the form of a nude man ((c.) 1986 Sotheby's Inc.)

Axes look intimidating, and certainly many of the commoners would have been skilled in their use, but they are unlikely weapons. Thrown, they would not have the range of other projectiles, even if the problems of balancing such a stone implement could be overcome. And they lack the reach of the competing shock weapons, such as the sword or thrusting spear.[130]

Axes in the codices are carried by persons or gods apparently attired for combat. But the garb worn is the ehuatl, not the tlahuiztli suit, indicating a more formal context, in the case of both gods and humans. Moreover, all of the ax-carrying humans are depicted in the same attire,[131] suggesting that they are specific functionaries. This interpretation is bolstered by the depiction of the ax as an execution device in association with the judge's seat[132] and in a decapitation scene,[133] as well as in an eighth-century Mayan execution scene.[134]

Knives are rarely mentioned as weapons of war. The *tecpatl* (literally., flint or fragment of flint) was a large flint knife used mainly for sacrificial purposes, also called an *ixcuahuac*. Another general term for knife was *itztli* (literally, obsidian or obsidian fragment), which also encompassed razors, lancets, and so forth. Knives were carried in battle (see fig. 14), but their major use in war-related events seems to have been in sacrificing captives and other victims.[135]

Which weapons were adopted and when depends, to some extent, on the offensive-defensive cycle in military development. Aztec armor and shields were adapted to the weapons they encountered, but technological developments were not as sophisticated in Mesoamerica as in Europe at that time. Given Mesoamerican technology, any material innovation in warfare could diffuse rapidly and came within the grasp of every group. The barriers to technological dissemination were social organizational constraints. Anyone could construct a macuahuitl, but only states could afford to support specialists who would spend the time necessary to learn how to wield the weapon in hand-to-hand combat. Weapons such as bows and ar-

Fig. 15. (facing page) Tribute list for the province of Hueipochtlan, depicting a variety of warriors' suits and accompanying shields. The glyphs along the left side represent towns, and indicated tribute includes four types of mantles (400 each, indicated by the "feathers"), five types of warrior suits and shields (one each of two suits and shields, and 20 each of three suits and shields, indicated by the flags), corn and beans (one bin of each), and *octli* (400 jars, indicated by the "feather"). (*Codex Mendoza*, MS Arch. Seld. A 1, fol. 31; courtesy of the Bodleian Library, Oxford)

(29
cccc. cargas
cccc. matillas de henequen
una pieça de armas de plumas ricas desta diuisa
una rodela de plumas ricas desta diuisa
xx. pieças de armas de plumas baladis amarillas desta diuisa
xx. rodelas de plumas baladis desta diuisa
xx. pieças de armas de plumas baladis desta diuisa
cccc. cantaros de miel de maguey espesa

rows or atlatls were used in generalized activity and in hunting, so even the simpler Chichimecs could acquire those skills, but the macuahuitl was used for warfare only by specialists, and Chichimecs were unlikely to master it. There were relatively few technological options available, and Aztec innovations were largely organizational. Even in this area, however, advances were not extensive. The major organizational development was in logistics, which permitted the prosecution of war at a great distance. But the Aztecs also pioneered the unprecedented reliance on naval capacity, which enabled them to wage extensive warfare within the basin of Mexico and to integrate the region. But both the substance and the amplitude of the offensive-defensive cycle were muted in Mesoamerica.

CHAPTER 7

Combat

THE predictable and stylized battle actions typical of the flower wars were largely missing from the Aztec battles of conquest. When wars were fought for effect, not for show, and when the goals were conquest, suppression of revolts, or retaliation, battle tactics and sites naturally varied with the targets and conditions.[1]

TIME OF ATTACKS

In general battles started in the morning, usually at dawn.[2] But even though dawn attacks were anticipated by the enemy, surprise attacks could sometimes be effected.[3] If the battle was not won during the day, the armies usually disengaged shortly before sunset.[4] Night attacks were uncommon, because the dark severely limited large-scale movements and troop control. But small-scale night raiding was common among some groups, such as the Mixtecs, Tzapotecs, and Otomies (the ethnic group, not the otontin military order).[5] The militarily sophisticated Aztecs generally carried out night assaults only against nearby (and thus familiar) targets and not during distant campaigns.[6] In short, they used the tactic only where difficulties of control and communication were minimized and they were confident of a relatively easy victory.[7]

SIGNALS

Smoke was used as a general signal to other camps and cities that there was war or that an army was approaching.[8] These signals were also used to initiate coordinated attacks,[9] but because they were prearranged—usually calls for assistance—they conveyed only previously agreed-on information.[10]

Nevertheless, the Aztecs accomplished a remarkable level of coordinated planning and control in their troop movements.[11] They could divide their army into smaller units for simultaneous attacks on a single objective[12] or on several dispersed objectives,[13] and they could coordinate joint land and water operations.[14]

For tactical communications the usual frontal attack was signaled by a variety of sound-making devices—drums and trumpets—accompanied by the shouts and whistles of the warriors, especially when they were winning.[15] The Aztec leader, either the king or a general, usually signaled the attack with a conch-shell trumpet, while the king of Tetzcoco signaled his troops with a small drum (see fig. 13), but other devices were also employed. The same sound that signaled attack also signaled retreat.[16] Fire was used as a signal in coordinated attacks only when the units were too far apart for audible commands.

Sound devices were effective in signaling the armies' advance, but warriors of each unit entered battle shouting the name of their town and beating their shields with their swords, so such devices were ineffective for maneuvers during the engagement. For that, the tall cuachpantli standards were used. Unit leaders wore standards and led their troops into battle.[17] If the cuachpantli bearer was killed or the standard was taken, the unit was thrown into disarray, and the Spaniards reasoned[18] that the Indian warriors fled because losing their standard was an evil omen.[19] Actually, this disarray was caused by more pragmatic considerations. Because the noise and confusion in battle made it impossible to rely on audible commands, sight was used, and the standard, towering above the fray, provided an easy sign indicating where and when the unit was advancing and retreating. Individuals and groups could keep in touch with their main body simply by observing the standard. And though the loss of the standard and the leader carrying it no doubt proved a major psychological blow to the rest of the unit, this setback was secondary to the loss of direction. Without the standard soldiers could not determine where their comrades were going, and they risked being cut off and captured by the enemy. The consternation shown by the army units had real tactical significance, and the loss of the standard-bearer did not mean divine displeasure and lead to dispersion; rather, it disrupted control and blinded the troops.

This use of the standard as a signaling device may have been an Aztec innovation.[20] Although pottery, mural, and sculptural depictions from earlier eras show similar standards, it is not known whether they functioned in the same fashion.[21]

THE ORDER OF BATTLE

Like their civilian attire, the battle dress of the Aztecs showed considerable variation, much of it the result of insignia and special attire granted to individuals to attest to their rank, class, past exploits, or membership in military orders. Offensive weapons were also socially skewed. Virtually everyone carried a shield, but the ichcahuipilli was restricted to warriors of demonstrated skill—tequihuahqueh and members of military orders. Lacking this armor, commoners were more vulnerable to the blows delivered to their unprotected head and body, and they died in greater numbers both in projectile barrages and in hand-to-hand combat.

The various weapons also carried different social connotations. Shock weapons were generally of higher status than projectile weapons, for at least three reasons. First, both slings and bows were regarded as plebian, since the latter were commonly used for hunting and they were the arms par excellence of the Chichimecs. Second, effective use of a macuahuitl or a staff weapon required considerable training and practice, which were reflective of class. The situation was much like that of late medieval European armies which were divided between the common archers and billmen, who required a much smaller investment in matériel and training, and the mounted, armored lancers of the nobility. And third, bows and slings were not as effective in combat as shock weapons, particularly against armored opponents. The atlatl was a projectile weapon, but it was revered because of its association with the gods and did not suffer from this stigma. Moreover, it had largely ceased being a utilitarian hunting tool—possibly because of its relatively short range—and its great penetrating power made it an effective military weapon, even against armored opponents.

In sum, then, elite warriors generally wore body armor, helmets, and tlahuiztli suits or ehuatl, carried shields (usually with a protective feather fringe on the bottom): in hand-to-hand combat wielded shock weapons (usually a macuahuitl but perhaps a club or thrusting spear); and also used atlatls and darts. Novice warriors (a category that included both nobles and commoners) lacked body armor but had shields; they wielded thrusting spears, clubs, and macuahuitl. Nevertheless, the bulk of the army was composed of nonspecialists, commoners who served as archers and slingers.[22] As might be expected, the fate of the combatants was largely determined by these differences in training and weaponry. Thus how, where, and when each weapon was employed must be considered.

Mesoamerican combat involved an orderly and recognized sequence of weapons use and tactics, usually beginning with projectile fire.[23] Although there were specialist archers and slingers, the opening salvo of projectiles was cast by all the combatants, employing whichever projectiles they possessed and causing considerable damage.[24]

Both of the archer's hands were needed to shoot the bow, so even if he was carrying a shield or had one attached to his left forearm, he could not use it to defend himself effectively. Consequently, archers were sometimes protected by shieldsmen who watched for and deflected incoming projectiles,[25] although this was not usual. There are few references to the Aztec archers' rate of fire, but a conservative estimate of six arrows per minute would exhaust all of their arrows in about three minutes. Likewise, the number of stones carried by slingers is unknown, but they, too, had a high rate of fire and probably used their ammunition even more quickly than the archers.

The distance at which fire was opened depended largely on the nature of the engagement, but the maximum projectile range was not exploited, even if the battle was joined in set-piece fashion between two armies. Battle descriptions indicate that the initial engagement took place at around 50 to 60 meters (55–66 yards), for several reasons. First, shorter ranges minimized difficulties in sighting targets and lessened the effectiveness of natural cover. Second, holding fire until shorter distances were reached allowed all the projectile weapons to be brought to bear (e.g., the shorter-range atlatl). Third, the closer the targets, the greater the projectile's penetrating power and the greater the effect of the limited number of projectiles soldiers could carry into battle. And fourth, lesser distances meant that the offensive army could exploit its firepower to injure the enemy, disrupt its formations, suppress return fire, or dislodge it from an entrenched position. In the case of an attack against a fortified position, however, the defenders would be more heavily supplied since they did not have to be mobile, and could thus initiate projectile fire at a greater distance.

The initial fusilage likely continued until the projectiles began to be depleted. The armies then closed during the waning moments of the mass barrage to take advantage of the covering fire,[26] as further delay would have needlessly exposed the warriors who had shot all their projectiles. It was during this advance that the atlatl was most used. It could not match the range of the bow and sling projectiles, but the darts could be thrown with maximum effect during the time required to close with the enemy, striking the opposing soldiers with enormous force and disrupting their formations. These were elite weapons wielded by soldiers advancing on the enemy.[27] But once in hand-to-hand combat the atlatl was cumbersome, since it was held in the right hand and prevented the use of a defensive parrying weapon. Moreover, the darts were quickly exhausted, as atlatl wielders apparently carried only a few; no more than four or five darts (and usually only three) are ever seen being held by a single warrior.[28] This may be an artistic convention intended to convey the presence of more such darts, but that seems unlikely, on three counts. First, the weapons are realistically presented in painted and carved depictions of atlatl-wielding warriors. Second, their likely use in the combat sequence (see below) argues in favor of limiting the number carried into battle, at least during the postclassic period. And third, they are not shown in a quiver or other container but loose, as one would expect for immediate combat use (see below).[29]

During the advance while the right hand was occupied with the atlatl, other weapons were held with the shield hand in a reversed position, handle forward.[30] But once the armies closed, shock weapons were used,[31] and the atlatl[32] was discontinued. It may have been attached to the shield[33] or, more likely, have simply been dropped. Although some soldiers continued projectile fire throughout the battle,[34] the slingers and archers probably remained back, since they were extremely vulnerable to shock-weapon attack, which inflicted the decisive injuries.[35] Once the armies closed, moreover, slingers and archers lost their massed targets and could strike only individually and opportunistically. They were also used to counter the enemy's archers and slingers and to harass reinforcements and prevent encirclement. Both this attack sequence and the role of the atlatl find support in a mural in the Temple of the Warriors at Chichen Itza and in scenes in various codices. Stela 5 at the classic Mayan site of Uaxactun depicts a Mexicanized warrior bearing an atlatl in the left hand and a bladed club in the right.[36]

The best and most experienced warriors initiated the clash between opposing armies in the hope of delivering a decisive blow. Particularly valorous kings sometimes led in battle, but usually the military orders preceded everyone. Of these, the cuahchic warriors advanced first. The cuahchicqueh fought in pairs and were sworn not to flee even in the face of overwhelming opposition. But they were not organized into offensive combat units, nor did they command troops; rather, they were superior individual fighters and were used largely as shock troops. They also acted as a rear guard if the army was forced to retreat[37] and as reinforcements for anyone in difficulty. Such was the reputation of the cuahchiqueh that, reputedly, two or three were deemed capable of routing an entire army. Once a cuahchic's foot was set in place, it was said, a hundred of the enemy could not budge him.[38]

After the cuahchicqueh came the otontin, followed by the veteran warriors, tequihuahqueh,[39] who led the first organized units. The leaders entered battle at the head of their respective units, which were composed of intermixed veteran and novice warriors so the veterans could support, teach, and watch over the youths in combat. The king usually entered the battle with his entourage of generals. This order of battle was essentially duplicated by each city as they advanced in separate units, with the Aztecs leading.[40]

Order was rigidly maintained in battle.[41] Anyone who broke ranks or caused confusion was beaten or slain, as was anyone who committed any hostility without the order of his leader.[42] Whenever warriors were killed or disabled, the rest closed ranks.[43]

The Aztecs placed considerable stress on orderly movements into and out of battle. Forward elements that advanced too rapidly could lose their cohesive front and intermingle with the enemy troops, presenting an opportunity for a devastating counterblow. If the army was forced back and its withdrawal turned into a rout, the resultant collision with the advancing support troops allowed an organized attacker to wreak havoc on the routed troops penned in by their own reinforcements.[44]

Combat units operated together to maintain a solid front so that the enemy could not penetrate and disrupt them. This tactic protected the other soldiers in the unit and reduced their immediate concern to fighting along the battle front rather than on all sides. Since only the soldiers directly facing an adversary could fight effectively, the units probably expanded along their front rather than forming blocks and remained only deep enough to prevent the breakthrough of enemy elements. Once the army had closed with the enemy and formed a broad front, skirmishing occurred by units as wholes,[45] but given the weapons employed, actual combat was inevitably an individual affair. If the unit's front broke, a rout was likely. It is doubtful that soldiers would remain on the battlefield in the face of sure extinction, especially not the commoners, who had the least to gain.

Battlefield tactics varied according to local conditions, opponents, and so forth, but the Aztec army generally tried to surround the enemy and assail it from all sides.[46] Attacking the flank while engaged in a frontal assault was practiced,[47] as were other formations.[48] The battle occurred largely between the warriors at the front of their respective armies, as only these could bring their weapons to bear. Thus, it was to the Aztecs' benefit to extend the front as much as possible, to take advantage of their usual numerical superiority, and thereby envelop the enemy troops and cut them off from reinforcements and resupply.

There are no accounts of battles from the individual soldier's view. But among the Indians taken to Spain was a young warrior who reenacted a battle scene that was described by Peter Martyr d'Anghera:

> In his right hand he carried a simple wooden sword, without the stones which ordinarily decorate this weapon, for the battle swords have their two edges hollowed out and filled with sharp stones fastened in with solid bitumen, so that these swords are almost as stout in battle as our own. . . . In his other hand he carried a native shield, made of stout reeds covered with gold. The lower extremity of this shield is decorated with a feather fringe, a cubit long. The shield was lined with tiger skin, and the centre of the exterior had colored feathers resembling our raw silk. Armed with his sword the slave advanced. He wore a robe of woven feathers, half blue and half red, and cotton trousers; a handkerchief was suspended between his hips and his leggins were fastened to his garments like a cuirass which is taken off without undoing the strings that fasten the leggins. He wore beautiful sandals. He then gave an exhibition of a battle; first hurling himself upon his enemies, then retreating; then he engaged another slave who served with him and was trained to these exercises. He seized him by the hair, as they do their enemies whom they capture with weapons in their hands, dragging them off to be sacrificed. After throwing the slave on the ground, he feigned to cut open his breast above the heart, with a knife. After tearing out the heart, he

wrung from his hands the blood flowing from the wound, and then besprinkled the sword and shield. This is the treatment they show prisoners.[49]

Little is known about the Aztecs' battle formations, but general considerations favor relatively open ranks in which the combatants are widely dispersed. This open formation is typically employed when fighting infantry of a similar nature to one's own, whereas a more densely packed closed formation is employed when withstanding a cavalry charge. Since there were no horses, the way Aztec weapons were used fostered an open formation.

In combat the left foot and shield are kept forward. In striking, the right foot advances to throw the body weight forward and permit the arm to achieve maximum extension while delivering the blow. Thereafter the soldier steps back, and the shielded left side is again forward to defend against a retaliatory blow. Thus, the lateral distance between friendly forces was the length of the extended arm and weapon—about two meters (6 feet) in the case of the macuahuitl. Thrusting spears were probably used for jabbing and some restricted lateral movement rather than being swung from side to side, since the holder is disadvantaged if an opponent makes it past the blade. The logical (and frequently depicted) placement of thrusting spears was between the macuahuitl warriors. With the spear's superior length the fighters would not be severely disadvantaged by distance from their opponents but could reach between the foremost combatants and strike at the opponent while simultaneously preventing them from slipping between the widely spaced swordsmen.

In addition to spacing, Aztec tactics must also have suffered from the technological limitations of their weapons, much as the tangless Bronze Age Greek swords were used primarily for piercing and not for slashing or parrying. Dislodging of the flint or obsidian blades of the Aztec weapons was apparently not a problem,[50] but they were fragile. Consequently, warriors probably made some effort to avoid direct blows to the blades; they may have used the flat of the weapon to parry and have struck with the bladed edges. But they were more likely to have deflected blows with the shield because parrying damaged their weapon and meant losing the initiative and the opportunity to strike back. Thus, macuahuitl duels are unlikely to have resembled European saber duels in which combatants struck and parried with the same weapon.

AMBUSHES

Ambushes were among the most successful and skillfully executed of the Aztec tactical maneuvers. They included simple attacks at physically disabling times and locations, such as at narrow mountain passes, where the advantage lay overwhelmingly with the attacker, or from seemingly deserted houses.[51] The most spectacular ambushes, however, were executed in battle and involved use of a feint in which the Aztec forces retreated as if the enemy were winning the struggle. If the feint was executed convincingly, the enemy advanced to press home its advantage. Once the enemy forces had been drawn into a compromised position, the Aztecs turned on them with additional troops, attacked them from behind, or used these troops to cut them off from tactical and logistical support.[52]

One feint described many times in the historical accounts involved the use of foxholes and cover.[53] During the war with Tecuantepec, King Axayacatl advanced at the front of his army. When the opponents attacked, he fell back to a place where his soldiers were hidden by straw, whereupon they attacked and won.[54] In the war against the Huaxtecs, King Moteuczomah Ilhuicamina formed his units and attacked, before feigning a retreat. This drew the Huaxtecs forward until two thousand armed cuahchicqueh and otontin warriors, camouflaged with grass, arose and destroyed them.[55] The same basic tactic was used in many other wars. In the war against Tolocan (Toluca), King Axayacatl and eight of his generals concealed themselves in straw-covered holes in the ground. When the Aztec army retreated past their location, they leaped out, killed the Toloca lords, and routed the army.[56]

Although disobedient rulers were sometimes killed, political assassination before battle was not a significant factor in Mesoamerican warfare. But in battle the ruler was a legitimate target, since his death could shorten the battle and the war.[57]

REINFORCEMENTS AND WITHDRAWAL

Replacing units in battle is dangerous and may open the army to renewed attack. Nevertheless, this operation is crucial, since both arms and the combatants' stamina are limited. The Aztecs were adept at both tactical reinforcement (adding men and units on the battlefield) and strategic reinforcement (adding men and units in a war). They commonly committed only some of their troops in a given battle and held the remainder in reserve,[58] although the best warriors were usually sent into battle first. The Aztecs could thus assess the enemy's strength and commit an appropriate force.[59]

The practice of holding troops in reserve until needed was common throughout Mesoamerica.[60] And if a Mayan example can be legitimately extended to other areas of Mesoamerica, reinforcements brought with them food and drink for the combatants as well as a resupply of projectiles and other arms.[61]

The Aztecs' open formation probably eased the maneuver, as new troops could easily approach the combatants from the rear and move up through the widely spaced fighting troops. Fresh troops probably moved forward on the allied combatants' right side, which offered them a better view than the shielded left side. Once at the front, the relief soldier could engage the enemy and allow his predecessor to fall back on the left.

How often new units relieved those currently fighting is uncertain.[62] One source put it at every quarter of an hour. While the precise length of combat for each unit probably depended on a variety of factors, including the ferocity of the fighting, nature of the terrain, and access to supplies,[63] reliefs suggest both regularity and relatively brief periods of combat, probably because of arms and ammunition limitations.

Stone blades shatter when they strike other weapons, but they usually do not when they strike cotton armor, flesh, or shields. Nevertheless, the breakage during combat must have been significant. While weapons with shattered blades can still be used effectively as clubs, their effectiveness is impaired. Thus the periodic withdrawal of troops during combat served not only to rest the men but also to allow them to trade weapons. Overnight or after battles, blades were probably replaced, and other arms were repaired.

Occasionally the opposition was too strong to continue hand-to-hand combat, so the army would fall back just enough to allow the archers, slingers, and atlatl wielders to use projectiles.[64] The same tactic also supported orderly withdrawals in the face of superior forces. When the entire unit or army was forced back, it moved in the direction of its camp, where additional projectiles could be retrieved to turn the tide against opponents who did not have a fresh supply.[65] The ability to conduct an orderly withdrawal was also necessary in a prolonged battle, as fighting did not generally continue at night.[66]

As noted earlier, the Aztecs also left two generals in Tenochtitlan for the purpose of strategic reinforcement.[67] Additional troops dispatched from Tenochtitlan were largely of use in relatively nearby battles, such as against Xaltocan or Xochimilco.[68] But reinforcements were also sent directly from Tenochtitlan to distant campaigns of extended duration, in one case after twenty days of combat.[69]

Some wars were quite long, but these were either flower wars or battles against cities that were sufficiently close that troops could be easily resupplied and reinforced.[70] Most battles to conquer a single city lasted for relatively short periods.[71] The length of wars depended on such factors as distance to the objectives, logistical difficulties, and differential strength. But the intensity of interest in conquering the objective was also a factor.

CONQUERING A CITY

If the defending army failed to acknowledge defeat and withdrew to the city or if the attackers flanked the defenders, the battle was carried to the city itself. The initial objective, however, was to induce the city to submit, not to destroy it. Thus, except in raids by non-Aztecs,[72] burning was largely restricted to temples and their associated buildings.[73] Firing a town's main temple was the ultimate sign of victory[74] and was a devastating blow, for several reasons. The temples were usually the most heavily fortified sites within the city, and burning them meant that the enemy had succeeded in penetrating and overcoming the strongest resistance. More pragmatically, the temple precincts also contained the city's armories. Thus, burning them deprived the embattled army of additional arms and war supplies, so the act was devastating even when it was accomplished by stealth or deception.[75] Burning the temples also signified that the local gods had been overcome, although their images were not necessarily destroyed. The Aztecs often removed them, along with their priests,[76] to Tenochtitlan, where the gods were housed in the coateocalli temple in the main plaza.[77]

Burning a city to accomplish its defeat was not common. But depending on the town's willingness to negotiate, the city might be burned if it did not surrender once its main temple had been fired.[78] When the Aztecs defeated Coaixtlahuacan, for example, the people fled to strongholds atop the nearby hills. Thereupon the Aztecs burned the temple, but they refrained from razing the city when its inhabitants pledged to pay tribute.[79] But when the lords of Alahuiztlan refused to submit and become tributaries, the city was razed.[80]

Burning the entire town was thus not an invariable consequence of defeat, although battles often led to this result when the clash was between major adversaries.[81] But burning a town did not mean its complete and eternal obliteration; if a defeated town was burned, its inhabitants were expected to rebuild it. Thus during the conquest of Tenochtitlan the Aztecs taunted the Spaniards and their allies by telling them to burn the city, because they knew that if the Spaniards won, the Aztecs would be forced to rebuild it anyway, and if the Aztecs won, they would force their enemies to rebuild it.[82]

FORTIFICATIONS

When fortifications were encountered, different battle tactics and timing were involved. Urban fortifications were not typical in postclassic central Mexico, but some cities had completely encircling walls, often high and occasionally constructed in concentric rings although usually not free-standing.[83] Other cities were fortified when a threat arose.[84] When the Spaniards attacked Tenochtitlan, walls, earthworks, and trenches were built.[85] Temporary breastworks in streets and atop houses were common, and they were ubiquitous during the battle for Tenochtitlan.[86] But even unprotected cities had fortified structures—usually the main temples and their enclosed precincts,[87] although other buildings also possessed fortified aspects.[88]

Another significant type of Mesoamerican fortification was the stronghold, detached from but associated with a city. It was usually atop a hill, where the advantage of height and a difficult ascent provided natural defensive additions to walls and battlements. From such heights simply rolling large stones down on attackers provided an effective first line of defense. However, these sites were vulnerable to siege if they were not equipped with adequate supplies of food and water.[89] When the residents fled to a detached fort near the town of Cuezcomaixtlahuacan, the Aztec army was foiled in its attempt to conquer them.[90] There was also a stronghold atop the island hill of Tepepolco, near Tenochtitlan,[91] as well as Aztec fortresses elsewhere.[92]

These fortified hilltop sites did not protect their cities, but they did serve two purposes. First, they could be used as places of refuge in the event of attack. When the Spaniards and their allies attacked the Matlatzincas, their warriors fought the Spanish party while the women and children, with their belongings, fled to the nearby fortress. When the battle grew even fiercer, the warriors also retreated to the stronghold.[93] Second, they could house additional warriors. When Cortés attacked Cuauhquechollan (Huaquechula), warriors emerged from the adjacent hilltop fort to fight the Spaniards.[94]

SIEGES

The mere existence of fortifications was not always a guarantee of safety in war. One of the Aztecs' main considerations in battle and in siege operations was to prevent outside help from reaching the defenders. Accordingly, army units were dispatched against neighboring towns in the region to ensure that they did not aid the enemy.[95]

If the war was not won on the open battlefield, the enemy could retreat behind fortifications—if, indeed, it had emerged in the first place. Under those conditions, unless the attackers gained entry through deceit or treason, they might simply withdraw in resignation. Barring this, three options faced the attacking army: breaching the fortifications, scaling them, or laying siege to the target.

Fortifications were frequently breached. In the war to conquer Oztoman, King Ahuitzotl's forces attacked the city, broke the wall and its fortress, and burned the temple.[96] Moteuczomah Xocoyotl's forces did the same in the war with Teuctepec.[97] Most such examples of breaching fortifications offer only scant details. But when the Aztecs attacked Xochimilco, the people reportedly retreated behind a defensive wall and wounded the attackers through holes constructed in it. (Whether these were loops through which arrows could be shot or merely holes to accommodate thrusting lances is unclear.) This strategy was overcome by the Aztecs, however, when they used sticks and digging implements to tear down the wall, precipitating a Xochimilca surrender.[98]

Unbreached fortifications could still be scaled, but this was uncommon. When the Aztecs tried to conquer the six-walled fortress of Quetzaltepec, scouts were sent at night to find a way to enter, as was standard practice, but they found none. As a result the Aztecs constructed wooden ladders, used them to scale the walls, and conquered the fortress.[99] During Cortés's absence the Aztecs attacked the Spaniards remaining in Tenochtitlan and scaled the walls of their fortress.[100]

If neither breaching nor scaling the walls succeeded, the remaining option was to lay siege to the city or fortress. The Aztecs could besiege towns within the basin of Mexico because of the ease with which canoes could be used to ferry supplies. But logistical constraints rendered sieges virtually impossible elsewhere. More than other tactics, sieges depended on factors external to the military skills of the forces involved. Time, expense, logistics, and the presence of potentially hostile groups adjacent to the target city affected siegecraft. Enemy resistance in the area could stiffen, and the besieged city might be reinforced and resupplied while Aztec supplies dwindled. Moreover, the Aztecs themselves could be attacked. So instead of sending a small army capable of defeating a city through a siege, the Aztecs sent a large army to overwhelm it.

Large siege machines did not exist in Mesoamerica, and only the weapons normally used in combat were available to the attackers.[101] Projectiles had harassment value in besieging fortifications, and atlatl darts and stones proved to be effective. Both could be lobbed over the walls of fortifications with telling effect,[102] and burning arrows were used to set buildings afire.[103]

Since extended sieges were usually not feasible, defensive fortifications could be rudimentary. Strongholds could doubtless have been built to withstand sustained sieges, and their absence reflects the limitations of the attacking army. Rather, such forts were temporary refuges where women and children could escape the fighting and, if the battle went badly, where the nobles and leaders could withdraw and hold out for a short period. During this time they could still negotiate the terms of surrender from a better bargaining position than if they had suffered outright defeat.

Given the potential of fortifications for defense, their infrequent use in postclassic Mesoamerica was probably linked to nontactical considerations. First, as noted above, the Aztecs had developed some countermeasures. Second, even if a city were to erect effective fortifications, the cost of manning the entire perimeter was enormous, particularly for sprawling agricultural towns, as opposed to the planned fortified cities of Europe. And the inhabitants were unlikely to be able to repulse a massed enemy at any given point along the walls. Furthermore, the likelihood of betrayal seriously reduced the value of such protection, particularly considering the expense involved. But third, and most important, the use of fortifications in Mesoamerica could not be divorced from the city's wider social networks. The city itself might be safe, but its fields and stores beyond the walls were still vulnerable. So were its smaller unfortified dependencies, and without these the city was lost anyway. In consequence, a static defense was a losing one. Only an active defense that defeated the enemy would enable the city to continue as the hub of a social network.

CHAPTER 8

Victory (or Defeat) and Its Aftermath

BATTLES were a major concern for the Aztecs, but, so, too were many collateral activities. Standards of conduct for combatants and other functionaries were enforced; follow-up actions were planned; and the captured, the wounded, and the killed had to be dealt with in a systematic manner.

MILITARY JUSTICE

Wartime rabble-rousers and malcontents were widespread, but not approved of, in Mesoamerica, certainly not by the Aztecs who wrote the following description:

> The subversive [lit., double-sided enemy] is a trouble-maker. He is excrement, he is feces. He causes discord among people [lit., He stretches out between people, among people]. He causes people to turn against one another. He incites people. He convinces people of lies [lit., He causes people to swallow saliva and slobber]. He pollutes people with lies [lit., He repeatedly spits in people's mouths]. He thrives on gossip [lit., His food is words]. He stirs people up, he upsets people, he agitates people.[1]

These and many other war-related matters were dealt with by a military tribunal. The four (or possibly five) main war leaders also acted as judges in military trials at the battlefield and could order the execution of capital offenders by public clubbing or stoning.[2] The judges were drawn largely from the noble class but also from among the exceptional warriors.[3]

Military justice covered virtually all aspects of martial conduct. If a soldier revealed the generals' plans to the enemy, he was considered a traitor and was killed and dismembered, and his accomplices, or those who had known of his treason, were enslaved. As noted earlier, any warrior who attacked the enemy without his leaders' command was killed, as were any who attacked before the signal or who left their units.[4] Anyone who fled when a withdrawal had not been ordered was punished with death, regardless of his social class.[5] And messengers who failed to deliver a leader's message truthfully were killed.[6]

The military leaders also resolved disputes over who had taken a captive. If two men claimed the same captive and if no one verified either claimant's story or had seen how the captive was taken, the leaders decided who should receive credit. If neither proved a better claim, the captive was dedicated to the Huitzcalco temple in Tenochtitlan, where slaves were sacrificed.[7]

Warriors, like everyone else, could also be punished for misbehavior in peacetime. This was done by the civilian judges, who were drawn from the ranks of the nobles and also from the commoners who had excelled in war.[8] Telpochcalli youths were also judged and sentenced for various infractions of their expected code of behavior, but by the tiachcauh.[9] And if informers who passed information to the Aztecs' enemies were caught in Tenochtitlan, they were executed and dismembered in the main plaza.[10]

VICTORY AND DEFEAT

The end of a battle also entailed its own problems, procedures, and difficulties. Some matters varied according to whether the Aztecs had won and under what circumstances. Others, such as dealing with the dead and wounded, were routine and were not dependent on the battle's outcome.

Defeat meant breaking off the engagement and withdrawing. Orderly retreat was signaled with drums, trumpets, and whistles, in the same manner as the attack.[11] But disengagement was accomplished without the warriors' turning their backs. Thus they could pull back beyond reach of swords and club, yet could continue firing covering projectiles at the enemy.[12] The cuahchic warriors formed the rear guard to cover the retreat of the rest of the army,[13] which, ideally, was orderly.

If a withdrawal covered the flight of women and children—as was often the case with the Aztecs' opponents—the warriors faced the enemy and fought a delaying action until their dependents were safe;

then they, too, retreated.[14] If there was no refuge, they all fled together, with the women and children in the middle.[15]

Sometimes, retreat discipline broke down, or an orderly withdrawal was neither possible nor desirable. When the troops at Itzyohcan were routed, for instance, they escaped by jumping into the river. The heavily armored Spaniards could not follow, since the Indians had destroyed the bridges.[16] As mentioned above, a disorderly withdrawal could easily turn into a disorganized rout, with disastrous consequences. But maintaining order in the ranks while pursuing a retreating opponent was sometimes even more difficult than maintaining it during one's own retreat, as pursuers often stopped to gather goods dropped in flight.[17]

Victory meant the imposition of tribute on the vanquished, an obligation owed to the Aztec king by the defeated town's nobility, although the tribute was actually divided among the Triple Alliance members. But decisions about the new tributary town were made by the Aztec king alone,[18] with the disposition of the defeated military leaders decided on by the Aztec war leaders.[19]

Defeated towns were frequently sacked in Mesoamerican wars.[20] But sacking was not inevitable, and it usually happened when the conflict had not been concluded by a negotiated halt or surrender. Enemies would ordinarily surrender before total defeat to save their cities from being sacked. Refusal to submit to Tenochtitlan merely meant that the Aztec army would march against that city, but submission before the battle could save it; tribute requirements would increase, but sacking would be avoided.

After the battle had been joined, sacking could still be avoided if the city surrendered. If not, sacking immediately followed the successful battle, but it could be stopped at any time if the enemy leaders surrendered. Sacking was the ultimate act and could be avoided as long as the vanquished retained something to grant the victors in return, even as little as surrendering themselves and pledging obedience.

Thus, in the war between Tetzcoco and Azcapotzalco, the Azcapotzalcas sacked cities allied with Tetzcoco while the latter's army was absent, since Tetzcoco had not surrendered and the other towns, as dependencies, could not.[21] But once a major town had been conquered, so, too, had its dependencies, rendering physical conquest of these additional towns unnecessary. Sacking was not merely an act of vengeance, but was one way soldiers were compensated, and when looting was prevented or curtailed for political reasons, the Aztecs paid the soldiers for their losses.[22]

Peace could always be restored, either by defeating the attacking army or by submitting, but the process was not an unconditional either/or: surrender had many permutations. Conquest might mean outright destruction and domination, but it could also merely be the point at which the destruction reached unacceptable levels, leading to surrender. Consequently, a "conquest" was not always clear-cut. Instead, there were grades of conquest: voluntary alliance, "voluntary" tribute, tribute under threat, submission under threat of war, submission during or after battle, and utter destruction.

In the actual peace process a noble envoy or delegation was dispatched to the enemy with the offer—usually, if it had been defeated, to become a tributary.[23] But if a city did not yield early, such as by pledging obedience to the Aztecs on first request or submitting on the approach of their army, battle was joined, and the terms of submission became more onerous.

The defending city would not initiate battle unless it felt it could actually prevail. But once the battle began, surrender usually followed, to save the city from imminent defeat[24] or to avert its destruction.[25]

The victors did not ordinarily make offers to the vanquished once battle had been joined and the fate of emissaries sent to negotiate a cessation was not always a happy one. When Cortés had already destroyed much of Tenochtitlan, for instance, he sent for a noble captured a few days before and asked him to negotiate a surrender by the Aztecs. The noble agreed and was received in Tenochtitlan with the respect due his rank, but the Aztecs then sacrificed him.[26] Similarly, when Aztec emissaries were sent to ask for help from the Tarascans against the Spaniards, they were killed because the Tarascans were suspicious of their true intentions.[27]

These suspicions arose, in part, because some segments of a community might sue for peace while others continued to fight. Furthermore, peace negotiations were often used as subterfuge. When Cortés attacked Xochimilco, the Indians negotiated for peace, but they did so to salvage their property and to delay the Spaniards until the Aztecs could come to their aid.[28] Similarly, the Aztecs began negotiations in order to use the time to resupply themselves.[29]

Another option was to withdraw to a stronghold. Such retreats bolstered a side's negotiating position, particularly since those taking refuge there usually included the political leaders. Open flight was another option taken by some and it had many variations. Dependents could get out of the city before the battle, leaving only combatants,[30] or the nobility and political leadership of the city might flee.[31] Both alternatives left the fate of the city dependent on the battle's outcome. But more common was flight after the city had been conquered. Thus, when the Aztecs conquered Amaquemecan (Amecameca), sixteen thousand people abandoned the town and fled to Huexotzinco.[32] The city's fate was then solely in the hands of the Aztecs, since they had conquered it and the citizens had not "ransomed" it by submitting.

Most radical of all was abandonment before the arrival of the attacking army. This was rare, but occasionally it was the only way to salvage anything at all. When Yancuitlan and Tzotzollan rebelled and killed some Aztec merchants, for example, the Aztec army marched on them. It reached Yancuitlan first and retaliated fiercely, killing even the elderly and burning the town. Two days later it reached Tzotzollan, only to find that the city had been burned by its own inhabitants, who had fled and could not be found.[33]

When all hope of a military victory was lost and the enemy recognized its imminent defeat, it laid down its arms as a sign of surrender.[34] Openly surrendering was an act of submission that could salvage something from the defeat.

Part of what determined the course of battle and its subsequent destructiveness was the degree to which the two sides shared the same premises: expectations of victory and defeat played a significant part in Mesoamerican warfare. Where concepts of what constituted victory or defeat were shared, destruction might be minimized, because the loser would recognize when defeat was inevitable and might quit. Where this view was not shared, as with the Chichimecs and, later, the Spaniards, battles might be bloodier, because the opponents would not recognize the pivotal point of defeat.

CAPTIVES

Taking captives was extremely important to the social, military, and political aspirations of the warriors. Accordingly, a major strategy in Aztec warfare was to capture rather than to kill the enemy.[35] Thus, even when he could as easily have been killed, an enemy was wounded so that he could not defend himself and, thus weakened, was dragged from the battleground.[36] The soldiers behind the front lines bound the wounded enemy warriors.[37] The captives' hands were tied behind their backs, and sometimes their feet were bound as well. Wooden collars called *cuauhcozcatl* were placed around their necks,[38] and they were sometimes placed in cages.[39] In one of the early battles under King Itzcoatl against Xochimilco, the Aztecs cut one ear from each captive,[40] but this action was atypical.

The captives' fate depended, in part, on the enemies' actions and how the town submitted. Towns that submitted on request or before combat began paid tribute, but their occupants were not taken captive (assuming no grievous offense had been committed, such as killing Aztec merchants). Once battle began, however, captives would be taken.[41]

The *Codex Mendoza*[42] depicts captives being taken by warriors of various statuses, from novices to cuahchicqueh (see fig. 2). However, all of the prisoners are dressed as warriors who have not yet taken a captive. No veteran warriors or members of military orders are shown captured, which doubtless reflects the true situation and is not merely an artistic convention. Novices and commoners were the likeliest prey, because they lacked the skill and experience to prevail in combat, especially against veteran soldiers, and they also made up the bulk of the combatants. In sum, the inexperienced and the unskilled formed the group upon which the skillful warriors preyed, built their reputations, and ascended socially.

At the same time, being taken captive was also to be avoided. Youths, in particular, strove so hard to avoid capture that they reportedly preferred being cut to pieces.[43] Rather than throwing down their arms and being taken prisoner, they fought on and were killed. And because warriors with greater skills and prestige risked more in being captured, they probably fought it with greater vigor, even to the death when feasible.

Seizure in combat did not irrevocably mean capture: the captors had to win or at least fight to a draw. Thus warriors taken by ultimately vanquished towns did not remain prisoners. But for a warrior to return home after he had been a bona fide captive was dishonorable.[44]

Captured enemies were enslaved and later sacrificed to the gods;[45] as a general rule, they were neither freed nor ransomed.[46] Most captives were taken to Tenochtitlan or other cities to be sacrificed, but not all. The first prisoner taken in battle was sacrificed on the spot.

His chest was cut open with a flint knife, and his heart was taken out.[47] During the Tecuantepec campaign, after the conquest of Miahuatlan, prisoners were immediately sacrificed before the army marched on.[48]

THE DEAD AND DYING

The cost in dead and wounded in premodern warfare depended on their armor and weapons and the way the two were wielded. Shields are normally carried on the left side in a right-handed population, and one might expect that side to be better protected as a consequence, but such is not the case. Sword wounds are predominantly on the left side—especially the left side of the head and neck and the upper left extremity[49]—because a right-handed slashing motion strikes the opponent's left where a right-handed defender is less able to parry blows. Staff weapons could slash equally well from either direction, but right-handed parrying also skewed these wounds to the left. And the crushing effect of swords, clubs, and staff weapons can break bones even when a blow is taken on the shield. Projectile wounds are randomly distributed over the unshielded portions of the body.

How bad wounds are is not simply a function of their severity but also of their type. Abdominal wounds are the worst (fatal over 90 percent of the time), followed by penetrating chest wounds.[50] Serious head wounds are frequently fatal, even more so in the case of projectiles than in the case of cutting weapons.[51] Puncture wounds are more serious than cutting or slashing wounds and cannot be treated so effectively, since they are likelier to involve internal bleeding.[52] And by Spanish accounts, thrusting swords caused most of the Indian deaths (by punctures).[53]

Among the military elite, body armor—shields, helmets, and ichcahuipilli—protected the most vulnerable areas, but this was not true of the unarmored commoners, which points to a heavy skewing of combat wounds and fatalities toward the lower classes and novice warriors. Moreover, their roles in combat placed the commoners at greater risk. Commoners were more likely to be wounded by projectiles, while the elites closed with the enemy to engage in hand-to-hand combat, in which projectiles played a less significant role.

Based on eighteenth- and nineteenth-century combat statistics, the ratio of dead to wounded is 1 to 4, with the killed, wounded, and missing amounting to 16 to 17 percent of the total army strength. There are no reliable statistics for the number of Aztec war dead. The available information is anecdotal, giving the number of Aztecs and allies killed versus the enemy victims in specific battles but not for every battle or even for complete campaigns, other than for the ill-fated Tarascan campaign. Consequently, the figures given are used advisedly[54] and may reflect the extremes: great success, as against Alahuiztlan and Oztoman; great failure, as against the Tarascans; and exceptionally disappointing results, as in Tizoc's campaign against Metztitlan. The great successes probably reflect conquest of an entire town and its civilian populace, while more modest successes probably reflect battles solely against armies.

In battle, designated individuals cared for the wounded and took them to medical specialists to be tended.[55] Drawing a parallel with Tlaxcallan the wounded were bandaged and taken away immediately so the enemy could not tell the damage it was inflicting.[56] Consequently, the dead did not litter the battlefield. But all the dead were identified, and their families were notified.[57] The fate of the bodies is unclear: those of nobles and valiant warriors were returned to their home cities, but, depending on circumstances, those of the commoners may have been cremated on the spot.

The numbers of captives taken and of warriors killed reflect differences not only in individual skills and numbers of combatants but also in the tactics employed. If an opposing army was surrounded, vastly more captives could be taken, since they and their archers and slingers could not escape. If the enemy forces were not surrounded, only the hand-to-hand combatants were likely to be captured. Consequently, the Aztecs would be expected to suffer fewer captives than their numerically inferior opponents, because the Aztecs were unlikely to be encircled. When an envelopment was accomplished, commoners would be more greatly represented among the captives, but when it was not, the captives were disproportionately drawn from the military elite.

THE RETURN HOME

When the war ended, the king or commanding general of the army ordered the teuctlahtohqueh judges to return home. There they were to inform the families of those who had died, so that there would be weeping for the dead.[58]

If he was not in battle himself, the king received news of the outcome by messenger. Runners were dispatched before the battle ended but after its outcome was clear. On arrival, the messenger was taken directly before the king to report and was thereafter confined until his report could be confirmed, even if the army was victorious. If the Aztecs had been defeated, the priests of all the temples wept over the deaths,[59] and the warriors entered the city in tears. They did not paint themselves, braid their hair, carry their shields, or use any drums or trumpets. They proceeded straight to the the temple of Huitzilopochtli, then spoke to the king, and then burned their weapons and insignia.[60]

If, on the other hand, the army had been victorious, a second messenger was sent to alert the king of the army's coming. It was received with happiness on the road, with drums and trumpets and the burning of copal incense. From Tenochtitlan, emissaries called *teuctitlantin* were sent to inform all the towns. Residents of the towns came with food and gifts to Tenochtitlan, where the army was received by everyone around the lakes.[61]

Those who had taken prisoners in the war were honored.[62] The families of the commoner dead were given clothing on behalf of the king, and those of the nobles were also given jewels, featherwork, and other finery. The leaders of each ward in the city visited the homes of the warriors in their wards, beginning with the unit leader of that calpolli. There they congratulated the soldiers and gave them ample supplies of food and clothing.[63]

In battles close to Tenochtitlan the dead were returned to the city. After four days of rituals and amid the lamentation of their families, their bodies (at least those of the nobles and valiant warriors), were burned at the temple of Huitzilopochtli.[64] Others were burned in the *cuauhxicalco* in the main plaza, and still others, in the various telpochcalli.[65]

The bodies of warriors could be either cremated or buried with their insignia, but the nobles were cremated.[66] Statues were made of nobles who had been lost in battle, and these were burned in place of their bodies along with their clothes and weapons.[67] Similarly, although merchants were not nobles, if a merchant died in battle, a statue of him was made from bound pine torches and placed in the merchants' temple and after one day it was burned.[68]

According to Aztec belief, all those who died in battle went to *ilhuicac*, the place of the sun, as did those who were captured in battle and later sacrificed. After four years in ilhuicac they were transformed into birds and butterflies and returned to earth.[69]

DISPOSITION OF CAPTIVES

Captives taken to Tenochtitlan were distributed among the wards. Each calpolli guarded and maintained a certain number, with the ward heads taking charge and honoring each of the captives as a god.[70] But not all captives were treated the same: noble captives were disposed of by the king as he desired; captive military leaders belonged to the victorious military leaders; and the rest belong to their individual captors.[71] Commoners made up the bulk of the captives, but not all of them could have counted for martial purposes.[72] All captives were important for displays of power and for ritual sacrifice, but only the combatants were important for status elevation.[73]

While the above situation was typical, anomalies did occur in Aztec conquests. In some cases wars were successfully fought without captives being taken. In the campaign against the southern Pacific coast towns, for example, King Ahuitzotl told the warriors to kill everyone and take no captives, because the battle was too far from home.[74] At other times the army was ordered not to kill any of the captives at the battle site but to bring them all back to Tenochtitlan.[75] Aside from the religious purpose for taking captives[76]—such as the sacrifice of captives, called *xipemeh* and *tototectin*[77]—and their status purposes, they were needed for political reasons, such as the coronation of a new king.[78] After his election the new king had to display his martial prowess by conquering cities and securing captives.[79]

The way captives were sacrificed varied widely, depending on the class of the captive, who had captured him, and the ceremony being celebrated. There were regular events such as the festivals held at the beginning of each month, and examples abound of sacrifices on these ritual days. For instance, captives were sacrificed at the feast to Huitzilopochtli.[80] During the festival of *Tititl* war captives were sacrificed following two days and nights of dancing.[81] Captives were also sacrificed to the gods Macuilxochitl and Xochipilli.[82] Tlacaxipehualiztli was a major sacrificial festival during which Xipe ToTec was honored by the sacrifice of prisoners, and even the enemy kings were invited to witness this event.[83] In Tlaxcallan, during the festival of *Coailhuitl* (which corresponded to Tlacaxipehualiztli in Tenochti-

Fig. 16. Gladiatorial sacrifice. A captive warrior, tethered to a sacrificial stone, is armed with a shield and a *macuahuitl* in which the stone blades are usually depicted as having been replaced with feathers (e.g., Códice Tudela 1980: 12r). His opponent is armed in the normal fashion. (Tovar 134; courtesy of the John Carter Brown Library, Brown University)

tlan), every town sacrificed the prisoners taken by its own warriors.[84] Sacrifices were held in towns throughout central Mexico.

Captives were also sacrificed for special occurrences other than feast days, such as celestial events. The New Fire ceremony marking the end of the fifty-two year cycle (the Mesoamerican "century") and, if all went well, the beginning of the next,[85] accounted for numerous sacrifices—two thousand prisoners from Teuctepec on one occasion.[86] Captives were also slain at the emergence of the morning star[87] and at solar eclipses.[88]

Many sacrifices were held when major temples were dedicated. For example, King Ahuitzotl brought captives from Quimichtlan and elsewhere to be sacrificed at the dedication of a temple in the ward of Tlillan.[89] Perhaps the most famous example was King Ahuitzotl's dedication of the main temple to Huitzilopochtli in Tenochtitlan, in which as many as 80,400 captives were sacrificed. Within Tenochtitlan, many prisoners were sacrificed at the *coateocalli* or *coacalco*, where the foreign gods were kept.[90] Others were sacrificed at night in the armories.[91]

Some captives, usually nobles and great warriors, were sacrificed in gladiatorial combat at the *temalacatl* (see fig. 16)[92] during the feast of Tlacaxipehualiztli.[93] The captive was taken to the round sacrificial stone, where he was painted with stripes. He was given four cudgels to throw, a shield, and a sword with its obsidian blades replaced by feathers. After drinking octli, he fought warriors—several, if he was a great warrior. First he fought four warriors of the military orders in a row—two jaguar and two eagle—and if he triumphed over each, he then fought all four together. If he still triumphed, then he fought a left-handed warrior. He fought until he was felled, whereupon he was stretched on his back, his chest was cut open, and his heart was torn out and dedicated to the sun. Then the body was flayed, and the skin was worn by the priests.

Captors did not kill their captives but brought them as offerings to the priests, who carried out the sacrifices, dragging the captives to the sacrificial stone if they faltered, and sacrificing them to Huitzilopochtli. After they were killed, the bodies were laid by the skull rack, and each warrior identified the one that he had captured. Then the body was taken to the captor's home, where it was eaten; the bones were hung in the house as a sign of prestige.[94] The heads of those who were sacrificed were skinned, the flesh was dried, and the skulls were place on the skull rack, the *tzompantli*[95] (see figs. 28 and 29). In the flower wars captives were also sought for sacrifice. But more probably died in combat than were captured.[96]

PART TWO

The History of Aztec Expansion

The armor they use in warfare is certain shirts like jupons, of quilted cotton the thickness of a finger and a half and sometimes two fingers, which is very strong. Over these they wear suits all of one piece and of a heavy cloth, which they tie in back; these are covered with feathers of different colors and look very jaunty. One company of soldiers will wear them in red and white, another in blue and yellow, and others in various ways.

The lords wear certain smock-like coats which among us are of mail but theirs are of gold or gilt silver, and the strength of their feathered garments is proportionate to their weapons, so that they resist spears and arrows, and even the sword. To defend the head they wear things like heads of serpents, or tigers, or lions or wolves, and the man's head lies inside the animal's jaws as though it were devouring him. These heads are of wood covered on the outside with feathers or incrustations of gold and precious stones, and are something wonderful to see. They carry shields of various kinds made of strong solid cane woven with heavy double cotton, and decorated with feathers and round plaques of gold. The shields are so strong that only a good crossbow can shoot through them, but arrows do not damage them. Although some of these shields have been seen in Spain, I should say they are not the kind used in warfare but in their dances and ceremonies.

The offensive arms are bows and arrows, and spears which they throw with crossbows made of another pole. The spearheads are of hard stone, or a fishbone that is very strong and sharp, and some spears have three points. Their maces have three points inserted in the same manner, so that in one thrust they produce three wounds. They have swords that are like broadswords, but their hilts are not quite so long and are three fingers wide; they are made of wood with grooves into which they fit hard stone blades which cut like a Tolosa blade. One day an Indian I saw in combat with a mounted horseman struck the horse in the chest, cutting through to the inside and killing the horse on the spot. On the same day I saw another Indian give a horse a sword thrust in the neck that laid the horse dead at his feet. They have slings with which they shoot very far, and many if not most of the warriors carry all these kinds of weapons in combat. It is one of the most beautiful sights in the world to see them in their battle array because they keep formation wonderfully and are very handsome. Among them are extraordinary brave men who face death with absolute determination. I saw one of them defend himself courageously against two swift horses, and another against three and four, and when the Spanish horsemen could not kill him one of the horsemen in desperation hurled his lance, which the Indian caught in the air and fought with for more than an hour, until two foot soldiers approached and wounded him with two or three arrows; he turned on one of the soldiers but the other grasped him from behind and stabbed him. During combat they sing and dance and sometimes give the wildest shouts and whistles imaginable, especially when they know they have the advantage. Anyone facing them for the first time can be terrified by their screams and their ferocity. In warfare they are the most cruel people to be found, for they spare neither brothers, relatives, friends, nor women even if they are beautiful; they kill them all and eat them. When they cannot take the enemy plunder and booty with them, they burn everything.

ANONYMOUS CONQUEROR

CHAPTER 9

The Preimperial Kings

WHEN the Aztecs entered the basin of Mexico, their political system was simpler than that of the city-states they encountered. Political control was divided among a weak paramount leader and the heads of the various calpolli, thus lacking strong centralization.[1] After some initial difficulties with the surrounding peoples the early Aztecs allied themselves with the city of Colhuacan and soon adopted the tlahtoani system of leadership common throughout the basin of Mexico.

The Aztecs' first tlahtoani, Acamapichtli, was not an Aztec but a member of a Colhuacan noble lineage that claimed direct descent from the Toltecs (see chart 1 for the genealogy of the Aztec kings). The Aztecs adopted the tlahtoani system because it was militarily superior to their own decentralized system, and they chose a foreign ruler to provide legitimacy and overcome the competing interests of the various calpolli leaders, which prohibited the elevation of an internal candidate.[2] But more importantly, the Aztecs had settled on a small island in the lakes, and they needed to establish (or legitimize) close relations with lakeshore cities, such as Colhuacan, to gain regular access to needed agricultural products. This they did, though the price was technical subordination to Acamapichtli, who consolidated political control over external matters (largely manifested as military power) while internal control remained in the hands of the calpolli leaders. However, Acamapichtli married the daughters of the twenty calpolli leaders, and the children of these unions inherited not only the mantle of nobility but traditional calpolli leadership roles as well.[3] This did not mean an automatic convergence of internal and external control because the calpolli leaders' power still

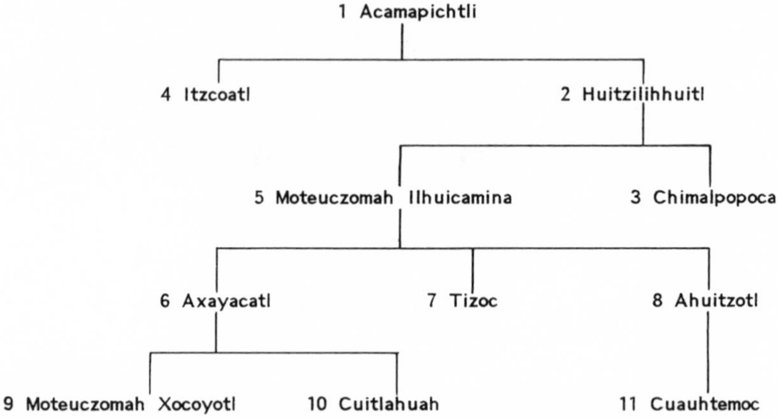

Chart 1. Chart showing the relationships of the Aztec kings, based on Durán 1967. For a reconstruction that differs slightly, see Carrasco 1984b: 60–61.

derived from their individual calpolli rather than from the tlahtoani, but the conflicts lessened.

Although the Aztecs fought battles before their adoption of the tlahtoani political system, these did not involve political expansion or incorporation of the vanquished and will not be considered here. The post-tribal wars began with the exploits of Acamapichtli, but the position of the Aztecs in a wider political context must be considered first.

The three earliest Aztec kings were not independent rulers but, like the kings of many cities, including Colhuacan, were subordinate to Tetzotzomoc, king of Azcapotzalco and leader of the Tepanec Empire, the most powerful polity in the basin of Mexico at that time (see map 2). Nearby Azcapotzalco dominated the western basin of Mexico, and the Aztecs became its tributary,[4] paying the Tepanecs in lake products and gaining access to the markets of the Tepanec cities.

Conquests by the Aztecs during this time were presumably under the aegis of the the Tepanecs of Azcapotzalco. This presents a number of difficulties in interpretation: when were the Aztecs the principal conquerors, when were they merely auxiliaries, and when did they wage war in pursuit of their own strategic goals as opposed to those of the Tepanecs? The Aztecs also fought on behalf of the

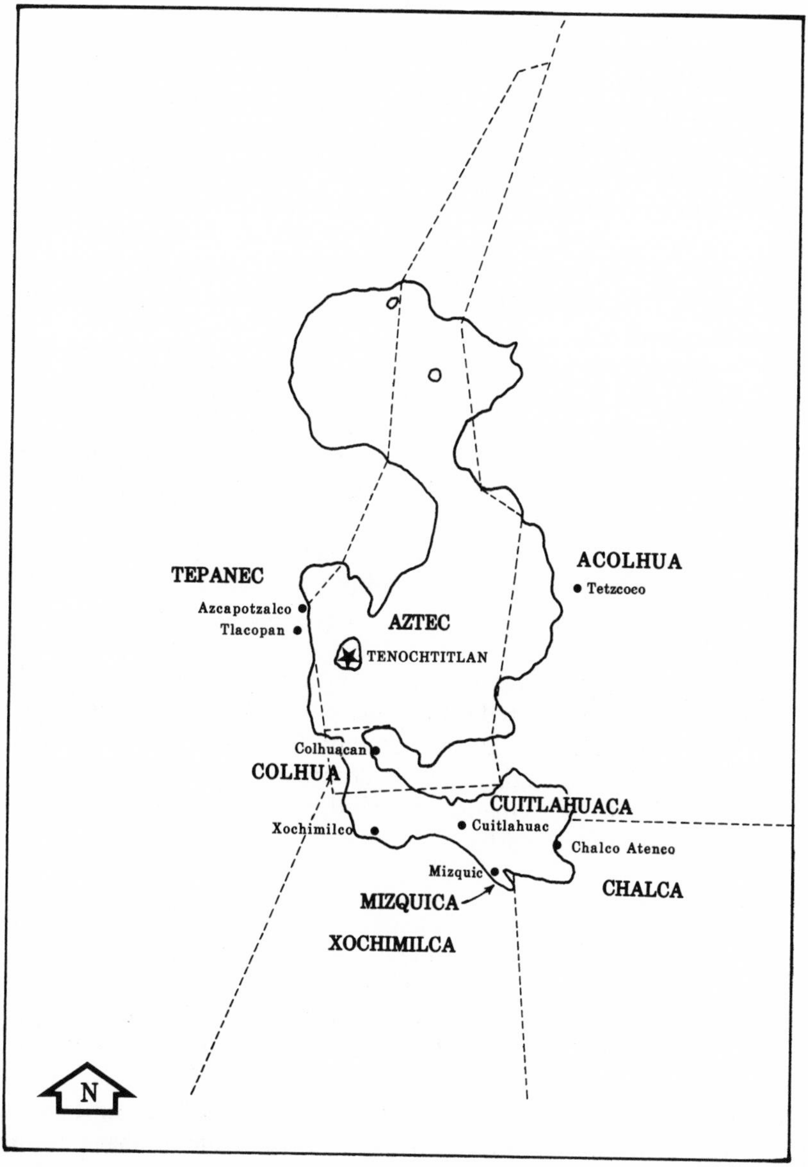

Map 2. Ethnic areas in the basin of Mexico (derived from Gibson 1964:14).

Tepanecs in many campaigns in which they had no obvious interest, but they were not mercenaries: assisting in their lords' wars was an obligation of all tributary relationships in Mesoamerica. This pattern was common in Mesoamerica and was one that the Aztecs continued and elaborated in their own empire, but it leaves their actual role in many conquests open to question. Did they provide the bulk of the army, or merely a few troops? Moreover, the Aztecs' role in these conquests may not have been as significant as depicted. Their accounts tend to exaggerate, and some Aztec claims of conquests (such as at Chalco) conflict with the accounts of the people supposedly conquered.

Whatever their participation in the Tepanec campaigns, the Aztecs did not determine goals or strategy. The towns the Aztecs conquered do not fall into any readily apparent pattern, because we lack sufficient information on the Tepanec expansion. The same would be true in trying to reconstruct the events of the Second World War solely from the accounts of only one of the smaller participants, such as New Zealand. Not only is the overall picture lost, but many significant battles appear unintelligible.[5]

Although they were tributaries, the Aztecs nevertheless benefited from conquests in which they engaged under the direction of the Tepanecs. Political supremacy belonged to the Tepanecs, but subordinates might be granted immediate political control, other benefits, such as the right to free passage and trade, spoils, and continuing tribute. Thus, being part of the dominant political system gave even subordinate participants enough derivative rights and benefits to bind them to the empire.

ACAMAPICHTLI "REED-FIST" (Ruled 1372–1391)

The earliest war during the reign of Acamapichtli (see fig. 17) began with Chalco in 1375 and lasted for twelve years.[6] However, it was not an ordinary war of conquest but one of the anomalous flower wars. The most common reasons the participants gave for fighting a flower war were to secure sacrificial captives and to provide combat training for the soldiers, but these explanations are incomplete. Recent explanations have emphasized the seemingly ritualistic and religious nature of the xochiyaoyotl battles, but they obscure their very sig-

Fig. 17. Acamapichtli ("Reed-fist"). (Tovar 93; courtesy of the John Carter Brown Library, Brown University)

nificant military and political purposes, which cannot be seen by examining a single occurrence at a single time. Rather, flower wars must be examined in context and through time, because their practice changed substantially.

The early xochiyaoyotl wars with Chalco were not mortal. For the first eight years of this intermittent combat, neither side tried to kill the soldiers of the other.[7] Rather, the xochiyaoyotl was a demonstration of martial prowess designed to determine dominance, so trying to kill one's opponents was not a primary goal. Thus, flower wars were not fought with all peoples. Weak opponents were simply conquered by force or frightened into submission, and wars with opponents too strong to be conquered were avoided if possible, frequently by preemptory submission. Between these extremes were potential adversaries who might be conquered, but only with difficulty, and these formed the xochiyaoyotl opponents.

Not all war between evenly matched opponents was avoided, nor were all such clashes necessarily flower wars. Sometimes there were compelling reasons to fight a difficult opponent, and at other times such clashes resulted from poor assessments of the enemy's strength. But since in wars between strong opponents the stakes were high and the outcome was uncertain, there was a clear preference for determining dominance through the xochiyaoyotl, in which superiority gradually became evident over a long period of time and at relatively low cost.

Because flower war objectives differed from those of ordinary conquest wars, so, too, did the order of battle. The projectile barrage of arrows, stones, and atlatl darts that began ordinary wars was absent, because demonstrating martial superiority was the primary objective. Consequently, killing by means that demonstrated no individual combat skills in either slaying the opponent or keeping from being slain played little part in the xochiyaoyotl. And there was a greater per capita reliance on shock weapons that required skill than was usual in ordinary combat.

After eight years of nonlethal combat with Chalco and no decisive demonstration of one side's dominance, the nature of the flower war changed: people began to be killed, but not the nobles.[8] Captives were taken by both sides, but the nobles were released and only the commoners died—presumably as sacrifices.[9] These changes accelerated the struggle for dominance, making it more costly to both sides, but stopped short of all-out battle that risked total defeat.

Flower wars do not necessarily reflect strategic military planning relevant to other conquest battles in which the Aztecs participated, but they do reflect something of the Aztecs' early political strategy. Chalco was an exceptionally rich agricultural region both near at hand and independent of the Tepanec Empire. Thus it presented an attractive and accessible target whose conquest could alleviate the Aztecs' food supply problems and eliminate their continued dependence on the Tepanecs. However, it was too large and powerful to be conquered outright—hence the recourse to a xochiyaoyotl. The twelve-year conflict during Acamapichtli's reign was the opening sequence in a flower war that ultimately spanned many decades. Neither side was vanquished, neither side demonstrated marked superiority, and neither side was apparently willing to risk the consequences of an all-out war.[10] But by carrying out a long-term, intermittent, and low-intensity struggle, the Aztecs could pressure the Chalcas and still engage in other military ventures.

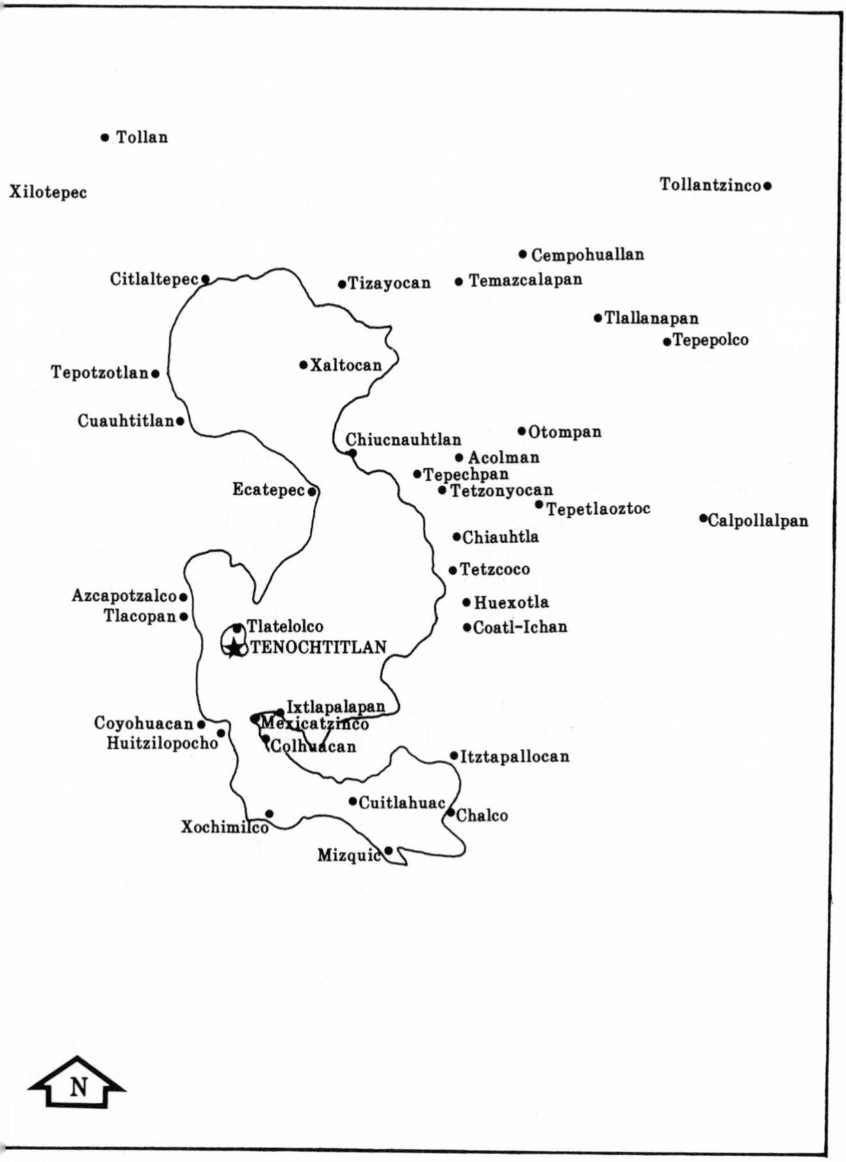

Map 3. Cities within and adjacent to the basin of Mexico accessible by easy marches over gentle terrain.

The Aztecs' earliest actual conquests were undertaken in conjunction with Azcapotzalco, as part of the Tepanec expansion and consolidation of the southern, eastern, and western portions of the basin of Mexico. The Aztecs conquered a group of towns—Xochimilco, Mizquic, and Cuitlahuac (in that order)[11] and secured the southern lakes area adjacent to the Tepanec Empire on the western shore.[12] They also participated in the conquest of Chimalhuacan on the eastern shore of Lake Tetzcoco[13] around the same time, but as a separate campaign, and then conquered Cuauhhuacan (Cuahuacan), on the western slopes behind Azcapotzalco.[14] There is also some evidence of conquests west beyond the basin of Mexico in the Matlatzinca area in the valley of Tolocan.[15]

Cuauht-Inchan was also reported as a conquest at this time (and confirmed by records of the "conquered" peoples)[16] (see map 3). However, this city is so far from the basin of Mexico across so much hostile territory that military conquest was probably not involved. Rather, because of the logistical constraints on projecting forces so far, and because the daughter of the "conquered" king was taken as a wife by the "conquering" king, this "conquest" probably reflects the establishment of an alliance secured by marital ties rather than actual martial defeat.

HUITZILIHHUITL "HUMMINGBIRD-FEATHER" (Ruled 1391–1417)

Huitzilihhuitl (see Fig. 18) became king on the death of his father, Acamapichtli, but since Tenochtitlan was merely one of many subordinate cities, the death of its king had relatively little consequence for the Tepanec Empire, which continued without disruption. The political relations of the Aztecs vis-à-vis their own subordinate towns also continued without significant disruption, because the ultimate guarantor of those relations was Azcapotzalco, not Tenochtitlan.

The Aztecs' relationship with the Tepanecs remained the same structurally, but Tenochtitlan rose in importance during Huitzilihhuitl's reign. The city continued to pay tribute to Azcapotzalco, but the amounts were reduced to a symbolic level—just two ducks, some fish and frogs, and other small lake products.[17] There were also significant changes in the Aztecs' military structure, status, and capability, and Huitzilihhuitl instituted the office of tlacochcalcatl (cap-

Fig. 18. Huitzilihhuitl ("Hummingbird-feather"). (Tovar 95; courtesy of the John Carter Brown Library, Brown University)

tain general and supreme head of the army) and gave it to his brother Cuauhtlecoatl (also known as Itzcoatl), who was to become the fourth Aztec king.[18] The Aztecs also expanded their tactical skills by practicing naval warfare from canoes.[19] Whether the boats played an active combat role at this point is uncertain, although armored canoes (*chimalacalli*) were used in battle as a source of projectile fire in the Spanish conquest. But the use of canoes sharply altered the local military situation, because until this time campaigns in the basin had relied largely on land travel around the lakeshore and the inadequate logistical support of tlamemehqueh (porters). Canoe transport could dispatch and resupply troops, greatly reducing the logistical problems within the basin of Mexico and opening both lakeshore and island cities to easier attack. Military operations were henceforth limited only by the supplies available rather than the limited amounts that could be carried on foot. Even more important, the Aztecs were no longer simply subordinates operating at the behest of the Tepanecs but could make political or military decisions independently.[20]

About five years into his reign Huitzilihhuitl assisted Azcapotzalco in an expedition against Xaltocan to the north,[21] continuing the Tepanec push to dominate the basin. Xaltocan's ruler, Pain, died and was succeeded by his uncle, Tzompantli, a noble from Metztitlan. According to Acolhua (Tetzcoca) accounts, the new ruler allowed the people of Xaltocan (who were Otomies) to pillage the neighboring towns at night (see map 3). Consequently the lords of Azcapotzalco, Tenochtitlan, and Tetzcoco raised an army, defeated Xaltocan, and forced Tzompantli to flee to Metztitlan.[22] Though this account provides an acceptable rationale for the conquest, the real reason was probably tied to political succession. Tzompantli was a leader without an established reputation in the area, and this jeopardized Xaltocan's political ties with other cities. A new king had to reassert his polity's dominance over its tributaries—usually by demonstrating martial prowess and resolve—or the political bonds would disintegrate. And Tzompantli's inability to control the actions of the Otomies may have been one example of his uncertain control. Whatever the case, Azcapotzalco, assisted by Tenochtitlan and Tetzcoco, successfully exploited Xaltocan's temporary weakness (see map 3).

Political control was poorly centralized in the northern basin because of the problems at Xaltocan, and the Tepanecs conquered much of the area during this campaign, including Xaltocan, Xilotepec, and Tepotzotlan, and probably the nearby centers of Tollan (Tula), Cuauhtitlan, Toltitlan, Tecciztlan (Tequizistlan), Tepanohuayan, Chiapan,[23] and Cuauhximalpan (Cuaximalpan).[24] Successful maintenance of a hegemonic empire typically requires a careful balancing of the conquerors' benefits in tribute and the tributaries' burden in paying. Nevertheless, Tetzotzomoc imposed a heavy tribute on the Otomies. As a result, many fled to the Acolhua region and settled at Yahualiuhcan and Mazapan,[25] depriving Tetzotzomoc of the manpower necessary to provide the tribute demanded, creating additional potential adversaries, and creating animosities that would haunt both himself and his successor.

Thereafter, the Aztecs participated in a number of conquests south of the basin of Mexico. Cuauhnahuac (present-day Cuernavaca, Morelos)[26] is recorded as an Aztec conquest (see map 4), but because Huitzilihhuitl took a daughter from Tezcacoatl, ruler of

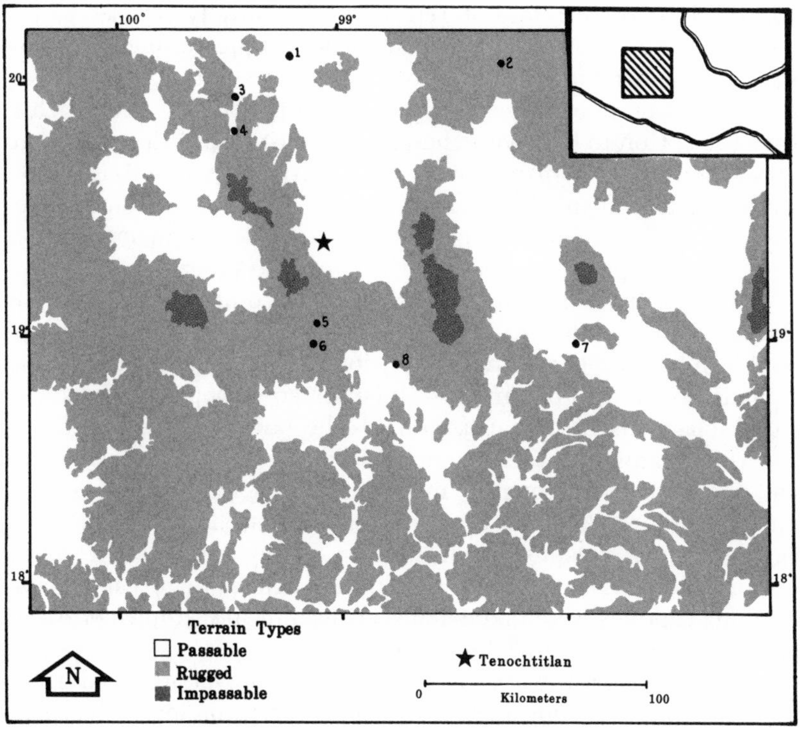

Map 4. Areas of campaigns by the preimperial kings. 1—Tollan; 2—Tollantzinco; 3—Xilotepec; 4—Chiapan; 5—Cuauhximalco; 6—Cuauhnahuac; 7—Cuauht-Inchan; 8—Yacapichtlan.

Cuauhnahuac, the "conquest" is more likely to have been a political alliance secured by marriage, similar to the one with Cuauht-Inchan. Two other towns in present-day Morelos were conquered by Huitzilihhuitl—Cuauhximalco (Coajomulco) and Yacapichtlan (Yecapixtla)[27]—but they were unconnected with Cuauhnahuac and were part of the struggle with Chalco, which was tentatively subdued for the first time the following year. However, Chalco neither pledged fealty nor paid tribute and quickly reasserted itself. Thus, this "victory" may have reflected a tactical success but not a strategic one.

The last major campaign of Huitzilihhuitl's reign was in the Acolhua area to the east, as part of the Tepanec effort to consolidate control. Ixtlilxochitl, lord of Tetzcoco, had initially acceded to Tetzotzomoc's demand that he make mantles for the Tepanecs.[28] Then, in a clear demand for an admission of vassalage, Tetzotzomoc began sending cotton to be woven every year, but in defiance, Ixtlilxochitl gave the cotton to his own tributaries. The timing of this campaign was propitious, for many towns nominally subject to Tetzcoco—Xaltepec, Otompan, Axapochco, Temazcalapan, and Tolcuauhyocan—secretly favored the Tepanecs,[29] probably seeing an opportunity to better their positions vis-à-vis the dominant polities.

Rather than risking a direct attack, Tetzotzomoc chipped away at the Acolhua domain little by little, and Ixtlilxochitl dared not oppose him because of internal opposition. But after consolidating the support of his loyal provinces—Tollantzinco, Tepepolco, Huexotla, Coatl-Ichan, and Acolman (Aculma)—he punished the traitorous towns.[30] Meanwhile, Tetzotzomoc raised an army from the western and southern basin towns,[31] met secretly at Aztahuacan, and attacked the loyal Acolhua town of Itztapallocan (Ixtapaluca) in the early morning, vanquishing it after an all-day battle. Ixtlilxochitl was unable to raise an army quickly enough to help,[32] and many Acolhua captives were taken and sacrificed in the temples of Azcapotzalco, Tlatelolco, and Tenochtitlan.[33]

Although the war had ostensibly broken out over breached tributary obligations, it continued the Tepanec consolidation of the basin of Mexico and eliminated a potential rival harboring dissident elements, such as the Otomies. This campaign resulted in the conquest of Otompan, Acolman, Tepechpan, and Tollantzinco, but Tetzcoco itself was not conquered until after the death of Huitzilihhuitl.[34]

CHIMALPOPOCA
"HE-SMOKES-LIKE-A-SHIELD"
(Ruled 1417–1427)

Chimalpopoca (see Fig. 19) succeeded to the throne at the age of ten on his father's death.[35] Like that of his father, Chimalpopoca's succession caused little disruption in the stability of the political system, as might have been expected in view of Tenochtitlan's subordinate position in the Tepanec Empire.[36]

During Chimalpopoca's reign the Aztecs aided the Tepanecs in their continued war against the Acolhuas of the eastern basin.[37] Though Tetzcoco was eventually conquered, it soon became a major

Fig. 19. Chimalpopoca ("He-smokes-like-a-shield"). (Tovar 97; courtesy of the John Carter Brown Library, Brown University)

rival of the Tepanecs again. Ten years after the conquest of Itztapallocan near the end of Huitzilihhuitl's reign, the Tepanec army attacked Huexotla and fought the Tetzcoco army for many days, going by canoe each day and returning at night before finally being repulsed.[38]

These Tepanec incursions were inconclusive, but decisive conquest was not the object. The purpose was to reduce the Tetzcoco's military capability and, even more importantly, to reduce support among Ixtlilxochitl's allies by chipping away at his domain and by demonstrating the Tepanecs' capacity to defeat him militarily. This strategy was apparently successful: there were many Tepanec sympathizers among the Acolhua cities, and Ixtlilxochitl was unable to consolidate his internal support. Thus, while his army fought the Tepanecs, Ixtlilxochitl remained in Tetzcoco for fear of treachery on the field and domestic intrigue in his absence.[39]

Three years later at Chiucnauhtlan, the Tepanecs again fought the Tetzcocas. The battle lasted many days, and Ecatepec and Acolman were sacked. But Tetzcoco was still too strong to attack directly, so Tetzotzomoc negotiated with Ixtlilxochitl's most important allies, the lords of Otompan and Chalco, to secure their neutrality in the war. Nevertheless, Ixtlilxochitl was able to gather support from many of his other subjects and allies, including Huexotla, Coatl-Ichan, Chiauhtla, Tepetlaoztoc, Tetzonyocan, Tepechpan, Chiucnauhtlan, Acolman, Ahuatepec, Tizayocan, Tlallanapan, Tepepolco, Cempohuallan, and Tollantzinco. With an army drawn from these cities and Tetzcoco, Ixtlilxochitl launched an attack against his former ally Otompan and against Tepanec subjects and allies in the northern part of the basin. He defeated Otompan, Xaltocan, Axapochco, Quemecan, Aztacan Quemecan, Temazcalapan, and Tollan, then Xilotepec and Citlaltepec, before turning south and conquering Tepotzotlan and Cuauhtitlan[40] (see map 3). Tetzotzomoc was not idle, however, and while the Tetzcoca army was attacking Cuauhtitlan, the Tepanec army struck back in the Acolhua area and sacked many of the undefended towns.[41]

What happened then is unclear. By one account the Tepanecs were defeated at Teptepec, and, after four years, Tetzotzomoc agreed to peace with the Tetzcocas.[42] By another, the Tepanec capital of Azcapotzalco was besieged until combat losses forced Tetzotzomoc to swear obedience to Ixtlilxochitl.[43] It seems very unlikely that Azcapotzalco was actually conquered, because within a year of its "defeat," Tetzotzomoc was able to gather enough support from among Tetzcoco's putative allies and subjects to threaten Tetzcoco once again.

With the help of Chalco, Otompan, Huexotla, Coatl-Ichan, Chimalhuacan, Coatepec, Itztapallocan, and Acolman, Tetzotzomoc attacked and defeated Tetzcoco. Disaffection with Ixtlilxochitl was high, and during this battle some of the people of Tetzcoco—the Chimalpanecs—turned on the king's supporters and killed them, forcing Ixtlilxochitl to flee to Tlaxcallan and Huexotzinco.[44] Though many vanquished rulers retained their thrones if they pledged allegiance, Ixtlilxochitl was either unwilling to do this or was considered too great a threat, so Tetzotzomoc ordered him killed.[45] But Ixtlilxochitl's son, Nezahualcoyotl, escaped to Tlaxcallan, where he remained for six years, returning only after the death of Tetzotzomoc in 1427.[46]

All of the major cities that participated in the conquest of Tetzcoco shared in the spoils. The Aztecs were given Teopancalco, Atenchicalcan, and Tecpan (near Cuitlahuac), and portions of the redistributed domain were also given to Tlatelolco, Coatl-Ichan, Acolman, Chalco, and Otompan.[47]

With the elimination of the last major rival to Tepanec domination in the basin, the Aztecs then engaged in a war of their own against Chalco, an occasional ally of the Tepanecs but a traditional Aztec enemy. The lords of the Chalca towns ordered walls built across a pass through their lands, with the result that the Aztecs could not travel through freely.[48] This was a breach of relations as well as an economic hindrance, and it appears to have been the precipitating factor in their "reconquest."[49] The ongoing flower war between the two city-states again changed its nature: both sides ceased freeing the nobles taken captive during the battles[50] and began sacrificing them, raising the cost of the war and spreading it more evenly across the social spectrum.

At this time trouble began between Azcapotzalco and Tenochtitlan, perhaps over the Chalca war but more probably because of the changing political situation in the basin. A militarily powerful Tenochtitlan was a desirable ally, but with Tetzcoco subdued, Tenochtitlan looked less like a necessary ally and more like a potential challenger. The traditional account maintains that the conflicts arose over water. Tenochtitlan was located on an island surrounded by brackish water, so the Aztecs asked for, and received, Tetzotzomoc's permission to draw water from the springs of Chapoltepec. But they also asked the Tepanecs to give them wood, stone, and lime to build an aqueduct, which was the sort of demand that a would-be lord might make to a potential subject, and thus it was both an affront to the Tepanecs and a provocation. Azcapotzalco immediately cut off all trade with the Aztecs, ordering that no more foodstuffs or merchandise be sent to Tenochtitlan, on pain of death. Guards were placed on the roads, and all contact between Tenochtitlan and the other cities was to be severed.[51] However, a number of non-Tepanec cities continued to sell goods to the Aztecs.[52]

Whatever the historical basis for this version, other events were probably more significant in bringing about the impending Tepanec war. The Tepanec political system depended largely on the skill and resolve of its leader. But Tetzotzomoc's death in 1427 was followed by a succession struggle among his sons.[53] Tetzotzomoc had named Tayauh to succeed him, but another son, Maxtlatl, seized power, murdered his brother, and assumed the throne of Azcapotzalco and the emperor's role, and he might have succeeded had the empire been more secure.

On the eastern side of the basin, the Acolhuas were disgruntled over their recent defeat and the loss of their lands. Many of the original city rulers had been replaced by Tepanec puppets, so there was a group of legitimate and disgruntled Acolhua pretenders, largely living in exile in states hostile to Azcapotzalco. Loyalties were deeply divided in the Tepanec cities on the western side of the basin as well. Maxtlatl's seizure of power was a breach in the legitimate (and consensually agreed-upon) rulership, and many other city rulers who were also descendents of Tetzotzomoc had an equally legitimate claim to the throne.[54]

It was during this unstable political situation that Chimalpopoca and his son, Teuctl-Ehuac, were killed. The most widely reported version of these events maintains that Maxtlatl ordered his soldiers to enter Tenochtitlan at night and kill the Aztec king and his son,[55] presumably out of fear of the growing power of Tenochtitlan, in retribution for Aztec pretentions, and from a desire to weaken that city and remove a threat to the empire. But this explanation seems unlikely, because Maxtlatl would not want to remove a young, untried ruler and permit his replacement by a much stronger and more experienced one.[56] The second and more plausible version of Chimalpopoca's death places the blame on his successor, Itzcoatl.[57]

CHAPTER 10

Itzcoatl
"Obsidian-serpent"
(Ruled 1427–1440)

THERE was a change in Tenochtitlan's succession system following the assassination of Chimalpopoca. In pre-imperial Tenochtitlan, strong and gifted leadership was not crucial because of the city's subordination to Azcapotzalco. Moreover, a council assisted the ruler and in the case of Chimalpopoca, his uncle, Itzcoatl, probably played a particularly large role.[1] But now there was no remaining direct heir and Itzcoatl took the throne in 1427 (see fig. 20), with profound consequences for Tenochtitlan's power structure.[2] He would rule until 1440.

Under strict hereditary succession the number of potential heirs is relatively limited. For example, inheritance of positions and titles through primogeniture, as in Great Britain, means that the eldest son automatically succeeds on the death of his father. If the eldest son dies, the next son then succeeds, and so on. But the more succession is determined by kinship, the likelier it is that an unsuitable candidate will emerge, because kinship rather than competence is the criterion for selection.

Moreover, much of the political elite is excluded from candidacy. If the logical successor is eliminated, other pretenders may come to power themselves. Or, in a system of somewhat loosely linked city-states, members of the royal family may break away and form their own dynasties when the old king dies, and they may do so with some legitimacy. Thus a system of succession that excludes many able candidates is potentially vulnerable to internal disruption, especially where allied cities are not structurally dependent on a centralized authority.[3]

Fig. 20. Itzcoatl ("Obsidian-serpent"). (Tovar 99; courtesy of the John Carter Brown Library, Brown University)

THE DEFEAT OF AZCAPOTZALCO

When Itzcoatl was elected king of Tenochtitlan, he was forty-six or forty-seven. He had been the tlacochcalcatl under Huitzilihhuitl,[4] and he had probably served in the same capacity under Chimalpopoca. A member of the immediate royal family, he was also a mature leader and skilled soldier and, consequently, was an able and likely contender for power. Legitimacy would now be largely a function of ability, at least within the upper nobility. Itzcoatl's legitimacy was confirmed through success; had he failed in the prosecution of the war he would probably have been deposed. He was still vulnerable to the pretensions of others with an equal right to govern, but several factors worked to his advantage. Chimalpopoca left no legitimate successor, Itzcoatl was more experienced than anyone else, and there were no other Aztec cities to provide a power base for potential challengers. Thus the very weakness and limited size of the Aztec domain proved an advantage to Itzcoatl, while the strength and much greater expanse and complexity of the Tepanec Empire proved a disadvantage to Maxtlatl.

Maxtlatl's main vulnerability was internal, not external. Once he eliminated the designated successor and assumed rule, there was little to restrain other equally legitimate pretenders who already ruled their own cities. Consequently, the cohesion of the Tepanec Empire was rent, Maxtlatl lost his secure power base, and he was challenged everywhere.

In the east Nezahualcoyotl, heir to the throne of Tetzcoco, left Tlaxcallan for Calpollalpan, seven leagues from Tetzcoco. There he received messengers from Chalco, Coatl-Ichan, and Huexotla seeking help against Maxtlatl, and at Oztopolco he also met with Axayacatl, who had been sent by Itzcoatl to offer help. Many other towns in non-Tepanec areas (Zacatlan, Tototepec, Tepeapolco, Tlaxcallan, Huexotzinco, Chalollan, and Chalco) joined Nezahualcoyotl to fight the Tepanecs. Acolman fell to the Tlaxcaltecs and Huexotzincas, and Coatl-Ichan to the Chalcas, and the kings installed by Maxtlatl were killed.[5] With Aztec help,[6] Nezahualcoyotl subdued the entire Acolhua province including Tetzcoco, although apparently not securely because he remained in Chiauhtla[7] (see map 3).

The Acolhua losses and the Aztec affront were provocative, but the Tepanecs did not retaliate immediately, although guards were again placed on all of the roads out of Tenochtitlan—the causeways of Tlacopan, Chapoltepec, and Tlatelolco[8]—and Itzcoatl had time to prepare. When he was ready, Itzcoatl sent his nephew, Tlacaelel, to Azcapotzalco, where he asked first if peace was possible. On learning that it was not, he smeared pitch on the king and feathered his head, as was done with the dead, and gave him a shield, sword, and gilded arrows—the insignia of the sovereign—and thus declared war.[9]

The Aztecs were helped in this war by Nezahualcoyotl, whom the Aztecs had assisted, and by Totoquihuaztli, the ruler of Tlacopan. The Tepanec city of Tlacopan was ostensibly subdued by the Aztecs and Acolhuas during the campaign against Azcapotzalco.[10] But in reality, there was no support for Maxtlatl in Tlacopan. Its ruler, Totoquihuaztli, was Tetzotzomoc's son and thus a legitimate pretender to the throne of the Tepanec Empire. His claim to the throne was as valid as Maxtlatl's, and the overall political situation in the basin of Mexico persuaded Totoquihuaztli to reassess his relationship to Azcapotzalco. As a consequence there was no real battle

Fig. 21. War with Azcapotzalco. (Tovar 101; courtesy of the John Carter Brown Library, Brown University)

for Tlacopan. Totoquihuaztli immediately "surrendered" as a result of a previous secret alliance with the Aztecs, and was named the new Tepanec king, for which he ultimately received a fifth of the booty and tribute taken and was given the province of Mazahuacan, the westward slopes of the valley of Tolocan, and the Otomies.[11]

The battle for Azcapotzalco lasted 114 days (see fig. 21) before the city was destroyed[12] in 1428. The Aztecs and Acolhuas, assisted by the Huexotzincas and Tlaxcaltecs,[13] defeated the Tepanecs, who fled into the mountains and to other Tepanec cities, many of which were conquered in turn.[14] This victory overthrew the Tepanec Empire, made Tenochtitlan an independent city-state, set the stage for the creation of the Triple Alliance of Tenochtitlan, Tetzcoco, and Tlacopan, and initiated the Aztec Empire.

Maxtlatl fled to Tlachco and obscurity, and the Tepanec kings were no longer recognized as lords but were considered tributaries of the Aztec Empire.[15] The Azcapotzalcas pledged lands, labor, and tribute, which the Aztecs divided, giving the most and best to their king, followed in declining portions by Tlacaelel, the other lords and nobles of Mexico according to their merits, the commoners who had demonstrated great valor, the various calpolli, and the gods and their temples.[16]

The overthrow of Azcapotzalco was only the first step in the creation of an Aztec Empire. Although the Tepanecs were deposed, their allies and tributaries were not automatically subject to the Aztecs but were simply freed from their tributary status. Consequently, a redefinition of relations followed, often through forceful reconquest.

The Tepanec city of Coyohuacan was sympathetic to Maxtlatl and chafed under their new subordination to the "traitorous" Tlacopan. While Aztec accounts allege that guards in Coyohuacan stopped, robbed, raped, and killed Aztec women en route to market,[17] the struggle for overall rulership of the Tepanec cities is a likelier reason. The people of Coyohuacan sought allies against the Aztecs among the peoples of Colhuacan, Xochimilco, Cuitlahuac, Chalco, and Tetzcoco, but without success,[18] and Coyohuacan was defeated (see fig. 22).[19] Thereafter, the Aztecs concentrated on the west and southwest area of the basin where the Tepanecs had been strongest, conquering Coyohuacan, Tlacopan, Huitzilopochco, Ixtlapalapan, and Colhuacan and, probably, Atlacuihuayan, Teocalhueyacan, and Mixcoac,[20] thus consolidating their power. Not every independent city-state in the area was conquered immediately, but this campaign did eliminate the threat of a Tepanec resurgence in the basin of Mexico.

SOCIAL CHANGES

With Tenochtitlan's emergence as the single most powerful city in the basin of Mexico, King Itzcoatl instituted a series of changes in the political, military, and social structures of Aztec society. To this point the Aztec tlahtoqueh's political power had been limited, because they were dependent upon the commoners for tribute. But the commoners, in turn, relied on the calpolli heads for access to lands and wealth, and the calpolli heads had their own interests. Now, however, the tlahtoani had lands and goods that were independent of the calpolli and their leaders, and by virtue of his position as mili-

Fig. 22. War with Coyohuacan. (Tovar 103; courtesy of the John Carter Brown Library, Brown University)

tary leader, they were his to distribute.[21] The tlahtoani could reward successful warriors and maintain the newly emerging nobility without the active support of the commoners, and he could elevate meritorious commoners (the cuauhpipiltin), separating them from the calpolli heads on whom they had been dependent. Thus he could create a body of soldiers primarily dependent on and responsive to him. Although the conquest did increase the calpolli holdings, commoners remained dependent on their calpolli for access to lands, but the nobles, including the calpolli leaders, received lands and wealth independent of the commoners, and the interests of the state (i.e., of the nobles) could be furthered without hindrance.[22]

This shift in relative power was rationalized as an explicit agreement with the people. According to Aztec accounts, the lords asked permission of the people to fight the Tepanecs,[23] but the fearful commoners did not want to fight them, and some even suggested that they deliver their god, Huitzilopochtli, to Maxtlatl as an act of obedience. The king persisted, however, and said that if the Aztecs lost the war, the people could kill the nobles and eat their flesh. The commoners agreed that they would be the nobles' tributaries, work in their houses, farm their lands, and carry their baggage in war if they won.[24]

What emerged from the Tepanec war was a more sharply defined class structure and a more independent elite tied more closely to the tlahtoani's interests. To secure his own position, Itzcoatl also instituted changes in the military structure, elevating his brothers and immediate relatives to the ruling council: Tlacaelel was chosen the tlacochcalcatl; Moteuczomah Ilhuicamina was chosen the tlacateccatl; Tlacahuehpan was chosen the ezhuahuancatl; and Cuauhtlecoatl was chosen the tlillancalqui.[25] Thereafter new officeholders were chosen at every royal succession, each new king choosing from among his own close relatives, and it was from among these that a successor was selected when the king died.[26] Moreover, these changes institutionalized the new system and provided for a more regular succession, the emergence of more skilled and experienced leaders, and some criteria for competence.

Another change in the system of social status that emerged (probably during Itzcoatl's reign) was the increased stress on taking war captives for sacrifice. This practice was part of the Mesoamerican tradition and predated the Aztecs, but as practiced by the pre-imperial Aztecs it was a matter of individual achievement. Taking captives now served the state in a direct way, by emphasizing its power and thus helping achieve Aztec ascendency in the hegemonic political world of fifteenth-century Mesoamerica.

THE TRIPLE ALLIANCE

By itself, Tenochtitlan lacked the power to consolidate the fledgling empire without engaging in numerous military operations and depleting its own strength. Tenochtitlan's partners were necessary to the continuation of the Aztec dominance, just as Aztec support was crucial to their own, because the Acolhua region had not yet been effectively consolidated, and Tlacopan's position vis-à-vis the other Tepanec cities remained insecure. But geographical location and not just power relationships determined the relative strength of the cities in the Triple Alliance. The Aztecs were situated between their two partners, Tlacopan on the west shore and Tetzcoco on the east. An island, Tenochtitlan was relatively secure from attack because, the Aztecs controlled the causeways and all areas where canoes could land. The same was not true of its partners, however. The Aztecs could secure the support of either ally against the other through bilateral arrangements, since Tenochtitlan posed an immediate threat (or security) for either city. Aztec forces could attack either city from numerous lakeshore locations, and Tlacopan and Tetzcoco were too far apart to reinforce each other quickly. Thus, the Aztecs were in both a geographical and a strategic position to coerce either ally or to use either bilaterally against the other.[27]

This balance-of-power strategy was apparently successful: there are no records of Tlacopan ever having opposed the Aztecs, possibly because it was more vulnerable to Aztec coercion than more distant Tetzcoco, with whom there were some difficulties. Thus Tlacopan was tied tightly to the Aztecs, and this bilateral configuration gave Tenochtitlan a preponderance of power from the outset of the Triple Alliance. The Aztecs' power grew to the point that they could defeat either or both of their partners without outside assistance, but the coalition remained important to Tenochtitlan. Destroying its partners would not place greater power in its hands; it would only deplete the Aztec army, reduce the allied forces, and eliminate two relatively reliable partners, thus undermining the Aztecs' own power.

Similarly, the further expansion of the Aztec Empire could have been accomplished through military conquest and subjugation, but only at great cost in time, money, and men. And since the purpose of the empire was not to usurp all the wealth of dominated regions but to extract moderate amounts from the existing tributary flow, there were several advantages to retaining the local leaders in office. It placed minimal administrative burdens on the Aztecs. It ensured the loyalty of the local populace to the local leaders. It placed the burden of maintaining local control on the local leaders rather than on the Aztecs. And it offered some incentive for the local leaders to submit without fighting a total war that would be costly to the Aztecs and would probably seriously damage or destroy the economy of the target region and ultimately reduce its value to the Aztecs. Since the terms of subordination were not harsh (particularly in view of the alternative), many towns submitted without more than a show of Aztec force.

EXPANSION OF POWER

Though Tenochtitlan was rapidly emerging as the dominant power, it was not yet beyond challenge, and the Aztecs engaged in a series of conflicts to eliminate potential rivals. Shortly after the initial consolidation of their empire, the Aztecs of Tenochtitlan fought their sister city, Tlatelolco, as they would intermittently for decades.[28] The dispute arose during the succession period following the death of Tlatelolco's king, Tlacateotl, who had been killed by the Tepanecs.[29] The defeat of Azcapotzalco had freed Tlatelolco from its subordinate political position, but it had also removed a political bulwark against Tenochtitlan's encroachment, and the loss of its own king made Tlatelolco particularly vulnerable at this time. Thus the conflict that broke out may have been an attempt by Tenochtitlan to dominate Tlatelolco or to prevent the rise of another, legitimate line of rulers that might pose a threat to Itzcoatl. But since Tlatelolco remained free of political obligations, it was probably an attempt by Tlacateotl's successor to preserve a favorable status vis-à-vis Tenochtitlan.

The Aztecs next helped secure the lands of their allies, the Acolhuas, on the eastern shore of the lake. Numerous Tepanec-dominated Acolhua towns had already been reconquered, and a joint Aztec-Acolhua army went to Chimalhuacan to negotiate with the remaining rebels. But despite the fledgling Triple Alliance's impressive victories against the Tepanec cities, the rebel towns refused to submit voluntarily. Consequently, the Triple Alliance armies fought and vanquished the main rebel city of Huexotla,[30] following which the remaining cities submitted easily, including Acolman, Coatl-Ichan, Teotihuacan, Tecciztlan, and Tepechpan.[31]

Aztec accounts attribute the next conquest to an affront:[32] asked by the Aztecs for stone to build a temple to Huitzilopochtli, the Xochimilcas refused. Acquiescence was an acknowledgement of vassalage, but refusal meant war. A further alleged provocation occurred when Aztec merchants and soldiers en route to Tenochtitlan with cotton were attacked and robbed by Xochimilca soldiers,[33] and subsequent Aztec peace overtures were refused.[34] But this version obscures the campaign's geopolitical purposes.

With both the eastern and western sides of the basin secured, the south was the next logical target.[35] In addition to security considerations, the southern portion of the basin was economically important as an area of exceptional agricultural productivity, and through it ran the two passes south out of the basin. Conquering this area would reduce the subsistence vulnerability of Tenochtitlan and permit unhindered movement into or through the region of present-day Morelos.

In the first attack the Aztecs were thrown back by a strong Xochimilca army. But Itzcoatl returned with reinforcements from Tetzcoco, Azcapotzalco, and Coyohuacan and the fighting resumed at the border of the Xochimilca territory. The Xochimilcas fell back to a defensive wall, from which they wounded many of the attackers, but the Aztecs tore it down. The Xochimilcas withdrew into their city, where they were pursued and defeated. The entire war lasted eleven days;[36] the Aztecs conquered Xochimilco, and its people fled into the mountains. By most reports the city was sacked, the temple was burned, and the land was divided,[37] although one account states that Tlacaelel ordered the soldiers not to loot the city and promised to recompense the soldiers for what they had lost.[38]

As the Aztecs continued their southern expansion, Mizquic fell next.[39] A small city adjacent to the newly conquered Xochimilca territory, Mizquic offered little difficulty and may have submitted without a battle at all. Then the Aztecs turned to Cuitlahuac, on the dual pretexts that it was impeding trade[40] and that the Cuitlahuacas had refused to attend a festival in Tenochtitlan.[41]

Cuitlahuac was relatively small, but it was located on an island between Lakes Xochimilco and Chalco and must have felt secure enough to refuse the Aztecs' blandishments. The Aztecs then sent envoys to the lords of nearby Chalco and Tlalmanalco to ensure that they would not aid Cuitlahuac.[42] Having thus eliminated outside assistance, the Aztecs determined to dominate and humiliate the city-state. The Aztecs sent youths (ages sixten to eighteen) who were below warrior age to fight Cuitlahuac. But so that they would not be defeated, the youths were outfitted in quilted armor and trained by captains, and veteran warriors were sent with them to defend the archers by deflecting arrows with their shields. This force marched from Tenochtitlan to Tecuitlatenco, where it embarked in one thousand canoes and, reaching the island, met and defeated the Cuitlahuacas.[43]

Nezahualcoyotl must have watched with some trepidation as Tenochtitlan conquered towns throughout the western and southern regions of the basin, gaining strength and subjects, and headed inexorably toward the eastern shore of the basin. An eventual conflict may have appeared inevitable, and also the outcome, At any rate, according to Acolhua accounts,[44] Tetzcoco submitted to Tenochtitlan by means of a feigned war. The armies of Tetzcoco and Tenochtitlan met at Chiquiuhtepec and fought, after which Nezahualcoyotl's army retreated to Tetzcoco, whereupon the king set fire to his city's temple as a sign of surrender. The war lasted only eight hours and took place by prior secret agreement.[45]

Even though Tetzcoco was given unprecedented privileges,[46] there were great benefits in this arrangement for Tenochtitlan. As the other major power in the basin of Mexico, Tetzcoco was a potential challenger, and war between the two cities would probably have proven costly and protracted. Tetzcoco's submission offered the Aztecs an extremely low-cost conquest with the appearance of forceful domination, which would enhance the Aztecs' perceived power and increase the likelihood that others would submit peacefully. This conquest also isolated the Chalca city-states in the southern basin of Mexico.

The Chalca city-states were independent and powerful, so despite the increasing severity of the intermittent conflict with the Aztecs, it did not seem perilous to the Chalcas. In fact, rather than seeking any opportunity to destroy the Aztecs, the Chalcas often sided with them in other conflicts; they aided Tetzcoco and Tenochtitlan in the war to wrest control from the Tepanecs, refused to assist Coyohuacan against the Aztecs, and agreed not to help Cuitlahuac against the Aztecs. Thus Chalco continued to fight Tenochtitlan, but without perceiving the ongoing struggle as mortal. To the Aztecs, however, the continued independence of Chalco was not merely a failure to seize economic control of the basin but also a serious threat to their security.[47]

All enemies were dangerous, but nearby enemies were particularly so: if the Aztec army launched a distant campaign, these local enemies could threaten their capital. Distant enemies posed a less immediate threat because of the time required to organize and march to Tenochtitlan, but nearby enemies suffered no such limitations. Consequently, leaving an unconquered enemy nearby meant that the Aztec army was an incidental hostage to the vulnerability of its capital. Thus Chalco was a serious threat, to Aztec dominance within the basin of Mexico and to Aztec expansion beyond it.

Unreliable allies also posed a threat to Tenochtitlan, as could be expected in a political system that did not institute structural changes among its tributaries and allies. But the Aztecs could exercise some control over their allies; when they went to war, they took their allied armies with them—primarily for military support, but also to remove them as threats in the basin of Mexico while the Aztec counterforce was absent. But the Aztecs could exercise no such control over enemies: these had to be endured or eliminated.

Nevertheless, Chalco was not conquered immediately, perhaps because it proved to be such a formidable opponent. But the continued state of intermittent war effectively isolated it in the southeastern corner of the basin and reduced its inhibiting effect on further Aztec expansion.

Having dominated virtually all of the southern, eastern, and western portions of the basin of Mexico, the Aztecs next sought to eliminate residual resistence from unconquered cities in the old Tepanec domains.[48] The resulting campaign was relatively easy: the Aztecs expanded into the north, conquering Tenanyocan (Tenayuca), Tepanohuayan, Toltitlan, Cuauhtitlan, and Xaltocan, possibly in 1434.[49] Cuauhximalpan, Tolocan, Xiquipilco, Xocotitlan, Matlatzinco (the area, not the town), and Chiapan were also conquered[50] (see map 5). Tollan, Ecatepec, Teocalhueyacan, Cuauhhuacan, Huitzitzilapan, and Tecpan submitted as well,[51] probably as a result of the Aztecs' demonstration of power in the region rather than through physical conquest.[52]

This campaign marked a significant expansion in Aztec strategic and logistical capabilities. Within the basin of Mexico, canoe transport allowed the Aztecs to mount campaigns with the tactical and logistical advantages of easy and swift troop movement and cheap resupply. But overland the army's tactical area was limited, and its operations required much more time because of the slower land movements and more difficult resupply. Still, extended campaigns

Map 5. (facing page) Itzcoatl's campaigns north, west, and south of the basin of Mexico and into present-day Guerrero. 1—Tollan; 2—Chiapan; 3—Xaltocan; 4—Xocotitlan; 5—Cuauhtitlan; 6—Toltitlan; 7—Cuauhhuacan; 8—Tepanohuayan; 9—Ecatapec; 10—Tenanyocan; 11—Xiquipilco; 12—Teocalhueyocan; 13—Tecpan; 14—Huitzitzilapan; 15—Cuauhximalpan; 16—Tolocan; 17—Cuauhnahuac; 18—Xiuhtepec; 19—Tzacualpan; 20—Yohuallan; 21—Teloloapan; 22—Itztepec; 23—Tepecuacuilco; 24—Quetzallan; 25—Tetellan.

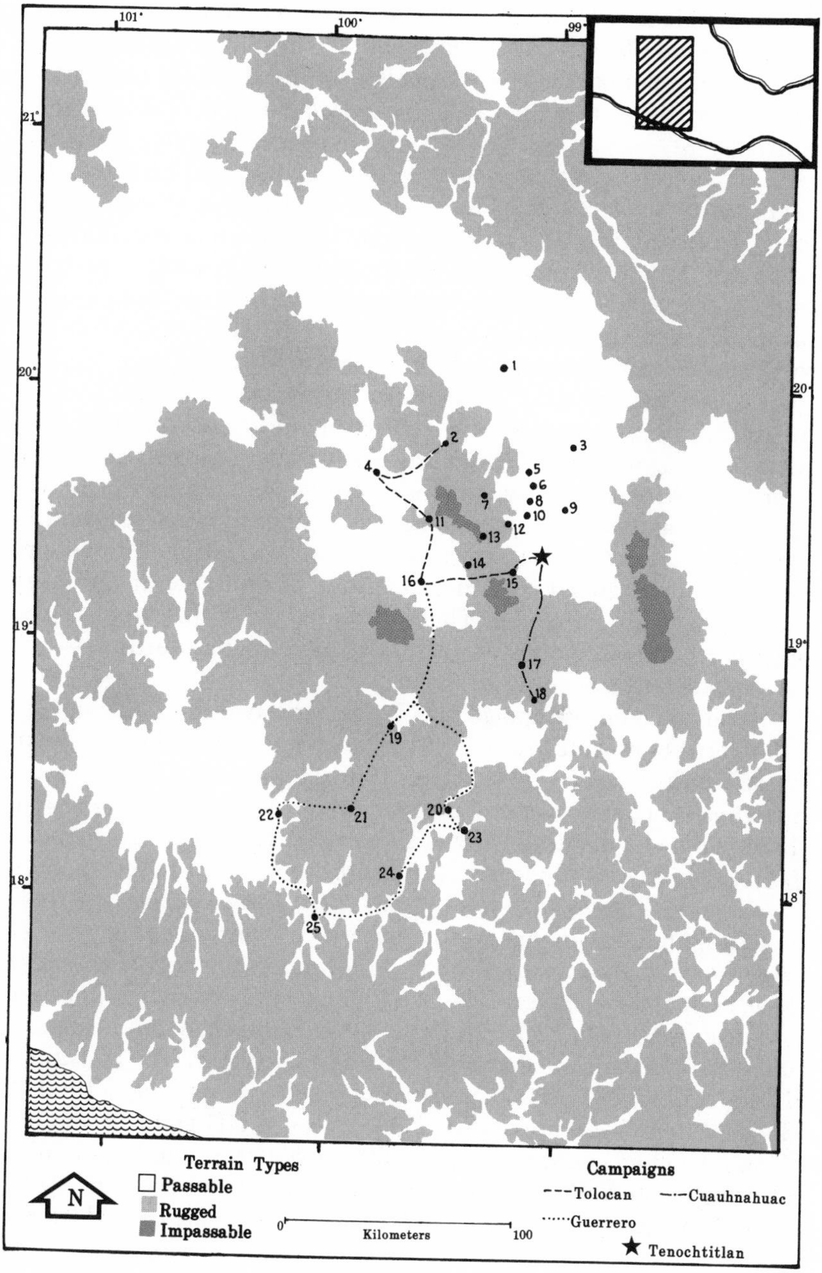
101°
100°
99°
21°
20°
19°
18°
1
2
3
4
5
6
7
8
9
10
11
12
13
14
15
16
17
18
19
20
21
22
23
24
25
Terrain Types
Passable
Rugged
Impassable
N
0
Kilometers
100
Campaigns
Tolocan
Cuauhnahuac
Guerrero
Tenochtitlan

were feasible as long as the army marched within the empire, where supplies could be gathered from tributary towns, but once beyond the imperial boundaries, the campaign could extend only two or, at most, three days' march because the army had to rely on the goods it carried.

In the early campaigns none of the towns actually conquered were more than three days' march from the basin of Mexico, but as part of the valley of Tolocan campaign, the Aztecs pushed well beyond the three-day limit and into present-day northeastern Guerrero.[53] Tzacualpan, Teloloapan, Itztepec, Tetellan, Quetzallan, Tepecuacuilco, and Yohuallan[54] were in an area previously under Tepanec influence,[55] and all submitted. The Aztecs filled a power vacuum that had existed since the defeat of the Tepanec Empire. But the costs of subduing the region by force strongly argue against an interpretation of outright military conquest. And because of logistical limitations, the Aztec army had a major incentive to use its power as economically as possible. Intimidation was the preferred method of conquest, and if the first battle could be won decisively, subsequent towns were likelier to submit, possibly without the entire army having to enter the region. This interpretation is supported by the lack of historical references to the conquest of these towns (which are merely listed as tributaries).

If the foregoing campaign did involve strictly military conquests, the shortest probable route (via Tolocan) required marching approximately 562 kilometers (348 miles; 18 to 29 days). Each battle would presumably consume an additional day (6 days), and there would likely be a rest day following each battle (6 days). Unless the post-battle rest days compensated for them, there were probably additional periodic rest days—every 7 days (3 to 4 days) in ancient Greek practice,[56] but possibly as frequent as every 5 days in Aztec practice (4 to 6 days).[57] As a result, the total minimum campaign time would have been 29 to 41 days (33 to 47 with rest days) and the cost of such a venture was high. Each xiquipilli (8,000 soldiers) on a campaign required 4,000 additional porters, totaling 12,000 men who consumed 11,400 kilograms (25,000 pounds) of grain per day, or a total of 330,600 to 467,400 kilograms (727,000–1,028,000 pounds) (for 29–41 days). Yet an enemy town of 20,000 inhabitants could easily field an army of equivalent size (drawing on the defensive army of 90 percent of the male population), and the surrounding area could supply more. Even if not as well trained as the Aztec troops, the defending army knew the terrain and presumably had allies close at hand, ample supplies of foodstuffs, and armories immediately accessible. Thus to ensure such a conquest the Aztecs would have had to dispatch an army of at least two and probably three xiquipilli, totalling 24,000 combatants and an additional 12,000 support personnel. This both tripled the food requirements and lengthened the campaign, because each xiquipilli began marching on succeeding days. An additional two days would be required for each march between battles, resulting in a campaign of at least 55 days (without formal rest days en route) and a food cost of 1,881,000 kilograms (4,147,000 pounds) of maize. Given this expense, it is likely that the Aztecs either entered the area with only a token force or they entered with an army but did not significantly penetrate the region or engage in any major battles.

Itzcoatl's last major campaign extended south of the basin of Mexico into areas adjacent to his previous campaign. Tenochtitlan, Tlacopan, and Tetzcoco sent a joint army to aid Xiuhtepec (3 to 4 days distant) in the conquest of Cuauhnahuac (2 to 3 days distant), with the result that both cities became tributaries.[58] But instead of marching as a single unit, the Aztecs divided their forces into three separate armies. The Aztec army went by way of Ocuillan to attack from the west (3 to 5 days' march), the people of Tlacopan went by way of Tlazacapechco to attack from the north (2 to 3 days' march), and the Tetzcocas went by way of Tlalquiltenanco to join the Xiuhtepecas and attack from the east and south (6 to 7 days' march if they marched via Chalco); the return for all armies was 2 to 3 days' march due north). The purpose of dividing forces was f they marched via Chalco: the return for all armies was 2–3 days' march due north). The purpose of dividing forces was not surprise, since intelligence traveled much faster than marching armies, but logistical and tactical. Marching by separate routes distributed the burden of supplying the army among a greater number of subject towns. But more significantly, it also ensured that the Triple Alliance could attack Cuauhnahuac from several sides simultaneously. Had the army proceeded en masse along one route, the numerically inferior Cuauhnahuacas could have attacked it at any pass, bottling up the larger army at a site where only a few troops could have engaged them at any one time, thus nullifying the Aztecs' numerical advantage. By approaching from several directions, the Aztec forces minimized the risk that the Cuauhnahuacas might try the same maneuver simultaneously against all advancing columns.

This southward thrust was the most ambitious Aztec expansion using overt military power during Itzcoatl's reign.[59] The target was far from Tenochtitlan, and the conquest required several armies, but the logistical difficulties were eased by the presence of an ally—Xiuhtepec—which enabled the troops to march for a number of days and still be reliably supplied. The Aztecs had consolidated areas within the basin of Mexico and extended into the west and southwest, and areas to the east were held by their Acolhua allies. Chalco remained unsubdued, but it was contained through the flower war and posed little offensive threat.

CHAPTER 11

Moteuczomah Ilhuicamina

"He-frowned-like-a-lord
He-pierces-the-sky-with-an-arrow"
(Ruled 1440–1468)

WHEN Itzcoatl died, his successor was again selected from among a group of high nobles. In addition to membership in the upper nobility, the primary characteristic required for royal succession was military prowess, because the tlahtoani's increasing power depended on continued Aztec success in war and the accumulation of booty, tribute goods, and distributable lands. Thus, Moteuczomah Ilhuicamina, the tlacochcalcatl during the Tepanec war, was elected the next king in 1440 (see fig. 23).[1]

The Aztecs had relatively limited concerns vis-à-vis conquered areas, demanding that they remain loyal, permit Aztec economic penetration in the form of merchants, pay their tribute, and aid the Aztecs as needed. Beyond these requirements, each conquered area was free to operate largely as it wished. The Aztecs were basically content to tap into the local tribute system at the highest level.[2] This strategy was partially effective while the empire was small, since an army could be dispatched on an ad hoc basis whenever problems arose and direct control was unnecessary. But because conquered areas retained their own political structures, officials, and interests, control became more problematic as the empire expanded, particularly during periods of succession when past military accomplishments were not always enough to guarantee the security and continuation of the Aztec Empire.

When the king died, the Aztecs' willingness and ability to use force was thrown into doubt, because power was bound up with the personality of the ruler. It was at these times that tributaries contemplating an attempt to break away would act. Thus, avoiding fragmentation of the empire was a key concern in selecting a successor,

Fig. 23. Moteuczomah Ilhuicamina ("He-frowned-like-a-lord He-pierces-the-sky-with-an-arrow"). (Tovar 109; courtesy of the John Carter Brown Library, Brown University)

and military prowess weighed increasingly heavily in the selection process. Once the ruler was chosen, his willingness to sustain the empire had to be demonstrated to his tributaries, so each king initiated his reign with a show of force.

Among Moteuczomah Ilhuicamina's first recorded conquests were the cities of Xochimilco, Azcapotzalco, Colhuacan, Coyohuacan, and Huexotla, in the basin of Mexico[3] (see map 3). However, since these cities had all been conquered by the previous king, Itzcoatl, they probably merely acknowledged vassalage and were not actually conquered anew.[4] But Moteuczomah Ilhuicamina did embark on a successful campaign to force recognition of his rule on the remaining independent cities in the basin.

Moteuczomah Ilhuicamina used the pretext of constructing a temple to Huitzilopochtli to consolidate his power in the basin.[5] He sent messengers to the lords of all the surrounding towns—Azcapotzalco, Coyohuacan, Colhuacan, Xochimilco, Cuitlahuac, Mizquic, and Tetzcoco—asking for help in the construction, to which they all agreed. Tenochtitlan was seen as overwhelmingly powerful since each city assessed its military prospects against the Aztecs on an individual basis. The important equation was how strong each city was in relation to Tenochtitlan, not how strong they all were. No city could know with certainty how much allied assistance the Aztecs could actually muster at any time. So while Moteuczomah Ilhuicamina's request was cast in terms of religious devotion, it was actually a test of political allegiance: acquiescence was a tacit acceptance of vassalage to the Aztecs, And refusal was an assertion of political independence. Thus the construction of Huitzilopochtli's temple was at least as much a measure of political fealty as of religious devotion, but the act could be rationalized as one of friendship and piety.

Only the Chalcas refused,[6] and to ignore their refusal would have encouraged other cities to follow Chalco's example.[7] On Tenochtitlan's request, therefore, armies were raised from Azcapotzalco, Tlacopan, Coyohuacan, Xochimilco, Cuitlahuac, and Tetzcoco.[8] The Chalcas were not defeated outright in this conflict. Both sides suffered many casualties and took many prisoners, including two hundred by the Aztecs,[9] who claimed victory. The victory may have been tactical but was not decisive, and conflicts with the Chalcas continued. However, this show of force was apparently sufficient to chastise the Chalcas and to maintain the cohesion of the empire. The only other dissension in the basin was another conflict with Tlatelolco: King Cuauhtlahtoa took advantage of the uncertainty associated with Tenochtitlan's succession to assert Tlatelolco's independence.

Having largely secured his hold on the empire, especially on cities within the basin of Mexico, Moteuczomah Ilhuicamina launched his first major campaign into present-day Morelos and Guerrero[10] to consolidate the conquests of his predecessor in the old Tepanec domain. This campaign included Cohuixco, Oztoman, Quetzallan, Ichcateopan, Teoxahuallan, Poctepec, Tlachco, Tlachmalacac, Chilapan, Cuauhteopan, and Tzompanhuacan (see map 6).[11] These towns had also been asked for specific items for building the temple of Huitzilopochtli, but instead they killed the king's messengers, so the Aztecs conquered them.[12] Chontalcoatlan, Tepecuacuilco, Tlalcozauhtitlan, and Ohuapan also became subjects at this time, but probably submitted peacefully after the conquest of other major cities in the region.

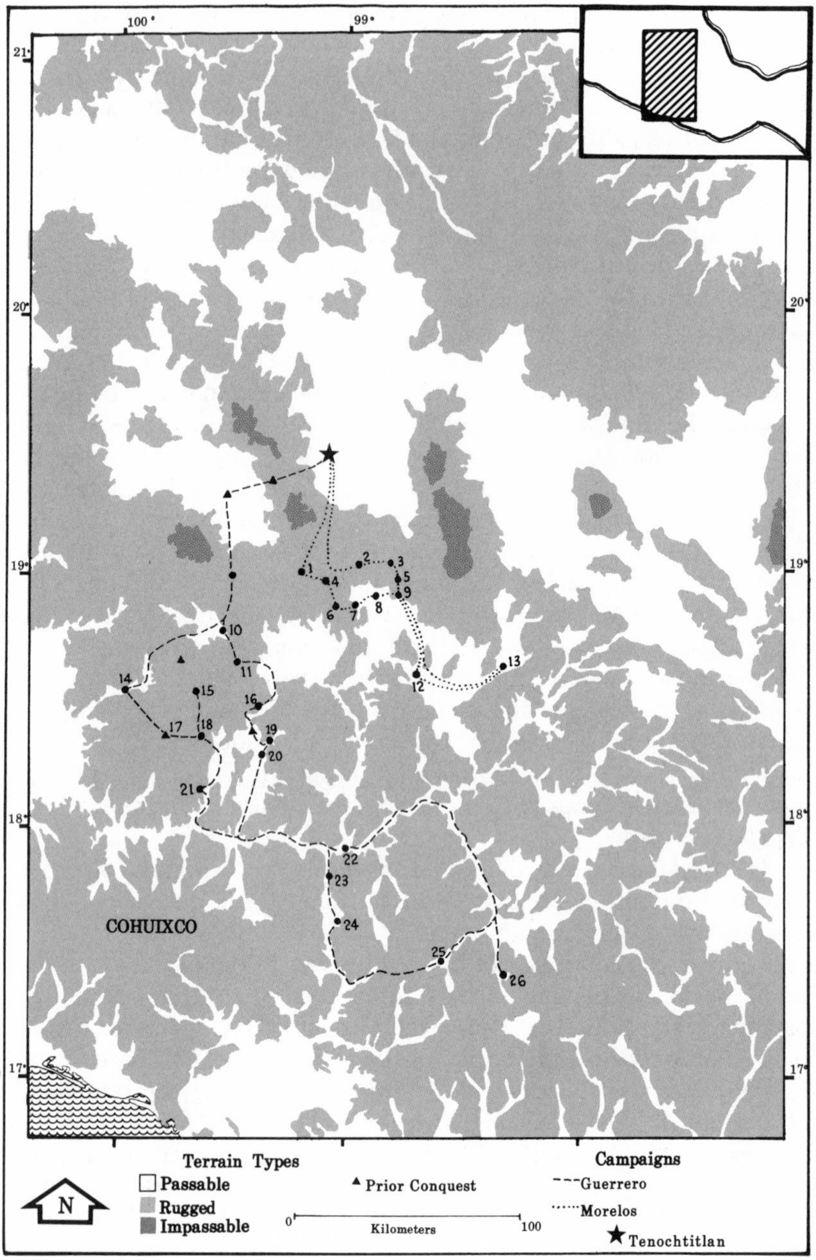

100°
99°
21°
20°
19°
18°
17°
1
2
3
4
5
6
7
8
9
10
11
12
13
14
15
16
17
18
19
20
21
22
23
24
25
26
COHUIXCO
Terrain Types
Passable
Rugged
Impassable
N
Prior Conquest
0
Kilometers
100
Campaigns
Guerrero
Morelos
Tenochtitlan

These towns were among the Aztecs' most distant conquests to date, which made Moteuczomah Ilhuicamina's feat a particularly effective demonstration of his power and ability. However, these conquests were the result not only of the king's abilities but also of the groundwork established by his predecessor.

By the shortest route, the entire campaign required a march of 835 kilometers (518 miles), or 26 to 44 days, plus additional days for battles, rest, and march spacing between the participating xiquipilli.[13] What made these distant conquests feasible was following Itzcoatl's itinerary so the army could draw logistical support from tributaries en route. The Aztec armies were never more than one or two days from a supporting town except for the southernmost extension (when they were four days away).

Cuauhnahuac and Ocuillan, both easily within the reach of Aztec armies, were also conquered (or reconquered).[14] Towns to the east and south of Cuauhnahuac were also probably acquired during this campaign: Tepoztlan, Xiuhtepec, Yauhtepec, Huaxtepec, Totolapan, Atlatlauhyan, Yacapichtlan, Tecpantzinco, and, possibly, Itzyocan[15] (see map 6), but it is likely that they simply capitulated following the defeat of Cuauhnahuac and Ocuillan. However, it is unclear whether this expansion was part of the Guerrero conquests.[16]

The army's passage also had a consolidating effect on the reat of the area. By marching through cities that were not targets of the immediate campaign, the Aztecs effectively solicited pledges of allegiance at a time that was most advantageous to themselves. The local rulers could either acknowledge support and provide the Aztec army with supplies, or they could oppose them militarily. Although the rulers knew that the Aztecs were approaching in full fighting form, they did not have enough advance notice to muster and retrain an army. Thus, even if the local rulers might have opposed the Aztecs under ideal conditions, they could not.

Map 6. (facing page) Moteuczomah Ilhuicamina's campaigns into present-day Morelos and Guerrero. 1—Ocuillan; 2—Tepoztlan; 3—Totolapan; 4—Cuauhnahuac; 5—Atlatlauhyan; 6—Xiuhtepec; 7—Yauhtepec; 8—Huaxtepec; 9—Yacapichtlan; 10—Tzompanhuacan; 11—Chontalcoatlan; 12—Tecpantzinco; 13—Itzyocan; 14—Oztoman; 15—Ichcateopan; 16—Tlachco; 17—Poctepec*; 18—Coatepec; 19—Tlachmalacac; 20—Tepecuacuilco; 21—Quetzallan; 22—Tlalcozauhtitlan; 23—Teoxahuallan*; 24—Chilapan; 25—Ohuapan; 26—Cuauhteopan. (*Approximate location.)

Around 1450 there was another major confrontation, in which Chalco was reportedly reconquered but with heavy Aztec losses, including two important leaders.[17] Whether or not this was the proximate cause, the nature of the war with Chalco underwent a major shift. The conflict had already changed from a flower war, in which only combatants died during the fighting, to one in which commoner captives were taken and sacrificed and then to one in which even noble captives were taken and sacrificed, although the combat itself had remained largely a display of individual courage and prowess. But in 1453 the arrow war began between Chalco and the Aztecs,[18] and battle tactics changed. Instead of emphasizing the martial skills and valor of hand-to-hand combat, now bows and arrows were introduced, initiating an element of indiscriminate death from projectile fire that afflicted nobles and commoners alike. The war had shifted from one of martial demonstration (albeit an increasingly bloody and classless one) to one of attrition by death in combat. The Aztecs doubtless initiated the change. Although they were unable or unwilling to commit their forces to a sustained frontal assault in which the stakes were very high, Chalco's position was eroding, and the Aztecs increased the pressure by encircling the Chalcas. This tactic escalated the war by cutting the Chalcas off from potential allies and depriving them of room to retreat. Although the Chalcas did not immediately succumb, their position was growing increasingly precarious.

There was relatively little military activity during the famine that spanned 1450–54, but the next campaign was directed toward the northern Gulf coast,[19] for the stated purpose of avenging the killing of Aztec merchants by the Huaxtecs in Xiuhcoac (Tziccoac) and Tochpan (Tuxpan).[20] Aztec merchants traded over a wide area and were repeatedly the objects of attack, possibly because they dominated the markets and were detrimental to other merchants, but more probably because of their intelligence functions.

Traveling throughout Mesoamerica, as we have seen, Aztec merchants were a prime source of information about such matters as roads, defenses, and political conditions, so their presence could easily have inspired hostility. Moreover, their political role was such that they may have been sent into areas as deliberate acts of provocation by the Aztecs to create an excuse for war. Such incidents were used by the Aztecs so often and over such a wide area that they cannot be understood as *reasons* for the wars but as *pretexts*. On the other side, what better way to signal a breach in relations than by killing these handy symbols of Aztec might, so even the innocent appearance of Aztec merchants may have stimulated hostile responses. In this instance, as in so many others, the killing of Aztec merchants prompted a military response.

To secure his position as king, Moteuczomah Ilhuicamina had to ensure the continued influx of tribute goods and lands—primarily for the nobles, on whom his position and authority increasingly relied. Thus he had to engage in war, but only successful war. Failure—particularly sustained failure—could have undermined his support among the nobles. So Moteuczomah Ilhuicamina chose to march, not on his only target but on his easiest. Many towns to the north had been conquered, and farther north lay the desert; the powerful Tarascan Empire lay to the west, the immediate south had been conquered, and further expansion at that time might have strained the Aztecs' logistical capacity; and directly to the east was the formidable enemy alliance of Tlaxcallan, Huexotzinco, Atlixco, and Cholollan. But to the northeast lay the Huaxtec area. The Huaxtecs were not strongly centralized, and much of the trek to the target area would take place through the lands of the Aztecs' ally, Tetzcoco, where they could expect a friendly reception and plentiful logistical support. Thus the Huaxtecs became the target. Moreover, a successful campaign would mean that, for the first time, the Aztecs would have direct and sustained access to ocean goods and products from the tropical lowlands.

On the way to the Huaxtec area the Aztec armies passed through Tollantzinco, which had been conquered previously (in 1450) by King Nezahualcoyotl of Tetzcoco.[21] When the Aztec armies arrived, they were well received and fed,[22] as they were throughout the dominated march area.[23] After reaching the northern Gulf coast region, the Aztecs defeated the Huaxtecs by use of a feint. During the battle they feigned retreat, drawing the pursuing Huaxtecs past a hidden contingent of two thousand warriors, who then attacked the flank and rear of the Huaxtecs and routed them.[24]

The Huaxtecs' defeat led to the conquest of the general area of Tochpan (see map 7). Numerous towns formed part of the conquests in the region, although some of these towns were associated with the earlier Tetzcoca expansion, including Pahuatlan and Cuauhchinanco,[25] which lay on the route to the target area. Thus, reliable logistical support was available to the Aztecs for the first five to eight

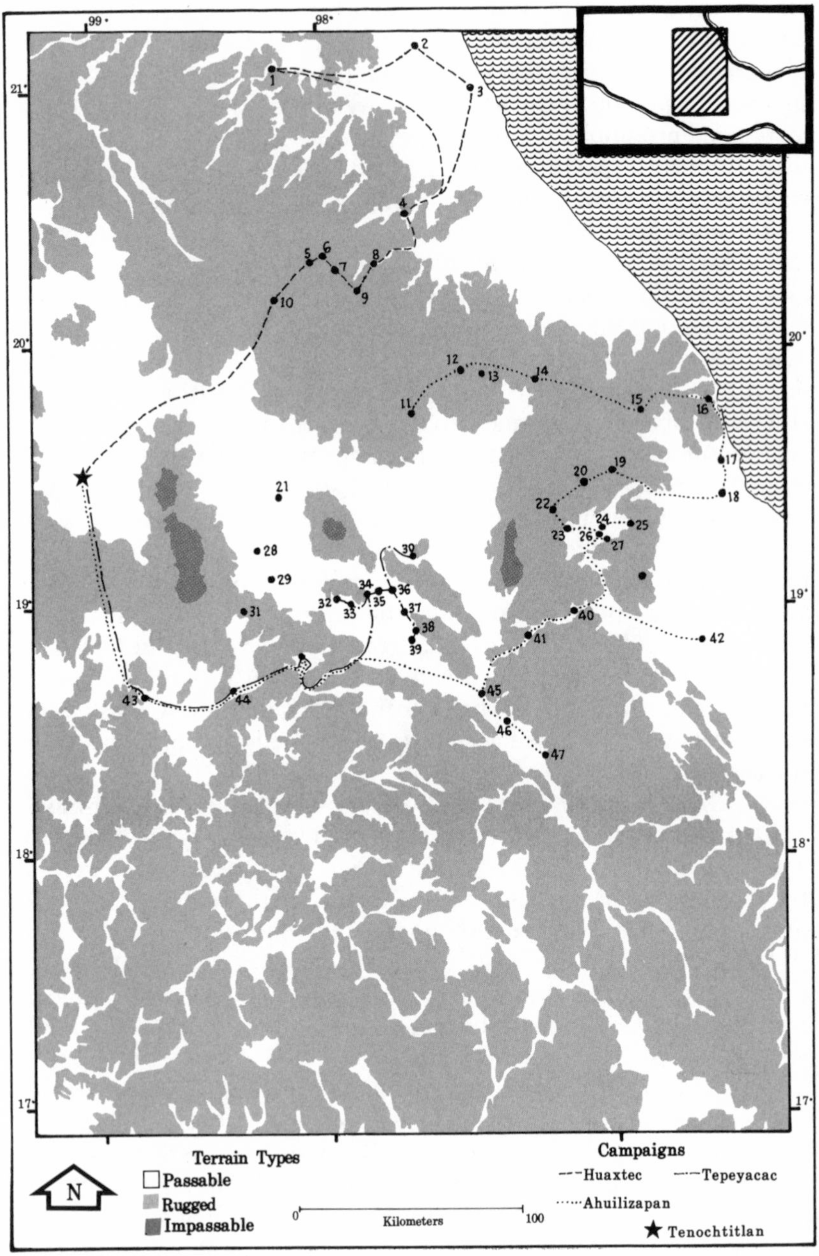

99°
98°
21°
20°
19°
18°
17°
Terrain Types
Passable
Rugged
Impassable
N
0
Kilometers
100
Campaigns
Huaxtec
Tepeyacac
Ahuilizapan
Tenochtitlan

days of the march (158 kilometers or 98 miles). But Xilotepec was also conquered,[26] as well as Tollantzinco, Hueipochtlan, Atotonilco (el Grande), Axocopan, Tollan, Itzcuincuitlapilco, Atotonilco (el Chico), Tecpatepec, Chapolicxitlan (Chapolycxitla), Chiconcoac (Chicoaque), Cuauhchinanco, Tlapacoyan. The Mazahuacan area also submitted to the Aztecs though probably with little or no armed struggle following the subjugation of Xilotepec.[27]

Tozapan, Xolotlan, and Tlapacoyan were also conquered during this campaign, as well as, probably, Xiuhcoac and Tamachpan on the march route.[28] These conquests would entail a total penetration of five to eight days (155 kilometers) to Tochpan, conquering towns en route and presumably taking supplies from them. Other towns listed as conquests are easily accessible from Tochpan and may have merely yielded to the inevitable.

As important as conquests were to the empire, the projection of the Aztec image of power was even more significant: news of Aztec successes had to be disseminated among friends and enemies alike. Accordingly, rulers from throughout the empire—Tetzcoco, Tlacopan, Xochimilco, Tlalhuican, Cohuixco, Matlatzinco, and Mazahuacan—were summoned to attend the feast of Tlacaxipehualiztli, dedicated to the god Xipe ToTec. They gave the Aztec king gifts, and captives were sacrificed.[29] This ceremony had the dual purposes of requiring the summoned rulers to affirm their fealty by attending and of displaying the power of the empire. The Aztecs could demonstrate by having conquered their enemies and taken them captive and could then sacrifice them amid considerable ceremony in what had become the largest city in the New World. Attending rulers re-

Map 7. (facing page) Moteuczomah Ilhuicamina's campaigns into present-day Puebla, the Gulf coast, and the Huaxtec region. 1—Xiuhcoac; 2—Tamachpan; 3—Tochpan; 4—Tozapan*; 5—Xolotlan; 6—Pahuatlan; 7—Cuauhchinanco; 8—Chapolicxitlan; 9—Tlapacoyan; 10—Tollantzinco; 11—Tzauctlan; 12—Tlatlauhqui-Tepec; 13—Macuilxochitlan*; 14—Tzapotlan; 15—Maxtlan*; 16—Quiahuiztlan; 17—Cempohuallan; 18—Oceloapan; 19—Tlahuitollan; 20—Teoixhuacan; 21—Tlaxcallan; 22—Quimichtlan; 23—Chichiquillan; 24—Tototlan; 25—Tlatictlan; 26—Tlatlactetelco; 27—Cuauhtochco; 28—Huexotzinco; 29—Cholollan; 30—Coatepec; 31—Atlixco; 32—Cuauht-Inchan; 33—Tecalco; 34—Tepeyacac; 35—Oztoticpac; 36—Acatzinco; 37—Tecamachalco; 38—Yohualtepec; 39—Tetl-Icoyoccan; 40—Ahuilizapan; 41—Coxolitlan; 42—Huehuetlan; 43—Tecpantzinco; 44—Itzyocan; 45—Teohuacan; 46—Cozcatlan; 47—Teotitlan; 48—Piaztlan. (*Approximate location.)

turned home with the knowledge of Tenochtitlan's enormous power, an experience that both tied the local rulers more tightly to the Aztecs and reduced the Aztecs' need to expend their forces.

Following the campaign into the Huaxtec area, the Aztecs again turned toward the south, against Coaixtlahuacan[30] and Tepozcolollan.[31] The region was ostensibly one of the easiest remaining targets and, unconquered, was an obstruction to further expansion. So the campaign was a logical expansion of the Aztecs' previous conquests. By one account the incident that gave rise to the war was Coaixtlahuacan's refusal to allow the Aztecs to pass through its territory.[32] Another version holds that the lords of Coaixtlahuacan had 160 merchants massacred and their wares taken; only merchants from Toltitlan escaped to bring the news to Tenochtitlan.[33]

To meet this challenge Moteuczomah Ilhuicamina summoned troops from Tetzcoco, Azcapotzalco, Tlacopan, Colhuacan, Coyohuacan, Tepeyacac (Tepeaca), Tolocan, Tollantzinco, Itzyocan, Acatzinco, and Cuauhtitlan, raising an army of 200,000 warriors, supported by 100,000 porters. The Coaixtlahuacas were aided by the Tlaxcaltecs and Huexotzincas,[34] powerful city-states to the east of Tenochtitlan and potential rivals for power in central Mexico, but the Aztecs successfully attacked, entered the city, and burned the temple. The people fled to the hills and negotiated their surrender from there, agreeing to become tributaries (see map 8).[35]

Several other nearby towns in this area were probably also conquered at this time, including Chinantla, Piaztlan, and Acatlan.[36] Much of the route taken in this campaign is uncertain, but the Aztec army passed through the area, if not the town, of Itzyocan,[37] so it probably left the basin of Mexico via Cuauhnahuac (since the Chalcas were still at war), passed through the previously conquered present-day Morelos area, by Itzyocan, and marched along accessible valleys almost directly southeast to the conquest area. The entire trek would have entailed a minimum march of 26 to 43 days (823 kilometers or 510 miles), exclusive of rest, combat, and regrouping

Map 8. (facing page) Moteuczomah Ilhuicamina's campaigns into the Gulf coast and the Huaxyacac region. See Map 7 for connecting routes to Tenochtitlan. 1—Itzyocan; 2—Chinantla; 3—Piaztlan; 4—Acatlan; 5—Cuauhtochco; 6—Ahuilizapan; 7—Cuetlachtlan; 8—Coaixtlahuacan; 9—Texopan; 10—Tepozcolollan; 11—Cozamaloapan; 12—Otlatlan; 13—Tochtepec; 14—Tamazollan; 15—Huaxyacac; 16—Mictlan; 17—Quetzaltepec; 18—Miahuatlan.

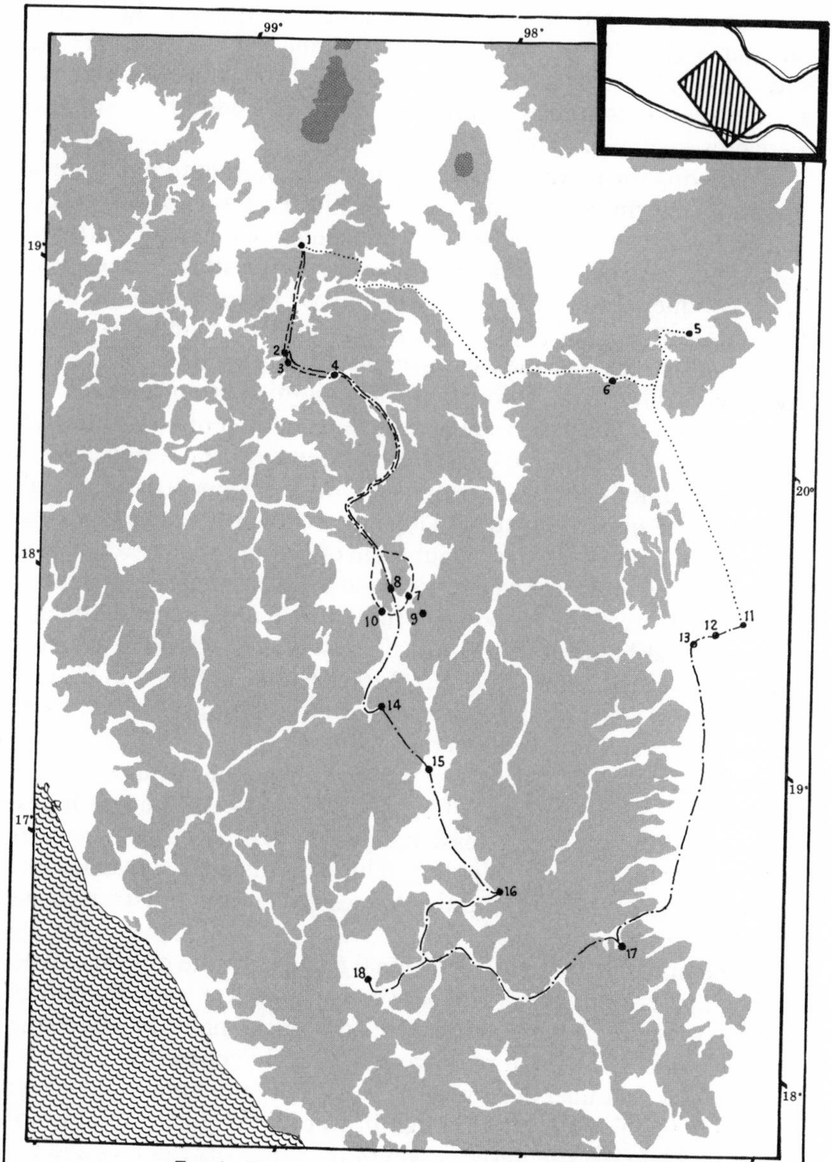

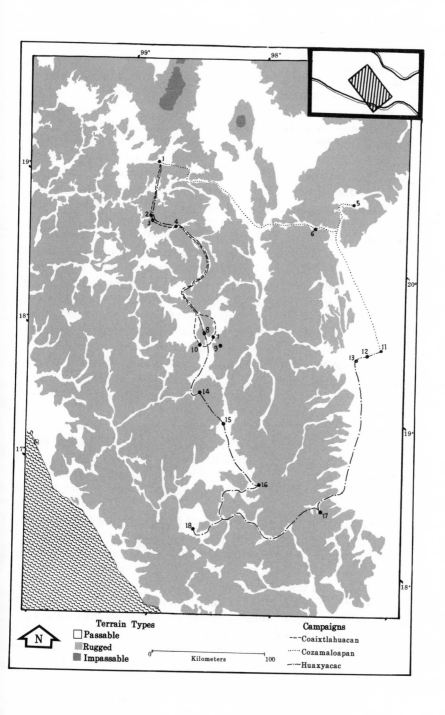

99°
98°
19°
18°
17°
20°
19°
18°
1
2
3
4
5
6
7
8
9
10
11
12
13
14
15
16
17
18
Terrain Types
Passable
Rugged
Impassable
N
0
Kilometers
100
Campaigns
Coaixtlahuacan
Cozamaloapan
Huaxyacac

days for the xiquipilli. It would have required 7,410,000 to 12,255,000 kilograms (16,336,000 to 27,018,000 pounds) of maize. Although such a journey would have been impossible through hostile territory, apparently no resistance was met en route, and additional supplies were presumably available.

Following the pattern adopted by Itzcoatl, Moteuczomah Ilhuicamina's initial thrust into the region was limited to clearly specified objectives. A few towns en route were conquered, not the entire region. The campaign was based on the support available from previously conquered towns and, in turn, laid the groundwork—in logistics, intelligence, and Aztec reputation—for later conquests. Again the Aztecs concluded their campaign with the sacrifice of the captives, with rulers from throughout the empire in attendance.[38]

Such power displays were an efficient method of controlling an empire, but they required constant maintenance, and Aztec failures and unanswered affronts became seemingly disproportionate challenges to the imperial system. Thus, the following year Cozamaloapan was conquered, as was Cuauhtochco the next year in retaliation for the killing of Aztecs (see maps 7 and 8). Nevertheless, manpower limitations forced the Aztecs to be judicious in responding to threats: not all could be dealt with immediately. Thus, when the Chalcas "revolted" at the same time that Aztecs had been killed in Cuauhtochco, the Aztecs were forced to choose which threat was the more immediate,[39] and they ignored the Chalcas.

In an action that was to have a major impact on the military, political, and social structures of Tenochtitlan, Moteuczomah Ilhuicamina strengthened and professionalized the military by establishing a telpochcalli in each calpolli.[40] This significantly expanded the body of trained soldiers, and the Aztecs thus vastly outstripped the forces of other city-states.

He instituted a series of additional changes in the military structure. Distinctions were drawn between all grades of warriors, reflecting the growing power and independence of the nobility. Uniforms, insignia, and symbols of rank were rigorously controlled.[41] He also established a number of sumptuary laws: only the king could wear a golden diadem in the city (though in war all the great captains and lords could do so as representatives of the king); only nobles and valiant warriors could wear sandals in the city; only nobles could wear plugs of gold and precious stones in their lips, ears, or noses, but great warriors could wear those of bone or wood; common soldiers could wear only the simplest type of mantle, and no cotton clothing. Thus, the importance of the nobility was further emphasized, both as a group and as individuals, and the maintenance of their position was increasingly tied to military success and continued imperial expansion.

The Aztecs next turned to the Gulf coast area, beginning a lengthy campaign with a major thrust and continuing at an intermittent low level between and during campaigns elsewhere.[42] Aztec ambassadors had been sent to Ahuilizapan (present-day Orizaba) and Cuetlachtlan (Cotaxtla) to ask for shells for their god—a standard gambit seeking an admission of vassalage (see map 7). The emissaries were killed, however, and the news was brought to Tenochtitlan by merchants from Ixtlapalapan.

Such occurrences were common in the history of Aztec expansion. If a city felt it was sufficiently strong to resist encroachment, it would reject Aztec brandishments, often with fatal results for the Aztec messengers. In the case of Cuetlachtlan the assessment of relative strength was not made in isolation or in ignorance of wider events in Mesoamerica. The Aztecs had just vanquished the Coaixtlahuacas but had suffered large casualties. This was learned by spies from Tlaxcallan and Huexotzinco in Tenochtitlan, and with Aztec military capability impaired these enemies seized the opportunity to thwart the Aztecs in the east. Thus they urged Ahuilizapan and Cuetlachtlan to revolt and promised to support them.

Individual city-states in central Mexico were vulnerable to conquest by stronger polities, so they attempted to form alliances as a matter of self-defense, usually with a regional power. But the Aztecs eventually dominated all the nearby and accessible cities and left no viable alternative alliance partners in the basin of Mexico. Given the Aztecs' considerable resources, no regional power was able to compete for allies close to the imperial heartland. But more distant regional powers could compete for towns adjacent to themselves or even farther from Tenochtitlan. Thus the alliance that, at one time or another, was made up of various configurations of Tlaxcallan, Huexotzinco, Atlixco, Chololllan, and Tliliuhqui-Tepec offered an alternative in its immediate vicinity and to the east. Groups seeking refuge from the Aztecs allied with other local powers and defended their borders.[43] These alliances offered significant advantages to the cities of the present-day Puebla/Tlaxcala valley. First, they would strengthen them by creating additional allies or alliance partners.

Moreover, they would offer free and safe access to coastal lowland areas possessing otherwise unavailable goods. Second, they would weaken the Aztecs by depriving them of additional tributaries, removing free trade and transit areas, and, perhaps most important, they would break Tenochtitlan's encirclement of the area, which was the Aztecs' primary long-term strategy for subjugating a powerful region.

So when the Aztecs demanded that Ahuilizapan and Cuetlachtlan submit, the Tlaxcaltecs, Huexotzincas, and Chololtecs urged that the emissaries be killed, and they promised assistance if the Aztecs retaliated. Given the Aztecs' momentary weakness, the great distance from Tenochtitlan, and the assurances of assistance from Tlaxcallan, Huexotzinco, Atlixco, and Cholollan, Cuetlachtlan felt sufficiently strong to resist the Aztecs' threats and killed the messengers. In response, Moteuczomah Ilhuicamina sent his army against Ahuilizapan and set up camp at the city's borders.[44] Despite the assistance of a large army from Tlaxcallan, Huexotzinco, and Cholollan,[45] the Aztecs conquered Ahuilizapan, taking 6,000 captives. The lords of Cuetlachtlan asked for peace and agreed to become tributaries, but in a marked departure from previous practice, the Aztecs named an Aztec governor, Pinotl, to rule them.[46] Also conquered on this campaign were Tlahuitollan, Tototlan, Cuauhtochco, Tlatlactetelco, Tzapotlan, Tepzolco (Tepzol), Coxolitlan, Teohuacan, Cozcatlan, Cuextlan (Cuetlachtlan?), Chichiquillan, Teoixhuacan, Quimichtlan, Tzauctlan, Macuilxochitlan, Tlatictlan, and Oceloapan, as well as Cuetlachtlan, Ahuilizapan, Maxtlan, Cempohuallan, Quiahuiztlan in the Totonac area, and possibly Tlatlauhqui-Tepec.[47] But most of these towns probably capitulated with the approach of the victorious Aztec army.[48]

The round trip to Alahuiztlan required twenty-four to forty-one days (780 km. or 484 mi.), exclusive of rest, combat, and regrouping days. If the towns to the north of Alahuiztlan were actually conquered, an additional five to nine days' journey (163 km. or 100 mi.) would have been entailed each way. Teotitlan (del Camino) also appears to have come under Aztec sway at this time.[49]

On their return from the Gulf coast the soldiers reached a place called Acachinanco, at the entrance of Tenochtitlan, where Moteuczomah Ilhuicamina received them. Then the army continued to the temple to Huitzilopochtli and paid reverence to the king and other leaders.[50] This campaign was of pivotal importance, coming at a time when the Aztecs were weakened. Abetted by Tlaxcallan, Huexotzinco, and Cholollan, the Cuetlachtlan challenge had presented the most serious threat to the Aztecs to date. The consequences of failure would have been disastrous for the cohesion of the empire.

Thereafter, the Chalca war was finally resolved. With the encirclement of Chalco now completed as a result of the Gulf coast campaign, the conflict reached the stage of a full-fledged war of conquest.[51] Small towns such as Itztompiatepec, Panohuayan, Atezcahuacan, and Tzacualtitlan Tenanco were taken.[52] Then, assisted by the Acolhuas, the Aztecs defeated the Chalcas and sacked the town of Chalco Atenco.[53] Many people fled to other Chalca towns, such as Tlalmanalco, Amaquemecan, Tenanco, Chimalhuacan, Tecuanipan, and Mamalhuazzocan, but the Aztecs pursued them and, during the following year, conquered these cities, too. The Chalcas agreed to pay tribute to Moteuczomah Ilhuicamina, and the Chalca lands were divided among the people of Tenochtitlan, Tetzcoco, and Tlacopan,[54] but sixteen thousand people abandoned Amaquemecan and fled to Huexotzinco.[55] With the final defeat of their sole remaining adversary in the basin of Mexico, the Aztecs finally consolidated control of the area.

The lords of the newly conquered Chalca towns met various fates. Some fled to friendly cities, and others were simply removed from their offices. The indigenous leaders in at least nine Chalca towns were replaced by Aztec military governors,[56] an unusual, but not unprecedented, action. The imposition of military governors (*cuauhtlahtohqueh*, sing. *cuauhtlahtoani*) was not a total usurpation of authority by the Aztecs. Rather, the new ruler usually had a legitimate, and noble, kin tie to his new subjects.[57]

Usually, local rulers were not completely removed; rather, they remained a vital element in the local government, continuing to make most of the day-to-day decisions. But they were subordinated to the paramount authority of the governor, who acted largely as an overseer. This usually occurred when the cities had militarily resisted incorporation, but it also occurred through natural attrition. When the ruler of a relatively weak city died (and possibly only when there was no appropriate successor), the Aztecs could impose their own choice with relative ease.[58] But the replacement rulers were acknowledged to be governors, not tlahtohqueh.

Installing an Aztec governor in subject towns, particularly troublesome ones, did not enable the Aztecs to control everything that was happening there. Indeed, without supporting troops the governors lacked a direct means of implementing Aztec wishes, and no significant bodies of troops appear to have been delegated for this purpose. Rather, the governors headed off the emergence of any major rival leadership that might have acted against Aztec interests or sought alliances with hostile outside groups. It is unlikely that extensive meddling in local affairs took place. Instead, the governors primarily served as barometers of local sentiment and as suppliers of intelligence about local matters to Tenochtitlan. Enforcement remained a matter of Aztec projection of power.

At this time the Aztecs fought a flower war with Tlaxcallan, Huexotzinco, Chalollan, and, probably, Tliliuhqui-Tepec.[59] This was the first in a series of escalating flower wars to be fought with the city-states of the present-day Puebla/Tlaxcala valley. It was aimed at engaging these opponents at a relatively low level of violence while putting them on the defensive, permitting Aztec expansion elsewhere, and continuing the encirclement and ultimate strangulation of these troublesome cities.

Moteuczomah Ilhuicamina's last major campaign was into the Tepeyacac region, and it was probably tied to this strategy (see map 7). Again, the rationale for the campaign was that merchants from the Triple Alliance had been murdered. Although the cities of the present-day Puebla/Tlaxcala valley apparently played no role here, later events and their proximity to Tepeyacac suggest a relationship. Thus the Aztecs may have been preempting future problems while tightening their encirclement of those cities. The king prepared for war and sent four envoys to Tepeyacac with a message and a shield, swords, and feathers as a warning of war, but it did not submit. So an army was assembled from many towns, including Azcapotzalco, Tlacopan, Cuauhtitlan, Acolhuacan, Tetzcoco, Chalco, Xochimilco, Colhuacan, Cuitlahuac, Mizquic, and Coyohuacan, and ordered to meet on an assigned day. After a few days' march it reached Cuauhpetlayo (Coyupetlayo or Coahuapetlayo), on the outskirts of Tepeyacac, where each unit set up camp.[60]

Scouts were sent out and reported that Tepeyacac had no defenses, garrison troops, or fortifications. The use of scouts to reconnoiter enemy fortifications was a common stratagem. Though unrecorded for many campaigns, it was doubtless employed by the Aztecs from the time of their first imperial excursions outside the basin of Mexico into areas where specific local conditions were unknown to them. The repeated use of this tactic clearly points to a primary interest in the outcome of the battles and not in the manner of their execution. Individual exploits remained important to the soldiers involved, but not to the state. The polity's interests were in the success of the battles and of the campaign. Thus, scouting an adversary's defensive posture was aimed at exploiting whatever weaknesses might be found.

After the scouts reported, the allied army divided into four units, which were sent, respectively, to Tecalco, Cuauht-Inchan, Acatzinco, and Tepeyacac. At dawn all four attacked at a signal and conquered and burned the four cities. The lords of Tepeyacac submitted and agreed to pay tribute.[61] Tecamachalco, Coatepec, Yohualtepec, Oztoticpac, and Tetl-Icoyoccan (Tecoyocan) also became subjects as a result of this campaign, but they presumably submitted following the fall of the first four towns rather than actually being subdued. Reaching the Tepeyacac region required only nine to fourteen days' march (275 km. or 170 mi.), most through friendly territory. But less than the usual two to four days was required in the combat area, because the armies divided and conquered towns simultaneously.

The Aztecs also expanded into the Gulf coast area, stretching on into the Huaxyacac region. According to the Aztec accounts, Moteuczomah Ilhuicamina had sent the pochtecah to Coatzacualco for goods, including gold dust, to adorn the temple of Huitzilopochtli. On their return via Tecuantepec they reached Mictlan (Mitla), where they were robbed and killed by order of the lords of Huaxyacac, and their bodies were left to be eaten by animals.[62] News of this was brought to Moteuczomah Ilhuicamina by merchants from Chalco, and an army was dispatched.

The city of Huaxyacac was attacked, the cuahchicqueh climbed the great temple and burned it, and the city was conquered,[63] as were the nearby cities of Mictlan, Miahuatlan, Quetzaltepec, and Tamazollan, and the Gulf coast towns of Cozamaloapan, Otlatlan, and Tochtepec[64] (see map 8). Coatzalcualco was not conquered but did give tribute.[65] Whatever the rationale for this campaign, it further encircled Tlaxcallan, Huexotzinco, and Atlixco, deprived them of potential allies, and continued the logical Aztec expansion and consolidation of areas to the east and south.

En route to Huaxyacac the Aztecs passed through tributary lands that provided logistical support, but thereafter the army must have lived off the land or have negotiated with towns en route, since its logistical capabilities were vastly exceeded.[66] Nevertheless, this campaign was made possible by the previous incursion against Coaixtlahuacan, which established at least a partial network of tributaries who would offer logistical support and intelligence.

But the Aztecs did not rely on tributaries or foraging alone for their logistical needs. They fell back on a range of strategies that took into account the political dependency of the transit areas. Where local tributaries already existed, these were relied on to provide obligatory supplies. Where they did not, the Aztecs' reputation could still compel considerable respect and, in effect, create new tributaries on the spot or at least induce support as the course of least resistance. If a town resisted—whether it was an incidental town or the target—it was conquered, if possible, and its supplies were taken to further the Aztecs' thrust or to support their return home. In addition to these manifestly coercive strategies the Aztecs also apparently relied on markets for resupply in areas that they did not want to disturb politically. But this last strategy underlies a persistent pattern of Aztec logistical expansion: conquest was less a qualitative than a quantitative matter.

There were many levels of Aztec conquest, based on political, military (strategic and tactical), and economic considerations. Thus, how different towns and cities supported the passing Aztec armies varied widely. Some towns of strategic importance, such as those dominating passes and those that could offer considerable resistance, were assessed lesser obligations—perhaps merely free passage for Aztec armies. Those towns capable of little resistance and having greater tributary importance were compelled to provide more support. In this the Aztecs far exceeded the other polities of central Mexico. Beyond their respective heartlands no others guaranteed outlying cities defense from hostile incursions, possessed the reputation on which Aztec power was based, or had the military or logistical capacity to project power as far as the Aztecs. Thus the Aztecs were in a dominant position, politically and militarily, and in extending their influence they were more concerned with the ability to mobilize and to project force than in its specific location. Consequently, to maximize their areas of dominance, they imposed markedly different administrative burdens on internal regions of the empire.

The city of Huaxyacac was an extreme in this regard. Because of its actions (and probably because of its strategic location so far from

Tenochtitlan), the city was destroyed, and the kings of the Triple Alliance each sent people to colonize it. Tetzcoco sent sixty men with their wives and children, as did Tlacopan, and Tenochtitlan sent six hundred. Moteuczomah Ilhuicamina appointed a relative, Atlahcol, to be their lord, gave the colonists great privileges, and ordered each nation to establish its own calpolli in the city.[67]

The creation of an Aztec enclave in Mixtec and Tzapotec lands was not an effort to create an effective fighting force there: the people were too few for that. However, they could provide intelligence for the Aztecs, much as the governors did, and ensure that supplies were gathered. The area was too far removed for the Aztecs to rely on the continual incidental relay of intelligence to Tenochtitlan, so a reliable center was established that could, among other things, oversee, but not effectively enforce, Aztec interests in the region.

CHAPTER 12

Axayacatl
"Water-mask"
(Ruled 1468–1481)

WHEN Moteuczomah Ilhuicamina died, his son Axayacatl was chosen to succeed him (see fig. 24).[1] Before his coronation Axayacatl undertook his first conquests, probably during the campaign season of 1468–69. Moteuczomah Ilhuicamina had been a powerful king and skilled military leader whose actions and reputation had kept the tributaries loyal, and imperial continuity required a leader of similar skills and inclination.

The king's investiture ceremony required captives, but the primary purpose of these conquests was to display the successor's martial skills and resolve,[2] as well as to shore up support among the most recently conquered and distant tributaries. Accordingly, Axayacatl led an army to the Tecuantepec region, and when the enemy attacked, he pretended to flee, withdrawing to an area where some of his soldiers were hidden. When the enemy passed, these soldiers attacked them, advanced, and conquered the city.[3] Axayacatl then conquered the entire area as far south as the Pacific port of Cuauhtolco (Huatulco). Although this was a very distant conquest, the transit route ran almost exclusively through areas of existing tributaries where the army could receive logistical support.[4] He returned to Tenochtitlan with honor and captives and was crowned (see map 9).[5]

During the same year (the campaign season of 1468–69), Axayacatl fought a flower war with Huexotzinco and Atlixco, continuing the pressure on the city-states of the present-day Puebla/Tlaxcala valley (see map 10). The Aztecs and their allies claimed victory, but King Totoquihuaztli of Tlacopan was killed in the war,[6] and the region's cities continued to resist Aztec expansion.

Taking advantage of the imperial uncertainties caused by the recent death of Moteuczomah Ilhuicamina and possibly that of Toto-

Fig. 24. Axayacatl ("Water-mask"). Tovar erroneously recorded Axayacatl as the eighth king rather than the sixth. (Tovar 113; courtesy of the John Carter Brown Library, Brown University)

quihuaztli, Cuetlachtlan revolted with the support of Tlaxcallan and killed the Aztec governor installed after their earlier conquest. Consequently, the Aztecs sent an army and reconquered them.[7]

Heretofore, conquered rulers had generally been retained in office after their defeat. The few exceptions involved the placement of Aztec governors over the local political system, but even then the local nobility still controlled much of the business of government. However, Cuetlachtlan's revolt marked a departure. Aztec accounts state that Cuetlachtlan's commoners came forward, saying the revolt was the fault of their lords, not of the people. When the rulers tried to flee, they were captured by the commoners, bound, and turned over to the Aztecs, who executed them. Not all of the local nobles were eliminated, since someone had to exercise local control in the absence of Aztec willingness to accept an expanded administrative role. So new leaders were selected, and a new Aztec governor was placed over them.[8]

These new rulers lacked the traditional tie to the commoners,

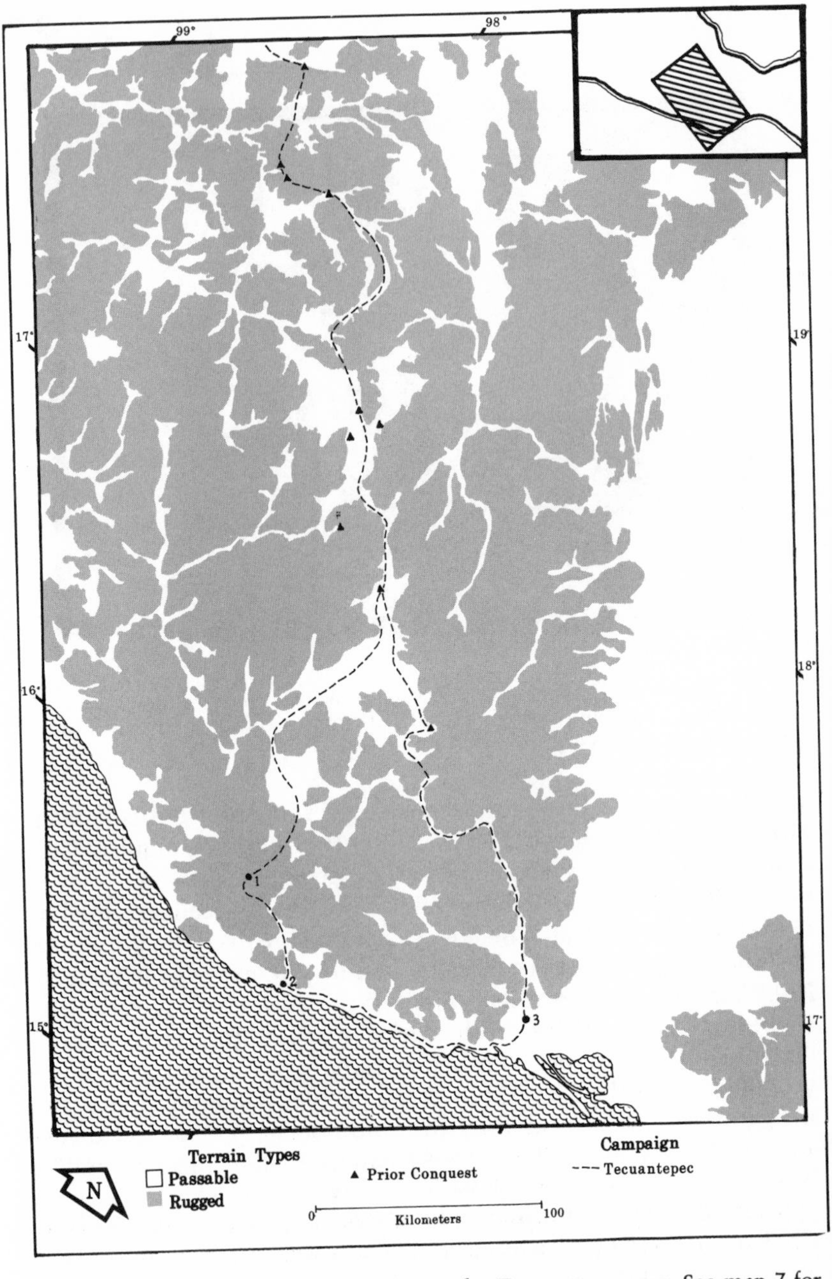

Map 9. Axayacatl's preinaugural raid into the Tecuantepec area. See map 7 for connecting routes to Tenochtitlan. 1—Xochitepec; 2—Cuauhtolco; 3—Tecuantepec.

probably faced some competition from the traditional heirs of the previous rulers, and were dependent on the Aztecs for the maintenance of their positions. But with this replacement of Cuetlachtlan's leaders, the Aztecs had signaled a willingness to alter local status relationships, deal directly with the people, and replace the existing leadership. The conditions of subordination for target towns (or at least towns that had previously been conquered and had then rebelled) had shifted from a quantitative continuum of relative harshness to the potential for a qualitative change.

Axayacatl further consolidated his control over the area by also conquering Totonacapan Cuauhxoxouhcan, Tetl-Icoyoccan, and Tlahuiliipan (see map 10).[9] Several other towns, including Tecalco, Tepeyacac, Oztoticpac, Matlatlan, Ahuilizapan, Cuezcomatl-Iyacac, Poxcauhtlan, Quetzaloztoc, Tlaollan, and Mixtlan,[10] were also incorporated or reincorporated into the empire at this time, although probably not by direct military action.[11]

Following this eastward thrust, there was a minor campaign to secure the area north of the basin of Mexico. The line of march probably proceeded almost directly north to Xochitlan and then Chiapan (both during campaign season 1472–73) before returning home (see map 11). Xilotepec, located in the valley through which the army must have traveled, was probably conquered at this time as well.[12]

But Axayacatl's most famous conquest, of Tenochtitlan's sister city, Tlatelolco, occurred in 1473 (see Map 3).[13] There had been repeated conflicts between the two cities previously.[14] Tlatelolco was not strong enough to sever its increasingly subordinate relationship with Tenochtitlan under normal conditions. But Aztec control had been weakened by the recent death of King Totoquihuaztli of Tlacopan and by Axayacatl's still fragile grip on the empire, and its position deteriorated further with the death of Tetzcoco's King Nezahualcoyotl in 1472.[15]

Nezahualcoyotl had been a major political figure in the Triple Alliance and a skilled military commander, so his death and the resulting succession problems were serious problems for the Aztecs. Nezahualcoyotl was succeeded by Nezahualpilli, aged seven, over opposition from his brothers, who sought to generate support from Chalco for their own candidacy.[16] As a result, a strong leader was gone, the new king was still weak, and there was dissension within the upper nobility.

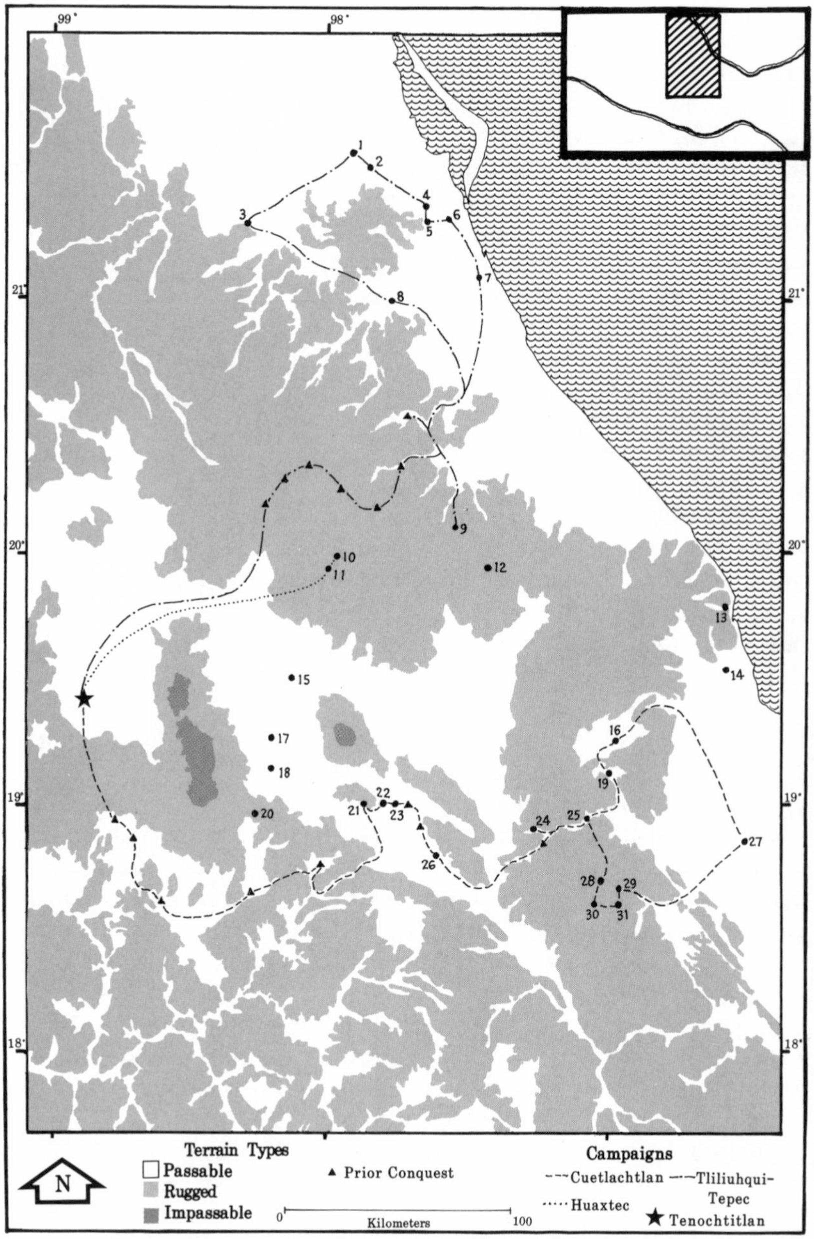

99°
98°
21°
20°
19°
18°
1
2
3
4
5
6
7
8
9
10
11
12
13
14
15
16
17
18
19
20
21
22
23
24
25
26
27
28
29
30
31
Terrain Types
Passable
Rugged
Impassable
N
▲ Prior Conquest
0
Kilometers
100
Campaigns
Cuetlachtlan
Tliliuhqui-Tepec
Huaxtec
Tenochtitlan

Nevertheless, Tenochtitlan was still a formidable opponent, so Tlatelolco's King Moquihuix sought assistance from other cities, including several subject to the Aztecs (Chalco, Xilotepec, Toltitlan, Tenanyocan, Mexicatzinco, Xochimilco, and Mizquic) as well as enemy cities (Cuachpanco and Matlatzinco). They promised assistance,[17] but Huexotzinco, Chalollan, Tlaxcallan, and Tliliuhqui-Tepec all refused,[18] which is somewhat puzzling since this was an ideal opportunity to defeat the Aztecs decisively and remove them as a threat. There are, however, three plausible explanations for their failure to act. First, Tlaxcallan and its allies may still have regarded their conflict with Tenochtitlan as a flower war and not as a serious military threat. Therefore the potentially adverse consequences of attacking Tenochtitlan and converting their conflict to a war of conquest may have outweighed any beneficial results. But this alone seems unlikely, given Tlaxcallan's support for Cuetlachtlan's rebellion to the east. Second, these city-states still retained their independence and were apparently unlikely to lose it soon under prevailing conditions. Thus provoking the Aztecs may have seemed unwise when they contrasted their slight potential gains with their enormous potential losses. Third, and most likely given the distances involved, a military penetration so deep into Tenochtitlan's territory would have left the Tlaxcaltecs and Huexotzincas vulnerable to reprisals while they were far beyond their own domains. Thus the refusal to assist Tlatelolco may have stemmed from a recognition of the liabilities to Tlaxcallan and Huexotzinco, rather than from a disinclination to fight Tenochtitlan.

Despite Moquihuix's secrecy, Axayacatl learned of his plea for assistance and attacked before Tlatelolco's supporters could arrive. Axayacatl placed troops under his best leaders at each of the roads running into the city to prevent the Tlatelolcas from escaping and

Map 10. (facing page) Axayacatl's campaigns into present-day Puebla, the Gulf coast, and the Huaxtec area. 1—Tanpatel*; 2—Occentepetl*; 3—Xiuhcoac*; 4—Tenexticpac*; 5—Tzapotitlan*; 6—Tamomox*; 7—Tochpan; 8—Micquetlan*; 9—Cuauhtlan*; 10—Zacatlan; 11—Tliliuhqui-Tepec*; 12—Tlatlauhqui-Tepec; 13—Quiahuiztlan; 14—Cempohuallan; 15—Tlaxcallan; 16—Tototlan; 17—Huexotzinco; 18—Chalollan; 19—Cuezcomatl-Iyacac; 20—Atlixco; 21—Tecalco; 22—Tepeyacac; 23—Oztoticpac; 24—Matlatlan; 25—Ahuilizapan; 26—Tetl-Icoyoccan; 27—Cuetlachtlan; 28—Poxcauhtlan*; 29—Quetzaloztoc*; 30—Tlaollan; 31—Mictlan.* (*Approximate location.)

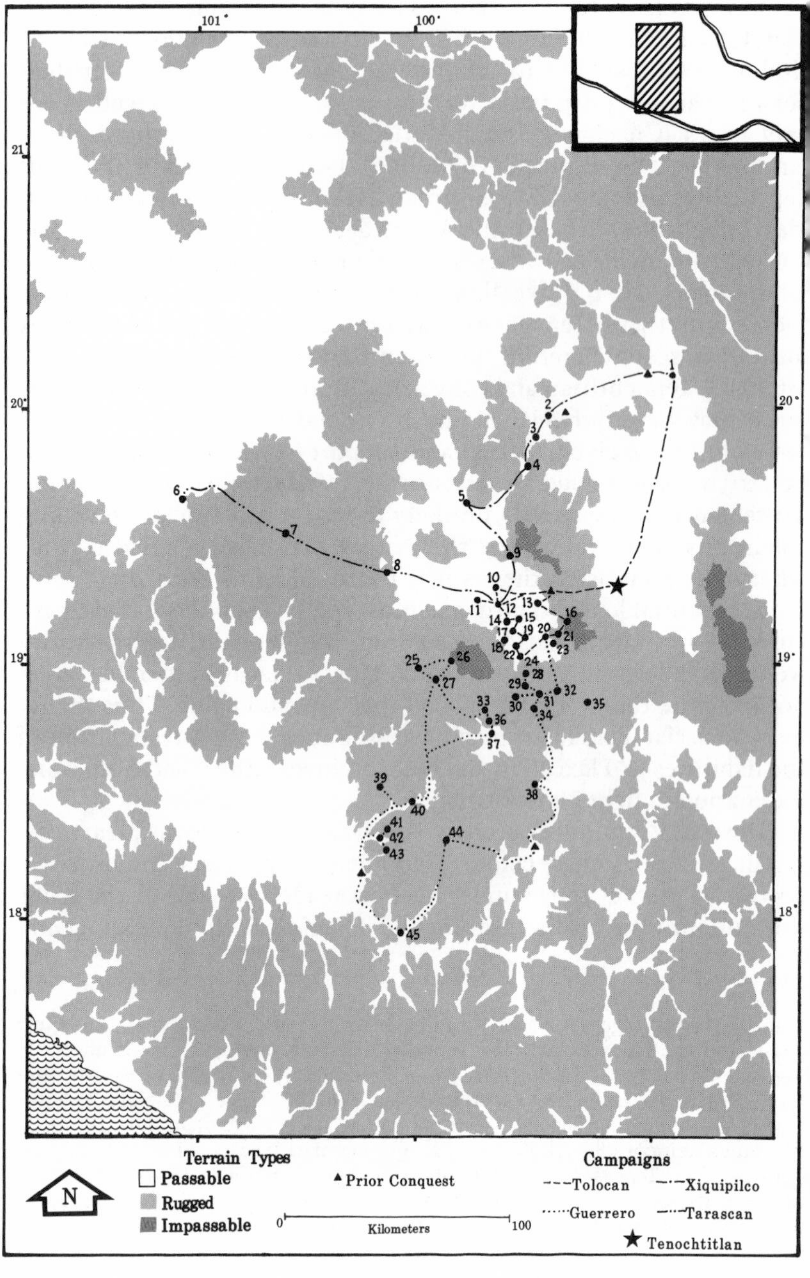
101°
100°
21°
20°
19°
18°
Terrain Types
Passable
Rugged
Impassable
Prior Conquest
0
Kilometers
100
Campaigns
Tolocan
Xiquipilco
Guerrero
Tarascan
Tenochtitlan
N

their reinforcements from entering. The Aztecs then began the attack, forcing the outnumbered Tlatelolcas back to the temple of Quetzalhuah near the marketplace,[19] where Axayacatl is credited with killing Moquihuix in single combat. Tlatelolco was defeated, losing 460 dead, and the temple was burned.[20]

After the battle people came to Tlatelolco from Xochimilco, Cuitlahuac, Mizquic, Mexicatzinco, and Huitzilopochco. Axayacatl killed the rulers of those towns, as well as the rulers of Colhuacan, Cuitlahuac, and Huitzilopochco.[21] Although the Xochimilcas had not aided the Tlatelolcas, they had not assisted the Aztecs in a timely manner, so their king, Xihuitl-Temoc, was also killed.[22] Axayacatl also placed an Aztec military governor over Tlatelolco.[23] Thus he punished those who had conspired with Tlatelolco, secured his hold over his tributaries, and generated greater loyalty among the successors of the executed rulers, as the Aztec manipulation of succession increased the number of local rulers who also had kin ties to Tenochtitlan.[24] Consequently, Tenochtitlan emerged stronger from this civil war.

Except for a small war with Huexotla the following year[25]—either the result of the Acolhua succession struggle or as part of the consolidation following the defeat of Tlatelolco—Tenochtitlan now had no challengers left in the heart of the empire. Axayacatl had successfully expanded north and south, and Tlaxcallan and its allies were safely contained to the east. The Aztecs next turned westward in a series of campaigns aimed at expanding and strengthening their flank and blocking any expansion of the Tarascan Empire, the only serious competitor to the west. The western conquests fall into

Map 11. (facing page) Axayacatl's campaigns into the valley of Tolocan, present-day Guerrero, and north of the basin of Mexico and the Tarascan incursion. 1—Atocpan; 2—Xochitlan; 3—Xilotepec; 4—Chiapan; 5—Xocotitlan; 6—Matlatzinco; 7—Tlaximaloyan; 8—Malacatepec; 9—Xiquipilco; 10—Calixtlahuacan; 11—Tzinacantepec; 12—Tolocan; 13—Ocoyacac; 14—Cozcacuauhtenanco; 15—Metepec; 16—Atlapolco; 17—Tlacotempan*; 18—Tlacotepec; 19—Tepemaxalco; 20—Capolloac; 21—Cuauhpanohuayan*; 22—Calli-Imanyan; 23—Xalatlauhco; 24—Teotenanco; 25—Temazcaltepec; 26—Cimatepec*; 27—Neucatepec*; 28—Zoquitzinco; 29—Maxtlacan; 30—Tenantzinco; 31—Tecualocan; 32—Ocuillan; 33—Cuitlapilco; 34—Malinalco; 35—Cuauhnahuac; 36—Coatepec; 37—Malinaltenanco; 38—Chontalcoatlan; 39—Amatepec; 40—Oztoman; 41—Acapetlahuayan; 42—Icpatepec*; 43—Totoltepec; 44—Poctepec; 45—Tonalli-Imoquetzayan. (*Approximate location.)

three periods reflecting different phases of the overall campaign. The first thrust was west into the valley of Tolocan during the campaign season of 1475–76. The next movement was south from Tolocan during 1476–77. And the final phase was directed north from Tolocan during 1477–78 (see map 11).

There were two Aztec pretexts for the first western incursion. One account states that the lord of Tenantzinco requested assistance against Tolocan; Tecualocan is named as the threat by another account. Another says that Aztec messengers sent to Tolocan for materials for the temple of Huitzilopochtli were refused and on that pretext the Aztecs began the war. However, the Tarascans had previously attempted to expand into the area between their empire and the Aztecs', attacking Xiquipilco. Although they were repulsed, the Aztecs sought to prevent an alliance between that region and the Tarascan Empire in Michhuacan (Michoacan).[26] Conquering the area would preempt Tarascan expansion in the region, enlist additional allies that would be particularly helpful in case of further expansion to the west, and create a logistical support area permitting more rapid movement of troops.

Unlike other areas of central Mexico, where there were many major city-states, the Tarascans lacked significant competitors in their area, yet they were powerful enough to persuade and/or force many other cities to become tributaries of their empire. But they were not immediately threatened by the Aztecs because of their distance from the basin of Mexico. In fact, the Tarascan consolidation was facilitated by the position between the two competing empires of smaller towns, which were forced to choose an alliance with one empire or the other.

Control of these small towns was politically necessary for the domination of the area and militarily pivotal for any further expansion. Thus, when the Aztecs expanded westward, Axayacatl ordered the army not to kill many Matlatzincas.[27] Accordingly, in the battle for Tolocan, Axayacatl again used deception and ambush to strike a decisive blow that would end the battle without killing large numbers of the enemy. He and eight of his leading warriors camouflaged themselves with straw. When the Aztec army feigned withdrawal, the Tolocas advanced, whereupon the hidden soldiers leaped out and killed the Toloca lords. Axayacatl personally took prisoners, the Tolocas fled, and the Aztecs burned their temple.[28] The king of Tolocan surrendered, and the image of the people's chief god, Coltzin, was taken back to Tenochtitlan, together with all the priests of the temple.[29] Also conquered in this campaign were the cities of Xalatlauhco, Cozcacuauhtenanco, Teotenanco, Metepec, Tepemaxalco, Tlacotempan, Tzinacantepec, Calli-Imanyan (Callimayan), and Tlacotepec, all in the easily accessible valley area.[30] Other towns likely to have formed a part of this thrust were Ocoyacac (Teouyacac), Calixtlahuacan, Atlapolco, Capolloac, and Cuauhpanohuayan (Quapouya), completing the conquest of the southern valley area.[31] However, these towns probably did not require more than the presence of the Aztec army to capitulate.

The Aztecs' next movement, as mentioned, was toward the south during the following campaign season (1476–77). It included the conquest of Tenantzinco and the reconquest of Ocuillan,[32] located in separate passes out of the valley of Tolocan. As the army moved south, Ocuillan was conquered first, followed by Tenantzinco.[33] The army probably marched south from Ocuillan, conquering towns as distant as Tonalli-Imoquetzayan, and including Chontalcoatlan, Poctepec, Icpatepec, and Amatepec.[34] Also conquered at this time were Tecualocan, Oztoman, Teotzacualco, Malinaltenanco, Cuitlapilco, Coatepec, Acapetlahuayan, Totoltepec, Tenantzinco, Maxtlacan, and Zoquitzinco, and, apparently, Neucatepec (Necantepec), and Cimatepec.[35] Cuauhnahuac was conquered during the same year, but by Ocuillan, not by the Aztecs.[36]

The next expansion in this campaign took place to the north. At this time (1477) the Aztecs ended the military governorship of Ecatepec imposed after the death of its king in 1465, and a new ruler was installed.[37] This may have been the result of matters that were strictly internal to Ecatepec, but its timing and the location of the town en route to the northern campaign suggest a connection. Whether or not the governor's rule had accomplished the ends for which it was originally imposed (and presumably it had), the newly reinstated ruler would have been eager to prove his support for the Aztecs and probably was an excellent ally in this campaign, supplying troops or providing logistical support.

The main target of this northern campaign, Xiquipilco, was conquered during the following campaign season (1477–78). Six thousand Xiquipilcas died in the conquest, and three thousand were captured.[38] Other towns conquered during this campaign include Xocotitlan, Xilotepec, and Atocpan (Actopan).[39] These towns are all accessible directly from the basin of Mexico, and a campaign staged from there would have benefited from the transportation and logistical advantages afforded by the lake. Based on the sequence in which the towns were conquered, however, the campaign was apparently launched through the valley of Tolocan. Xocotitlan was easily accessible from Xiquipilco, as was Atocpan to the northeast as the army passed through the previously conquered towns of Chiapan and Xochitlan. The return was probably directly south to Tenochtitlan.

These campaigns occupied most of their armies, but the Aztecs also used their military successes in one part of the empire to buttress their control of other parts. After the conquest of the Matlatzinca territory, the Aztecs sent messengers to Quiahuiztlan and Cempohuallan on the Gulf coast for feathers for the festival of *Tlatlauhqui-Tezcatl* (see map 10),[40] and this veiled threat resulted in the two cities' acquiescence without the use of force.[41] The consequences of refusing the Aztec request were all too apparent to the solicited cities. The Aztecs' ability to commad respect at such distance was doubtless a reflection of their success in the western campaigns and the additional areas added to the empire.

Following the completion of the western campaigns, the Aztecs imposed a military government in Tolocan in 1479,[42] which may have been a strictly internal political or successional matter. But thereafter the Tarascan war began (probably in campaign season 1479–80), suggesting that the Aztecs were ensuring their support in an area crucial to a thrust farther west[43] (see map 11).

Accounts of the Tarascan campaign agree on the general outlines but conflict on the details.[44] By one account[45] the Aztecs and their allies fought the Tarascans at Matlatzinco (present-day Charo) but, outnumbered 32,000 to 50,000, were badly defeated. The army returned to Tzinacantepec, one of Tolocan's subjects, with only 100 warriors each from Tetzcoco, Acolhuacan, Tlacopan, Xochimilco, and Chalco, 10 each from the Otomies, mountain groups, and Chinampanecs, and only 200 Aztecs.[46] By another account[47] the Aztec army set up camp at the lagoon near Tzinapequaro (roughly the location of Matlatzinco), and spies were dispatched. The Tarascan army was on a nearby plain and the spies allegedly tunneled to their tents and overheard the strength of the army and their weapons. Although outnumbered 40,000 to 24,000, the Aztecs attacked, but they finally withdrew to Ecatepec with only 200 Aztecs, 400 Tetzcocas, 400 Tepanecs, 400 Chalcas, 400 Xochimilcas, 300 Otomies from Cuauhtlalpan, and practically none from the lowlands.[48] The only significant conquest of this campaign was Tlaximaloyan, which lay on the probable route of march and was doubtless conquered on the way in.[49] By all accounts the Aztecs were soundly defeated, which was unusual, but so, too, was the Tarascan failure to follow up on the victory.[50] The explanation of both these anomalies lies in the logistical situation.

Like the Aztec Empire, the Tarascan was based on a system of alliances that depended on the perception of power. The area into which the Aztecs marched, though part of the Tarascan Empire, was not part of its political core; it was an area primarily composed of ethnic Matlatzincas, whose loyalty to the Tarascans was largely pragmatic. The Aztecs were probably seeking a tactical victory over the Tarascan army, since a significant defeat could have undermined the perception of Tarascan power and precipitated a shift of alliances by non-Tarascan towns in the region.

One possible reason for the Aztecs' defeat was that they were permitted to enter beyond their secure lines of supply or communication. Thus, the Aztecs could not readily acquire additional goods, men, or arms, and with no means of resupply their arrows would have been exhausted rapidly, in contrast to the Tarascans'. This would not only have exposed them to unanswered arrow fire but also have meant the loss of covering fire for withdrawing and replacing their troops in combat. The Tarascans could easily have brought in fresh troops. The inevitable outcome was an extremely heavy casualty rate among the Aztecs.[51] But the Tarascans' failure to follow up on their decisive victory probably reflects both the Aztec success in securing the areas between the rival empires and the Tarascans' logistical inability to dispatch and supply troops at great distances. The Aztecs' defeat was unequivocal, but its effects were contained.

Other wars followed this defeat, because the empire required shoring up through military exploits, a need made all the more acute by the defeat the Aztecs had suffered and by their enormous loss of experienced soldiers. Thus, a year after the Tarascan campaign (campaign season 1480–81?), the decision was made to complete the *cuauhxicalli* (eagle vessel, to hold human hearts taken from sacrifices) of the temple of Huitzilopochtli in Tenochtitlan, which required war captives for sacrifice. Although religious demands for sacrificial captives are often cited as reasons that Mesoamerican wars were fought, irregularly occurring religious events, such as the construction or dedication of a temple, were chosen by the leaders as occasions especially demanding captives. So while religious occasions supplied the rationale for war, they were politically manipulated and were rationalizations for wars rather than causes. A war was begun with Tliliuhqui-Tepec (see map 10).[52] Zacatlan also fought the Aztecs at this time, probably as an ally of Tliliuhqui-Tepec.[53] Tliliuhqui-Tepec was unconquered in the apparent xochiyaoyotl, but seven hundred captives were taken for sacrifice.[54]

At this time (campaign season 1480–81), news came of some Aztec and Tetzcoca merchants who were killed at Tochpan, and the Aztec army reconquered the area.[55] Also listed as conquered during this campaign, but probably without much actual combat, were the towns of Tamomox (Tamuoc), Tenexticpac, Occentepetl ("another mountain," not a town name), Tanpatel, Tzapotitlan (Tetzapotitlan), Xiuhcoac, and Micquetlan, as well as Cuauhtlan en route.[56]

The probable route taken depends on the conquest sequence and the logistical demands of the army. Assuming that Tochpan was conquered first, the army probably marched from Tenochtitlan, up the Teotihuacan valley to Tollantzinco, and then along the previous conquest route via Xolotlan, Pahuatlan, Cuauhchinanco, Tlapacoyan, Chapolicxitlan, and Tozapan, to Tochpan (an error in the sequence of conquests would merely require reversing the route). On the return the army probably simply retraced its route. Cuauhtlan was easily accessible from the lowlands by marching up the Apolco River in the unlikely event that it had to be physically conquered. Here, as with all of Axayacatl's conquests except the successful conquest of Tecuantepec and the unsuccessful campaign against the Tarascans, there were numerous conquests but little extension beyond existing areas of reliable logistical support.

CHAPTER 13

Tizoc
"He-has-bled-people"[1]
(Ruled 1481 to 1486)

WHEN Axayacatl died in 1481, the news was sent immediately throughout the land. Emissaries traveled to Tenochtitlan from tributary cities, as did enemy rulers from Tlaxcallan, Huexotzinco, and Chalollan, secretly and at night.[2]

There are many possible reasons for attending an enemy ceremony: goods were distributed, prestige might be achieved, relations might be renewed, and enmities and alliances might be discussed. But an even more pressing reason was to avoid unnecessarily incurring the wrath of a powerful state. An Aztec invitation contained a considerable element of the mailed fist, and even enemies maintained some levels of intercourse that might be jeopardized. Though the enemy rulers might attend, however, they could not be seen to do so, as that would reflect poorly on their own perceived power. It was enough that the rulers were aware of these arrangements. Thus, attendance by enemy rulers was a barometer of the state's power.

Tlacaelel was allegedly offered the kingship and declined;[3] but this is unlikely, for at least two reasons. First, he had not been a major military leader of the Aztec army under Axayacatl and thus was not ideally positioned to be elevated to the throne.[4] Second, and probably more important, Tlacaelel was old by this time. Even during the reign of King Moteuczomah Ilhuicamina he had been too old to accompany the army on the Coaixtlahuacan campaign,[5] and as the empire expanded, maintaining the network of tributaries increasingly rested on the martial and political attributes of the king. Every time a king died, the empire underwent a period of uncertainty and potential fragmentation, so selecting an older king would ensure more frequent turnovers in rule—something to be avoided if at all possible.

Fig. 25. Tizoc ("He-has-bled-people"). (Tovar 111; courtesy of the John Carter Brown Library, Brown University)

Tizoc, who had been the tlacochcalcatl under Axayacatl, was elected king (see fig. 25),[6] and notice of his selection was immediately sent throughout the empire.[7] He is credited with having conquered some towns (see fig. 26), but of all the Aztec kings Tizoc is notorious for his lack of military success.[8]

As had become customary, the king designate embarked on a campaign to secure captives for his coronation. This was necessary to demonstrate the military power of the Aztec empire and the ability of the new king. Several alternatives were suggested as the target for Tizoc's conquest, including Michhuacan and the recently rebelled Cuetlachtlan, but it was decided that the campaign should be directed toward the northeast, against Metztitlan and Itzmiquilpan (see map 12).[9] After summoning troops from the Chalcas, Chinampanecas, Tolocas, and Matlatzincas, Tizoc assembled the entire army[10] at Tetzontepec (85 km. or 53 mi.; 3 to 4 days, from Tenochtitlan and 120 km. or 74 mi.; 4 to 6 days, from Tolocan). It proceeded to Atotonilco (80 km. or 50 mi.; 3 to 4 days), reportedly reaching it the next day (but clearly not) and then marched to Metztitlan (40 km. or 25 mi. to the town proper; 1 to 2 days).

The battle site was probably some 24 kilometers (15 miles) from Atotonilco, and the distance could have been covered in a long day's march. Metztitlan was much smaller than Tenochtitlan and could not have fielded a very large army of its own, but it had the advantage of location. The Metztitlan valley is relatively narrow and some 30 kilometers (19 miles) long, with the town of Metztitlan located about halfway from the entry point (from the direction of Atotonilco). Its mountainous sides limited both maneuvering room and the number of combatants that an attacker could bring to bear. Thus it was in Metztitlan's interest to fight just inside the valley, where its numerical inferiority was minimized, its army had room to fall back as necessary, and the town of Metztitlan would not be immediately endangered.

Fig. 26. Detail from the Stone of Tizoc, showing Tizoc taking a captive representing a conquered town. Tizoc is depicted in Toltec attire and with the smoking-mirror left foot characteristic of Tezcatl-Ihpoca. (Courtesy of the Museo Nacional de Antropología, Mexico)

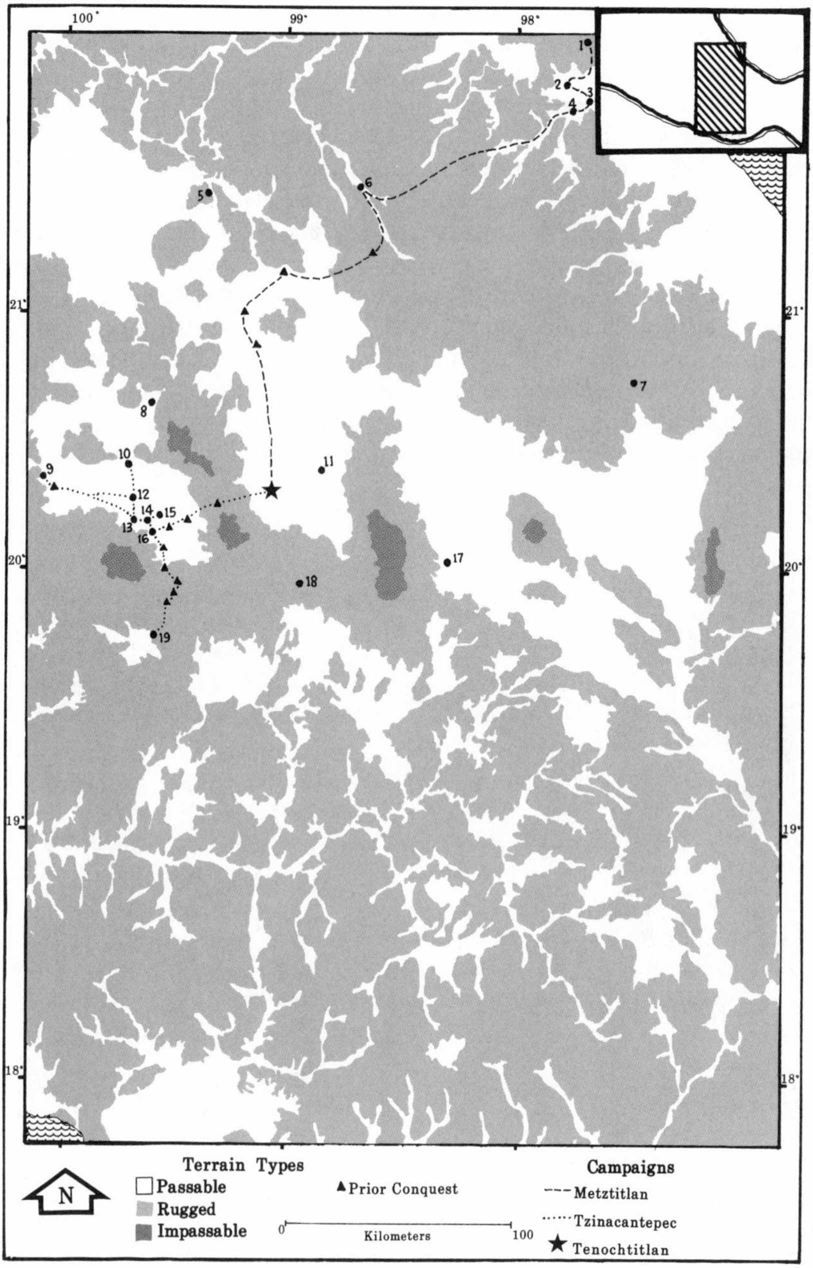
100°
99°
98°
21°
20°
19°
18°
1
2
3
4
5
6
7
8
9
10
11
12
13
14
15
16
17
18
19
Terrain Types
Passable
Rugged
Impassable
Prior Conquest
0
Kilometers
100
Campaigns
Metztitlan
Tzinacantepec
Tenochtitlan
N

The selection of Metztitlan as a target was a poor one, since a numerically inferior opponent was offered the advantage of a superior defensive position. Moreover, the Aztecs needed to secure a victory and not merely stave off a defeat, and because of the limited time allowed by their supplies, they had to take the offensive without being able to outflank their opponents. This exposed the Aztec warriors to a far greater likelihood of injury or death, while the warriors of Metztitlan were content to fend them off, wear them down, and slowly withdraw, trading off land for the enormous casualties being taken by the offensive forces.

The Aztecs claimed a victory but took only forty prisoners in the battle—some from Metztitlan but mostly Huaxtecs—and lost three hundred of their own warriors before returning to Tenochtitlan.[11] They did not conquer the town of Metztitlan, nor is it likely that they conquered Itzmiquilpan but probably fought their armies at the Metztitlan battle site. Other towns conquered in the Huaxtec area, including Tlatlauhqui-Icxic, Micquetlan, Tamachpan, and Occentepetl ("another mountain," not a town name),[12] were probably not directly involved in fighting, at least not at their own cities, but acquiesced to Tenochtitlan's traditional dominance.[13] Four of the six lowland towns had been conquered by the Aztecs previously, and the remaining two may have been as well, with the record now lost.[14]

Although he lost more men in the raid than he took, Tizoc maintained that he had taken the required number for the coronation.[15] He may have been referring to the sacrificial captives needed for religious purposes, but his statement reflected a misunderstanding of the power purposes of the preinaugural raid. Nevertheless, the inauguration proceeded: rulers from all over the empire were invited, and Tizoc became king.[16]

Two years after the start of Tizoc's rule there was a war between Cuauhnahuac and Atlixco[17] in which the Aztecs apparently took no part, perhaps because of their own campaign (the campaign season of

Map 12. (facing page) Tizoc's preinaugural raid against Metztitlan and the Huaxtec area and into the valley of Tolocan. 1—Occentepetl*; 2—Tamachpan; 3—Tochpan; 4—Micquetlan*; 5—Itzmiquilpan; 6—Metztitlan; 7—Tlatlauhqui-Tepec.; 8—Tecuauhcozcac*; 9—Cillan*; 10—Tozxiuhco*; 11—Tetzcoco; 12—Tecaxic; 13—Tzinacantepec; 14—Iczoxochitlan; 15—Tolocan; 16—Tlacotepec; 17—Huexotzinco; 18—Cuauhnahuac; 19—Ecatlapechco*. (*Approximate location.)

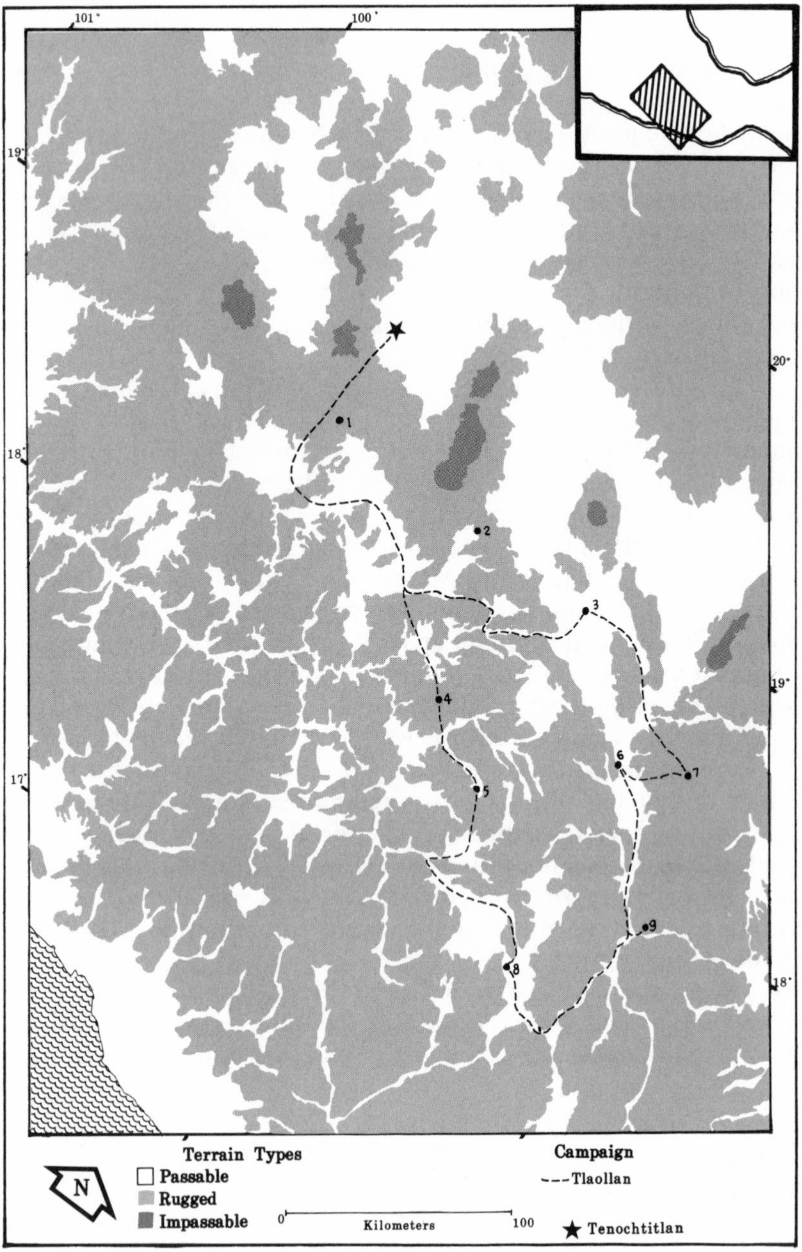

Map 13. Tizoc's campaign into the Huaxyacac area. 1—Cuauhnahuac; 2—Atlixco; 3—Oztoticpac; 4—Xochiyetla*; 5—Tilmatlan*; 6—Teohuacan; 7—Tlaollan; 8—Yancuitlan; 9—Mazatlan. (*Approximate location.)

1483–84) directed toward the Gulf coast, where several towns had rebelled. Chicpantlan[18] and Tlaollan[19] were reconquered, and references to the sacrifice of captives from Toztlan and Oztoticpac indicate that these towns were involved as well,[20] although there is no evidence that the army actually marched as far as Toztlan. The Aztec army probably conquered Oztotipac en route and continued as far as Tlaollan, with Toztlan participating in the battle there (see map 13). Such a campaign would still require a round trip of some 735 kilometers (456 miles) or 23 to 38 days exclusive of days for combat, rest, or regrouping.

Tizoc's poor war record as king reduced the Aztecs' credibility as a military power, and there were revolts throughout the empire. The revolt in the Matlatzinca area[21] began when the people of Tzinacantepec killed an Aztec tribute collector (calpixqui).[22] This revolt was put down, and Tzinacantepec was conquered, as was Tlacotepec,[23] in a campaign that probably began at the end of 1484 and extended into 1485. Several other towns in the Matlatzinca area are also listed as conquests, including Tecuauhcozcac, Cillan, Tozxiuhco (Toxico), Tecaxic, Ecatlapechco, Tonalli-Imoquetzayan, Tolocan, and Iczoxochitlan,[24] but they appear to have been of little significance during this campaign and probably submitted once Tzinacantlan and Tlacotepec had been reconquered.[25]

Both cities were nearby (no more than 4 to 5 days round trip) and within established logistical-support areas (see map 12). The bulk of the conquered towns are nearby and even those at some greater distance are easily accessible, so an actual march could easily have been accomplished but may not have been necessary. Only the two southern towns posed any difficulty, requiring a mountainous passage, but they were on established conquest routes and could have been approached if the need had arisen.

The only other major military venture during Tizoc's reign was Tetzcoco's war with Huexotzinco. Led by Nezahualpilli, the Tetzcoca forces vanquished the Huexotzincas and sacked their city, without direct Aztec participation.[26] This war either preceded or was concurrent with the Matlatzinca war, a circumstance that might explain the lack of Aztec participation.

There remain a few towns listed as conquests that are so scattered or remote that they do not fit easily into any of Tizoc's campaigns. These include Teohuacan, Mazatlan, Yancuitlan, Tilmatlan, Xochiyetla, Tlappan, Tonalli-Imoquetzayan, and Ecatepec, which

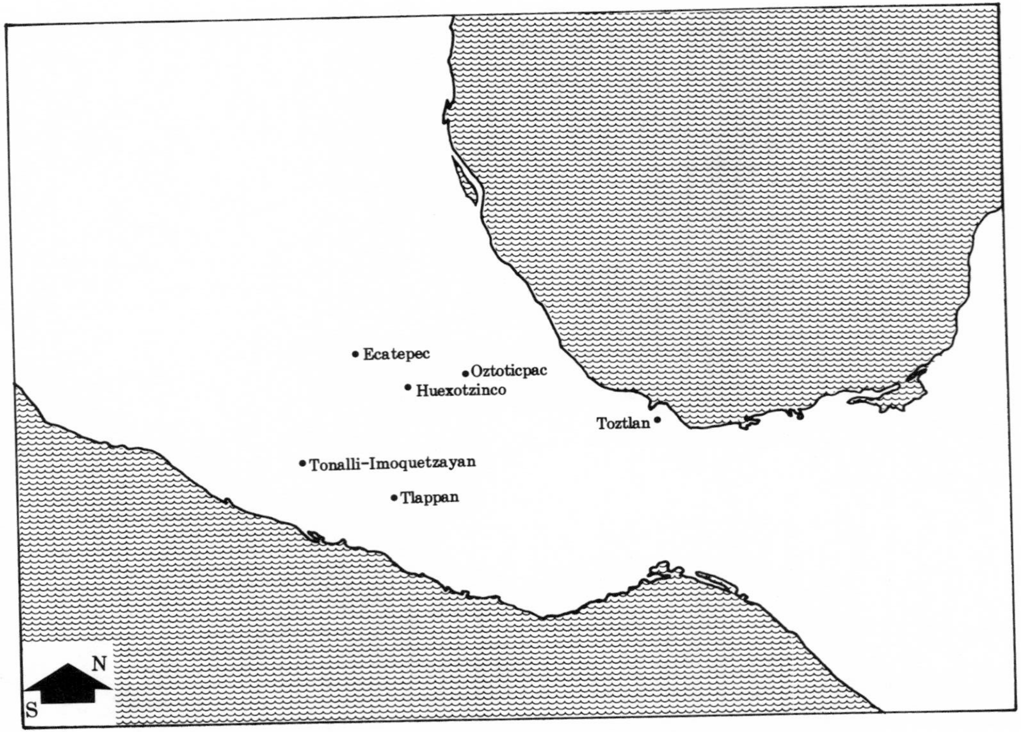

Map 14. Scattered conquests undertaken during the reign of Tizoc.

were probably among the many rebellious cities.[27] But they probably capitulated voluntarily or were reconquered on a case-by-case basis. With the possible exception of Toztlan, Tizoc's scattered conquests remained well within the existing area of logistical support, although this area was probably deteriorating (see map 14).

In 1486 Tizoc agreed to return home rule to the Chalca towns.[28] The reasons for this decision are unclear. Perhaps the Chalcas were now sufficiently aligned with the Aztecs to permit them home rule. But given Tizoc's weak record, the decision may reflect his unwillingness to enforce military rule any longer, which may have contributed to his downfall.

Despite his poor combat record Tizoc did institute changes in Aztec society reflecting military concerns, declaring that the Huexotzincas were such good warriors that no soldier would be given the insignia of a valiant warrior unless he had captured one.[29] It seems paradoxical that Tizoc would increase the requirements for rising in military status when his own record was so weak, but it may simply have been an attempt to encourage greater effort and to place responsibility on the soldiers for his poor performance. The change also reflects the accelerating requirements for military advancement, however, and an increasing division between the noble and commoner classes. Tizoc may have been forced to adopt this course of action by the growing numbers of commoners seeking social mobility through martial accomplishments—a consequence of Moteuczomah Ilhuicamina's having increased the number of telpochcalli.

In ordinary wars of conquest most of the prisoners taken were commoners, both because they were more numerous than nobles and because they received poorer military training. Thus, taking a commoner prisoner would not necessarily reflect great martial skill or daring. In a flower war, however, a primary goal was to demonstrate individual martial skills, those involving the use of shock weapons. The supporting commoners, at least those not in the telpochcalli, were largely (perhaps totally) absent from these conflicts. The net effect was that fewer prisoners were taken and when they were, it required considerably more skill. Tizoc's new standard thus further reduced the chances of commoners' rising in class through military exploits by requiring that they excel in a flower war (i.e., against Huexotzinco), the very type of conflict in which they were least represented.

Tizoc's reign did not reflect an attempt to change imperial strategy. He made no structural changes in his army, in the role of nobles, in the rule by local tlahtohqueh, or in rule by power. He lost the offensive and concentrated (to the extent he did) on putting out brushfire revolts. The longer his reign continued, the more the Aztec empire eroded. Because the system was held together by threat of military reprisal, internal revolts were even more dangerous than failed campaigns, the former arose from a perception of Aztec weakness, while the latter were thrusts into unconquered and unknown areas and might require more than one effort to succeed. Tizoc forgot (or never realized) that the key to keeping the empire together was maintaining the appearance of power, which required constant attention. His was a failure of implementation.

Tizoc's reign lasted only four or five years, cut short by poison administered by his subjects,[30] and news of his death was immediately sent throughout the empire.[31] The general reasons for doing away with Tizoc involved the withering away of Aztec influence and control of the empire and were readily apparent. But the specific reasons—who would dare kill the king and why—are not recorded, although an examination of the effects of Tizoc's reign suggests some possibilities.

Any sustained lapse in maintaining the Aztecs' reputation meant a shrinkage of the empire and a corresponding reduction in tribute goods and lands that went disproportionately to the nobility. So Tizoc's failure to maintain the empire struck directly at their interests and undermined their support. Consequently, there may have been considerable motivation among the nobility for his removal. General ill feeling against the king was probably inadequate for any single individual to have taken the undoubted risk of harming someone so exalted and powerful.

Tizoc's poor performance had reflected on the chances of his apparent successor, the tlacochcalcatl Ahuitzotl.[32] Kings were drawn from a limited pool of upper nobles who had good military records. Though the tlacochcalcatl position gave its occupant an advantage in any succession selection, it did not guarantee it, and this was probably even more the case during the reign of Tizoc. Performance was a critical criterion, and regardless of ability, service under a militarily poor king—whether because of his timidity in prosecuting war or because of his poor tactical directions—diminished the tlacochcalcatl's chances to ascend to the throne. Thus, he had a considerable interest either in forcing more wars or in eliminating the king.

Since few wars were conducted under Tizoc and fewer still successful ones, Ahuitzotl watched the daily erosion of his position as heir apparent. Discounting the suggestion that Lord Techotlallah of Ixtlapalapan employed witches to kill him,[33] there is no good evidence to indicate who might have killed Tizoc. But the apparent lack of reaction among the noble class, the exalted position of the king, which would certainly deter the commoners, the daily erosion of the position of the nobility, and the specific undermining of Ahuitzotl's position as successor indicate that Tizoc was eliminated by the nobility, and the noble who benefited most was Ahuitzotl.

CHAPTER 14

Ahuitzotl
"Otter"[1]
(Ruled 1486 to 1502)

WHEN Tizoc died in 1486, he was succeeded by Ahuitzotl (see fig. 27). Whether or not he was responsible for his predecessor's demise, there was tremendous pressure on Ahuitzotl to perform well, to reassert Aztec dominance, and to recement the ties between Tenochtitlan and its tributaries. He proved to be one of the most energetic and successful Aztec kings.

As was customary, news of Tizoc's death was immediately sent throughout the land, but in this case it doubtless took on added significance. Subject towns were to come to Tenochtitlan and by so doing declare their loyalty,[2] thus automatically providing an assessment of the state of the empire. At the outset of Ahuitzotl's reign the Aztecs were experiencing problems with their allies as a result of Tizoc's weak leadership. But this difficulty was transitory, and it could be remedied by the reassertion of strong leadership. A more significant problem arose from the lack of cohesiveness in the imperial army.

The ideological underpinnings of the Aztec Empire were the upper classes, abetted by the priesthood, and both groups benefited disproportionately as the empire expanded. Whatever the individual Aztec commoner's inclinations, the calpolli system operated to ensure his obedience. The calpolli leadership called up troops, distributed rewards, and recorded the soldiers' deaths. But even more significant, the calpolli leadership controlled all access to lands for commoners. So in addition to positive incentives the Aztec state possessed considerable coercive power to ensure the compliance of the common soldiers. Moreover, the lower classes benefited indirectly from the influx of tribute goods, the greater flow of trade, the acquisition of new calpolli lands, and the opportunities that wars

Fig. 27. Ahuitzotl ("Otter"). Tovar erroneously recorded Ahuitzotl as the fifth king rather than the eighth. (Tovar 105; courtesy of the John Carter Brown Library of Brown University)

presented for social advancement. Thus, even though their gains were less than those of the elites, the lower classes probably favored the imperial expansion.

The elites and commoners of the other Triple Alliance cities also shared many of the benefits enjoyed by the people of Tenochtitlan. This was less true of other allies, who shared in the booty of successful campaigns but not in the control of vanquished peoples or in their annual tribute. The allied elites still benefited more than the commoners, whose potential rewards were small while their risks were great. Allied towns were required to supply a specified number of troops for specific campaigns, but since neither the local calpolli leaders nor the commoners benefited from the conquests the way their Aztec counterparts did, there were fewer positive incentives for commoner soldiers to remain in the field once the campaign was under way. Differences in allegiance and rewards were common, but their impact depended largely on the perception of the army—the

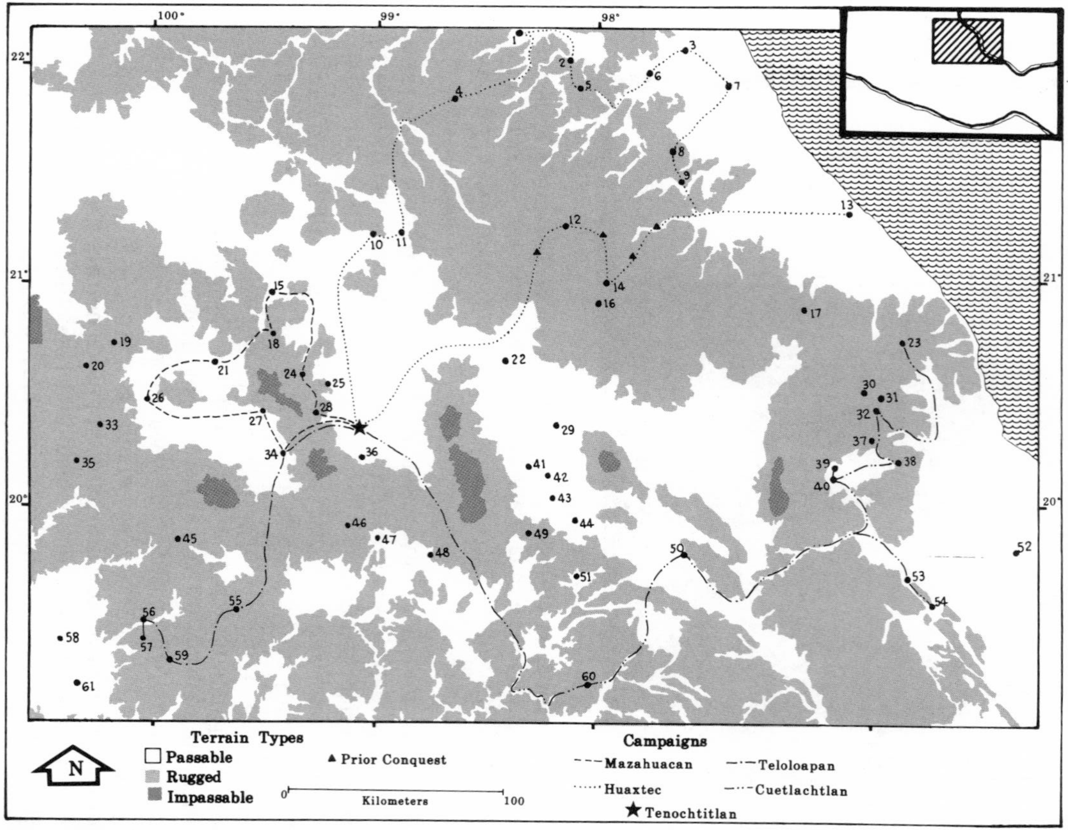
Terrain Types
Passable
Rugged
Impassable
Prior Conquest
0 Kilometers 100
Campaigns
Mazahuacan
Teloloapan
Huaxtec
Cuetlachtlan
Tenochtitlan
100°
99°
98°
22°
21°
20°
N

more powerful it was, the more muted the dissension. Following Tizoc's reign dissension was rife.

As was also customary, the newly designated king engaged in a war of conquest to provide captives for his coronation. For Ahuitzotl, this first campaign was against the cities to the north and northwest of the basin of Mexico, including the area referred to generally as Mazahuacan, where discontent and rebellion were rampant. The Aztec army and its allies marched to Chillocan and to Xiquipilco, which they conquered, as well as Cillan and Xocotitlan[3] (see map 15). But defections during the campaigns must have been high, particularly before Aztec dominance had been reasserted, and Ahuitzotl issued an order that no one was to leave after the initial conquests on pain of death.[4]

To avoid the attrition likely among the allied troops during the usual rest day after battle and to surprise Chiapan, the Aztecs marched on the city the same day. However, their approach was discovered by sentries, the city was warned, and a battle ensued. While the Tetzcocas, Tepanecs, Xochimilcas, and Chalcas engaged the enemy directly, the Aztecs entered the city secretly with the help of come of Chiapan's inhabitants. It was this ability to circumvent defenders and conquer an objective that made traitors so dangerous and disliked in Mesoamerica, although in a situation of constantly shifting alliances and multiethnic polities, traitors must have been pervasive. Once inside, the Aztecs captured the main temple, took the

Map 15. (facing page) Ahuitzotl's campaigns into present-day Guerrero, Puebla, the Gulf coast, the Huaxtec area, the valley of Tolocan, and north of the basin of Mexico. 1—Huexotla; 2—Xiuhcoac; 3—Tamapachco; 4—Mollanco; 5—Tlatlauhqui-Icxic*; 6—Micquetlan*; 7—Tochpan; 8—Tetzapotitlan*; 9—Tozapan*; 10—Tecpantepec; 11—Atocpan; 12—Xolotlan; 13—Nauhtlan; 14—Zacatlan; 15—Xilotepec; 16—Tliliuhqui-Tepec*; 17—Tzapotitlan; 18—Chiapan; 19—Tlalpoxahua; 20—Tlaximaloyan; 21—Xocotitlan; 22—Apan; 23—Acatlan; 24—Cuauhhuacan; 25—Atizapan; 26—Cillan*; 27—Xiquipilco; 28—Chillocan; 29—Tlaxcallan; 30—Xiuhteczacatlan*; 31—Tepechiapan*; 32—Xicochimalco; 33—Zitacuaro; 34—Cozcacuauhtenanco; 35—Tozantlan; 36—Xochimilco; 37—Teopochtlan*; 38—Tlallocatepec; 39—Patlanalan; 40—Quimichtlan; 41—Huexotzinco; 42—Totolapan*; 43—Chololllan; 44—Totomihuacan; 45—Zoltepec; 46—Cuauhnahuac; 47—Yauhtepec; 48—Huaxtepec; 49—Atlixco; 50—Cualtepec; 51—Huehuetlan; 52—Cuetlachtlan; 53—Cuauhxayancatihuayan*; 54—Coyolapan; 55—Teticpac; 56—Oztoman; 57—Alahuiztlan; 58—Cutzamala; 59—Teloloapan; 60—Chinantlan; 61—Axochitlan. (*Approximate location.)

priests and other officials prisoner, and burned the building. When the soldiers of Chiapan saw this, they fled.[5] The army also conquered Xilotepec, Cuauhhuacan, and Cozcacuauhtenanco.[6]

The entire campaign was relatively close to the basin of Mexico through easy terrain. The army apparently marched northwest to Chillocan and then crossed the mountains into the valley of Tolocan. Once there, Xiquipilco, Cozcacuauhtenanco, and Cillan were all within easy reach over level ground. Then the army turned northeast and marched up valleys to Xocotitlan, Chiapan, and Xilotepec. At that point it moved east and south to Cuauhhuacan and then returned to Tenochtitlan.

Thereafter Ahuitzotl was crowned before the rulers of all the subject towns.[7] Enemy lords from Michhuacan, Metztitlan, Tlaxcallan, Huexotzinco, Chalollan, Tliliuhqui-Tepec, and Yopitzinco declined to attend, though lesser officials from Yopitzinco and Chalollan were sent.[8] These lords had attended the ceremonies of previous Aztec rulers, and their rejection of this invitation reflected the lowered esteem in which the Aztecs were now held.

Reasserting Aztec power was a major concern of the nobles who depended on the income from Tenochtitlan's tributaries, and it must have been a matter of considerable personal concern to Ahuitzotl as well. Tenochtitlan could ill afford another weak leader, and the fate of any such leader would probably be swifter than Tizoc's but equally final.

Apan was also conquered at this time,[9] probably to consolidate the Aztec Empire and reassert its dominance, but this was a simple effort requiring only a march up the Teotihuacan valley and then a short trek to the east on a level plain. Despite Ahuitzotl's conquests the state of the empire was poor following four or five years of neglect under Tizoc, and Ahuitzotl quickly undertook a second major campaign. This time he went into the Huaxtec region, which, like many other areas of the empire, had rebelled. During the campaign season of 1487–88 the army marched to Cuauhchinanco (165 km. or 102 mi.; 5 to 9 days), where it received support. Thereafter, the Aztec army fought and conquered the Cuextecs.[10] Xolotlan, Xiuhcoac, Tochpan, Tetzapotitlan, and Nauhtlan were also conquered,[11] as were several other towns in the region, including Tozapan, Tamapachco, Micquetlan, Tlatlauhqui-Icxic, Huexotla, Mollanco, Atocpan, Tecpantepec, and Zacatlan (see map 15).[12] Given the descriptions of the campaign and the route taken, it seems likely that, except for Huexotla,[13] the armies of these towns were defeated and the individual towns submitted without having been visited by the Aztecs. Other towns to the east must have supplied troops to oppose the Aztecs, since many captives from these towns were subsequently sacrificed in Tenochtitlan, along with the Huaxtecs. The campaign stretched 565 kilometers (350 miles) and would have required 18 to 29 days of march, exclusive of days for combat, rest, and regrouping.[14]

The captives taken during the campaign were sacrificed as part of Ahuitzotl's dedication of the temple of Huitzilopochtli in Tenochtitlan, which his predecessor had begun. Ostensibly a religious occasion, it served more as a pretext for the exercise of military power and renewed Aztec prowess. In this area Ahuitzotl had been impressively successful. Although his coronation ceremony had been treated with disdain by the enemy states, Ahuitzotl performed so effectively in his first two campaigns that once again an Aztec ceremony could be used to impress and intimidate. Now, in addition to rulers of cities within the empire, many enemy lords attended the temple dedication, including the rulers of Huexotzinco, Chollollan, Tlaxcallan, Tecoac, Tliliuhqui-Tepec, Zacatlan, Metztitlan, Michhuacan, and Yopitzinco.[15] Doubtless attempting to compensate for previous lapses, the Aztecs put on a display of military power unprecedented in size. A reported 80,400 men were sacrificed, from Huexotzinco, Tlaxcallan, Atlixco, Tliliuhqui-Tepec, Chollollan, Tecoac, Zacatlan, Xiuhcoac, Tozapan, Tlappan, and the Huaxtec area[16] (see figs. 28 and 29).

With the Aztec reputation greatly restored, Ahuitzotl could ease his control over internal matters, and he continued his predecessor's return of home rule to the Chalca cities. Many cities received their rulers in 1486, but several other towns were not permitted home rule until 1488, and still others were deferred until 1493.[17] The return of the Chalca rulers was subject to confirmation by the Aztec king,[18] which probably went beyond the largely pro forma confirmation accorded other tributaries. Moreover, the king manipulated the internal political structure of at least one of the towns to lessen its military autonomy.[19]

The reason home rule was returned to the Chalca towns so gradually was strategic. By relinquishing control gradually, Ahuitzotl could do at least two things. First, he could assess the tenor of the local rule to see if anything adverse to Tenochtitlan's interests was happening. Second, he could show how he had dealt with rebellious

Fig. 28. Templo Mayor, with temples to Huitzilopochtli and Tlaloc, and skull rack. (Tovar 122; courtesy of the John Carter Brown Library, Brown University)

towns elsewhere and thus could implicitly warn the Chalcas. But the return of home rule was generally in Tenochtitlan's interests. Direct control was costly: it reduced revenues from the administered towns, increased local hostility, and diminished the effectiveness of control over local matters. Eliminating the position of military governor removed an additional and significant power base for any potential contender for Tenochtitlan's throne.

As internal control loosened, however, control over the empire tightened, and Ahuitzotl's next major campaign was into the present-day Guerrero area in response to the rejection of Tenochtitlan's overtures. The main target was Teloloapan,[20] which had become a tributary under Itzcoatl. But now the city was acting as if it were independent. The lords of Teloloapan had refused Ahuitzotl's invitation to attend the dedication of the temple of Huitzilopochtli, and in response, King Ahuitzotl sent noble emissaries to talk to them, presumably the following year (campaign season 1488–89).

The four lords and eight commoners sent by the king only reached Teticpac where they were told that the road was blocked with large trees and cacti, so they returned to Tenochtitlan.[21] Closing the road confirmed Teloloapan's treason, so Ahuitzotl decided to make war on it. Led by the king, the allied armies met at Teticpac (125 km. or 78 mi.; 4 to 7 days) to rest and then marched on Teloloapan (an additional 38 km. or 24 mi.; 2 days) and conquered it.

The lords of Teloloapan told Ahuitzotl that they had been misled by the people of Oztoman and Alahuiztlan[22] who were also in rebellion. Three days later the people of Teloloapan provided food for the army and guided the Aztecs to Oztoman (40 km. or 25 mi.; 2 days), bypassing the closer town of Alahuiztlan (32 km. or 20 mi. from Teloloapan) and deferring its conquest.

The people of Oztoman refused to pay tribute to the Aztecs, so the army attacked, broke through the fortifications, burned the temple, and killed the people, sparing only the children. Then they sent emissaries to Alahuiztlan (8 km. or 5 mi.) asking for tribute, which the town refused to give, and the Aztecs attacked and razed

Fig. 29. Base of the skull rack (*tzompantli*) at the Templo Mayor. (Courtesy of the Instituto Nacional de Antropología e Historia, Mexico)

that city as well. All of the adults were killed in Alahuiztlan and Oztoman, and more than forty thousand children were taken and distributed throughout the rest of the empire.[23] The reason the towns were conquered in that sequence lies in the previous pattern of loyalties: Alahuiztlan had not been conquered by the Aztecs, but like Teloloapan, Oztoman had been an Aztec tributary, so its hostility was the more serious and had to be dealt with first.

Teloloapan, Oztoman, and Alahuiztlan were repopulated by married couples from the heart of the empire, two hundred each from Tenochtitlan, Tetzcoco, and Tlacopan, as well as people from other towns in the empire, totaling nine thousand couples.[24] When they reached the area, the people divided into three groups, the largest going to Oztoman. Those staying in Teloloapan acted as the garrison of that town, since it had not been depopulated as had the other two cities.[25]

This campaign displayed considerable economy of purpose. By attacking cities that had refused to attend the ceremony in Tenochtitlan, the Aztecs demonstrated both their military power and the consequences of disloyalty or open hostility. The campaign itself encouraged submission by demonstrating that the fate of the conquered cities was partially in the hands of the vanquished: those who cooperated received more favorable treatment than those who did not. Moreover, it placed considerable value on splitting existing alliances. The Aztecs were also able to further their own strategic goals by placing armed and loyal people at the border with Michhuacan, adjacent to the enemy Tarascan Empire.[26]

The Tarascan Empire has been a persistent problem in the analysis of Aztec political and military expansion.[27] It was an empire of considerable geographical expanse, population, and military power, but what this represented to the Aztecs is unclear. Some writers consider the Tarascans militarily superior and the Aztecs' likely successors as the dominant power in central Mexico.[28] Except for the outcome of a few clashes, however, such an interpretation finds little support in the data.

There were few fortifications in most of Mesoamerica, and of those most were urban. The Tarascans' situation was radically different: they erected a series of fortifications along their border with the Aztecs at key points dominating the valleys along which a conquering army would be likely to march. These sites were (from north to south) Tlalpoxahua (Tlalpujahua; not a proper Nahuatl town name),

Tlaximaloyan, Zitacuaro, Tozantlan, Cutzamala, and Axochitlan.[29] Moreover, the Tarascans ensured their control of these areas by replacing local rulers with their own leaders,[30] thus providing secure locations to which the Tarascan army could march to meet an impending invasion.[31] The Aztecs did not match these fortifications with their own.[32]

This strategy marked a major and expensive shift in imperial systems. By fortifying, manning, and defending fixed borders, the Tarascans no longer controlled the area through power but relied on force —the harbinger of a territorial system. This was not a full-blown territorial system, because the Tarascans continued to function internally in a hegemonic manner,[33] but it was a marked departure in perimeter defense. While all other major polities had the rudiments of such systems in their core areas, any substantial political expansion quickly exceeded these limited regions. But the Tarascans formed a distinct culture in central Mexico, reinforced by their linguistic distinctiveness and compounded by their relative geographical isolation. Thus they possessed a larger and more cohesive core region from which to build than most polities in central Mexico.

One reason the Tarascans may have adopted this border defense strategy involved intelligence. Unlike many other polities, Tarascan speakers were unrepresented in the Aztec Empire, so Tarascan spies could not easily slip into Aztec areas. The Otomí-speaking Matlatzincas living within the Tarascan Empire could, but they may not have been trusted by the Tarascans. A second reason may have been Tarascan fear of Aztec expansion. The Aztecs had been successful throughout much of Mesoamerica, and in the region between the two empires—the valley of Tolocan—Tarascan penetration had been repulsed while the Aztecs subdued the entire area. Thus, erecting fortifications may have been the only feasible way to keep the Aztecs from further chipping away at the borders of the Tarascan Empire.

Tarascan adoption of this defensive system can also be understood in terms of the relative offensive capability of the competing empires. Although neither side had fared well in its expansionistic efforts against the other, the Aztecs had shown a capacity for major long-range incursions, and their superior numbers, alliance networks, and logistical system gave them a marked offensive advantage over the Tarascans. Thus, direct competition meant eventual defeat for the Tarascans.

The more territorially based Tarascan system required considerable manpower and revenue, either actual in imperial expenditures or potential in local resources diverted to maintain the fortifications. This situation had three logical consequences. First, the number of men available for use elsewhere in the empire was reduced, which decreased the perception of the polity's power. Second, limited manpower meant that the system of fortifications could not be increased indefinitely. Moreover, attempts to control local political offices meant that administrative costs were increasing. And third, the territorial system was considerably less flexible than the hegemonic system, which could adjust its defenses more rapidly and create new areas of vulnerability. Consequently, the increased costs of maintaining this system limited the size of the Tarascan Empire. The Tarascans' control over dependent areas was greater, but it was achieved by sacrificing geographical expanse: it was, in essence, a defensive strategy.

Nevertheless, the Tarascan fortifications had several advantages. First, they provided intelligence about the approach of enemy troops. Messages dispatched by runners traveled considerably faster than did marching armies. Thus, even if the Tarascans were unaware of an Aztec advance until it reached the border, they would then be warned in sufficient time to muster an army and advance well before the Aztecs reached the main Tarascan cities. Second, the Aztecs were faced with the option of either conquering these fortifications or bypassing them. These strongholds could be conquered, because they were usually manned with small forces, but doing so would consume considerable time and supplies and correspondingly reduce the Aztecs' chances of success against the Tarascan main forces. Alternatively, the strongholds could be bypassed, but since the fortifications were located in the best passes, bypassing them meant marching through more rugged terrain with a corresponding loss of time. If, however, the Aztec army decided to proceed along the main pass without conquering the strongholds, their rear would be vulnerable to harassment and the fortification's troops could endanger additional logistical support. Containing troops could be left behind to defend against raids from the encircled defenders, but this would also reduce the Aztec forces. And third, a stabilized and fortified frontier effectively stymied the standard Aztec tactic of chipping away at empires by continually conquering frontier towns. Thus, although there were disadvantages in permanently fortifying a border, building strongholds was an educated gamble by the Tarascans about where and why the Aztecs would attack. This defense was predicated on the logistical constraints on Mesoamerican armies, since the Tarascans did not erect barriers to the north or south.

Towns located between the competing empires were faced with the dilemma of selecting their masters: neutrality was not feasible in the context of expanding imperial systems. For many the fortunes of war removed any choices they may have had. But for others alliances were viable options, and while many people allied with the Aztecs, many others chose the Tarascans, including some who had fled from the Aztecs.[34] Thus, many of the people manning the Tarascan border fortifications were Matlatzincas, not ethnic Tarascans. Given the alliance nature of Mesoamerican polities, it is unlikely that the Tarascans completely trusted them. Nevertheless, these border Matlatzincas were useful and, perhaps, more expendable.

The Aztecs' conquest and fortification of Teloloapan, Oztoman, and Alahuiztlan was quickly followed by another campaign into present-day southern Guerrero, probably in the campaign season of 1490–91. It was a logical extension of the earlier conquests but also began in earnest the Aztec strategy of gradual encirclement of the Tarascan Empire. This campaign resulted in the conquest of Tlappantzinco, Tototenanco, Atl-Chayahuacan, and Cuauhtepec.[35] Iztac-Tlallocan, Pochtlan, and Tototepec are also likely to have fallen,[36] and other towns in the area also submitted, influenced by the Aztec demonstrations of power. Among these were Tlalcozauhtitlan, Tlappan, Acatl-Iyacac (Acatepec), Nexpan, Acapolco, Cihuatlan, Nantzintlan, Coyocac, Xolochiuhcan, Xiuhtlan, Tzohuilpillan, Acalecan, and Tetellan (see map 16).[37]

The campaign's probable route was south from the basin of Mexico to the Pacific coast. Then the army turned north, going up the coast as far as Acalecan before backtracking and marching northeast to Tenochtitlan.[38] Tribute was a universal purpose of expansion, but another purpose was to outflank the Tarascan fortifications; creating an active front against the Tarascans was apparently not an aim, since the Aztecs did not take advantage of it. Nevertheless, by beginning the encirclement of Michhuacan, the Aztecs gained an unguarded, albeit distant, approach to the enemy heartland, which was necessarily a security concern for the Tarascans. Of equal importance, the Aztecs effectively deprived the Tarascans of outside aid and room to retreat in that direction. As with other powerful enemies, the encirclement of the Tarascans was not an immediate

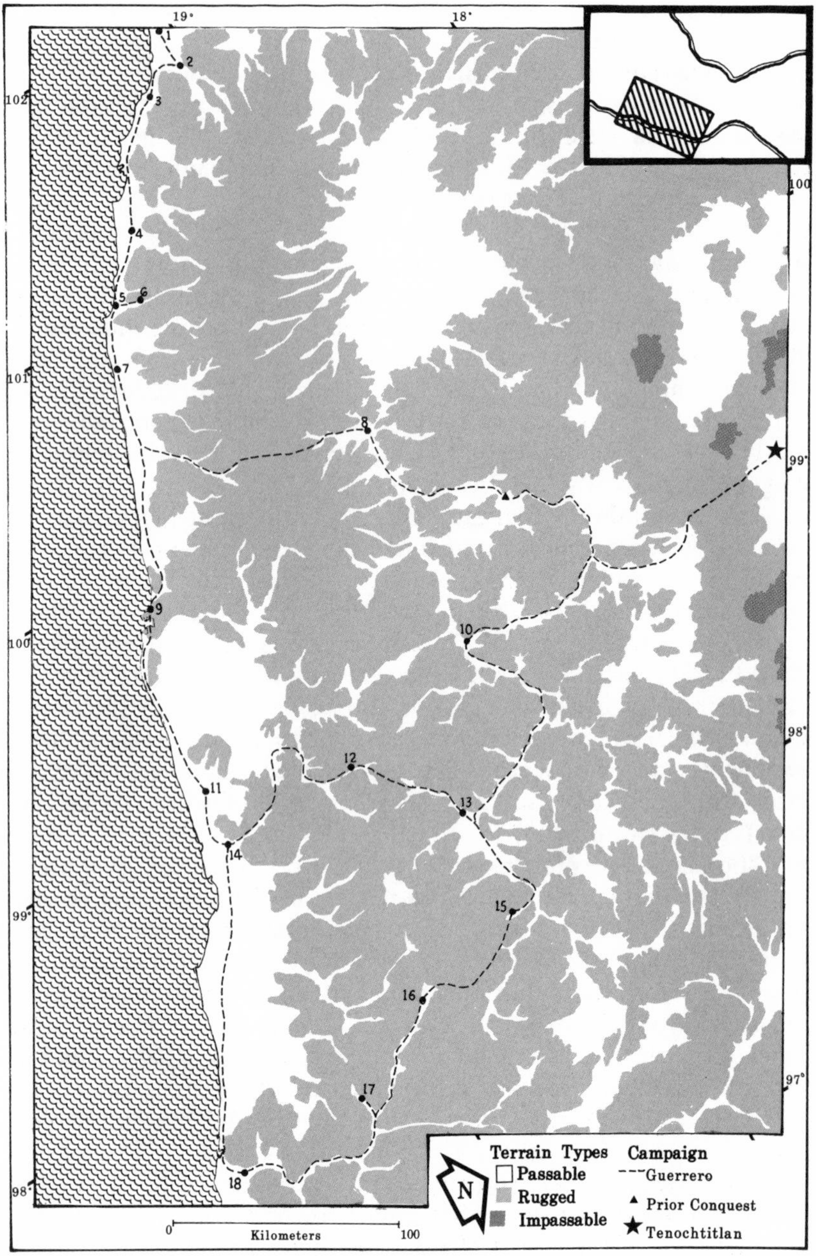

19°
18°
102°
101°
100°
99°
98°
100
99°
98°
97°
1
2
3
4
5
6
7
8
9
10
11
12
13
14
15
16
17
18
Terrain Types
Passable
Rugged
Impassable
Campaign
Guerrero
Prior Conquest
Tenochtitlan
N
0
Kilometers
100

priority but was to be a gradual process taking years. Meanwhile, Ahuitzotl's concerns were elsewhere.

The next campaign took place in 1491–92 and was directed toward the rebellious Gulf coast of present-day Veracruz.[39] The army marched out of the basin of Mexico, through present-day southern Puebla, and into central Veracruz, conquering the towns of Chinantlan (Chinauhtla), Coyolapan, Cualtepec, Cuextlan, Quimichtlan, Tlallocatepec, Acatlan, Totomihuacan, and Xicochimalco (see map 15),[40] further consolidating Aztec control of the empire.

During the same season, and either as part of the same campaign or as one of a series of consolidating actions near the basin of Mexico, the Aztecs fought the Cuauhnahuacas, and Tetzcoco's King Nezahualpilli fought Totolapan,[41] possibly as part of a flower war with Huexotzinco.[42] Nezahualpilli gave captives from Huexotzinco, Tzotzollan, and Totolapan to Ahuitzotl, and they were sacrificed in Cuauhnahuac.[43]

A flower war at this level of violence required substantially fewer warriors than a war of conquest, so its simultaneous exercise was easily within the capacity of the Triple Alliance, but the incidence and ferocity of these clashes was increasing. Many of the allied cities fought flower wars against the same group of enemy cities. In this case the Tetzcocas under Nezahualpilli apparently played the main role, not the Aztecs, and Xochimilco fought Atlixco in 1490,[44] which may have been connected with the Huexotzinco xochiyaoyotl. The Aztecs also fought a xochiyaoyotl with Atlixco soon after, in 1492.[45] Following the Huexotzinca war and the wars to the east, the Aztecs also conquered Atizapan, just to the north of Tenochtitlan,[46] probably as an isolated action.

Ahuitzotl next turned south in a major campaign (1494) into the Huaxyacac region which had thus far been neglected. The stated reason for this campaign was to reconquer Xaltepec which had rebelled, and this campaign largely consolidated prior conquests in the region.

Map 16. (facing page) Ahuitzotl's campaign along the Pacific coast of present-day Guerrero. See map 15 for connecting routes to Tenochtitlan. 1—Acalecan; 2—Tzohuilpillan*; 3—Xiuhtlan*; 4—Xolochiuhcan*; 5—Coyocac; 6—Nantzintlan*; 7—Cihuatlan*; 8—Tetellan; 9—Acapolco; 10—Tlalcozauhtitlan; 11—Nexpan; 12—Acatl-Iyacac; 13—Tlappan; 14—Cuauhtepec; 15—Tlappantzinco; 16—Pochtlan; 17—Iztac-Tlallocan*; 18—Tototepec. (*Approximate location.)

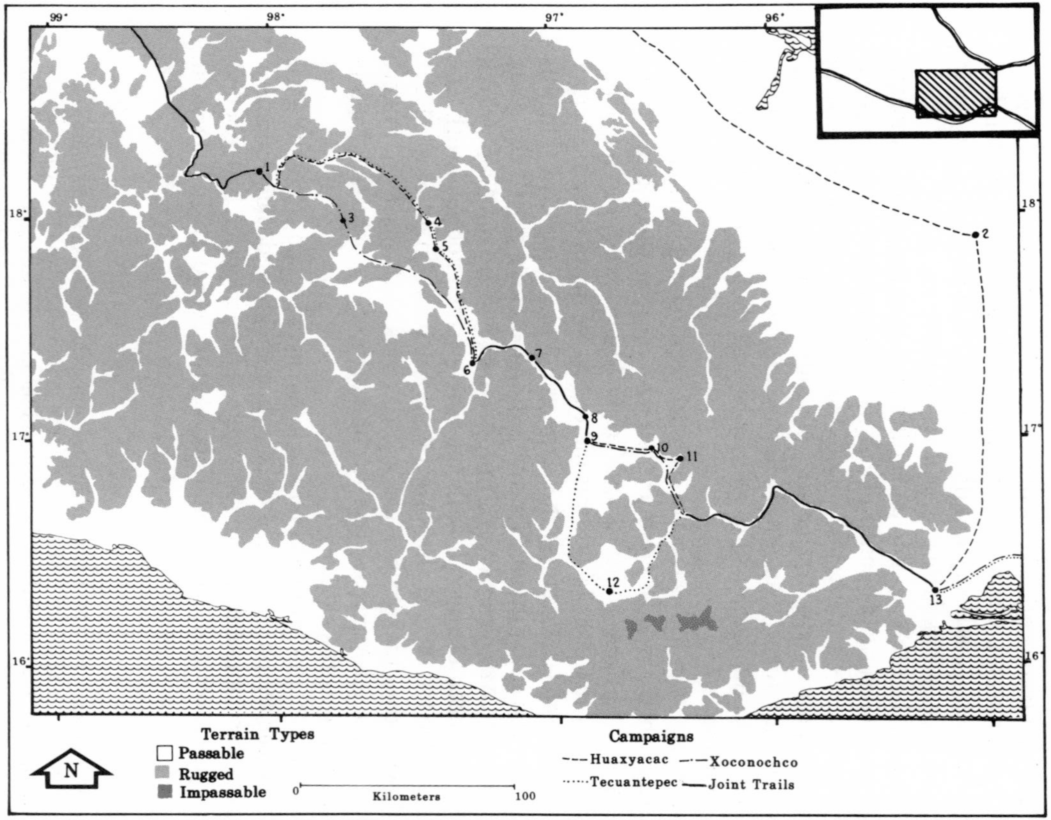
99°
98°
97°
96°
18°
17°
16°
1
2
3
4
5
6
7
8
9
10
11
12
13
Terrain Types
Passable
Rugged
Impassable
N
0
Kilometers
100
Campaigns
Huaxyacac
Xoconochco
Tecuantepec
Joint Trails

Other towns conquered on this campaign were Mizquitlan, Cuauhpiloayan, Teotzapotlan (Tlapotlan), Ayotochcuitlatlan, Mictlan, and Tlacotepec (see map 17).[47]

A year or two after the Huaxyacac region campaign, there was another flower war with Tliliuhqui-Tepec (135 km. or 84 mi.; 4 to 7 days) in which many Tetzcocas died.[48] The following year (1496), Zoltepec (in present-day west Mexico) (125 km. or 78 mi.; 4 to 7 days), was conquered, apparently as an isolated event and not as part of a campaign[49] (see map 15).

Building on his recent consolidation of the Huaxyacac area, Ahuitzotl directed his next major campaign into the Tecuantepec region around 1497. It was ostensibly precipitated by the murder of merchants from Tenochtitlan, Acolhuacan, Cuauhtitlan, Toltitlan, and the Tepanec towns, as well as Tenanyocan, Cuetlachtepec, Xochimilco, Cuitlahuac, Mizquic, and Chalco. These southern coastal lands had been at least partially conquered before, but they were difficult to secure because they were so far from Tenochtitlan. In an effort to quell future rebellions Ahuitzotl resolved not only to retaliate but also to make a major demonstration of power: he would kill 2,000 people for every merchant who had been killed.[50]

An army was raised in eight days by drawing soldiers from the basin of Mexico and areas to the west, north, and east.[51] The army was told to kill everyone, adult or child, because it would be too far to take captives back to Tenochtitlan,[52] but 1,200 captives were brought back from Tlacuilollan.[53]

The Aztec army conquered Miahuatlan and Izhuatlan (see maps 17 and 18) and then, with guides from these cities, headed to Maxtlan (Amaxtlan) and Tecuantepec.[54] Also conquered in this campaign were the towns of Xochitlan (Izquixochitlan, Xochtlan), Tlacuilollan, Chiltepec, Apanecan, and Acapetlahuacan.[55] Amextloapan, Nacazcuauhtlan (Cuauhnacaztitlan), and Quetzalcuitlapilco (Quetzalcuitlapillan) were also conquered,[56] apparently capitulating on the demonstration of Ahuitzotl's superiority. The entire trek covered 1,900

Map 17. (facing page) Ahuitzotl's campaign into the Gulf coast and the Huaxyacac area. See map 15 for connecting routes to Tenochtitlan. 1—Chinantlan; 2—Cuauhpiloayan; 3—Chillan; 4—Mizquitlan*; 5—Tlacotepec; 6—Xaltepec; 7—Ayotochcuitlatlan; 8—Huaxyacac; 9—Teotzapotlan; 10—Tlacuilollan; 11—Mictlan; 12—Miahuatlan; 13—Tecuantepec. (*Approximate location.)

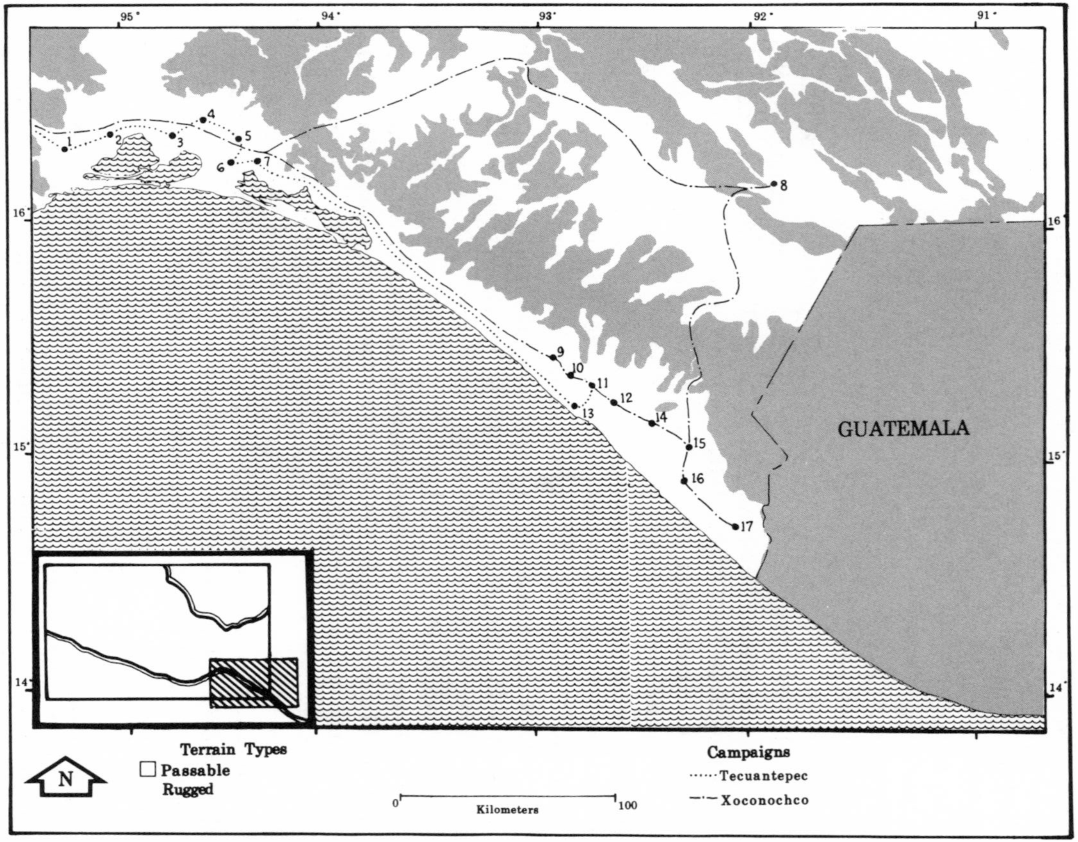
95°
94°
93°
92°
91°
16°
15°
14°
1
2
3
4
5
6
7
8
9
10
11
12
13
14
15
16
17
GUATEMALA
N
Terrain Types
Passable
Rugged
0
Kilometers
100
Campaigns
Tecuantepec
Xoconochco

kilometers (1,200 miles), requiring 59 to 99 days, exclusive of days needed for combat, rest, and regrouping. However, only 300 kilometers (190 miles) of that trek extended beyond the area of previous logistical support, requiring a round trip in that portion of 9 to 16 days.

On the army's return messengers were sent ahead, partly to notify local lords of its approach and ensure a proper reception. But the primary purpose of the messages was to spread the news of the army's success and compel the local rulers to acknowledge their allegiance. The leaders' only alternative was to revolt openly, but both the speed with which the Aztecs would appear and their new campaign success doomed that option.

The army went to Huaxyacac to rest and then marched on to Tepeyacac, Itzyocan, Chalco, Cuixtepec, Amaquemecan, Tlalmanalco, and Tlapechhuacan, Tlapitzahuayan (where a temple to Tezcatl-Ihpoca was located), Ixtlapalapan (where a temple to Huitzilopochtli was located), Mexicatzinco, and finally to Tenochtitlan.[57]

As part of the emphasis on public recognition of military skills and exploits, the king granted insignia commemorating great deeds to the deserving warriors. Ahuitzotl adopted the quetzal feather crest devices captured in the Tecuantepec campaign as part of his own insignia.[58]

Thereafter, the Aztecs continued the pressure on the enemy city-states to the east by engaging in a flower war against Atlixco in 1499.[59] But Huexotzinco entered the battle, too, and its participation appears to have been the more significant (see map 15).

The Aztecs engaged in only one more major campaign during Ahuitzotl's reign, in the region south of Tecuantepec. Two reasons are given for this campaign. First, Aztec merchants were attacked and killed at Xolotlan, Ayotlan, Mazatlan, and Xoconochco. Second, Xoconochco, Mazatlan, and Xolotlan had allegedly retaliated against Tecuantepec for having submitted to the Aztecs.

Map 18. (facing page) Ahuitzotl's campaigns into the southern Huaxyacac area and adjacent areas of present-day Guatemala. See map 15 for connecting routes to Tenochtitlan. 1—Tecuantepec; 2—Xochitlan; 3—Amextloapan*; 4—Nacazcuauhtlan*; 5—Quetzalcuitlapilco*; 6—Izhuatlan; 7—Maxtlan*; 8—Comitlan; 9—Mapachtepec; 10—Xolotlan*; 11—Acapetlahuacan*; 12—Xoconochco; 13—Chiltepec*; 14—Huitztlan; 15—Huehuetlan; 16—Mazatlan; 17—Ayotlan. (*Approximate location.)

The pochtecah's version of these events offers a tale of valiant and prolonged siege before the Aztecs eventually overcame insuperable obstacles and singlehandedly vanquished the enemy towns,[60] but the actual events are more mundane. Though militarily successful, Ahuitzotl's 1497 incursion into the Tecuantepec region was not sufficiently impressive to warrant local concern that the Aztecs could or would return at will. Moreover, during the three or four years following the initial conquests Aztec merchants trading in the rich coastal lands were in considerable danger. While Ahuitzotl undoubtedly knew of the situation, conditions elsewhere in the empire and the enormous physical and financial cost of mounting a further Tecuantepec campaign forestalled any immediate action in the region. But the situation finally deteriorated to the point that no viable alternative remained, and an army was dispatched under the tlacochcalcatl, Moteuczomah Xocoyotl.

The army was again raised in eight days and left Tenochtitlan, marching via Chalco, Cocotitlan, and Huaxyacac. It continued on to Mazatlan and set up camp at the pass to the city. The army attacked Mazatlan the next day and destroyed everything by noon, and the old people, women, and children fled into the mountains.[61] The troops then conquered Ayotlan, Xolotlan, and Xoconochco[62] (see maps 17 and 18) but declined to push farther south into the rich provinces of Cuauhtemallan (Guatemala), Atl-Popoca, Popoca-Tepetl, and Tlatla-Tepec. Also likely to have been subdued during this campaign were the towns of Mapachtepec, Acapetlahuacan, Huehuetlan, Huitztlan, Comitlan, Chillan, and Xaltepec.[63]

Thereafter, Ahuitzotl died, either of wounds[64] or of a strange withering disease.[65]

CHAPTER 15

Moteuczomah Xocoyotl
"He-frowned-like-a-lord The-younger"
(Ruled 1502–1520)

NEWS of Ahuitzotl's death in 1502 was sent by messengers throughout the empire.[1] Moteuczomah Xocoyotl, who was to be chosen as Ahuitzotl's successor, was in the valley of Tolocan, nine leagues (38 km. or 23 mi.) to the west, when he learned of the king's death (see fig. 30).[2]

As was traditional, Moteuczomah Xocoyotl engaged in an early war. The targets were Nopallan and Icpatepec,[3] which had refused to pay tribute to the Aztecs: Moteuczomah Xocoyotl gathered an army and marched to conquer them and take captives for his coronation (see map 19).[4] There were other, undated, conquests in the area, but these probably occurred later, since this was a preinaugural raid with a specific and circumscribed purpose.

Messengers were sent two days ahead of the army to advise towns along the route of its coming so that supplies could be gathered.[5] In advance of the battle soldiers entered the enemy towns at night to scout their fortifications and military preparations.[6] The army was ordered to take the captives to Tenochtitlan rather than to kill them, but in the heat of battle the soldiers began killing everyone in Nopallan, and they burned the houses and temple. When the people called for mercy, Moteuczomah Xocoyotl ordered that the destruction cease and that the Nopaltecs and Icpatepecas bring tribute.[7] Following the successful prosecution of this campaign Moteuczomah Xocoyotl was crowned in Tenochtitlan. The kings of Tlaxcallan, Huexotzinco, Chalollan, Tliliuhqui-Tepec, Michhuacan, Metztitlan, and the Huaxtecs secretly attended the coronation.[8] Once in power, Moteuczomah Xocoyotl instituted major changes in Aztec society. Some of these may have been an attempt to absorb the grow-

Fig. 30. Moteuczomah Xocoyotl ("He-frowned-like-a-lord The-younger"). (Tovar 117; courtesy of the John Carter Brown Library, Brown University)

ing members of the nobility, but the roots of many of these changes are to be found in the ill-fated reign of Tizoc.

The king's support lay among on both commoners and nobles, but after decades of cultivating the nobility and securing its loyalty with economic goods gained by conquest, the Aztec rulers had the hereditary nobility firmly allied behind them. The calpolli did not emerge as a powerful force because potential leaders from the commoner class were made meritocratic nobles. Thus they were both separated from the calpolli leadership and tied to the king through the same economic interests that bound the hereditary nobility. This helped secure the king's position vis-à-vis the commoners, but he was still vulnerable to noble intrigues, as evidenced by Tizoc's demise. To avert a threat from that quarter, Moteuczomah Xocoyotl broadened his base of support and diluted the power of any competitors by instituting social changes that accentuated the distinctions between nobles and commoners. He replaced all the commoners who were serving as royal servants with nobles, and he removed the officials installed by Ahuitzotl, including the ward heads and captains of hundreds of men; they were reportedly put to death.[9] He greatly widened the gap between nobles and commoners, in types of service, in rewards, and in attire, and these differences extended to both combat garb and peacetime wear. Among Moteuczomah Xocoyotl's new decrees was one declaring that only the king could wear a gold diadem in Tenochtitlan, although in war all the great nobles and war leaders could wear one, since in that capacity they represented the king. Also, only great nobles and valiant warriors could wear sandals in Tenochtitlan.[10] Commoner soldiers could wear only the simplest mantles and were proscribed from decorating or embroidering them in any way that would distinguish their wearers from the other common soldiers.[11] He created additional insignia of martial prowess and introduced the custom of cutting the hair of the major warriors and war leaders in the style of otontin warriors.[12]

Although these changes suggest a diminution of commoner roles in the court of Moteuczomah Xocoyotl, such an outcome is improbable in a strict sense. Increasing the requirements for elevation to meritocratic noble status reduced the likelihood of individual advancement, but it did not foreclose it and, in fact, guaranteed the rise of only the ablest commoners. Actions were not taken against existing meritocratic nobles, as that would have undermined the king's own position by strengthening the calpolli leadership, to whom those dispossessed would be forced to turn. Rather, the stringent social changes were aimed at stabilizing an already large Aztec nobility, and they paved the way for changes in the status of nobles from elsewhere in the empire.

By excluding commoners from his service, Moteuczomah Xocoyotl created positions for more nobles. This helped integrate the empire by drawing the sons of nobles from throughout the land to Tenochtitlan, where they could also be taught, indoctrinated, controlled, and, incidentally, held hostage,[13] although many probably also had kin ties to the Aztec nobility.[14] Thus with one simple move the king changed a coercive policy into one that conveyed honor and prestige on the "hostages" and that was carried out largely through normative means (although the iron fist was always there). He also now relied on these foreign nobles to counterbalance his internal support. Many of them participated in the internal affairs of Tenochtitlan, and because they owed their presence to the king, their inter-

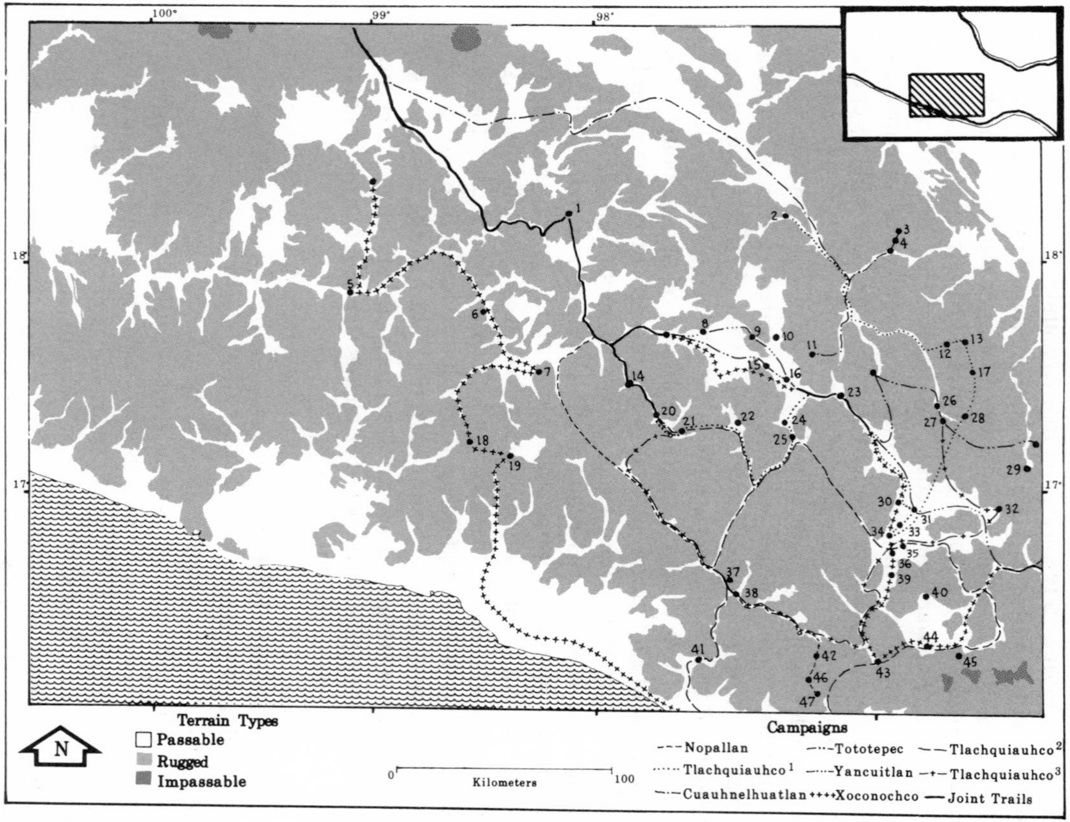
100°
99°
98°
18°
17°
1
2
3
4
5
6
7
8
9
10
11
12
13
14
15
16
17
18
19
20
21
22
23
24
25
26
27
28
29
30
31
32
33
34
35
36
37
38
39
40
41
42
43
44
45
46
47
N
Terrain Types
Passable
Rugged
Impassable
0
Kilometers
100
Campaigns
Nopallan
Tototepec
Tlachquiauhco 2
Tlachquiauhco 1
Yancuitlan
Tlachquiauhco 3
Cuauhnelhuatlan
Xoconochco
Joint Trails

ests were more aligned with his than with those of the Aztec nobility. Thus, Moteuczomah Xocoyotl increased his support among nobles throughout the empire and diluted the position of the Aztec hereditary and meritocratic nobles, but without providing additional support to the calpolli leaders and commoners.

Early Aztec military efforts had drawn on virtually all of the empire's resources, but because of his predecessor's expansion, his own internal reforms, and the general population increase, the Aztec army was large enough to deal with multiple simultaneous threats during Moteuczomah Xocoyotl's reign. Several armies could be fielded at the same time, undertaking concurrent campaigns, which allowed the Aztecs to deal more effectively with simultaneous disruptions and thus reinforce their reputation for relentlessly redressing affronts. With the large forces at their disposal the Aztecs could go far afield without leaving their home undefended, but they now rarely used maximum force against a given threat.

During his second year of rule (campaign of 1503–4) Moteuczomah Xocoyotl reportedly sent emissaries south to the province of Tlachquiauhco (Tlaxiaco) to request a *tlapalizquixochitl* tree. This veiled demand to acknowledge vassalage to Tenochtitlan was refused by Malinal, the lord of Tlachquiauhco.[15] Moteuczomah Xocoyotl ordered that no man or woman over fifty was to be spared, because they were the ones responsible for this rebellion.[16] Malinal was killed in the battle, and Tlachquiauhco was conquered along with all its subject towns (see map 19).

Continuing the consolidation of the region, the army marched to the boundaries of Xaltepec and Cuatzonteccan. There the king di-

Map 19. (facing page) Moteuczomah Xocoyotl's campaigns into the Huaxyacac area. See map 20 for connecting routes to Tenochtitlan. 1—Piaztlan; 2—Caltepec; 3—Cuauhnelhuatlan; 4—Mazatlan; 5—Tlalcozauhtitlan; 6—Teochiyauhtzinco*; 7—Tlachinollan*; 8—Tlacaxolotlan; 9—Texopan; 10—Coaixtlahuacan; 11—Huauhtlan; 12—Yolloxonecuillan; 13—Tliltepec; 14—Icpatepec; 15—Yancuitlan; 16—Nocheztlan; 17—Itzcehuitepec; 18—Malinaltepec; 19—Citlaltepec; 20—Quimichtepec; 21—Tlachquiauhco; 22—Achiotlan; 23—Tzotzollan; 24—Xaltepec; 25—Cuatzonteccan*; 26—Xaltianquizco; 27—Atepec; 28—Iztitlan; 29—Tototepec; 30—Ixtlahuacan; 31—Huaxyacac; 32—Mictlan; 33—Xalapan; 34—Teotzapotlan; 35—Macuiloctlan; 36—Chichihualtatacallan; 37—Iztac-Tlallocan*; 38—Centzontepec; 39—Texotlan; 40—Amatlan; 41—Tototepec; 42—Icpatepec; 43—Coatlayauhcan; 44—Miahuatlan; 45—Quimichtepec; 46—Teuctepec; 47—Nopallan. (*Approximate location.)

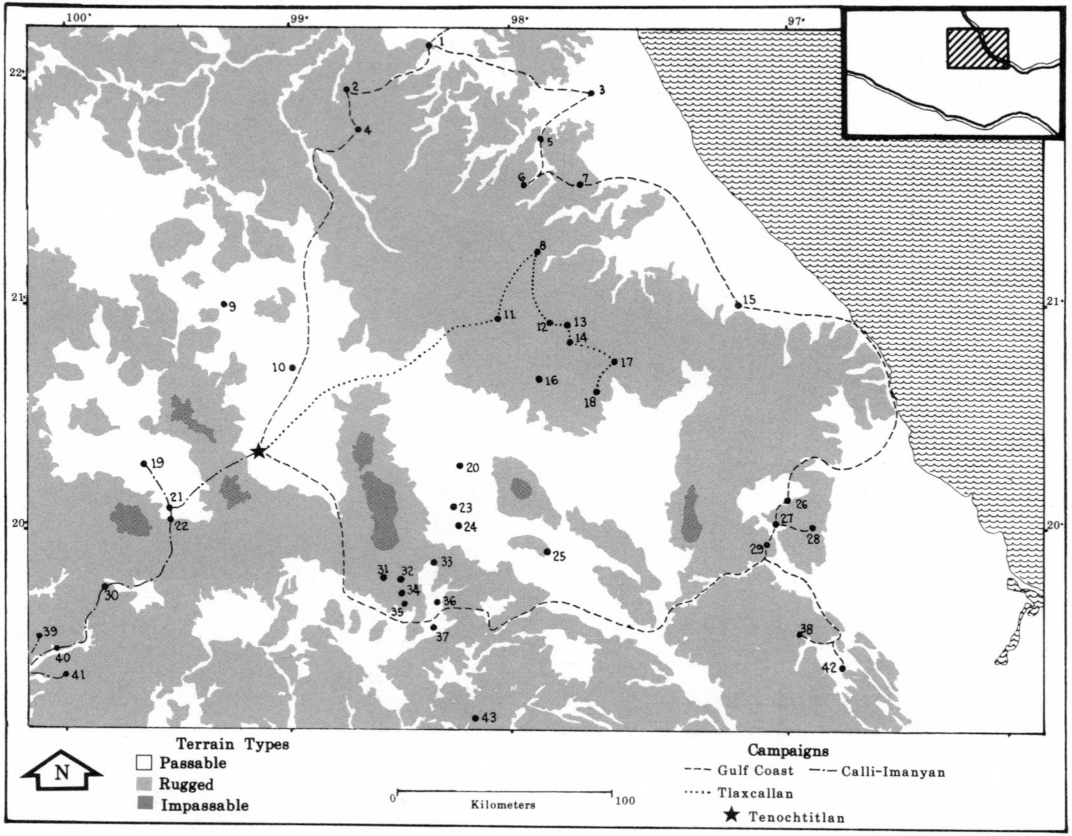
100°
99°
98°
97°
22°
21°
20°
Terrain Types
Passable
Rugged
Impassable
N
0
Kilometers
100
Campaigns
Gulf Coast
Calli-Imanyan
Tlaxcallan
Tenochtitlan

vided his forces, sending the Aztec, Acolhua, and Tepanec armies by different roads to avoid the whole army's being held in a pass by inferior numbers. Scouts were sent into the city and returned at dawn with intelligence. In the ensuing battle the king and others scaled the fortifications, climbed the temple, and set it afire. When the enemy saw this they lost heart and surrendered.[17] Also conquered in this campaign were Achiotlan, Caltepec, Xaltianquizco, and Icpatepec.[18] Other towns probably conquered during this campaign include Quiyauhtepec, Tliltepec, Yolloxonecuillan, Itzcehuitepec, Atepec, Iztitlan, and Quimichtepec.[19] Although they may have been subdued during other incursions into the region, the conquests of Ixtlahuacan, Huaxyacac, Xalapan, and Teotzapotlan most plausibly occurred at this time.[20] The campaign stretched 1,000 kilometers (620 miles) round trip and would have required 31 to 53 days of march, exclusive of days for combat, rest, and regrouping.

In 1504 the Aztecs again fought Tlaxcallan[21] (see map 20) in the latest in a series of flower wars. The xochiyaoyotl opponents had already been loosely encircled, but now the Aztecs tightened the noose, and the level of violence rose throughout this reign. Moteuczomah Xocoyotl marched toward Tlaxcallan to the town of Xiloxochitlan, where the armies fought. As the battle went against the Aztecs, they sent to Tenochtitlan for reinforcements, and a relief army marched via Tetellan and Tochimilco, south of Cuauhquechollan, but they were defeated, too. A more massive campaign launched against Tlaxcallan also failed.[22] The Aztec conflict with their xochiyaoyotl adversary had clearly escalated to a level more closely approximating a war of conquest. As it did so, the fighting became more intense, not simply because of the more desperate

Map 20. (facing page) Moteuczomah Xocoyotl's campaigns into present-day Guerrero, Puebla, the Gulf coast, the Huaxtec area, and the valley of Tolocan. 1—Huexolotlan; 2—Tlachinolticpac; 3—Micquetlan*; 4—Mollanco; 5—Atlan*; 6—Pantepec; 7—Tetzapotitlan*; 8—Xicotepec; 9—Tollan; 10—Tzompanco; 11—Panco*; 12—Tlachiyauhtzinco; 13—Teoatzinco*; 14—Atzomiatenanco; 15—Toztepec*; 16—Tliliuhqui-Tepec*; 17—Tlatlauhqui-Tepec; 18—Tecozauhtlan; 19—Tecaxic; 20—Tlaxcallan; 21—Calli-Imanyan; 22—Tetenanco; 23—Huexotzinco; 24—Chololllan; 25—Tepeyacac; 26—Cuauhtochco; 27—Cuezcomatl-Iyacac; 28—Izhuatlan; 29—Atzaccan; 30—Zoltepec; 31—Tetellan; 32—Tochimilco; 33—Atlixco; 34—Atzitzihuacan; 35—Cuauhquechollan; 36—Itzteyocan; 37—Itzyocan; 38—Tecpanayacac*; 39—Tlatlayan; 40—Oztoman; 41—Poctepec*; 42—Cihuapolhualoyan*; 43—Piaztlan. (*Approximate location.)

position in which the Tlaxcaltecs and their allies found themselves but also for structural reasons. As the targeted area shrank under the Aztec assaults so, too, did the Tlaxcaltec lines of communications and logistical support, and battles were increasingly fought in their territory, where they enjoyed an advantage in intelligence, resupply, and familiarity with the terrain—factors that simultaneously disadvantaged the Aztecs.

At this time Moteuczomah Xocoyotl successfully fought Cuauhnelhuatlan[23] (see maps 19 and 20), following on the heels of a major famine, to which the war's purpose, circumscribed goals, or both, were likely tied.[24]

The number of campaigns Moteuczomah Xocoyotl carried out in the Huaxyacac region was unprecedented. Several factors may have contributed. First, the increased size of the empire simply offered more opportunities for disruption, and pacifying efforts in any given locale were less likely to have effect beyond the immediate vicinity. Second, the increase in raids may have been necessary after the disastrous reign of Tizoc, despite Ahuitzotl's successful, albeit scattered, conquests in the area. Third, lacking an established, institutionalized, and effective logistical system in the region, plundering by Aztec troops may have occurred and thus have incited greater local hostility. And fourth, the probable new Aztec policy of dispatching a force into the region sufficient to conquer the objective was not politically adequate to control the region after the army's withdrawal. But much of the reason for the repetitive thrusts into the Huaxyacac region was also structural. The number of campaigns increased over time because of their cumulative effect. The earliest campaigns were targeted on specific and circumscribed goals, and during those, potential logistical support, routes, and obstacles were scouted. Then on subsequent campaigns more towns in the area were taken through conquest and intimidation. The earlier campaigns were also used to establish which towns could be convinced to cooperate, which could be coerced, which would have to be forced, and how many troops it would require. But because the imperial system did not demand territorially continuous conquest, areas were subdued in varying degrees and over considerable time, an approach consistent with the Aztec pattern of encirclement and eventual conquest of obstinate areas. Once towns and regions beyond (and thoughout) the Huaxyacac area had been conquered, further conquest became easier. The Aztecs now faced less danger in trying to subdue still unconquered areas, because there was little likelihood these towns would be reinforced from outside (which permitted the Aztecs to assess the actual threat more precisely and dispatch a commensurate force). Moreover, the Aztecs could draw on the existing tributary towns interspersed throughout the region for arms, men, and logistical support. But without instituting structural changes in local polities, this system still depended on the cooperation of the conquered.

Either Moteuczomah Xocoyotl's first thrust was too weak to achieve all its aims or the people of the Huaxyacac region were alarmed at this incursion and resisted, so a further campaign was launched into the Huaxyacac area, probably in campaign season 1505–1506 (see maps 19 and 21). This campaign was ostensibly precipitated by the killing of Aztec merchants whom Moteuczomah Xocoyotl had sent to Tototepec and Quetzaltepec to secure some goods (either precious stones, called *huitziltetl* according to one version, or sand for lapidary work, according to another). Although the merchants gave the lords of Tototepec rich mantles and explained their mission, they were killed,[25] and the roads were closed. These events was related to Moteuczomah Xocoyotl by other merchants, and he sent additional merchants to investigate. Traveling day and night disguised as Huexotzincas, they learned that the account given Moteuczomah Xocoyotl was true and quickly returned to Tenochtitlan.[26] Whatever the specific truth of this account, it does point to a lack of Aztec control in the region.

Moteuczomah Xocoyotl told the kings of Tetzcoco and Tlacopan what had happened; they agreed on war and ordered double supplies prepared because of the trip's length. Allied towns were told to gather their forces at Ocotepec and then march to Xaltianquizco to meet the armies of Tenochtitlan, Tetzcoco, and Tlacopan. The only major obstacle the army encountered on this trek was the Quetzalotli-Itempan River, which cut their path. When scouts failed to find a better route, the army built reed rafts and crossed, but the delay must have been considerable.

The Aztec army numbered 400,000, and when it reached Tototepec, the soldiers entered and burned the temple and royal houses and slaughtered all the people above nine years of age. The Aztecs took 600 captives, the Acolhuas 400, and the Tepanecs 350,[27] and Quetzaltepec was also conquered.[28]

At this time another flower war was fought with Huexotzinco, Atlixco, and Cholollan (see map 20).[29] But instead of sending only a

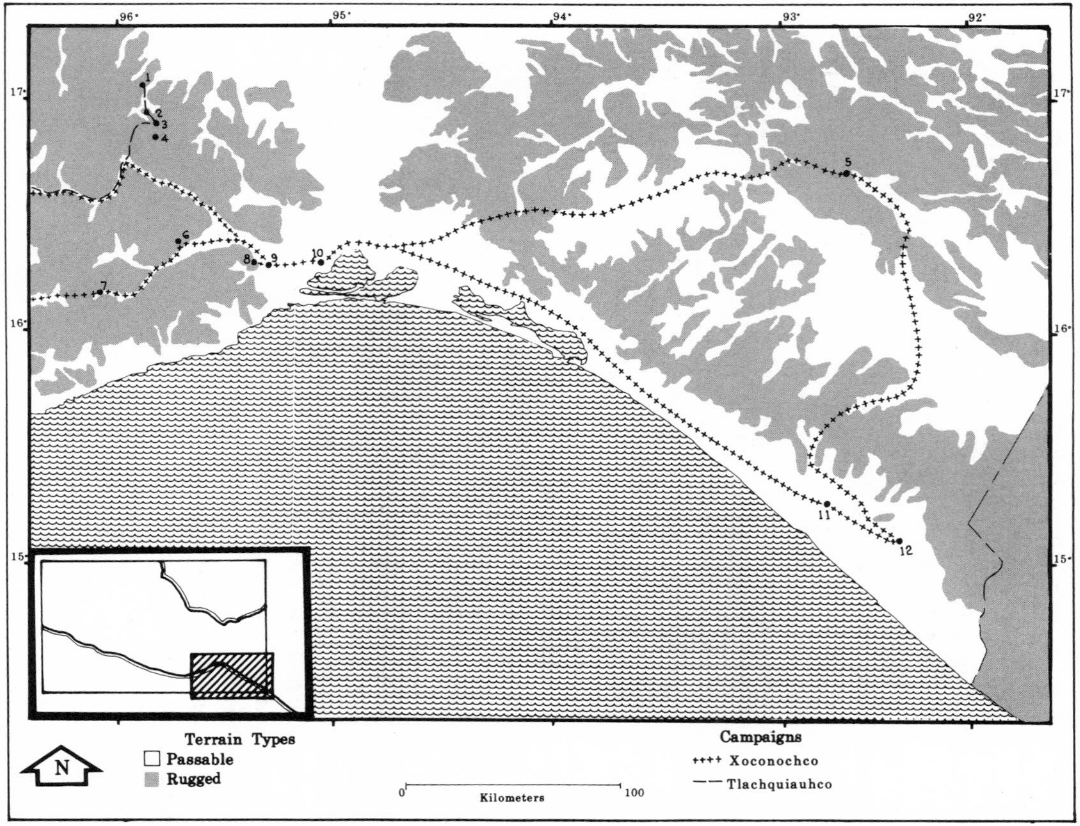
96°
95°
94°
93°
92°
17°
16°
15°
1
2
3
4
5
6
7
8
9
10
11
12
N
Terrain Types
Passable
Rugged
0
Kilometers
100
Campaigns
++++ Xoconochco
— Tlachquiauhco

small military contingent, the Aztecs and their allies dispatched a force of 100,000 men—presumably for intimidation rather than primarily for use in combat, as they adhered to the traditional flower war method of initiating combat with limited numbers of combatants. The army gathered at Atzitzihuacan, a subject of Papayocan, and the battle began with 200 Aztec warriors.[30] Nevertheless, the large acompanying forces could be drawn on for more rapid replacement of individuals; the war also displayed the forces available to the Triple Alliance if the xochiyaoyotl itself failed to achieve intimidation and ultimate capitulation. However the fighting did not go well for the Aztecs, and many nobles and war captains were lost, including Moteuczomah Xocoyotl's brother. The returning army entered Tenochtitlan in silence and without decoration, and the soldiers burned their weapons.[31]

Thereafter, yet another incursion took place into the Huaxyacac area: the cause this time was the rebellion of Yancuitlan and Tzotzollan (see Maps 19 and 21). The campaign may have been a continuation of the previous one. But Durán[32] cites the Triple Alliance's poor performance in the flower war with the Huexotzincas as the cause for the rebellion, and Torquemada[33] states that the entire area was in rebellion, which was a predictable reaction if Tenochtitlan was thought to be powerless or badly crippled as the result of a major military loss. Furthermore, the Aztecs had also failed to accomplish an overwhelming show of force in the region previously.

Despite their earlier losses, the Aztecs raised a 200,000-man army[34] and marched on Yancuitlan. Aztec soldiers entered the city at night and returned with a prisoner for interrogation. The next day they attacked, killing even the old people and burning the houses. After the battle the army rested, but the following day it approached Tzotzollan and found the city abandoned, everyone having fled; despite a four-day search no one was found.[35]

The Aztec army then marched to the fortified city of Quetzaltepec. As usual, scouts were sent to enter the city at night and bring

Map 21. (facing page) Moteuczomah Xocoyotl's campaigns into the southern Huaxyacac area and adjacent areas of present-day Guatemala. See maps 19 and 20 for connecting routes to Tenochtitlan. 1—Alotepec; 2—Quiciltepec*; 3—Quetzaltepec; 4—Itzcuintepec; 5—Tzinacantlan; 6—Huilotepec; 7—Izquixochitepec; 8—Guiengola; 9—Tecuantepec; 10—Izquixochitlan; 11—Xoconochco; 12—Huitztlan. (*Approximate location.)

back information, but they were unable to get in. The city had many houses and people within its fortifications. The first wall was five brazas wide (1 braza = 1.67 meters or 5.5 feet) and three high; the second, third, fourth, and fifth were similar; and the sixth was six brazas wide and two high. Unlike the armies of most other cities, Quetzaltepec's army did not emerge to fight the Aztecs in open fields, probably because of the impressive Aztecs victories.

Siege tactics were not well developed in Mesoamerica, because logistical constraints severely limited the time a large army could remain stationary in the field. However, bent on severely putting down the rebellion in the region and also concerned that fortified Quetzaltepec dominated a crucial route from the Gulf to the Huaxyacac area and could offer continual impedence to Aztec travel if left unchastised, Moteuczomah Xocoyotl ordered the construction of more than two hundred wooden ladders, with which the army scaled the walls.[36] Quetzaltepec resisted for several days, but the three armies assaulted the town from different directions and finally conquered it.[37] Also probably conquered during this campaign were the towns of Tlacaxolotlan, Texopan, Coaixtlahuacan, and Nocheztlan, in the Yancuitlan area,[38] and Itzcuintepec, near Quetzaltepec.[39] The route and duration of this advance were similar to those of the previous incursion into the area. Probably during the same campaign season (1506–1507), Totollan (the region of Piaztlan) was conquered, as was Teuctepec,[40] where 2,800 captives were taken.[41]

Tototepec was also conquered,[42] as was Tecozauhtlan (Tecozauhtepec), since captives from Tzotzollan, Teuctepec, and Tecozauhtlan were sacrificed during the New Fire Ceremony celebrating the end of the fifty-two solar-year calendrical cycle in 1507. Also probably conquered during this phase of the campaign were Texotlan, Tzollan, Tozac, and Zacatepec.[43] This latter phase required a trek southwest, rejoining the main route at Icpatepec before returning to Tenochtitlan. The entire campaign stretched 1,400 kilometers (870 miles) and required 44 to 74 days of march, exclusive of days for combat, rest, and regrouping.[44]

Following the second Huaxyacac incursion the Aztecs fought yet another flower war, apparently in 1508.[45] The primary objective was Huexotzinco, but many of the cities of the region seem to have been involved (see map 20).[46] The Aztecs claimed victory, but they lost many men and took few prisoners. The loss of so many men was the result of a shift toward a more conquest-oriented approach. Under these conditions the Huexotzincas probably took the defensive and thus suffered fewer casualties. It is apparent, in any case, that the nature of the struggle had changed, and the Aztecs did succeed in conquering the nearby city of Cuauhquechollan[47] and probably Itzteyocan[48] and Itzyocan,[49] further tightening the encirclement of the region.

Thereafter, probably in 1509, the Aztecs marched on the province of Amatlan (Amatitlan; see map 19),[50] but the army encountered unexpected snow and blizzard conditions in the mountains, and many soldiers died.[51] The Aztecs reached Amatlan with too few soldiers to conquer it—a serious blow to the Aztec efforts to establish credibility as a power in the region.

A short hiatus began around 1510, when strange celestial events were observed.[52] These were felt to have astrological significance, and wars throughout the land are said to have stopped.[53] Astrological predictions were important in Aztec culture, and dire ones may have led to the cessation of some campaigns, but a major strategic retreat is unlikely. Indeed, the lull was brief. Whether or not these celestial events were interpreted as presaging ill fortune for the Aztecs (and whether or not this was an interpretation by the Aztecs or by those who would rebel), numerous towns revolted throughout the empire, initiating a difficult period for the Aztecs.

Because political stability depended on the cooperation of vanquished peoples and their belief in the Aztecs' ability to punish any disobedience, the entire empire could not be forcibly subdued and controlled at any one time. The revolts that followed the astronomical phenomena of 1510 were so far-flung and widespread that the Aztecs were incapable of dealing with all of them in both an effective and timely manner.

When towns in the area of southern Huaxyacac rebelled, Moteuczomah Xocoyotl began another campaign and conquered Icpatepec, Malinaltepec, Xochitepec, and Izquixochitlan in 1511 or 1512,[54] along with Izquixochitepec, Huilotepec, Tecuantepec, probably Miahuatlan and Coatlayauhcan[55] and, probably, Tzinacantlan, Huitztlan, and Xoconochco (see maps 19 and 21).[56] It was probably during this campaign that the Tzapotecs were tied into the empire, although the Aztecs did not conquer their fortress of Guiengola, nor was this necessary. Passage through the area was more important to the Aztecs than domination and tribute extraction per se, so transit rights were negotiated.[57] It was most likely on the return portion of the campaign that Malinaltepec was conquered, along with Citlaltepec, Tlachinollan, Teochiyauhtzinco, and Tlalcozauhtitlan.[58]

The next conquests were probably in the same campaign season (1511–12). Tlachquiauhco was conquered, and 12,210 captives were taken to be sacrificed, leaving no one in the town (see map 19). The Yopitzincas had plotted to kill the Aztecs garrisoned at Tlacotepec by treachery, but this plan was discovered, and the Aztec army attacked and conquered them, taking 200 captives. Nopallan was conquered as well, 140 men being taken captive, but many Aztecs died, including twenty important men.[59] Chichihualtatacallan, Quimichtepec,[60] and the province of Tototepec were also conquered, as were Chilquiyauhco and Alotepec.[61] The conquest of Chilquiyauhco, although undertaken during the same campaign season, was doubtless a separate and independent enterprise[62] (see map 20).

Concurrent with the third thrust into the Huaxyacac area, the Aztecs fought another flower war, in which they took 140 captives. The fighting focused on Tlaxcallan first, then on Huexotzinco, and finally on Atlixco.[63] This apparent effort to divide the three allies and subdue them individually did not succeed immediately, but it exacerbated existing tensions.

Still, the multiple simultaneous engagements strained Aztec resources, leaving the empire vulnerable in other areas. So when the people of Cuetlachtlan also maltreated the Aztecs as an indication of rebellion, the Aztecs—who were occupied with both the xochiyaoyotl and the campaign in Huaxyacac—did nothing about it.

After the third Huaxyacac campaign (probably in 1514–15), the Aztecs entered Chichimec territory by way of the Huaxtec region. There they conquered Quetzalapan and took 1,332 captives while losing 95 Aztecs.[64] Although Quetzalapan is rather far to the south for a campaign entered from the area indicated, numerous conquests undertaken during the reign of Moteuczomah Xocoyotl stretch between that city and the Huaxtec region. Thus, most of these otherwise unascribed Huaxtec and coastal region towns were probably conquered at this time: Mollanco (Ollan), Tlachinolticpac, Huexolotlan, Cuextlan, Micquetlan, Atlan, Pantepec, Tetzapotitlan, Toztepec, Cuauhtochco, Cuezcomatl-Iyacac, Atzaccan, Izhuatlan, Tecpanayacac,[65] and razed Cihuapohualoyan. Two towns in the vicinity of Huaxyacac were also conquered, though possibly in independent actions: Macuiloctlan[66] and Cuezcomaixtlahuacan, which was not destroyed, as its inhabitants fled to a fortified stronghold.[67]

The Aztecs next fought their only other war with the Tarascans. The Aztec army went west, beyond the valley of Tolocan, to the fortified border of the Tarascan Empire, where the armies of the two empires met and fought, with many deaths on both sides. Although the Aztecs failed to capture the battle site, they succeeded in taking many captives and booty.[68] This was the Aztecs' first direct confrontation with the Tarascans since Axayacatl's defeat, and it was an extension of Ahuitzotl's strategic encirclement of Michhuacan.

The next significant event was not an Aztec war or conquest but the upheaval that followed the death of Nezahualpilli, king of Tetzcoco.[69] When he died in 1515, Nezahualpilli left several legitimate sons, all potential heirs, but none had been designated the king's successor. The eldest son, Tetlahuehhuetzquitih, was not capable of ruling: two others, Coanacoch and Ixtlilxochitl, both had the ability but favored their older brother. Taking advantage of this succession crisis to promote Aztec interests, Moteuczomah Xocoyotl opposed the likely choices and instructed the electors to select another of Nezahualpilli's sons (and Moteuczomah Xocoyotl's nephew), Cacama, to be king. The electors were the lords of the Acolhua towns and of Tenochtitlan,[70] and opinions were divided over who should be Nezahualpilli's successor. Coanacoch sided with Moteuczomah Xocoyotl's faction, but Ixtlilxochitl opposed Cacama and fled to the mountains of Metztitlan, where he received support. Returning with an army, Ixtlilxochitl conquered many Acolhua towns; established fortifications at Papalotlan, Acolman, Chiucnauhtlan, Tecacman, Tzompanco, and Huehuetocan, and fought both Moteuczomah Xocoyotl and his own brothers, Cacama and Coanacoch.

The Aztecs manipulated succession elsewhere in the empire, but in the case of Tetzcoco they were unsuccessful, and civil war followed. Tetzcoco controlled a large political area from which it could draw support but which it also had to appease, so an unacceptable heir in Tetzcoco could cause a breakup of the alliance. Since the Aztecs needed Tetzcoco's support, a persistent effort by Moteuczomah Xocoyotl to impose his own choice of successor could have alienated the Acolhua cities and, by weakening the Triple Alliance, have undermined the Aztec position throughout the empire. To avoid overt Tetzcoca hostility, Moteuczomah Xocoyotl agreed to a peace between the contending parties in which Cacama was recognized as ruler, but only of those cities not held by Ixtlilxochitl.[71]

Around 1515 a real war began when the 100,000-man Aztec army attacked Tlaxcallan.[72] In the conflict the Aztecs took only 40 prisoners, Tetzcoco 20, Tlacopan 15, and Tlatelolco 5. As punishment for their poor performance the king made the officers wear maguey fiber mantles and forbade them to wear sandals or to enter the palace for a year.[73] But Tlatlauhqui-Tepec, an ally of Tlaxcallan, was also conquered around the same time, as was nearby Tepeyacac later during the same campaign. Also probably conquered as a result were Xicotepec, Panco, Tlachiyauhtzinco, Teoatzinco, Atzomiatenanco, and Tecozauhtlan.[74] While individual battles did not always favor the Aztecs, the cumulative effect was to strangle Tlaxcallan further. In response to this increased military pressure from Tenochtitlan, Tlaxcallan attempted to centralize its alliance structure, which reduced the independence of its allies.

At this time fighting broke out between Huexotzinco and Tlaxcallan, but the reasons are unclear. The dispute may have been over spheres of influence since these city-states had clashed earlier;[75] but it is most likely that Tlaxcallan's attempt to assert its dominance alienated the previously dominant Huexotzinco. In the clash the Tlaxcaltecs destroyed the Huexotzincas' fields, causing many to die from starvation, so the Huexotzincas and their lords fled to Tenochtitlan and Amaquemecan, where they were granted refuge.[76] Huexotzinco now sought an ally that would give the Huexotzincas sufficient support to free them from Tlaxcaltec domination; hence it allied with the Aztecs.

While Huexotzinco wanted help in resisting Tlaxcaltec encroachment, the Aztecs were seeking an ally who would assist in the ultimate downfall of Tlaxcallan. But if the Aztec goal was to be accomplished, Huexotzinco's independence was doomed. Huexotzinco's political importance depended on its role as a fulcrum in the Tenochtitlan-Tlaxcallan regional balance of power. Without another power to play off against its current ally, Huexotzinco's importance was vastly reduced. Its significance lay largely in the power it could add to its partners, not in what it wielded alone. Thus the interests of Huexotzinco and Tenochtitlan were fundamentally divergent.

In one of the two campaign seasons following Nezahualpilli's death (1515–16 or 1516–17) the Aztecs launched another campaign into the Huaxyacac area (see map 19). The war began because Tlachquiauhco had stopped paying tribute and was interfering with the passage of goods from the Pacific coast and Tecuantepec to Tenochtitlan. Among the towns conquered in that incursion were Tlachquiauhco, Iztac-Tlallocan, Centzontepec, Texocuauhtli (not a place name but possibly the name of a mountain; probably near Nopallan), Mictlan, and Xaltianquizco.[77] Also conquered around this time was Calli-Imanyan near Tolocan, as a separate action, along with Tetenanco, Zoltepec, Tlatlayan, Oztoman, Poctepec, and Tecaxic (see map 20).[78]

There was also another flower war with Tlaxcallan at this time, in which the Aztec warriors who had been defeated in the previous xochiyaoyotl redeemed themselves. The disgraced warriors undertook the war on their own initiative, taking many prisoners, and the king pardoned them.[79] But this renewed success against Tlaxcallan was short-lived. By the next war Huexotzinco had reallied with Tlaxcallan.[80] The Aztecs and Huexotzinco allegedly fell out over the Aztec sacrifice of Tlaxcaltec prisoners to the goddess ToCih, which so offended the Huexotzincas that they burned ToCih's temple in Tenochtitlan, and hostilities broke out. But this was a rationalization: the fundamental reason for the break in relations between Tenochtitlan and Huexotzinco centered on their long-term political differences. Tlaxcallan, Atlixco, Huexotzinco, and Chalollan were united because of their opposition to Aztec expansion, but as the foregoing indicates, theirs was a fragile alliance, and by 1519 Chalollan had split with the others and become an Aztec ally.[81]

In one of his final campaigns Moteuczomah Xocoyotl sent an expedition into the Chichimec lands, via the Huaxtec region, and conquered Mazatzintlan and Zacatepec.[82] Two other towns listed as conquests—Tzompanco and Tollan—are sufficiently close to Tenochtitlan that their subjugation could have been carried out at any time.[83]

How far the Aztecs might have expanded had the Spanish conquest not cut their rule short we cannot say. But there is little evidence that the Aztecs had already achieved their height and were on the wane. Rather, they appear to have been expanding on all fronts, at least over the long term. For example, an Aztec presence had been established in the area of present-day Tabasco/Campeche at Xicalanco and Cimatlan, possibly as a step toward further expansion into the Yucatan peninsula.[84]

CHAPTER 16

The Spanish Conquest

THE Spanish conquest ended large-scale and coordinated use of Aztec and allied troops. Thereafter numerous Indian warriors from central Mexico fought other Indian groups, but on behalf of the Spaniards.[1] Often these warriors used indigenous arms and armor, but they gradually adopted Spanish arms, direction, and tactics.[2]

Much of the battle between Cortés and Moteuczomah Xocoyotl—between Spaniard and Aztec—has been cast in terms of a titanic struggle of cultures and of ideas.[3] There undoubtedly was such a clash, but arms and armor, strategy and tactics, and, most important, the imperial political structure itself supplied the pattern the Conquest was to follow.

Cortés and his men landed on the coast of present-day Veracruz in the spring of 1519.[4] They left the coastal region on August 16 and journeyed inland, entering Tlaxcaltec territory on August 31.[5] The Spaniards fought two main battles with hostile Tlaxcaltec forces. Though hard pressed, they won (on September 2 and 5), and the Tlaxcaltecs admitted them to their capital.[6]

In the context of Tlaxcallan history this defeat may seem anomalous. The Tlaxcaltecs had fought numerous battles against the Aztecs and others, and while they had lost many, they had never been decisively defeated. Rather, they remained in a state of economic and political siege, continually pressured by Aztec incursions. Why, then, did the loss of two battles lead to their capitulation to the Spaniards, particularly since their losses had been no worse than in previous battles and their military leaders were still undaunted?

TACTICS

One perspective on the Conquest sees the Spaniards' success resting on their superiority in technology and in tactics. It is true that the conquistadors did introduce many new things: technological innovations such as sailing ships, guns, crossbows, and steel swords and lances; animals such as horses and war dogs; and ideological concepts such as the militant Christianity of the Spanish reconquest, a European concept of appropriate social, political, and economic structure, and a Western notion of war and combat. However, the Spaniards also encountered alien technologies, plants, animals, and ideological and social concepts, and while the superiority of one set of ideological concepts over another is largely a matter of perspective, the superiority of Spanish technology was not immediately obvious.[7]

It is true that cannons, guns, crossbows, steel blades, horses, and war dogs were advances on the Aztecs' weaponry. But the advantage these gave a few hundred Spanish soldiers was not overwhelming. In any case, individual Aztec warriors were shown to be the equal of any Spanish soldier, and the Aztecs in general proved remarkably adaptable. Individual warriors are reported as having grabbed the horsemen's lances and thereby neutralized them.[8] One conquistador recorded a case in which a warrior successfully defended himself against three or four Spanish horsemen. When they could not bring him down, one of the Spaniards threw his lance at the Indian, who caught it and fought for another hour before being shot by two archers and then stabbed.[9] But no matter how effective the skill and valor of individuals are, it is the performance of armies that is decisive.

Accounts by conquistadors provide the best descriptions of Aztec tactics, but some of these tactics may not have been used previously, because the Aztecs had never faced the Spanish weapons and tactics.

Guns, especially cannons, proved so effective that they may not have been muzzleloaders but breech loaders which were normally found on ships during the sixteenth century. Such weapons, with multiple replaceable breech chambers, could sustain a very high rate of fire and would have proved daunting.[10] With its penetrating power, gunfire was also more effective in breaking up organized advances than any indigenous weapons, and it was not a respecter of social status. But the Aztecs were quick students, soon observing that the noise and smoke were of no consequence and that the shot went in a straight line. Thus, when the cannons fired, the warriors would dodge to the sides, as they also did against muskets.[11] But firearms were not the decisive factor. In fact, in the final days of the Conquest the Spaniards' gunpowder was so low that they tried to build a catapult.

Another factor favoring the Spaniards was their use of cavalry and mounted lancers. Before the Conquest, as noted earlier, the Aztecs used an open formation in their battle stance, since the denser closed formation is basically a tactic used to repel massed mounted attacks and was thus unknown to them. But open formations were ineffectual against cavalry charges. Nevertheless, the Aztecs quickly adopted strategies aimed at minimizing the effectiveness of the horse, but a major shift in tactics would have required considerable time, since it would involve retraining professional warriors. Closed formations were not adopted, apparently because while they might have cured the problem of a massed cavalry attack, they would also have created a better target for Spanish gunners. Consequently, organizational changes played only a minor role in the Aztecs' adaptation to the Spanish challenge; ineffective tactics were abandoned, but new ones were not adopted. Instead, the responses were largely technological. Devices and practices were adopted that aimed directly at these novel threats.

The Aztecs initially met the Spaniards in set-piece battles in open areas amid fields of maize and maguey.[12] While the Indians often held their own and more, open fields allowed the Spaniards to take the fullest possible advantage of their horses and guns. Hence the Indians increasingly adopted countertactics aimed at minimizing the advantages of horses.[13] For instance, when the Aztecs fell back in battle, they did so to areas, such as towns and ravines, where the Spanish cavalry could not be used to advantage.[14] Once repositioned, the Aztec warriors turned and reformed firm lines to continue the battle.[15]

Most of the advantages were not with the offensive, however, and the Aztecs were quick to use defensive measures. Passive traps were frequently built. Pits containing sharpened stakes were constructed in the streets of cities and covered with wood and earth so that they would not be readily detected.[16] Hidden pits were dug in the water-filled canals to trap the Spaniards, and sharpened stakes were driven

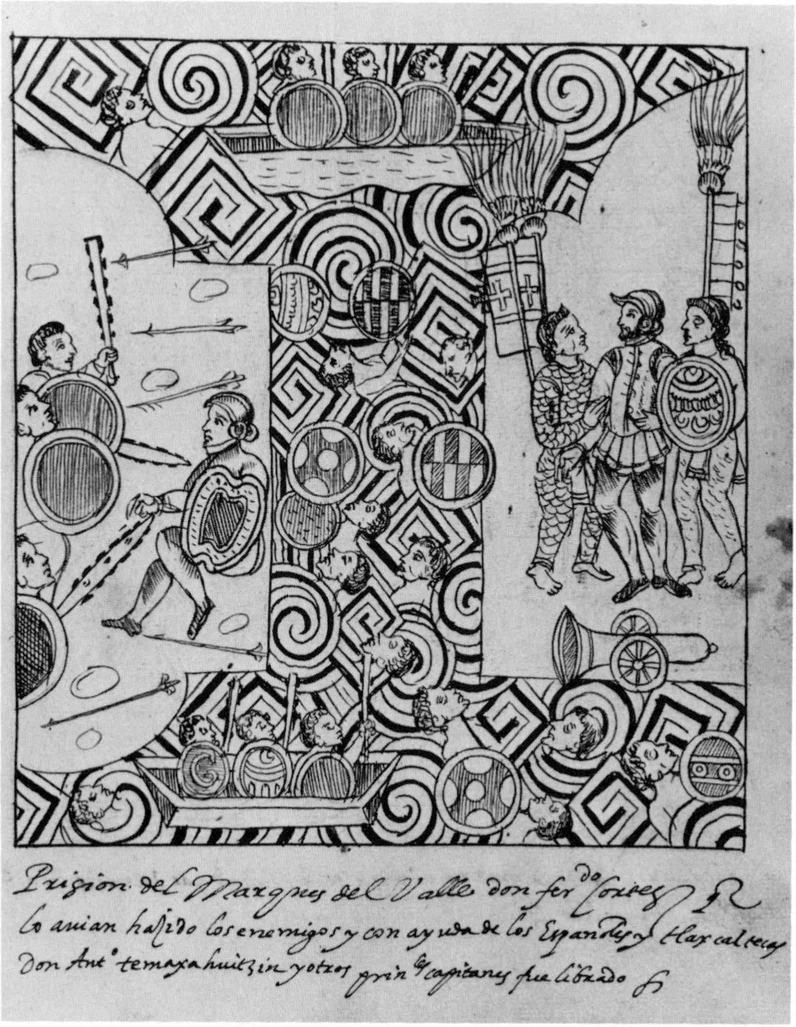
Prigion del Marques del Valle don ferdo Cortes q
lo avian hasido los enemigos y con ayuda de los Españoles y tlaxcaltecas
don Antº temaxahuitzin y otros prin capitanes fue librado

Fig. 31. Spaniards fighting the Aztecs during the siege of Tenochtitlan. Note the Indians' arms and armor, both the rectangular and the lancelet *macuahuitl*, the Spaniards' cannon, and the use of canoes. (Diego Muñoz Camargo, *Descripción de la ciudad y provincia de Tlaxcala*, 275r; 242 Hunter Collection, University of Glasgow Library)

Fig. 32. Tlaxcaltec entry into the Tenochtitlan ward of Tetzicuauhtitlan during the Spanish siege of the city. Note the defenders' arms and armor and their use of canoes. A head is placed on what appears to be a rudimentary skull rack (*tzompantli*). (Diego Muñoz Camargo, *Descripción de la ciudad y provincia de Tlaxcala*, 274r; 242 Hunter Collection, University of Glasgow Library)

into the shallow lake bottom to impale boats.[17] The dike system in the basin of Mexico was selectively destroyed in an effort to drown the enemy in low-lying areas.[18]

Most of the innovative tactics adopted were static, however; the Spaniards had to be drawn into an appropriate position or maneuver. Thus, feints were used against the Spaniards, as they had been in traditional Mesoamerican warfare, and they were adapted to the circumstances of the day. During the siege of Tenochtitlan, for example, the Aztecs lured the Spaniards into positions on the causeways where they were open to attack from canoes[19] (see figs. 31 and 32). The Aztecs also subjected the attacking Spaniards to coordinated assaults by land and water,[20] warriors often firing from armored canoes (chimalacalli) that were impervious to gunfire.

Moreover, the circumstances of the Conquest led to night actions by the Aztecs, despite their previous rarity. Night was a time of harassment during which the Aztecs yelled, whistled, and subjected the Spaniards to showers of arrows, darts, and stones from both land and canoes.[21] But these attacks proved to be neither very committed nor sustained,[22] although they had a significant psychological impact.

STRATEGY

Another explanation of the Spaniards' success focuses on competing ideologies: the Spaniards represented a dominant culture and viewed themselves as having a superior place in the world. In other words, Christianity is seen as naturally triumphing over the paganism of the heathen Indians, or Western Enlightenment over native superstition. But while perceptions on both sides played a role, appeals to grand clashes are unnecessary to explain the events of the Conquest.

The Spanish conquest is now seen as a major watershed in the history of the New World: the transition from the pre-Columbian world to the post-Columbian. But at that time and to the people involved—at least to the indigenous peoples—it was not. The Spaniards were simply another group, albeit an alien one, seeking to gain political dominance in central Mexico, and one that ostensibly did not represent a danger to the Tlaxcaltecs. When they first met, the Tlaxcaltecs could probably have defeated the Spaniards, and they certainly could have after the Spaniards' initial flight from Tenochtitlan. They did not because the Spaniards presented an opportunity. Here was a potential ally, and in customary Mesoamerican fashion the Tlaxcaltec leaders sought an alliance with them against their traditional enemy, the Aztecs. Thus, despite some internal dissent the Tlaxcaltecs befriended the Spaniards, and Cortés and his men entered the city of Tlaxcallan on September 23.[23]

Cortés now possessed formidable military backing, and with thousands of Tlaxcaltec warriors he entered Tenochtitlan on November 8, 1519,[24] though why he was allowed to do so is not easily explained. The traditional explanation is that Moteuczomah Xocoyotl thought Cortés was the returning god Quetzalcoatl. This or some other supernatural factor, such as the strange astronomical events that allegedly preceded the Spaniards' arrival, may have played a part in Moteuczomah Xocoyotl's reluctance to fight, but their impact is difficult to assess, and they are probably post hoc rationalizations. However, at least three more tangible factors may have contributed to the king's inaction.

First, in much of Mesoamerican warfare the perception of power was as effective as the actual force wielded, often more so. Thus a direct attack on a city as mighty as Tenochtitlan was unlikely and unexpected in the absence of some other crisis that could have weakened it internally. Competing city-states and enemy empires were held in abeyance by their real perception of Aztec power, but this perception was completely lost on the Spaniards. Although warned by the Tlaxcaltecs, the Spaniards had little basis for judging. They had fought the Tlaxcaltecs and thus knew of the Indians' skill, but the Spaniards felt themselves to possess superior weapons, doubtless believed themselves to be naturally superior, and were essentially ignorant of the size and power of the forces available to the Aztecs. Consequently, the normal respect and awe Moteuczomah Xocoyotl would have been accorded, even by enemies, was not felt by the Spaniards. Thus the Aztecs' first line of defense against enemy aggression—their perceived power—was ineffective against unknowing outsiders.

Second, because of Mesoamerican political and military conventions the Spaniards and their entourage were not treated as an invading army. An attacking army in Mesoamerica did not come unannounced. Whether or not an attacking army was formally preceded by ambassadors, everyone knew a war was in the offing, and the causes for it were frequently known as well. But such was not the case with the Spaniards. There was no reason for war, and their avowed intentions were peaceful. Moreover, since many areas of

Mesoamerica were not tightly integrated into larger political systems, even potential enemies were often permitted to pass through as long as they were not actively hostile. Moreover the presence of avowed enemies, even in Tenochtitlan, was not unusual. Although Aztec inactivity in the face of the Spanish approach appears naive in retrospect, the nature of the Spaniards was unclear to the Aztecs: they did not appear hostile, despite having defeated the Tlaxcaltecs and the Chololtecs, and they sent no ambassadors declaring war, although they did disregard the messages sent by the Aztecs. Thus their status was ambiguous; they could have been a group approaching to seek an alliance. So instead of meeting the Spaniards at some distance from Tenochtitlan and fighting them there as they would have met an enemy force, the Aztecs permitted them to enter their capital, as they would have if they were peaceful. However, this decision may have been colored by the next factor to be considered.

Third, the timing of Cortés's entry was fortuitous, as it was for many of his later actions. He entered Tenochtitlan toward the end of the harvest season, in early November. The elite military orders would have been available to fight at that time, but most of the army, the commoners, were heavily engaged in harvest activities. Moreover, the Spaniards arrived well before the festival of Panquetzaliztli, which marked the beginning of the first major campaigns. The religious festival was not an absolute brake on military activities, but it was the time that supplies, recruitment, and training were all scheduled for completion. Military activities before then had to contend with the problem of a preoccupied agrarian populace and a military apparatus not fully prepared for battle. This unpreparedness had not been a problem previously, since all Mesoamerican polities shared the same limitations. The Spaniards, however, did not: they lived off the land and were unconcerned with the long-term welfare of the populace, seizing or coercing whatever food or manpower they required from the local leadership. The Tlaxcaltecs suffered from the same logistical shortcomings as the Aztecs, though to a lesser degree, but they would never have attacked Tenochtitlan at this time—had they dared to at all—if the choice had been theirs alone. However, prodded by the Spaniards and presented with an unprecedented opportunity, the Tlaxcaltecs sent accompanying troops. Thus, the timing of the Spanish entry was fortuitous: the Aztecs did not expect a major military challenge at this time, and they would have been reluctant to commit the forces necessary to deter one because of the economic disruptions this would have caused. Thus Cortés was able to approach and enter the capital without serious opposition.

Within a week of entering the city, the Spaniards seized Moteuczomah Xocoyotl and held him prisoner.[25] Instead of resisting, the king submitted and even remained on friendly terms with the Spaniards, but the Aztecs saw this behavior as a sign of weakness. Moteuczomah Xocoyotl also ordered gold given to the Spaniards, and he imprisoned one of his close kinsmen in a nearby province who had refused to bring it.[26] Criticism of the king began to mount, but too-vigorous denunciation was dangerous. King Cacama of Tetzcoco was both vocal and premature in his, and Moteuczomah Xocoyotl still wielded considerable power. He imprisoned Cacama and replaced him on the throne with Cuicuitzcatl.[27]

Perhaps Moteuczomah Xocoyotl was biding his time, trying to find a way to bind the Spaniards to him politically and break their potentially dangerous alliance with Tlaxcallan. One traditional means of securing alliances was through marriages with Aztec nobles, and perhaps this was the reason Moteuczomah Xocoyotl offered Cortés one of his daughters in marriage. However, Cortés declined on the basis that he was already married.[28] Whatever the truth of the matter, the king's internal support was crumbling. Even the priests grew opposed, declaring that the gods Huitzilopochtli and Tezcatl-Ihpoca had told them that the Spaniards were to be killed. Perhaps in an effort to sway him, Moteuczomah Xocoyotl warned Cortés of the threat and told him to leave, but in vain.[29]

While holding Moteuczomah Xocoyotl prisoner, Cortés received word that another party of Spaniards had landed in Veracruz intent on arresting him, so Cortés left to deal with that threat. In his absence Pedro de Alvarado provoked a crisis that led to the Spaniards' expulsion from the city. During a festival to Huitzilopochtli the Spaniards attacked and massacred the noble celebrants, provoking a major battle.[30] Despite Cortés's return, the fight was going badly for the Spaniards, so Moteuczomah Xocoyotl was brought before the people to order them to desist. But the king had appeared too weak for too long to have any remaining credibility, and in fact the ruling nobles had already replaced him as tlahtoani with another lord, Cuitlahuah ("Excrement-owner"),[31] king of Ixtlapalapan. Moteuczomah Xocoyotl's orders were spurned, and in the ensuing fight he was killed. Spanish accounts contend that he was struck by stones thrown by the Aztecs;[32] Indian accounts maintain that he was killed by the Spaniards.[33] Cortés and his men fled Tenochtitlan on the night of July 1, 1520, and went to Tlaxcallan, where they were received in friendship. Many Spaniards were killed in the flight from Tenochtitlan, as were many Aztec nobles, including King Cacama of Tetzcoco, who had been Cortés's prisoner.[34]

Cortés remained intent on conquering the Aztecs, but given the effectiveness with which the Spaniards had been expelled from Tenochtitlan and the losses they had suffered, a frontal assault was unwise. Instead, the Spaniards began a series of attacks on Aztec tributaries near Tlaxcallan. By adopting this strategy, the Spaniards were guaranteed a refuge: they had allies at their backs, and they could mount assaults on locations too quickly for Tenochtitlan to respond. Notable among these battles was the defeat of the Aztec troops at Tepeyacac.[35] The success of this strategy bolstered the Spaniards' reputation as conquerors, but two factors other than military prowess contributed to their victories. First, these battles took place well after the normal Mesoamerican campaign season, when the Aztecs had limited troops available to meet Spanish attacks. Since the Aztecs were the defensive force, the limited availability of men was exacerbated by their having to station troops at or near all of the likely targets, because Tenochtitlan was too distant for reinforcements to be sent in a timely manner. Also, their manpower reserves were too limited to secure every potential target, and demands for agricultural labor prevented them from dispatching a force large enough to mount a direct attack on the Spaniards in Tlaxcallan. Second, as with all new Aztec kings, Cuitlahuah's special priority was establishing his power and credibility with his tributaries. This goal took on added urgency since the Spaniards represented a nucleus around which dissident elements could form alliances. Thus, Cuitlahuah and many of the available troops were doubtless engaged in the immediate demands of imperial consolidation rather than in focusing directly on the Spanish threat.

How Cuitlahuah's selection as king was received by the Aztecs' tributaries and how successful he would have been in consolidating the empire is unknown, because he died of smallpox eighty days after his election. Any efforts he made at consolidation were lost. Cuauhtemoc ("He-descends-like-an-eagle") was selected as his successor, and the process of consolidation began once again.

Times of succession were typically favorable opportunities for dissatisfied tributaries to rebel, and now there was a double succession crisis caused by the successive deaths of two kings. Equally significant, there was a new power with whom an alliance could be made in opposition to the Aztecs. But instead of making a major display of power that would have secured the loyalties of his tributaries—which may have been beyond his ability under the circumstances—Cuauhtemoc adopted a conciliatory approach. He sent messengers to all the towns to announce his ascendancy and tried to bind the local rulers to him by giving precious stones to some and remitting the tribute of others. And as the harvest ended and more men became available, he sent troops throughout the empire to guard against the Spaniards.[36] But his conciliatory actions were interpreted as signs of weakness.

Cuauhtemoc's efforts to keep the empire together were not entirely successful. Some local rulers met secretly with Cortés and sought aid. Others, such as the ruler of Cuauhquechollan, received assurances of support from the Spaniards and, in turn, supplied intelligence that enabled them to conquer the town.[37] The disaffection of numerous local rulers and the opportunity the Spaniards offered to break free of Aztec domination allowed the Spaniards to conquer a number of city-states to the south and west of Tlaxcallan (see fig. 33). After a series of such victories the Spaniards again marched toward Tenochtitlan.

When the Spaniards fled Tenochtitlan, Cuitlahuah remained in power, but to consolidate his hold he and Coanacoch killed the puppet ruler Cuicuitzcatl, who had been put on the throne of Tetzcoco by Moteuczomah Xocoyotl during his imprisonment by the Spaniards.[38] Coanacoch succeeded to rule in Tetzcoco, but because he was weak or had lost important support with the death of Cuitlahuah, Coanacoch met Cortés as he approached Tetzcoco and received him in peace. Some of Tetzcoco's subjects also asked for peace, including the city of Coatl-Ichan. Thus the Spaniards did not challenge Tenochtitlan directly; instead, they undermined the capital's support in the region, predictably in the Chalca and Acolhua areas. This strategy deprived the Aztecs of men and supplies that now flowed to the Spaniards, and it gave them a growing area of relative safety within which they could operate. Their strategy would have been even more effective, but additional cities desiring to ally themselves with the Spaniards, such as Tlalmanalco, Amaquemecan, and Chimalhuacan, were prevented by powerful cities still loyal to the Aztecs, such as Ixtlapalapan.[39]

Fig. 33. Spanish attack, aided by Tlaxcaltec allies, on Ayotochcuitlatlan (Cuicatlan). Note the cotton armor (*ichcahuipilli*) of the attackers, their insignia, shields, and swords (*macuahuitl*); and the *cuauhololli* (clubs), bows and arrows, shields, and quivers of the defenders. (Diego Muñoz Camargo, *Descripción de la ciudad y provincia de Tlaxcala*, 277r; 242 Hunter Collection, University of Glasgow Library)

Had the Aztecs seized the opportunity to engage the Spaniards in open and sustained battle, they might still have possessed the numerical superiority to overwhelm them. But they did not, for several reasons. First, as discussed, Spanish horses, tactics, and weaponry placed the Aztecs in a vulnerable position in frontal assaults on open terrain. Second, through a combination of threats and reprisals the Spaniards had augmented their own allies and decreased or cut off many of Tenochtitlan's, so the Aztecs' numerical superiority was seriously eroding. Third, simply occupying a defensive position while the enemy exhausted its logistical support was a traditional Mesoamerican response. But the superiority of the Aztecs' defensive position was undercut because the offensive fell during the agricultural cycle, Aztec tribute had been diverted in an effort to shore up poorly consolidated support, and the Spaniards were willing to plunder vanquished towns. Nevertheless, stalling was in the Aztecs' immediate interest, since each day that passed without a Spanish victory increased the likelihood that the Spaniards' allies would fade away and that the Aztecs would be reinforced from outside. Fourth, and perhaps conclusive, with disobedience widespread throughout even the heartland of the empire, dispatching an army from Tenochtitlan was exceptionally dangerous. If the Aztecs advanced on the Spaniards, Tenochtitlan would be left open to attack by others, which, if successful, would result in an Aztec defeat regardless of their tactical success in the field. Under these conditions no all-out preemptive assault was undertaken against the Spaniards by mainline forces from Tenochtitlan.

Having converted many potential enemies into allies, the Spaniards mounted attacks against neighboring cities from Tetzcoco, although not all of these were successful. Twelve days after their reception in Tetzcoco, for example, the Spaniards and their Tlaxcaltec allies failed to subdue Ixtlapalapan. The Ixtlapalapanecs deliberately drew the Spaniards and their allies into the city and then broke the dikes that kept the lake water out of the low-lying town. It was immediately flooded, and the attackers were forced back, narrowly escaping annihilation.[40] Cortés also struck to the north, marching against Xaltocan, which he failed to conquer.[41] But these setbacks did not prevent cities such as Otompan and Mizquic from seeking Spanish alliances. The Spaniards also freed several friendly towns, defeating the Aztecs stationed in Chalco, Tlalmanalco, and their dependencies.[42] But the struggle for control was not easily won, and the

Aztecs reacted to their defeat in the Chalca area by dispatching a punitive expedition against towns that had befriended the Spaniards,[43] making the consequences of rebellion clear to the wavering.

Maintaining loyalty was a serious matter for the combatants. Both sides were relying on their perceived power to retain their allies; some defeats were accepted as expectable, but direct challenges to either side's ability to aid its allies were serious. Consequently, when Chalco and Tlalmanalco sought aid from Aztec attack, Cortés dispatched Gonzalo de Sandoval to help. The Spaniards and their allies routed the Aztecs and also conquered Huaxtepec and Yacapichtlan.[44]

Not only must the enemy be defeated, but security must be maintained after the victorious army has withdrawn. Neither side had enough troops to permanently man all of the opponent's likely targets. But this was not a war in which towns were simply passive spoils; they took an active role in the formation of their own alliances. Without internal support the Spaniards could not have defeated the Aztecs in many towns, and once they had done so, the lack of troops meant that the Spaniards' new allies were largely dependent on their own resources to maintain their status. After the Spaniards won the battle at Chalco, for example, they returned to Tetzcoco. The Aztecs planned a counterattack by canoe, but word of the assault reached the Chalcas. Although the Spaniards were too far away to be summoned in time, the Chalcas asked for and received assistance from the Huexotzincas and repulsed the Aztecs.[45]

After securing much of the eastern portion of the basin of Mexico, Cortés conquered and burned Tepoztlan on April 5, 1521. Thereafter, the lords of Yauhtepec and Cuauhnahuac pledged fealty to the Spanish king,[46] severing the Aztecs' southern lines of support. The Spaniards then marched north, back into the basin of Mexico, and unsuccessfully attacked Xochimilco before returning to Tetzcoco.[47]

On May 13, 1521, the Spaniards left Tetzcoco for the major assault on Tenochtitlan. They divided, marching north and south around the lakes to their positions at the three major causeways into Tenochtitlan.[48] The battle did not go smoothly, and the Spaniards suffered major setbacks that led many of their allies to desert.[49] Added to these reversals was a newfound appreciation of the Spaniards' mortality.

The heads of those sacrificed in Aztec ceremonies were skinned, the flesh dried, and the skulls placed on the skull rack (tzompantli).[50]

This was done to the captured Spaniards during the battle for Tenochtitlan (see fig. 32). Their hands and feet were cut off and their faces were skinned and sent, with the horses' heads, to enemy cities.[51] More than simple show or religious devotion, these acts were calculated to intimidate their enemies, reinforce Aztec military prowess, and, in this case, show Spanish vulnerabilities.

Despite occasional reversals, the war was going in the Spaniards' favor, largely because of the timing of the assault and their strategically superior position. The war had disrupted the planting of the previous season, and battles had been actively waged in the basin of Mexico since early January. Both factors affected the foodstuffs available to Tenochtitlan, and reserves were dangerously low because the fighting had freed many towns on which Tenochtitlan was dependent. Compounding these difficulties, the Spaniards cut off all additional food supplies entering Tenochtitlan via the causeways, and they built thirteen ships to intercept supplies shipped into the city by canoe.[52] Moreover, Tenochtitlan's freshwater supply was severed on May 26, when the Spaniards destroyed the aqueduct bringing water into the city from Chapoltepec.[53]

As the battle swung in favor of the Spaniards, many of their Indian allies returned to help them once again, on July 15, notably, the warriors from Tetzcoco.[54] The Aztecs' situation worsened, and they sought aid from the Matlatzincas to the west beyond Spanish control. However, the Spaniards intercepted the Matlatzinca army and forced it away from the basin of Mexico.[55] The Matlatzincas then turned south and attacked Cuauhnahuac, which requested assistance from Cortés. Although sending Spanish troops to aid them would seriously weaken their forces in the siege of Tenochtitlan, failing to do so would undermine their alliances with other cities. Accordingly, Cortés sent the troops and still continued to hold his own in the siege.[56]

Eventually, the combined pressure of enemy forces, the gradual destruction of Tenochtitlan, the starvation of the city's populace, and the smallpox epidemic recently introduced into the capital led to the final defeat. On August 13, 1521, after three months of combat, King Cuauhtemoc was captured as he tried to flee the city by canoe.[57]

Conclusion

All the men wore great feather crests and they carried drums and trumpets, and their faces were coloured black and white, and they were armed with large bows and arrows, lances and shields and swords shaped like our two-handed swords, and many slings and stones and fire-hardened javelins, and all wore quilted cotton armour. As they approached us their squadrons were so numerous that they covered the whole plain, and they rushed on us like mad dogs completely surrounding us, and they let fly such a cloud of arrows, javelins and stones that on the first assault they wounded over seventy of us, and fighting hand to hand they did us great damage with their lances, and they kept on shooting and wounding us. With our muskets and crossbows and with good sword play we did not fail as stout fighters, and when they came to feel the edge of our swords little by little they fell back, but it was only so as to shoot at us in greater safety.

BERNAL DÍAZ DEL CASTILLO

CHAPTER 17

Conclusion

AZTEC warfare changed during the expansion of Tenochtitlan's empire, and one explanation of military developments holds that any change in the offense provokes an adjustment in the defense, and vice versa. But in the Aztec case, there was little of this development in technological aspects of warfare. However, increases in scale caused alterations in fortifications, logistics, response time, and the degree of imperial control exercised over local rulers.

Although they continued to be successful, Aztec forces were limited, and this became more obvious as the empire expanded. Adequate forces could neither be committed year round nor be dispatched everywhere; therefore, conquest scheduling became a key factor in imperial control. In the earliest campaigns troops were not left to control the conquered areas, nor were auxiliary support troops dispatched great distances. Later, troops were left intermittently, and tributaries supplied aid in areas distant from Tenochtitlan or where entire regions remained unconquered. Still later this practice was augmented with the replacement of some conquered rulers to ensure greater local control. Areas that had not been conquered recently or through which troops had not passed were less secure. This became increasingly the case as the commitment of large numbers of troops to one theater of operations reduced their presence elsewhere.

Historical accounts vary as to Aztec successes. Those of earlier wars record few defeats, while accounts of later wars include more. There are two causes: the first is chronicler bias. Recent reversals loomed larger in the memories of the chroniclers and their informants, while only the highlights of earlier campaigns were retained. Second, the Aztec approach to expansion had changed in scale. The earliest expansions beyond the basin of Mexico were not continuous and were not undertaken against determined opposition. Rather, conquests were spatially discontinuous, relying on intimidation as well as force and combining preselected targets with opportunistic conquests. Later campaigns were extended farther, posing greater logistical problems. Victories became more difficult and reversals more common, not as an indication of a less successful strategy or execution but as a function of the spatial extent of the Aztec expansion.

The goal of most campaigns was outright conquest, but because of a combination of relative strength, terrain, and distance, some competitors proved difficult to conquer in a single campaign or without a prolonged siege, which was usually logistically infeasible. When this situation arose, two separate but related strategies were adopted: encirclement and the xochiyaoyotl.

Encirclement was not a distinct tactic adopted against a strong opponent but merely one phase in an escalating conflict. If a frontal assault was ineffectual or if its continuation appeared costly, the Aztecs generally fell back on encirclement, although this strategy could require decades and involve the subjugation of the towns surrounding the opposing forces. Its purpose was to cut the enemies off from their allies and reduce their ability to retreat through the piecemeal conquest of enemy territory in successive battles.

Encirclement could be adopted alone or in ordinary wars of conquest, but it was frequently used in conjunction with flower wars. In the latter case the xochiyaoyotl was one part of an escalating conquest strategy. A flower war was the beginning phase of a protracted conflict that would evolve into a war of conquest. It was basically a demonstration of martial skills, and as such, it differed markedly from ordinary wars of conquest. As demonstrated by the use of ambushes, circumvention of battling armies, and firing of enemy temples, the Aztec leadership was not overly concerned with *how* victories were won in wars of conquest. But in the xochiyaoyotl outright conquest was not the immediate issue—the point was to make a show of military superiority—so how the wars were fought was of pivotal significance. Individual deportment was a major concern, and battling armies fought by established conventions. Accordingly, tactics involving stealth or trickery that were acceptable in wars of conquest were avoided in flower wars.

One purpose of flower wars was to demonstrate the ultimate

futility of resistance because of the superiority of the Aztec troops. Taking advantage of their numerical superiority would not accomplish this. The enemy would merely adopt its traditional defense-in-depth strategy, and the war would devolve into one of conquest. It was the Aztecs' lack of initial success in this type of struggle that had prompted the flower war in the first place. Consequently, to show off individual ability, the xochiyaoyotl was fought with equal numbers of warriors on each side, and it could be conducted with far fewer warriors than a war of conquest.[1]

A second purpose underlying flower wars was attrition. Those forces actually engaged in combat were equal, but the numerically inferior side normally suffered more because its losses represented a greater percentage of its overall forces. Similarly, since combatants were relieved periodically, the numerically superior side could withdraw soldiers more frequently and give them longer rests. Thus the larger opponent enjoyed advantages that were telling in the long run: a xochiyaoyotl ultimately resulted in a weakened opponent.

A third purpose of flower wars was to allow continued hostilities against a determined opponent at a low level of intensity. Few troops were required, yet a successful flower war contained the threat and permitted the Aztecs to carry out simultaneous wars and expansion elsewhere.

But propaganda was perhaps the most significant purpose of flower wars. Even if the Aztecs did not subdue their opponents outright in a war of conquest, engaging them in a xochiyaoyotl permitted a continued show of force and resolve as a warning to other city-states. Flower wars kept their opponents on the defensive (they were inevitably fought in the enemy's territory), and a significant show of could lead to some realignment of the enemy's allies.

If the enemy did not yield to Aztec pressure in a flower war, the conflict became increasingly mortal. This was especially likely after encirclement was complete and the xochiyaoyotl had sapped the opponent's best manpower. As the superior force the Aztecs controlled the nature of the conflict, changing it as it suited their purposes.

In short, flower wars were an efficient means of continuing a conflict that was too costly to conclude immediately. They allowed the Aztecs to encircle and undercut their opponents, to chip away at enemy territory and cut off allied support, to use their numerical superiority to reduce the strength of their opponents, and to continue their military exploits elsewhere in the empire. Thus they were a cost-effective approach to a persistent military problem.

The frequently reported Aztec rationale for flower wars with Tlaxcallan was that these conflicts provided a source of sacrificial captives close to Tenochtitlan, offered convenient training for the Aztec soldiers, and allowed Tlaxcallan to remain unconquered for these purposes, even though the Aztecs could have conquered it at any time. Although this reasoning has been roundly criticized as an Aztec rationalization for an inability to subdue the Tlaxcaltecs, it contains considerable truth. This is demonstrated in the wars with Tlaxcallan.

The Aztecs did not undertake the outright conquest of Tlaxcallan (or of their other xochiyaoyotl opponents) because they did not want to divert the necessary men and resources, for a variety of reasons. The troops were needed elsewhere in the empire; to divert these for an all-out push against Tlaxcallan would have been risky. If the Aztecs had tried unsuccessfully to conquer Tlaxcallan, their control elsewhere in the empire could have been undermined, and the king's position in relation to the nobles and calpolli heads could have been jeopardized.

Unquestionably, the Aztecs benefited both in military training and in the taking of captives in flower wars. Training as a function of the xochiyaoyotl was a real concern in relation to elevating and seasoning warriors, though certainly not in the sense of fighting a weaker opponent. Such a circumscribed war, however, could be undertaken without risk of total loss. It is likely that the Aztecs could have subdued the Tlaxcaltecs had they wanted to, given their greater manpower and resources, but the cost would have been very high. It was with just such a situation that flower wars (as modified by the Aztecs) were designed to contend. A flower war was largely an exercise in power, but one that also entailed very real strategic benefits for the Aztecs.

CONTROL

The Aztecs did not tightly integrate tributary areas into the empire. Conquered city states continued substantially as before, trading with their traditional marketing partners, retaining existing economic ties, and merely paying the Aztecs their due. Conquered towns afforded support for the Aztecs, not security, so there was little incentive or need to conquer territory in a geographically continuous fashion. And since tributaries were in little added danger from "enemy" attack in the region, leaving some towns unconquered did not endanger the conquests. Thus not having to subdue everyone in the area made the process of conquest easier, for the conquered towns could then be used for support in further penetration of the region.

Although the foregoing account describes the usual means of Aztec conquest, there were differences in degrees of conquest according to its distance. Towns close to Tenochtitlan were often forcibly subdued, while distant ones were often lightly incorporated. Beyond the central Mexican area Aztec interests changed. The security of Tenochtitlan was less threatened, and fewer obligations were negotiated. Also, many of these distant regions possessed only slight political integration, so security was of less concern (except to thwart others, as in the cases of Tlaxcallan and Cuetlachtlan). Other matters took on more pivotal importance, such as logistics, passage, economic goods, and tactical position vis-à-vis potential targets. Thus forceful conquest and incorporation would have generated great resistance while the Aztecs were in a precarious tactical situation, especially considering the more limited interests the Aztec state had in these distant tributaries. However, this shifting of concerns with distance changed as the Aztecs' political situation changed and as the empire grew in complexity, gaining more reliable support in some areas.

Accordingly, the political complexion of the empire was far from uniform, and areas had widely differing obligations. Likewise, the significance of rebellions varied. While all revolts struck at the perceived power of the empire, only towns near potential allies posed major political threats to the Aztecs, and only towns controlling pivotal transit zones posed real economic and political dangers. Hence the Aztecs reacted to the various revolts with different approaches.

There was no comprehensive imperial policy, simply Aztec policy and the policies of the subordinates, who were free to conduct their affairs—both internal and external—as they desired so long as they did not conflict with those of the Aztecs. Thus wars by and between tributaries were frequent, but these were tolerated because they did not affect relationships with the Aztecs. The tribute assessments owed the Aztecs would not change, but the victor could gain substantially in more tribute from new towns. The right to enlarge one's territory may have been regarded as sacrosanct and too troublesome for the Aztecs to try to alter. But another reason such internal wars might have been tolerated was that they exhausted tributaries militarily, destabilized them, and reduced their threat to the Aztecs.

However, the Aztecs would stop internal wars that did not benefit them, usually those in areas where there was no major power. These internal wars were unlikely to result in an alliance among the combatants, but they could add to the stature of individual kings, changing the power disparity and thus posing a danger of rebellion.

Some cities sought Aztec aid against enemies before being incorporated into the empire (e.g., Tzinacantlan against Tolocan and Xiuhtepec against Cuauhnahuac), but tributaries rarely did. The Aztecs apparently saw external attacks on their tributaries as attacks on themselves and responded accordingly.

The Aztecs had not only to create an empire but to maintain it as well, and the key to their success was the formation of alliances. Early Aztec alliances were relatively fluid, since no polity truly dominated the other city-states. But when the Aztecs achieved ascendancy, political relations—both friendly and hostile—crystallized. Temporary, limited alliances changed to ones of greater permanence, with the subordinate towns losing autonomy but gaining peaceful relations, greater trade, and a certain stability.

Since power determined many alliances, towns situated between the Aztecs and another formidable polity chose allies on the basis of perceived advantages. These choices were multifaceted: the coercive reasons for allying with one side or the other were obvious; the beneficial reasons took the form of trade and access to a wide range of goods through the central Mexican marketing sphere.[2] One detrimental consequence of severing relations with the Aztecs was that the nobility would be deprived of many elite goods.

Rewards also influenced alliance patterns. Gifts and honors were routinely accorded to Aztec and allied warriors, but extraordinary awards were also given on occasion. For example, for siding with the Aztecs the city of Tlalmanalco was given the right to hold the regional market that had previously belonged to Chalco, the Aztecs' primary foe in that war.[3] And when the Aztecs conquered Coaixtlahuacan, they sacrificed its ruler and made his brother, Cozcacuauh, lord of the city as a reward for having provided crucial military information.[4] Town lordships were conferred as a reward primarily on the basis of loyalty and martial prowess, although legitimate genealogical claims to the title were also important. These rewards were crucial to the maintenance of the empire.

Although the system was born of conquest, the Aztecs did not institute major structural realignments in their tributaries, so personal ties—either of friendship or of intimidation—served to hold the empire together. In their infrequent attempts to control tributaries directly, the Aztecs imposed military governors, though usually only when conquest had been followed by rebellion. This did not signal a structural shift in systems but was merely one of a series of temporary coercive measures the Aztecs could use against recalcitrant cities. Even then, local rulers were usually retained unless they were likely to establish some threatening outside alliance (e.g., Cuetlachtlan with Tlaxcallan and Tolocan with Michhuacan). This policy did, however, soothe succession disruptions and achieved continuity in local (albeit subservient) policy.[5]

The Aztecs also occasionally established garrisons and, to a lesser extent, colonies for both internal control and external security functions, but the relatively few people involved played only a small role in the political control of the local populace. Garrison troops and colonists became increasingly common in the Aztec system of imperial control, but a major presence would have upset the earlier alliance system. Alliances were maintained by power, so the relationships between the Aztecs and their tributaries tended to wax and wane as their perceived costs and power differentials shifted. But establishing significant fortifications, garrisons, and colonies would have stabilized the relationship and locked the locals into it on a long-term basis, undermining local rule, raising the local cost beyond that of merely being a tributary, and increasing the likelihood of rebellion. In short, stationing large contingents of Aztecs in tributary regions would have altered the power balance and required more direct control of local affairs at a significantly higher cost.

Because their troops were not tied down in garrison duty, the Aztecs were able to demonstrate overwhelming force. The larger the client state, the better, since it could maintain order more easily, but under a policy of direct rule (which requires garrisons), the disposable troops are few, the local garrison troops are finite, and the perception of power declines. Though garrisoned troops can be withdrawn in the event of war elsewhere, if they are integral to the political control of the place where they are stationed, withdrawing them weakens the local situation and encourages revolts.

The Aztecs did not limit the use of garrisons simply as a matter of policy. Given their manpower needs elsewhere, they could not disperse troops to garrisons year round. Rather, garrisons were either manned for brief periods or were staffed with only a few troops. The locations most often noted as garrisons were adjacent to frontiers near enemies, for example, along the Tarascan frontier, near present-day Pánuco, at Coatzacualco, and near the Tlaxcallan frontier. Locations within the Aztec Empire were transitory or, as in the case of Huaxyacac, in an area of uncertain support since transit rights to the south were essentially negotiated and not won through outright victory in war. Under these circumstances intelligence from the garrisons was more significant than their force.

The absence of garrisons is also associated with the general lack of fortifications. Even Tenochtitlan lacked major fortifications, although this absence has been explained in two ways.[6] First, Tenochtitlan was protected by its location on an island which permitted entry only by several easily defended causeways.[7] Second, drawing on European analogies,[8] fortifications demarcate political boundaries. Thus small states possess fortifications in their nuclear areas, while large ones possess them on the periphery of their territories.[9] But these explanations depend on an erroneous reading of the nature of the Aztec state and its military strategy.

Perimeter defense and minimal manpower were adequate for low-intensity threats, but high-intensity threats were met by sending concentrated mobile forces forward to intercept the opponent. The battles were usually beyond the fortifications, which were used as a supporting infrastructure for offensive operations.[10] Border fortifications could be surrounded, besieged, and bypassed but not easily conquered. They were created not to stop invasions but to pass on intelligence and to threaten the invading enemy's supply lines and troop movements. There were few fortifications in postclassic Mesoamerica, possibly because of limitations in wall-construction techniques. Most of the fortifications took advantage of strong locations, such as hilltops, where the defensive works could be built largely as walled embankments rather than as free-standing walls. Without such natural advantages Mesoamerican defensive works were inadequate as passive defenses capable of repelling invaders. Instead, an active defense was crucial in most cases. The mere existence of fortifications was not always a guarantee of safety in war. But whether they provided adequate protection depended on the exigencies of the conflict: how far away from home the enemy was, how good its logistical support in the region was, how near hostile groups were, and how determined the enemy was, among others.

The Aztecs created "buffer states" at the periphery of the empire that paid tribute in service and arms rather than in goods sent to the center. But since the empire was expanding, this was a transitional situation, and the buffer zones' tribute apparently shifted from service to goods as the frontier moved on. The main imperial troops were drawn from the basin of Mexico and adjacent areas; the main role of tributaries was passivity and logistical support. Buffer states probably helped only in wars against their traditional enemies, and since these were usually the adjacent polities, the loss of buffer-state assistance as the imperial borders expanded was relatively minor. But even though border states offered only rudimentary military assistance, they remained responsible for maintaining order locally. Thus they freed Aztec troops from this occasional necessity and provided important intelligence, logistical support, and arms supply, as well as some military support.

BENEFITS OF EMPIRE

Tribute was an economic benefit, but the tribute system was modified to serve political purposes as well, by tying the empire together. Earlier changes in the tribute system are unrecorded, but it was apparently reorganized by Moteuczomah Xocoyotl.[11] Each tributary town had a traditional relationship with its subject towns from which tribute goods flowed. From at least the time of Moteuczomah Xocoyotl's reorganization, the traditional flow of tributary goods from subject to cabecera (the local political center) was tied into an expanded tribute system. Tributary towns were organized into larger tributary "provinces," each of which was organized around a tributary capital (see fig. 15), with tribute goods now moving from subject to cabecera to provincial capital to imperial capital.[12] It was a rationalized reform: the system was not traditional, since no previous empire had been large enough to require such a reform. Nor did the system simply develop along the lines of the historical sequence of Aztec conquests.

The tributary provinces listed in the *Matrícula de tributos* (a native-style, Conquest-era pictorial tribute record) often grouped together towns of similar ethnic affiliation, but this grouping was primarily an attempt to cluster towns on the basis of proximity, regardless of when they had been conquered. Rather than keeping records on the status of each tributary town's payment, the new system bureaucratized the system and made it much more efficient. Now each cabecera was responsible for the payments by its dependent towns, each provincial capital was responsible for the payments by its tributary towns, and Tenochtitlan was concerned only with the receipts of its thirty-eight tributary provinces. Restructuring the system in this manner enabled each level to place responsibility for providing the appropriate tribute payment on the next-lower level, freeing it from concern for the entire system.

A second change instituted by Moteuczomah Xocoyotl was in scheduling. The time at which goods were paid under the original system is unclear. But perishables should logically be brought when ready, not according to an arbitrary schedule, while nonperishables can be sent at any time. During Tetzotzomoc's reign Tetzcoco paid Azcapotzalco on a yearly schedule, and several towns in the Cuauhnahuac area paid tribute to Tetzcoco six times a year during the reigns of Nezahualcoyotl and Nezahualpilli.[13] Under the system reorganized by the Aztecs, tribute was paid on a regular basis either annually; four times a year (in a sequence of 80, 100, 80, 100 days); or every 80 days, possibly keyed to specific festivals (Tlacaxipehualiztli, Etzalcualiztli, Ochpaniztli, and Panquetzaliztli).[14] These four festivals were at the beginning of the second, sixth, eleventh, and fifteenth months, so tribute payments would not have been equally distributed throughout the year. Rather, they were distributed around the military campaign season, which lasted six months of 20 days each, or 120 days.

The scheduling system was established not for the convenience of the tributaries but, aside from its economic function, to bring subjects into the capital at times most guaranteed to impress them.[15] Equally important, the more frequent schedule also served as a barometer of the tributaries' loyalties. Since tributaries took their payments to Tenochtitlan, requiring payment at least four times a year rather than once kept the king better informed about their loyalty. By keeping aware of the state of his tributaries this frequently, in the event of revolt, the king could mobilize the armies sooner and keep the rebellion from spreading.

The third reorganization of the tribute system involved its personnel. Only two tribute collectors were required per province. However, many of these provinces were far from Tenochtitlan, and there remained a possibility of rebellion, not just by indigenous rulers but by Aztec nobles.

Commoners posed little danger of usurpation, because they could never claim ownership of the goods they collected. But commoners could not be tribute collectors, because collectors had to deal with local nobles, and they had to do so from a superior position. The status problem would be eliminated if a noble were made the tribute collector, but he might claim the goods and property and create an independent power base, since most nobles had at least some potential claim to legitimate rule. This would have been a particular problem during periods of succession in Tenochtitlan, and to avoid this, meritocratic nobles were appointed to these positions. They possessed sufficient status to embody the authority of the Aztec state and to deal with the local nobles, but they could not be legitimate contenders for succession.[16]

In addition to its obvious economic purposes and consequent control functions, the tribute system also affected interpolity relations. What was required—as opposed to how much—could be manipulated to serve the Aztecs' political purposes. As part of its tribute, for example, Tepeyacac was required to give captive warriors from Tlaxcallan, Chalollan, and Huexotzinco.[17] This Aztec demand served to exacerbate relations between these independent enemy city-states and Tepeyacac, a potential ally.

MOTIVATIONS FOR CONQUEST

The pattern and the mechanics of Aztec expansion are fairly clear, but they do not explain *why* conquests were undertaken. As indicated previously, religion did play a part in warfare, but its precise role is unclear, and attributing an expansionistic motivation to it seems unwarranted.

Motivations, even if ideological, are not monolithic. In this case they varied, inter alia, according to the participants' class, city of origin, and degree of political integration into the Aztec Empire. Religious orthodoxy in Tenochtitlan solidly supported the state and its imperial aspirations, probably because the state was so successful and the various cults and temples benefited economically. Religious motivations may have penetrated to the lowest ranks of Aztec society, but they were unlikely to have been shared by people elsewhere in the empire or even within the Triple Alliance, who did not participate in the benefits of expansion in the same way the Aztecs did.[18] But even in Tenochtitlan, other general motivations played a more important role.

Aztec ideology held that anyone could advance through the social ranks through individual effort and military skill. However, differences in the way men of the various social classes were trained, the weapons they used, the way they were deployed on the battlefield, and the type of war they fought heavily skewed the rewards toward the nobility.

In ordinary wars of conquest wielders of shock weapons—disproportionately nobles—took most of the captives in battle since they were the combatants who actually came face to face with the enemy and had the skills to exploit opportunities. Although commoner archers probably killed many combatants, the standardized armory arrows did not allow the archer to be identified (and hence credited). Commoners made up the bulk of the armies and also the bulk of the prisoners, especially those fighting as part of their war service, since they had less training and skill than the telpochcalli warriors and markedly less than the nobles. But taking these commoners prisoner did not necessarily reflect great martial skill or daring, and because so many captives were taken in wars of conquest, the social significance of having done so diminished with time.

In flower wars, on the other hand, a primary goal was to demonstrate individual martial skills, and since this involved the use of shock weapons, commoners were largely absent. The net effect was that fewer prisoners were taken and that doing so required considerably more skill. Thus the likelihood of social advancement for the lower class was reduced, in terms of both access to a battle in which captives were taken and success once the battle began.

Nevertheless, social advancement provided some motivation for the individual warrior for taking captives, but at the state level it was more a rationalization for war than its cause or purpose. Much of the reason for taking prisoners was not simply that the gods needed them but that the captives enabled the Aztecs to make a display of power in Tenochtitlan to reinforce their image and might.

By using captives as a measure of military success and advancement, the state dovetailed its own interests in acquiring captives with the development of an effective and highly motivated military. Captives were also necessary to complete kingly succession. Thus extremely heavy emphasis was placed on the taking of captives in Aztec social life, military structure, state organization and control, and religious cosmology.

But even if religion justified war, and possibly even fostered it, religious mandates were not simply followed as demanded by Aztec beliefs but were manipulated by the state. Although religious festivals required captives, how many were needed turned on political considerations, and many celebrations were emphasized or deemphasized accordingly.

Instead of looking at the religious ideology of the populace, we can find the reason for wars by examining motivations in the upper levels of Aztec society, where such decisions were made. Thus, while much about Aztec warfare can be understood on a strictly tactical basis, the reasons for the Aztecs' expansion were embodied in their social world.

Both internal and external political factors fostered expansion. In times of war the tlahtoani's powers were strengthened, and the almost perpetual state of war kept these powers extended beyond their peacetime norm. The king enjoyed great military powers and was titular head of the nobility, but calpolli heads, not the king, held a similar role vis-à-vis the commoners. Thus in dealing with the commoners the king acted through the calpolli heads, a system that served as a brake on his power. The calpolli heads had to be consulted before general warfare could be ordered, because only through them could the chain of command select, order, train, equip, and unite the troops in the numbers needed and at the time necessary. But the king could send the military orders into battle (or permit them to go) without regard to calpolli wishes. And in becoming meritocratic nobles, commoners left the calpolli heads' authority and came under the king's control, creating an independent body of troops. But initially any cessation of war threatened the king's powers, because civil mechanisms might reassert themselves, injuring the office as well as the officeholder. As the nobles became more dependent on the king and as his command over the troops of foreign cities grew, the calpolli heads' position diminished. They increasingly adopted the role of middlemen, balancing the interests of their constituents (in order to stay in power) and the king's wishes (in order to continue receiving booty and tribute goods).

Support for an Aztec king—by the nobility, calpolli heads, commoners, and foreign polities—was not entirely automatic. Selection alone was not the legitimating criterion of Aztec kingship. The system would not simply maintain itself: imperial Aztec kings embarked on military campaigns to validate their position and leadership qualities and to demonstrate a continuing willingness to consolidate the system and extend it.

Times of succession were dangerous in all Mesoamerican city-states, since there was no guarantee of continuity in policy or in ability. This consideration worked against the selection of older candidates for king, because frequent turnovers of leadership were to be avoided. There was the added danger of internal instability arising from succession disputes, particularly in city-states with hereditary succession, because unqualified rulers might emerge, and potential competitors would be created in the siblings. Tenochtitlan had a relatively stable system because selection was achieved by consensus among pretenders and power holders. But Tenochtitlan still faced external dangers, so the deaths of the Aztec kings had increasing significance for the empire over time, while those of the tributary kings decreased in importance.

The normal difficulties associated with succession created problems for Tenochtitlan in retaining control of the empire. A poor or inactive king threatened the empire, the nobles' economic welfare, and the possibility of advancement of the king's heir apparent. Maintaining the empire was a motivation for continued warfare, and the kings' self-preservation was an incentive to avoid defeat. This emphasis on success fostered a concentration on easier targets of conquest, which dovetailed with the Aztecs' logistically induced tendency to chip away at empires rather than to attack them directly. It also maximized the likelihood of military success, minimized the risk of failure, and thus strengthened the tlahtoani's position. The empire was required to at least maintain itself for imperial reasons, and it was impelled to expand for internal reasons. Although they contributed to this expansion, religious motivations were the handmaidens of empire and not its impetus.

DOWNFALL

Despite their military power, vast political network, and motivations to conquer, the Aztecs nevertheless fell to the Spaniards, swiftly and finally. This was not the defeat of an inferior set of beliefs by a superior one: whatever their motivations, the Aztecs were a match for the Spaniards. Ideology was not the determining factor in the Aztecs' loss, at the level either of armies or of individuals. But ideology was important at the political level, for it played a role in structuring the Aztec Empire.

Much of the Aztecs' defeat can be understood by examining the advantages and disadvantages of the way their imperial system was structured. The advantages this system offered Tenochtitlan were a relatively large tribute return, few administrative or control costs, and an expanded area of trade, achieved at the relatively low cost of mounting periodic military campaigns.[19] However, these advantages were met with equal disadvantages. Because the Aztec system relied on creating alliances of individuals, classes, and city-states, its power fluctuated. As a result, political integration was fragile and depended on the perception of Aztec strength and resolve so that compliance was largely self-generated rather than dependent on structural changes. The system was a viable one—indeed, even an efficient one—in the absence of a major competing power around which disaffected members could unite. But this vacancy was filled by the Spaniards. The Spanish conquest was not one of superior arms and wills but one that took advantage of existing cleavages within the system to split the empire, turn its members on the Aztecs, and rend it asunder.

Glossary

Achcauhtli Executioner; keeper of the arms; military trainer.
Atlachchimalli Woven-cane shield.
Atlatl Spear or dart thrower.
Cacalomilli Lands designated to produce war supplies.
Cabecera Spanish term for the local political capital of a *tlahtoani* (q.v.).
Cactli Sandals.
Calmecac School primarily for nobles.
Calpanpilli Son of a concubine.
Calpixqui Tribute collector.
Calpoleh *Calpolli* (q.v.) headman.
Calpolli Ward.
Chichimecs Barbarians; less sophisticated peoples to the north.
Chimalacalli Armored war canoe.
Cihuacoatl "Woman snake," the king's adviser.
Cotzehuatl Warrior's greaves.
Cuachpantli Standard worn on unit leaders' backs to designate their unit.
Cuacuahtin Eagle warriors.
Cuahchic "Shorn one," warrior in the military order of that name.
Cuauhcalli Meeting house of the military orders.
Cuauhchimalli Wooden shield.
Cuauhcozcatl Collar used to bind war captives.
Cuauhnochteuctli One of the four main Aztec war leaders.
Cuauhololli Wooden war club with a spherical head.
Cuauhhuehueh Old warrior.
Cuauhpilli *Macehualli* (q.v.) raised to noble status.
Cuauhtlahtoani Military governor.
Cuauhtlalli Battleground between two enemies.
Cuauhtlocelomeh Eagle-jaguar warriors.
Cuauhtlahtoh Chief.
Cuauhxicalli Ritual "eagle vessel" used to receive sacrificial hearts.
Cuauhyahcatl Great captain.
Cuexpalchicacpol Youth who failed to take captives in war.
Ehuatl Warrior's feather tunic.

Estancia Spanish term for a spatially distinct but politically incorporated *calpolli* (q.v.) of a main town.
Huitzauhqui War club with stone blades.
Ichcahuipilli Body armor of quilted cotton.
Itztli Obsidian; obsidian blade.
Ixcuahuac Sacrificial knife.
Macana Taino word imported and used by the Spaniards for *macuahuitl* (q.v.).
Macehualli Free commoner.
Macuahuitl Wooden sword with stone blades.
Macuahuitzoctli War club with four knobs at the head, topped by a pointed tip.
Mahuizzoh chimalli Ornate display shield.
Matemecatl Warrior's armbands.
Matzopetztli Warrior's wristlets.
Maxtlatl Breechcloth.
Mayeh Commoner laborer permanently attached to the lands of the nobility.
Micomitl Quiver for arrows.
Milchimalli *Cacalomilli* (q.v.).
Minacachalli Three-pronged dart thrown with the *atlatl* (q.v.).
Mixiquipilli *Micomitl* (q.v.).
Ocelomeh Jaguar warriors of the ocelotl military order.
Octli Fermented beverage made from maguey sap; pulque.
Oquichtli Man, referring to a warrior.
Otlachimalli Shield made of woven cane with a heavy double cotton backing.
Otomitl "Otomi" warrior of the *otontin* military order.
Pilli Noble by birth.
Pillalli *Pilli*'s (q.v.) lands.
Pinolli Toasted maize flour mixed with water to form a beverage.
Pochtecatl Merchant.
Quetzalcoatl Patron god of the *calmecac* (q.v.).
Quimichin Spy.
Tecpatl Flint; flint knife.
Telpochcalli *Calpolli* (q.v.) school, usually for commoners.
Telpochtlahtoh Instructor of youths in the *telpochcalli* (q.v.).
Telpochyahqui Youth who took a captive in war unassisted.
Tematlatl Sling.
Tepoztopilli Thrusting spear.
Tequihuah Veteran warrior.
Tequihuahcacalli *Cuauhcalli* (q.v.).
Teuccalli *Teuctli*'s (q.v.) house.
Teucpilli *Teuctli*'s (q.v.) son.
Teuctlahtoh *Tlahtoani* (q.v.) subordinate to another tlahtoani.
Teuctli Lord.
Tezcatl-Ihpoca Patron god of the *telpochcalli* (q.v.).
Tiachcauh Master of youths in the *telpochcalli* (q.v.).

Titlantli Ambassador.
Tlacateccatl General.
Tlacacochcalco Armory.
Tlacalhuazcuahuitl Blowgun.
Tlacochcalcatl Supreme head of the army.
Tlacochtli Fire-hardened dart thrown with the *atlatl* (q.v.).
Tlacohtli Slave.
Tlahtoani Ruler of a province or town; king.
Tlahtohcamilli Lands of the *tlahtoani* (q.v.).
Tlahtohcapilli *Tlahtoani's* (q.v.) son.
Tlahuitolli Bow.
Tlahuiztli suit Limb-encasing gear worn by elite warriors.
Tlalmaitl *Mayeh* (q.v.).
Tlamani Captor.
Tlamemeh Professional porter.
Tlateconi Ax.
Tlatzontectli *Tlacochtli* (q.v.).
Tlazohpilli Son of a legitimate wife.
Tlemitl Fire arrow.
Tlillancalqui One of the four main Aztec war leaders.
Topileh Constable.
Tzompantli Skull rack.
Xahcalli Straw hut or dwelling.
Xiquipilli 8,000; a basic army size.
Xochiyaoyotl "Flower war," a war not for conquest.
Yaochimalli War shield.
Yaoihtacatl War victuals.
Yaomitl War arrow.
Yaoquizqui Soldier.
Yaotequihuah Leader of the youths in the *telpochcalli* (q.v.); a veteran warrior; a war captain.
Yaotlalli *Cuauhtlalli* (q.v.).
Yaotlapixqui Scout.

Notes

Chapter 1

1. I am using the traditional system of classification in Mesoamerica, which groups general time periods into archaic, preclassic (or formative), classic, and postclassic. An alternative system resulted from a School of American Research conference held in Santa Fe, New Mexico, in 1972 (the results of which are published in Wolf 1976). While this system may be more suitable for archaeology, it is superficially awkward and has not been universally adopted (particularly in Mexico).

2. Grennes-Ravitz 1975.

3. Durán 1967, 2:84 [chap. 9].

4. Mendieta 1971:129; Torquemada 1975–83, 4:322 [bk. 14, chap. 2]; Zorita 1971:134.

5. Torquemada 1975–83, 4:110–11 [bk. 12, chap. 6].

6. Casas 1967, 2:400–401 [bk. 3, chap. 215].

7. Clavigero 1787, 1:108; Torquemada 1975–83, 4:111 [bk. 12, chap. 6].

8. Torquemada 1975–83, 4:322–23 [bk. 14, chap. 2].

9. Mendieta 1971:129; Motolinía 1971:345 [bk. 2, chap. 12].

10. Clark 1938, 1:95.

11. For example, ambassadors were sent to request a *tlapalizquixochitl* tree (Torquemada 1975–83, 1:270–71 [bk. 2, chap. 69]), gold (*Códice Ramírez* 1975:131; Durán 1967, 2:225 [chap. 27]), and shells (*Códice Ramírez* 1975:128).

12. Casas 1967, 1:347 [bk. 3, chap. 67]; Clavigero 1787, 1:370; Hernández 1946:63 [bk. 1, chap. 20]. In the case of Tepeyacac (Tepeaca), a declaration in the form of shields and mantles was sent to the rulers (Durán 1967, 2:155–56 [chap. 18]; Mendieta 1971:129). Early in their history, when the Aztecs revolted against the Tepanecs of Azcapotzalco, Itzcoatl sent Tlacaelel to anoint the king of Azcapotzalco with pitch, used for the dead, and give him arms as a sign of war (Acosta 1604, 2:477–79 [bk. 7, chap. 12]; Clavigero 1787, 1:370; Durán 1967, 2:78 [chap. 9]), but in that instance the Aztecs were rebellious tributaries, not conquering lords. Clavigero (1787,

1:370) states this was the practice when one king challenged another, but this claim is not substantiated in the other sources or by events.

13. Díaz del Castillo 1908–16, 2:79 [bk. 6, chap. 92].

14. For example, the gods allegedly spoke to the priests, as when Huitzilopochtli and Tezcatl-Ihpoca said they wanted to leave that land unless the Spaniards were killed (Díaz del Castillo 1908–16, 2:149 [bk. 6, chap. 108]).

15. Díaz del Castillo 1908–16, 4:166 [bk. 12, chap. 154].

16. Anonymous Conqueror 1963:175.

17. Anonymous Conqueror 1963:179; Román y Zamora 1897:96 [bk. 1, chap. 6].

18. Díaz del Castillo 1908–16, 1:241–42 [bk. 4, chap. 66].

19. Ixtlilxóchitl 1975–77, 2:181 [chap. 72].

20. Sahagún 1975:22, 33.

21. Torquemada 1975–83, 1:218–19 [bk. 2, chap. 46], 1:263 [bk. 2, chap. 66].

22. If a commoner was born on the day 12 *cipactli* or the twelve days following it, it was thought that he would be a brave warrior. When the male child was born, he was bathed and adorned with a shield and four small arrows. His umbilical cord was bound with these and entrusted to the father, if he was a skilled warrior, or to other warriors, who took it and buried it on the battlefield, believing that the child would grow to be skilled in war. It was also thought that one born on 1 *ocelotl* or the twelve days following it or on 1 *calli* would die in war, that one born on 4 *olin* would either take captives or die in war, that one born on 1 *mazatl* would become a brave war leader and not flee in battle (Sahagún 1957:3–9, 93, 186), and that those born on 4 *ehehcatl*, 10 *tochtli*, or 1 *tecpatl* would also become brave warriors (Sahagún 1957:49, 53, 77).

23. For example, on 1 *xochitl* the king gave favors to his war leaders and noble warriors. And on 1 *miquiztli* the nobles and warriors honored Tezcatl-Ihpoca (Sahagún 1957:26, 33).

24. Sahagún 1954:57.

25. Paralleling the warrior ranks, priests who had taken only one captive were called *tlamacazcayahqueh* (sing. *tlamacazcayahqui*), and those who had taken three or four captives were called *tlamacazcatequihuahqueh* (sing. *tlamacazcatequihuah*) (Clark 1938, 1:94; Sahagún 1977, 1:162 [bk. 2, chap. 25], 1951:75). Nevertheless, the role of priests in warfare is unclear. Although Sahagún mentions priests who have taken captives, he does so in a discussion of religion, not war, so the reference may be an incidental one detailing all the things priests could permissibly do, rather than what they customarily did. In other sources warrior priests are largely ignored, casting doubt on their significance, except for the *Codex Mendoza* (Clark 1938, 2:64r, 65r). Page 64r shows a series of warriors—from lowest novice to highest cuahchic—taking captives while page 65r presents a similar series of pictures, but of people identified by Clark as priests. The term used in the codex is *alfaqui*, an Arabic word meaning doctor of laws and signifying someone trained in religion. Given the inattention paid warrior priests in the other sources, the great attention paid the alfaqui, plus the uncertainty of the term itself as relating to priests, this page may not refer to priests per

se. Rather, it may simply refer to the elite—those educated in the *calmecac* rather than in the more plebian *telpochcalli* (see chapter 3). This would encompass both priests and noble warriors. Consequently, it is possible that priests qua priests did not play a significant part in Aztec warfare and that those who did, did so in their military rather than in their sacred capacity. However, elsewhere in the codex (Clark 1938, 2:71r), the sixteenth-century scribe appended a note explaining that where he had used the term alfaqui, *sacerdote* (priest) should be understood. This casts some doubt on the foregoing interpretation but does not void it completely, since what a priest was, as opposed to the other members of the calmecac, is unclear. However, Frances F. Berdan (personal communication) points out that the individuals on page 65r all bear the red facial mark denoting priests, but she also points out that the *Codex Mendoza* is essentially a secular manuscript, virtually ignoring things sacred. Thus, the resaon for including these priests in the commentary on war is not clear. In any event the question of the true significance of priests in battle remains open.

26. Clark 1938, 2:64r; Sahagún 1954:52.

27. Bandelier 1880:98; Berdan 1982:105; Brundage 1972:159; Canseco Vincourt 1966:57–63; Conrad and Demerest 1983, 1984; Hagen 1962:162, 164, 170; Katz 1974:164–68; F. Peterson 1962:152–53; Soustelle 1970:101, 213; Vaillant 1966:217.

28. Bray 1968:186; Brundage 1972:100; Canseco Vincourt 1966:101; Davies 1974:96, 229; Hicks 1979:88; Katz 1974:168; Monjarás-Ruiz 1976: 254; F. Peterson 1962:153; Soustelle 1970:214; Vaillant 1966:223–24.

29. Isaac 1983a, 1983b.

30. Casas 1967, 1:347 [bk. 3, chap. 67]; Clavigero 1787, 1:371; Hernández 1946:66 [bk. 1, chap. 20]; Mendieta 1971:130; Motolinía 1971:347 [bk. 2, chap. 13]; Torquemada 1975–83, 4:324 [bk. 14, chap. 3].

31. Thus, in their flower war with Chalco, the victorious Aztecs stationed guards lest the defeated enemy tried to return to the battlefield (Durán 1967, 2:143 [chap. 16]).

32. Hernández 1946, 1:65 [bk. 1, chap. 20].

33. Durán 1967, 2:418–419 [chap. 55].

34. Moriarty 1969.

35. Fried 1967:26.

36. For an overview of anthropological approaches to warfare, see Ferguson 1984a.

37. Barlow 1947, 1949a; Gibson 1971; Holt 1976, 1979; Kelly and Palerm 1952:264–317.

38. Finer 1975:85–86; Tilly 1975a:73.

39. Gorenstein 1966:60–63.

40. Bosch Gimpera 1966:14; Gibson 1971:392; Gorenstein 1966:46.

41. Gorenstein 1966:60–63.

42. Caso 1928:147–48; *Colección de documentos inéditos . . . de América* 1864–84, 4:532; Frías y Frías 1906:21; Gómez de Orozco 1927: 175; Paso y Troncoso 1905–48, 4:120, 165–66, 185, 194; 5:113; 6:61–62, 105, 123, 149; Ramírez Cabañas 1943:24; Vargas Rea 1944–46, 7/1:104; 7/5:26; 7/8:20–21.

43. Bernal 1966; Borgonio Gaspar 1954–55; Bosch Gimpera 1966; Caso 1966; Corona Núñez 1966; Davies 1972, 1977; Gorenstein 1963, 1966; Jiménez Moreno 1966; Paddock 1966a, 1966b, 1966c; Palerm 1956; Phillips 1979.

44. In contrast, Skinner (1977b:308–45) suggests that, in traditional China, the distribution of military might is greatest at the periphery of a political system and least at the center.

Chapter 2

1. For the historical growth of empires as a result of the ability to physically link and administer them, see Taagepera 1968, 1978a, 1978b, 1979.

2. For a more detailed consideration of the relationship of imperial system to the Aztec economy and the structure of their society, see Hassig 1985:3–150.

3. Luttwak 1976.

4. E.g., Caplow 1968. Modern coalition theory offers considerable insights into the way alliances are formed and why, but the idea that they form as minimal winning coalitions is not entirely warranted in this case. Normally, forming the smallest dominant coalition allows each partner to retain the largest share of power and spoils, but this is inapplicable in the hegemonic case for two main reasons, one practical and the other structural. First, forming the smallest winning coalition depends on an accurate assessment of the competitors, a capability largely lacking in Mesoamerica. Second, because hegemonic empires are held together by the perception of the empire's power, a minimal victory is inadequate: an empire must impress its power on the conquered so that local rulers continue their obedience based on that perception. As a result, Mesoamerican coalitions formed in different ways than would have been predicted by modern coalition theory.

5. Goldberg and Findlow 1984:378.

6. Although some revolts were reactions to events in the Triple Alliance, others probably resulted from purely internal factors, such as the death and succession of the polity's own rulers. However, there is inadequate information to test this thesis. There may, in fact, have been more revolts near the heart of the empire (see Holt 1976:61), reflecting the greater length of time these provinces were under Aztec domination. But what constituted a "revolt" is unclear: all records of "revolts" cannot be taken at face value (see chapters 9–15).

Chapter 3

1. E.g., Bandelier 1880; Borgonio Gaspar 1954–55; Bray 1968:187–90; Canseco Vincourt 1966:75–80; Davies 1972; Monjarás-Ruiz 1976:244–46; Orozco y Berra 1978, 1:206–7; F. Peterson 1962:155–56; Piho 1972a, 1974; Soustelle 1970:42–47; Stenzel 1976; Vaillant 1966:217–20.

2. One problem in assessing rank of soldiers in the Aztec army lies in interpreting the terms employed in their descriptions. It is difficult to distinguish (1) when a term refers to general classifications of warriors, such as

"officers" or "noncommissioned officers"; (2) when it refers to a specific classification or group of warriors, such as "major" or "colonel"; and (3) when it denotes people in general but may also be applied to warriors, such as the term *men*. For example, the Aztecs used *oquichtli* and *huei oquichtli* in discussing warriors, but these merely meant "man" and "great man," respectively, and did not reflect either general or specific classifications of warriors. Other general terms had more applicability, such as *yaoquizqui*, "soldier." But considering such terms to denote ranking introduces more problems than it clarifies.

3. As an example, the Tlaxcaltec army apparently had a single supreme commander, but the political authority that directed him was divided among four coleaders. When they sent directives opposed by the war leader, they sent them three times and also sent word to the captains of each army unit not to obey the supreme commander's orders to the contrary (Díaz del Castillo 1908–16, 1:256 [bk. 4, chap. 69]; Ramón y Zamora 1897:287–88 [bk. 2, chap. 6]).

4. Sahagún 1954:77.

5. This discussion of social organization is based largely on Carrasco (1971:351–56).

6. Anonymous Conqueror 1963:168–69.

7. Cortés 1971:199.

8. Clark 1938, 1:89; Hernández 1946:23 [bk. 1, chap. 4]; Sahagún 1952:49.

9. Durán 1967, 2:120 [chap. 14], 213 [chap. 26]; Mendieta 1971:124; Sahagún 1952:55.

10. Durán 1967, 1:49 [chap. 5]; Sahagún 1952:49.

11. Sahagún 1954:75.

12. Sahagún 1952:49.

13. See Chapter 4 for a discussion of the demographic calculations.

14. Clark 1938, 1:89; Hernández 1946:23 [bk. 1, chap. 4]; Sahagún 1952:49.

15. Sahagún 1952:49–50; translation by J. Richard Andrews.

16. Sahagún 1952:50–51; translation by J. Richard Andrews.

17. Sahagún 1954:53–55.

18. Sahagún 1954:52.

19. Acosta 1604, 2:442 [bk. 6, chap. 27]; Clark 1938, 1:91–92; Durán 1967, 1:48 [chap. 5]; Sahagún 1952:53.

20. Sahagún 1952:54.

21. Zorita 1971:139.

22. Sahagún 1952:57.

23. Sahagún 1952:49.

24. Durán 1967, 1:48 [chap. 5]; Sahagún 1952:49, 59–61; Zorita 1971:138.

25. Sahagún 1954:71–74.

26. Seler 1960, 2:771–72. For English translations see Seler 1939.

27. Acosta 1604, 2:442 [bk. 6, chap. 27]; Durán 1967, 2:316–17 [chap. 41]; Hernández 1946:24 [bk. 1, chap. 5]; Sahagún 1952:59.

28. Sahagún 1952:59–60; translation by J. Richard Andrews.

29. Sahagún 1952:60; translation by J. Richard Andrews.
30. Sahagún 1952:59–61.
31. Zorita 1971:135.
32. Durán 1967, 1:189 [chap. 21]; Sahagún 1954:71; Torquemada 1975–83, 3:275 [bk. 9, chap. 13].
33. Sahagún 1952:63–65.
34. Acosta 1604, 2:442–43; Durán 1967, 1:191 [chap. 21]; Sahagún 1954:72.
35. Durán 1967, 1:50 [chap. 5].
36. Durán 1967, 1:105–1506 [chap. 10].
37. Sahagún 1954:72.
38. Sahagún 1954:75.
39. Sahagún 1954:76.
40. Clavigero 1787, 1:329; Durán 1967, 1:50 [chap. 5]; Mendieta 1971:124; Sahagún 1954:154.
41. Durán 1967, 1:67 [chap. 6]; Sahagún 1954:56, 65; Zorita 1971:267.
42. Weapons were only worn when the people went to war.
43. Sahagún 1954:76.
44. Clark 1938, 1:93–94.
45. Sahagún 1952:55.
46. Clark 1938, 1:93; Sahagún 1954:76.
47. Clark 1938, 1:93.
48. Sahagún 1954:76.
49. Clark 1938, 1:93.
50. Sahagún 1954:77.
51. Durán 1967, 1:67 [chap. 6].
52. Sahagún 1954:77.
53. Sahagún 1954:77, 87. Because of conflicting terminology—*tlacochcalcatl, tlacochteuctli, tlacateccatl,* and *tlacateuctli*—and supporting descriptive material in several sixteenth-century sources, Piho (1972b) suggests the bifurcation of the tlacochcalcatl and tlacateccatl positions into noble (tlacochteuctli and tlacateuctli) and commoner (tlacochcalcatl and tlacateccatl) offices by the time of the Spanish conquest. Nevertheless, the data are ambiguous, with some individuals of undoubted noble status, such as Moteuczomah Xocoyotl, described as the tlacochcalcatl. It may be that the terms are variable titles for the same position.
54. Sahagún 1954:87.
55. Códice Ramírez 1975:76; Durán 1967, 2:211–12 [chap. 26].
56. Casas 1967, 1:346 [bk. 3, chap. 66].
57. Clavigero 1787, 1:365–66.
58. Clavigero 1787, 1:366–67.
59. Clavigero 1787, 1:366.
60. Durán 1967, 2:211–12 [chap. 26]; Sahagún 1952:54.
61. Durán 1967, 2:211–12 [chap. 26].
62. Durán 1967, 2:211–12 [chap. 26].
63. *Crónica mexicana* 1975:344 [chap. 34]; Torquemada 1975–83, 4:329–30 [bk. 14, chap. 5].

64. Díaz del Castillo 1908–16, 1:22 [bk. 1, chap. 3], 1:42 [bk. 1, chap. 9], 1:118 [bk. 2, chap. 34]; Durán 1967, 2:167 [chap. 19]; López de Gómara 1965–66, 2:102; Muñoz Camargo 1892:14.
65. López de Velasco 1971:16.
66. Sahagún 1954:76.
67. Clark 1938, 1:93; Sahagún 1952:54.
68. Durán 1967, 1:114 [chap. 11].
69. Durán 1967, 1:67–68 [chap. 6].
70. Zorita 1971:93.
71. Sahagún 1954:52.
72. Sahagún 1951:45, 1957:26, 1970:15.
73. Sahagún 1954:51–52.
74. Durán 1967, 2:209 [chap. 25].
75. Sahagún 1954:74.
76. Sahagún 1959:92.
77. Sahagún 1959:5.
78. Sahagún 1959:5–6.
79. Sahagún 1959:6.
80. Nuttall 1891b:39.
81. McAfee and Barlow 1946:196.
82. Chimalpahin 1965:220 [relación 7]; *Crónica mexicana* 1975:553 [chap. 78], 599 [chap. 88]. The *Crónica mexicana* lists Ahuitzotl's insignia as the *cuauhxolotl*. (See fig. 15 for a picture of the cuauhxolotl warrior's suit.) What this represents is unclear: the word is not listed in Molina (1970) or Siméon (1981). If it is correct as spelled, the word should mean "Xolotl [double or servant] associated with trees [or wood] or eagles." It is possible, though unlikely, that it may have been an error for *cuauhxilotl*, which is a tree.
83. Torquemada 1975–83, 4:329 [bk. 14, chap. 5].
84. Torquemada 1975–83, 1:253–54 [bk. 2, chap. 61].
85. Durán 1967, 2:460–62 [chap. 61]; Sahagún 1954:88.
86. Acosta 1604, 2:316.
87. Although I am not in total agreement, for further consideration of the structure of the Aztec military see Davies 1972; Monjarás-Ruiz 1976; Orozco y Berra 1978, 1:206–208; Piho 1972a, 1974; Stenzel 1976.
88. Hernández 1946:23 [bk. 1, chap. 23]; Mendieta 1971:124.
89. Sahagún 1952:53–54.
90. Katz 1974:148; Velasco Piña 1979. The office of cihuacoatl was prominent only during its occupancy by Tlacaelel. This has been interpreted either as the result of Tlacaelel's personal qualities, elevated the otherwise less important office, or as an overstatement of Tlacaelel's significance by later chroniclers, who exalted their own ancestors (Davies 1974: 66; 1980:21). However, Carrasco (1984b) offers a significant argument for the importance of Tlacaelel based on his position in the Aztec succession hierarchy.
91. *Códice Ramírez* 1975:57–58; *Crónica mexicana* 1975:268 [chap. 15].

92. Durán 1967, 2:103 [chap. 11].
93. E.g., Torquemada 1975–83, 1:148 [bk. 2, chap. 17]; 1:209 [bk. 2, chap. 43]; 1:252 [bk. 2, chap. 60].
94. *Crónica mexicana* 1975:268–69 [chap. 15]; Durán 1967, 2:99 [chap. 11].
95. E.g. *Crónica mexicana* 1975:335 [chap. 33].
96. Durán 1967, 2:100 [chap. 11].
97. Durán 1967, 1:113 [chap. 11].
98. Piho 1974:173; Sahagún 1954:73; 1975:106.
99. Sahagún 1952:49–50.
100. Acosta 1604, 2:441 [bk. 6, chap. 213]; *Códice Ramírez* 1975:76.
101. Durán 1967, 2:194 [chap. 23], 1:115 [chap. 11].
102. Clark 1938, 1:93–94. Clark misidentifies the otomitl's macuahuitl as an atlatl, as may be seen by comparing the more clearly depicted weapons held by the other warriors in the picture.
103. Durán 1967, 1:114 [chap. 11].
104. Clark 1938, 1:93–94.
105. Durán 1967, 1:114 [chap. 11].
106. See *lámina* 82 of *Códice Vaticano* 1964–65:185 for a picture of a cuahchic warrior wearing the open-weave maguey fiber mantle (Durán 1967, 1:114 [chap. 11]).
107. Orozco y Berra (1978, 1:207) maintains that the eagle warriors and cuahchicqueh were noble orders, while the jaguars and otontin were commoners. Brundage (1972:111) suggests that the otontin were limited to the people of Tlatelolco. However, there appears to be little support for these views.
108. Also see Sahagún 1959:47, 101, 110.
109. Mendieta 1971:152; Sahagún 1954:43.
110. Clark 1938, 1:97.
111. Durán 1967, 1:113 [chap. 11]; *Códice Quinatzin* 1975:*lámina* 12.
112. Sahagún 1969:110; Stenzel 1976.
113. Sahagún 1959:32, 47.
114. Acosta 1604, 2:442; *Códice Ramírez* 1975:76.
115. *Códice Quinatzin* 1975:*lámina* 12.
116. Orozco y Berra 1978, 1:198 [bk. 2, chap. 2].
117. *Crónica mexicana* 1975:359 [chap. 38].
118. Durán 1967, 2:283 [chap. 37], 2:305 [chap. 40].
119. Durán 1967, 2:287 [chap. 38].

Chapter 4

1. Mendieta 1971:129; Motolinía 1971:345 [bk. 2, chap. 12].
2. Casas 1967, 1:347 [bk. 3, chap. 66]; Mendieta 1971:129; Zorita 1971:134.
3. This idealized view of Aztec warfare, in which early accounts are largely accepted as accurate, is found in many modern accounts; e.g., Berdan 1982:105–109; Bray 1968:186–94; Canseco Vincourt 1966:90–99; Hagen

1962:173; Katz 1974:164–68; F. Peterson 1962:155–60; Soustelle 1970:204–11; Thompson 1933:119–22; Vaillant 1966:217–23.

4. *Crónica mexicana* 1975:291–93 [chaps. 22–23].

5. *Crónica mexicana* 1975:606 [chap. 90].

6. *Crónica mexicana* 1975:358.

7. *Crónica mexicana* 1975:291–93 [chaps. 22–23].

8. To be consistent with my treatment of gentile names, *pochtecah* should be anglicized as "poctecs." I have, however, decided to point up the word's shift from gentile name to profession name by not anglicizing it, using instead *pochtecatl* for singular and *pochtecah* for plural. This is at variance with the traditional spelling *pochteca*, which has become entrenched in the Mesoamerican literature. For further comment, see the Preface.

9. Sahagún 1959:24.

10. Sahagún 1959:7–8.

11. Ixtlilxóchitl 1975–77, 2:161 [chap. 62]; Sahagún 1959:21–22; 1970:42.

12. Mendieta 1971:129; Motolinía 1971:345 [bk. 2, chap. 12].

13. Tochpan (Torquemada 1975–83, 1:251 [bk. 1, chap. 59]), Tecuantepec (*Códice Ramírez* 1975:68), Huaxtecs and Cuetlachtlan (*Códice Ramírez* 1975:128–29; *Crónica mexicana* 1975:326 [chap. 31]), Tepeyacac (*Crónica mexicana* 1975:306 [chap. 27]), Xiuhcoac and Tochpan (*Crónica mexicana* 1975:310 [chap. 28]), Coaixtlahuacan (*Crónica mexicana* 1975:334 [chap. 33]; Durán 1967, 2:185 [chap. 22]), Mictlan (*Crónica mexicana* 1975:354–55 [chap. 37]), Xochtlan, Amaxtlan, Izhuatlan, and Xolotlan (*Crónica mexicana* 1975:537–38 [chap. 75]), Xolotlan, Ayotlan, Mazatlan, and Xoconochco (*Crónica mexicana* 1975:550 [chap. 78]), Xaltepec and Cuatzonteccan (*Crónica mexicana* 1975:597 [chap. 88]), Tototepec and Quetzaltepec (*Crónica mexicana* 1975:602–604 [chap. 89]), Yancuitlan and Tzotzollan (*Crónica mexicana* 1975:614 [chap. 92]).

14. Sahagún 1959:17–18.

15. Sahagún 1959:3–4, 6–7.

16. Sahagún 1970:42.

17. Mendieta 1971:129; Sahagún 1959:6.

18. *Crónica mexicana* 1975:325 [chap. 31].

19. Clavigero 1787, 1:355.

20. Mendieta 1971:129.

21. Díaz del Castillo 1908–16, 1:256–57 [bk. 1, chap. 69].

22. Cortés 1971:109 [letter 2].

23. Acosta 1604, 2:409 [bk. 6, chap. 10]; Clavigero 1787, 1:345, 355; Sahagún 1954:72.

24. *Crónica mexicana* 1975:634 [chap. 96].

25. *Crónica mexicana* 1975:568 [chap. 81].

26. *Crónica mexicana* 1975:614–15 [chap. 92].

27. *Crónica mexicana* 1975:258 [chap. 12], 539 [chap. 75]; Torquemada 1975–83, 1:188 [bk. 2, chap. 33], 1:206 [bk. 2, chap. 42], 1:278 [chap. 72].

28. Díaz del Castillo 1908–16, 2:273–74 [bk. 9, chap. 130]; Durán 1967, 2:156 [chap. 18].

29. *Crónica mexicana* 1975:582 [chap. 84].
30. Torquemada 1975–83, 1:225 [bk. 2, chap. 49].
31. Torquemada 1975–83, 1:276–77 [bk. 1, chap. 71].
32. *Crónica mexicana* 1975:600 [chap. 89], 609 [chap. 91].
33. *Crónica mexicana* 1975:544 [chap. 76], 613 [chap. 92].
34. Cortés 1971:102–108.
35. Mendieta 1971:129–30; Motolinía 1971:346 [bk. 2, chap. 12]; Torquemada 1975–83, 4:323 [bk. 14, chap. 2].
36. Cervantes de Salazar 1971, 1:128 [bk. 1, chap. 15].
37. Cortés 1971:73–74 [letter 2], 218 [letter 3]; Díaz del Castillo 1908–16, 1:285 [bk. 4, chap. 78].
38. Aguilar 1963:152.
39. Cortés 1971:83–84 [letter 2].
40. Cortés 1971:369 [letter 5]; Durán 1967, 2:74 [chap. 8].
41. Sahagún 1954:56–58.
42. Cortés 1971:197 [letter 3].
43. Evidence for this pattern is based on eighteenth-century data (Florescano 1969:94).
44. Castillo Farreras 1969.
45. Broda 1976:61. The seasonal nature of battles refers to offensive, not defensive, wars.
46. López de Gómara 1965–66, 2:145.
47. Anonymous Conqueror 1963:179.
48. *Crónica mexicana* 1975:538 [chap. 75]; Durán 1967, 2:336 [chap. 43].
49. Anonymous Conqueror 1963:179.
50. *Crónica mexicana* 1975:335 [chap. 33], 551 [chap. 78]; Torquemada 1975–83, 1:278 [bk. 2, chap. 72].
51. *Crónica mexicana* 1975:539 [chap. 75].
52. Durán 1967, 2:80 [chap. 9].
53. *Crónica mexicana* 1975:440–41 [chap. 57].
54. Ixtlilxóchitl 1975–77, 1:374. Although large armies are frequently mentioned, an army of this size is highly unlikely, especially at this time.
55. *Códice Ramírez* 1975:127; *Crónica mexicana* 1975:481 [chap. 65]; Ixtlilxóchitl 1975–77, 2:79 [chap. 31].
56. E.g., Díaz del Castillo 1908–16, 1:118 [bk. 2, chap. 34]; Díaz 1963:8; Durán 1967, 2:211–13 [chap. 26].
57. *Crónica mexicana* 1975:307 [chap. 27]; Díaz del Castillo 1908–16, 2:253 [bk. 8, chap. 128]; Durán 1967, 2:167 [chap. 19].
58. *Crónica mexicana* 1975:335 [chap. 33].
59. Bray 1968:187; F. Peterson 1962:155; Thompson 1933:105, 119.
60. Muñoz Camargo 1892:16. The 100-man Tlaxcaltec units may simply reflect a smaller population, so that towns and calpolli were each responsible for fewer men marching under their own leaders, a situation less likely under the more populous Aztecs.
61. Anonymous Conqueror 1963:168; Clavigero 1787, 1:371; *Crónica mexicana* 1975:307 [chap. 27].
62. E.g., F. Peterson 1952:62; Vaillant 1966:218.
63. Bandelier 1880:116, 118.

64. *Crónica mexicana* 1975:419 [chap. 51], 543 [chap. 76], 599 [chap. 88]; Durán 1967, 2:167 [chap. 19].

65. Sahagún 1954:88.

66. For example, Tlaxcallan also possessed four different standards, reflecting its quadripartite division. The ruling town of Ocotelolco's standard was a *quetzaltototl* (resplendant quetzal) over a crag. Quiahuiztlan's standard was an arrangement of quetzal plumes compacted to form a crest or fan, called a *quetzalpatzactli*. Tepeticpac's standard was a fierce wolf on a rock with a bow and arrows held in his paw. And Tizatlan's standard was a white heron (Muñoz Camargo 1892:102, 1981:225v–226r).

67. Clark 1938, 1:57.

68. Aguilar 1963:139; Clark 1938, 1:57.

69. Anonymous Conqueror 1963:168.

70. Díaz del Castillo 1908–16, 1:231 [bk. 4, chap. 63]; 1:265 [bk. 4, chap. 73].

71. Díaz del Castillo 1908–16, 4:117 [bk. 12, chap. 151].

72. Durán 1967, 1:105–12 [chaps. 10–11].

73. Clavigero 1787, 1:368–69, 371–72; Hernández 1946:66 [bk. 1, chap. 20]; Sahagún 1957:26, 91.

74. Hernández 1946:66 [bk. 1, chap. 20].

75. Cervantes de Salazar 1971, 1:137 [bk. 1, chap. 22].

76. Sahagún 1954:51.

77. Durán 1967, 2:313 [chap. 41].

78. Sanders 1970:449; accepted in Sanders, Parsons, and Santley 1979: 162, 184.

79. These estimates are based on Denevan's reconstruction of the population ratios of Sanders and Cook and Borah for this area (Denevan 1976a: 81–82).

80. Calnek 1976:288; 1978:316, accepted by Sanders, Parsons, and Santley 1979:154. Hardoy (1973:154–55) estimates a population for Tenochtitlan of 300,000, based on a recorded 60,000 houses in the city.

81. Zorita 1971:183–84.

82. Bandelier 1880:98; Cook and Simpson 1948:25–26. Dobyns (1983: 175) also follows Cook and Simpson, but estimates the number of warriors at 20 percent of the total population and calculates that military activity involved every able-bodied adult male.

83. There is a lack of consensus about the pre-Columbian population, but the "west" stable population model at Level 3 (Coale and Demeny 1966) is the likeliest approximation. This population model fits sixteenth-century Peru (N. D. Cook 1981), and since this was the closest cultural, genetic, and epidemiological fit with central Mexico, I am using it in my discussion, although the results should be taken advisedly.

84. However, Durán (1967, 2:427 [chap. 56]) mentions a call-up extending to men as young as eighteen.

85. Borah and Cook 1960:71.

86. *Crónica mexicana* 1975:539 [chap. 75]; 551 [chap. 78]; 598 [chap. 88].

87. *Crónica mexicana* 1975:598 [chap. 88].

88. Hernández 1946:97 [bk. 2, chap. 7].

89. Motolinía 1950:215 [bk. 3, chap. 8].

90. Anonymous Conqueror 1963:179. However, Sahagún (1951:169, 178, 179) expressly mentions only three, one at Acatl-Iyacapan, one at Cuauhquiayahuac, and one at Tezcacoac, but indicates the existence of a fourth at Tlacatecco (Sahagún 1954:63), all located within the temple compound at Tenochtitlan.

91. Anonymous Conqueror 1963:179; Casas 1967, 1:270 [bk. 3, chap. 51]; Tapia 1963:42; Torquemada 1975–83, 3:224 [bk. 8, chap. 13].

92. López de Gómara 1965–66, 2:152 [chap. 74]; Hernández 1946:97 [bk. 2, chap. 7].

93. Díaz del Castillo 1908–16, 2:65 [bk. 6, chap. 91].

94. Solís y Rivadeneyra 1753:328 [bk. 3, chap. 14]. In Tetzcoco the royal armory was located in the king's palace adjacent to the hall of justice (*Códice Quinatzin* 1975:*lámina* 12; Ixtlilxóchitl 1975–77, 2:97 [chap. 36]).

95. Anonymous Conqueror 1963:179; López de Gómara 1965–66, 2:160 [chap. 79].

96. Durán 1967, 2:236 [chap. 29].

97. Clavigero 1787, 1:350; Torquemada 1975–83, 4:334 [bk. 14, chap. 7].

98. *Crónica mexicana* 1975:335 [chap. 33].

99. *Crónica mexicana* 1975:335 [chap. 33], 598 [chap. 88]; Durán 1967, 2:156 [chap. 18]. When King Ahuitzotl led a massive army on a campaign to the Gulf coast, Tenochtitlan was virtually depopulated of all but women. After the army's departure, everyone fasted for four days and throughout the campaign, and everyone made sacrifices to Huitzilopochtli by drawing blood from their own tongues, ears, arms, and legs. While the army was gone, the wives rose at midnight, started fires, and swept the streets. Afterward, they bathed, but not their faces or heads, and then prepared corn cakes to present to the gods. They entered the shrines to offer prayers and incense to the gods and then slept, but they arose before dawn to sweep the streets again, which was done also at noon and at sunset (*Crónica mexicana* 1975:539–40 [chap. 75]; Durán 1967, 2:164–65 [chap. 19], 2:359 [chap. 46]).

100. Sahagún 1954:69.

101. Zorita 1971:266–67 [art. 18].

102. *Crónica mexicana* 1975:539 [chap. 75].

103. *Crónica mexicana* 1975:327 [chap. 31].

104. *Crónica mexicana* 1975:538 [chap. 75], 551 [chap. 78].

Chapter 5

1. *Crónica mexicana* 1975:578 [chap. 83], 605 [chap. 90].

2. *Crónica mexicana* 1975:598 [chap. 88].

3. Durán 1967, 2:358 [chap. 46].

4. Acosta 1604, 2:443 [bk. 6, chap. 27]; Clark 1938, 1:92; Durán 1967, 1:50 [chap. 5]; Sahagún 1952:53.

5. *Crónica mexicana* 1975:328 [chap. 31]. An alternative construction of the Nahuatl word for carriers is *tlamemeh* (sing. *tlameme*). This rests on a present tense form, rather than on the preterit, as presented in the body of the text.

6. *Boletín* 1940, 11:16; Borah and Cook 1963:90; Cuevas 1975:52–53; Archivo General de la Nación, Reales Cédulas Duplicadas 3-17-9.

7. Based on rates given by Benedict and Steggerda 1937:182.

8. Hassig 1985:32–34.

9. *Crónica mexicana* 1975:329–30 [chap. 32], 394 [chap. 46]; Durán 1967, 2:111 [chap. 12].

10. *Crónica mexicana* 1975:394 [chap. 46].

11. *Crónica mexicana* 1975:582 [chap. 84].

12. Clavigero 1787, 1:350; Torquemada 1975–83, 4:334 [bk. 14, chap. 7].

13. *Crónica mexicana* 1975:359 [chap. 38].

14. *Crónica mexicana* 1975:609 [chap. 91].

15. *Crónica mexicana* 1975:312 [chap. 28], 546–47 [chap. 77], 552 [chap. 78]. The Aztec army was received and well supplied by many towns—Tollantzinco, Huaxyacac (Oaxaca), Tepeyacac, Itzyocan (Izucar), Chalco, Amaquemecan (Amecameca), Tlapechhuacan, Cocotitlan, and Tecuantepec.

16. *Crónica mexicana* 1975:540–41 [chap. 75]; Durán 1967, 2:158 [chap. 18].

17. Durán 1967, 2:168 [chap. 19].

18. *Crónica mexicana* 1975:331 [chap. 32]; Durán 1967, 2:179 [chap. 21].

19. Engels 1978:18.

20. Díaz del Castillo 1908–16, 4:3, 5 [bk. 10, chap. 137].

21. McNeill 1982:2.

22. For example, when the rebelling Teloloapan surrendered to King Ahuitzotl, its people immediately supplied the Aztec army with intelligence about other rebellious towns in the area, gathered supplies for the journey, and provided guides for the army (*Crónica mexicana* 1975:525–26 [chap. 72]).

23. *Crónica mexicana* 1975:600–601 [chap. 89].

24. Sahagún 1954:51.

25. Hernández 1946:62 [bk. 1, chap. 20].

26. *Crónica mexicana* 1975:294 [chap. 23].

27. *Crónica mexicana* 1975:359 [chap. 38].

28. For example, a forced march was used when the people of Cuetlachtlan and Cempohuallan (Zempoala) rebelled and killed the Aztec emissaries sent to collect their tribute (*Crónica mexicana* 1975:343–45 [chap. 34]).

29. On the campaign against the Pacific coastal towns of Xolotlan, Ayotlan, Mazatlan, and Xoconochco, the army marched from one major town to the next, where it was received, fed, and spent the night. And when the army arrived in Huaxyacac (Oaxaca), it stayed for two days and rested before proceeding (*Crónica mexicana* 1975:552 [chap. 78]).

30. Maurice 1930:212.

31. Engels 1978:20.

32. Neumann 1971.

33. Clausewitz 1943:276–77.

34. Clausewitz 1943:275.

35. Neumann 1971.

36. Clausewitz 1943:275.

37. U.S. Army 1971a:11.

38. U.S. Army 1971a: 16.
39. U.S. Army 1971a: 11.
40. The distance actually ranges from 2 to 5 meters (6.5 to 16.5 feet), but the maximum distance is used to avoid numerous casualties from a modern explosive projectile attack, a factor that need not be considered here (U.S. Army 1971b: C-2).
41. Dupuy and Dupuy 1970: 97.
42. Sekunda 1984: 23.
43. Rees 1971: 21–22.
44. Palerm 1973: 73–74.
45. Bustillos Carrillo 1974: 20, 56, 63, 113.
46. Dupuy and Dupuy 1970: 97.
47. There is some support for a column of twos in the depiction of warriors in the Tenochtitlan ward of Popotlan (depicted in the Mapa de Popotla; Caso 1947 and Glass 1964: 142, plate 94), although it is far from definitive.
48. Cortés 1971: 140–41 [letter 2]; Díaz del Castillo 1908–16, 4: 81 [bk. 11, chap. 145].
49. *Crónica mexicana* 1975: 605–606 [chap. 90]; Sahagún 1957: 93.
50. Cortés 1971: 148 [letter 2], 169 [letter 3]; Díaz del Castillo 1908–16, 4: 3 [bk. 10, chap. 137].
51. *Crónica mexicana* 1975: 539 [chap. 75], 632 [chap. 96]; Hernández 1946: 64 [bk. 1, chap. 20].
52. Sahagún 1954: 51–52, 1957: 70.
53. Scholes and Adams 1957: 60, 92, 128–29, 160, 195–96, 227.
54. *Crónica mexicana* 1975: 605 [chap. 90]; Hernández 1946: 64 [bk. 1, chap. 20].
55. *Crónica mexicana* 1975: 307 [chap. 27], 605 [chap. 90]; Durán 1967, 2: 319 [chap. 41]; Torquemada 1975–83, 1: 259 [bk. 2, chap. 63].
56. Cortés 1971: 145–46 [letter 2]; *Crónica mexicana* 1975: 274 [chap. 16]; Díaz del Castillo 1908–16, 4: 17 [bk. 10, chap. 17].
57. Díaz del Castillo 1908–16, 2: 28 [bk. 5, chap. 86]; Durán 1967, 2: 74 [chap. 8].
58. *Crónica mexicana* 1975: 603 [chap. 89]; Durán 1967, 2: 417 [chap. 55], 2: 436 [chap. 57].
59. Cortés 1971: 168 [letter 2]; *Crónica mexicana* 1975: 522 [chap. 71]; Sahagún 1975: 37.
60. Aguilar 1963: 139.
61. Díaz del Castillo 1908–16, 2: 280 [bk. 9, chap. 132], 4: 32 [bk. 11, chap. 141].
62. Díaz del Castillo 1908–16, 4: 28 [bk. 10, chap. 137].
63. Cortés 1971: 223 [letter 3]; Díaz del Castillo 1908–16, 4: 18 [bk. 10, chap. 139], 4: 28 [bk. 10, chap. 140], 4: 81 [bk. 11, chap. 145].
64. Clausewitz 1943: 279–80.
65. E.g., Torquemada 1975–83, 1: 200 [bk. 2, chap. 38].
66. For example, in the war against Cuextlan, King Ahuitzotl encamped at the outskirts of the enemy city and divided the army into two parts, each responsible for its own camp (*Crónica mexicana* 1975: 481 [chap. 65]).
67. *Crónica mexicana* 1975: 553 [chap. 78].

68. *Crónica mexicana* 1975:331 [chap. 32].
69. *Crónica mexicana* 1975:331 [chap. 32], 401 [chap. 47].
70. *Crónica mexicana* 1975:307 [chap. 27].
71. *Crónica mexicana* 1975:307 [chap. 27].
72. Durán 1967, 2:157–58 [chap. 18].
73. *Crónica mexicana* 1975:307 [chap. 27], 359 [chap. 38].
74. Durán 1967, 2:157 [chap. 18].
75. Hernández 1946:63–64 [bk. 1, chap. 20].
76. *Crónica mexicana* 1975:331 [chap. 32].
77. Caso 1963:869. The evidence is compelling largely in the absence of references to women accompanying the Aztec armies. However, the Tarascan army is recorded as expressly not including women (*Relación de Michoacán* 1977:188–89).
78. Hernández 1946:64 [bk. 1, chap. 20].
79. Durán 1967, 2:186–87 [chap. 22].
80. Torquemada 1975–83, 1:200 [bk. 2, chap. 38].
81. *Códice Ramírez* 1975:129; Durán 1967, 2:186–87 [chap. 22].
82. Díaz del Castillo 1908–16, 4:128 [bk. 12, chap. 151].
83. Clark 1938, 1:95; *Códice Ramírez* 1975:129, Durán 1967, 2:157 [chap. 18], 186–87 [chap. 22].
84. *Crónica mexicana* 1975:307 [chap. 27], 583 [chap. 84], 599 [chap. 88], 619–20 [chap. 93].
85. *Crónica mexicana* 1975:620 [chap. 93].
86. *Crónica mexicana* 1975:606 [chap. 90].
87. Durán 1967, 2:282 [chap. 37].

Chapter 6

1. Turney-High 1949:9–15.
2. Sahagún 1970:37.
3. Durán 1967, 2:39 [chap. 4].
4. Miller 1973:106; Séjourné 1966:49, 276–77, 283.
5. Kampen 1972:162.
6. Cook de Leonard 1971:225.
7. Nuttall 1891a:197.
8. Sahagún 1975:11.
9. E.g., Bushnell 1905; Coggins and Shane 1984:46, 103, 104; Noguera 1945:*lámina* 7–14; 1958:*lámina* 7–14; Pasztory 1983:262.
10. Joyce 1920:plate 17; Noguera 1945; 1958; Nuttall 1891a:182–83.
11. Bushnell 1905; Nuttall 1891a:184.
12. Porcacchi da Castiglione Arretino 1980:23; Sullivan 1972:188–89. For an example from Chichen Itza, see Coggins and Shane 1984:47.
13. *Crónica Mexicana* 1975:377 [chap. 41]; Díaz del Castillo 1908–16, 1:112 [bk. 3, chap. 31]; 1:238 [bk. 4, chap. 65]; 1:285 [bk. 4, chap. 75]; 2:65 [bk. 6, chap. 91]; 4:72 [bk. 11, chap. 145]; Sahagún 1951:124.
14. Linné 1937:63.
15. Sahagún 1951:124.
16. Kubler 1984:83; Nuttall 1891a:186.

17. Díaz del Castillo 1908–16, 1:285 [bk. 4, chap. 78] 1:238 [bk. 4, chap. 65].

18. Durán 1967, 2:121 [chap. 14]. The atlatl was in widespread use throughout the Americas (Mason 1884) and was still being used in central Mexico in the twentieth century (Beyer 1925; Linné 1937:63).

19. Nelson 1899:152–53.

20. Peets 1960:109.

21. Since the darts used by the Aztecs were smaller than the spears used in these tests, their range was doubtlessly greater than the studies indicate (Browne 1940:213).

22. Howard 1974:104.

23. Browne 1940:213.

24. Solís y Rivadeneyra 1753, 1:82 [bk. 1, chap. 19].

25. Clavigero 1787, 1:367.

26. Sahagún 1975:40; Solís y Rivadeneyra 1753, 1:82 [bk. 1, chap. 19]. For examples of central Mexican projectile points, see Tolstoy 1971:276–83.

27. Sahagún 1975:40.

28. Helmut Nickel:personal communication; Yadin 1963, 1:9.

29. However, López de Gómara (1965–66, 1:88) states that each Mayan warrior carried two quivers of arrows.

30. Fernández de Oviedo 1979:113–14.

31. Durán 1967, 2:167 [chap. 19].

32. Sahagún 1954:53.

33. Durán 1967, 2:208 [chap. 25].

34. Sahagún 1951:124–25; 1975:40.

35. Díaz del Castillo 1908–16, 1:231 [bk. 4, chap. 63]; 4:314 [bk. 13, chap. 166].

36. Mendieta 1971:130.

37. Pope 1923:334–40.

38. Pope 1923:368–69.

39. Coles 1979:171; Pope 1923:369.

40. Farfán 1579:124r.

41. Sullivan 1972:188–89.

42. Anonymous Conqueror 1963:19; *Crónica mexicana* 1975:441 [chap. 57]; Díaz del Castillo 1908–16, 2:65 [bk. 5, chap. 91]; Durán 1967, 2:208 [chap. 25]. Depictions of Aztecs with slings are rare. However, a drawing (orignial now lost) of a native Mexican soldier that was published by Gemelli Careri (1976:61) probably derived from the *Codex Ixtlilxochitl* (Glass and Robertson 1975:148). In that picture the warrior is clad in only a maxtlatl and armed with a macuahuitl, sling, and shield. He has also apparently taken a trophy head.

43. Korfman 1973:37.

44. Sherwin-White 1983:304.

45. Korfman 1973:38–40.

46. Díaz del Castillo 1908–16, 1:238 [bk. 4, chap. 63].

47. Aguilar 1963:152; Díaz del Castillo 1908–16, 4:116–17 [bk. 12, chap. 151].

48. Korfman 1973:40.

49. Yadin 1963, 1:10.
50. Carrera Stampa 1949:10.
51. Cortés 1971:133 [letter 2]; Díaz del Castillo 1908–16, 1:285 [bk. 4, chap. 78]; 2:65 [bk. 5, chap. 91].
52. Nickel n.d.
53. Díaz del Castillo 1908–16, 4:308 [bk. 13, chap. 166].
54. Solís y Rivadeneyra 1753, 1:82–83 [bk. 1, chap. 19].
55. González Rul (1971) provides dimensions for the reconstructions in the National Museum of Anthropology in Mexico.
56. Nickel n.d.
57. Nickel n.d.
58. Gay 1972:47; Wicke 1971:18–19.
59. Miller 1973:365.
60. E.g., Graham and Euw 1977:27, 33, 41. For a possible example of a mutilated wooden effigy of a thrusting spear (but which is labeled a macuahuitl), see Coggins and Shane 1984:108. One Mesoamerican codex (*Códice Vaticano* 1964–65:*lámina* 81) has a picture of what may be an additional type of staff weapon. This device is the size of the man wielding it, with the handle taking up two-thirds to three-fourths of the weapon's total length, and the head accounting for the remainder. The rectangular head is blunt on the end, while both sides are lined with stone blades. It is uncertain whether this picture accurately reflects Mesoamerican armament, however. The codex is not an original, but a copy probably made in Italy and certainly by a non-Indian painter. Thus the weapon may be a distortion of either the thrusting spear or the macuahuitl.
61. Díaz del Castillo 1908–16, 2:65 [bk. 6, chap. 91]; 2:251–52 [bk. 8, chap. 128]; 4:29 [bk. 10, chap. 140]. *Itzcuahuitl* is listed as another term for the macuahuitl by Macazaga Ordoño (1983:66) and by Aguilera (*Códice de Huamantla* 1984, 2:26). Although this is a logical possibility, I have found no references to such a weapon in sixteenth-century materials, and it is not listed in the dictionaries of either Molina or Simeon. However, *itzcuauhtli* (obsidian eagle) is listed, and it seems likely that itzcuahuitl is merely a misreading.
62. Follett (1932:387) shows a wedge-shaped blade that may have been from a macuahuitl.
63. Anonymous Conqueror 1963:169; Clavigero 1787, 1:106–107; Martyr d'Anghera 1970, 2:202 [decade 5, bk. 10]; Sullivan 1972:158–59, 172–73. "Turtle dung glue" is mentioned by several sixteenth-century writers, but it is apparently metaphorical and refers to the appearance of the substance, as actual turtle dung was not a Mesoamerican adhesive (Martínez Cortés 1974).
64. Fernández de Oviedo 1979:113.
65. It is possible that the never pictorially represented two-handed macuahuitl actually refers to the thrusting spear, leaving the macuahuitl as the one-handed sword.
66. Acosta 1604, 2:440 [bk. 6, chap. 26]; Aguilar 1963:139; Anonymous Conqueror 1963:169; Díaz del Castillo 1908–16, 1:232 [bk. 4, chap. 63]; Tapia 1963:29.

67. Díaz del Castillo 1908–16, 1:66 [bk. 2, chap. 18]; 1:228 [bk. 4, chap. 62]; Dorantes de Carranza 1970:35. Bartolomé de las Casas (1967, 1:347 [bk. 3, chap. 66]) concurs about the keenness of these swords but says that the blades were easily lost.

68. González Rul (1971) provides dimensions for the reconstructions in the National Museum of Anthropology in Mexico.

69. Nickel n.d.

70. Compare the Real Armería example with Muñoz Camargo 1981: 277v, 279v.

71. Morris, Charlot, and Morris 1931, 2:plates 76, 116.

72. Bonampak 1955. This could be a poor depiction, however; the overall design of the weapon is similar to an axlike club held by a Mayan warrior on stela 3 at Itzimte (Euw 1977:11).

73. Acosta 1604, 2:440 [bk. 6, chap. 26].

74. Clark 1938, 1:21.

75. Seler 1960, 2:594; Sullivan 1972:188–89.

76. Sullivan 1972:188–89.

77. Seler 1960, 2:592. For an example of a morning-star club from the classic Mayan, as well as classic Mayan warrior attire, see Furst 1978:120. See also Corson 1976:184.

78. See examples from western Mexico during the classic period (Baumbach 1969:31, 51, 60).

79. Clark 1938, 1:20; Clavigero 1787, 1:365–66; Nuttall 1891b:34.

80. Anonymous Conqueror 1963:169; Nuttall 1891b:35.

81. Nuttall 1891b:35; Porcacchi da Castiglione Arretino 1980:23.

82. Sullivan 1972:160–61, 174–75.

83. Díaz del Castillo 1908–16, 2:65 [bk. 6, chap. 91].

84. Aguilar 1963:139; Casas 1967, 1:348 [bk. 3, chap. 66].

85. See examples in Pasztory 1983:279, 285.

86. The few examples of square or rectangular shields in pictorial sources, such as the *Códice Tudela* (1980) and the *Codex Magliabechiano* (Boone 1983), may represent artistic variations and, in any case, are carried by executioners.

87. See examples from throughout the Mayan area, especially figurines from Jaina Island, the murals at Chichen Itza, and the murals at present-day Cacaxtla, Tlaxcala. The rectangular shields may have been diagnostic of Maya and Maya-influenced cultures. However, see stela 31 at Tikal, showing a warrior, probably from Teotihuacan, holding a similar shield (Jones and Satterthwaite 1982: figs. 51–52). Alternatively, the style may have been widespread during the classic period.

88. López de Gómara 1965–66, 2:81.

89. Anonymous Conqueror 1963:169; Clark 1938, 1:20; Nuttall 1891b: 34; Seler 1960, 5:665. For an extended discussion of the designs of shields, insignia, and so forth, see Berdan and Anawalt n.d.

90. Carrera Stampa 1949:10.

91. E.g., Sullivan 1972:160–63, 173–79. See the excellent example held by a warrior figurine from classic Veracruz in Sotheby's 1984:lot 135.

92. Miller 1973:109.

93. Euw 1977:11.

94. The existence of a long hanging fringe on shields may explain the widely reported but never pictorally represented roll-up shield mentioned above. For extended descriptions and pictures of Aztec shields, see Nuttall 1891b, Seler 1960, 2:509–619, Sullivan 1972.

95. Sahagún 1959:83–85.

96. Durán 1967, 2:208 [chap. 25].

97. Anonymous Conqueror 1963:169.

98. Nuttall 1891b:47.

99. Díaz del Castillo 1908–16, 1:118 [bk. 2, chap. 34].

100. Bray 1968:189; Hagen 1962:172; Vaillant 1966:219.

101. Landa 1973:52.

102. Landa 1978:16, footnote.

103. Durán 1967, 2:208 [chap. 25].

104. Anawalt 1981:39–46; Seler 1960, 2:546–47, 575–77.

105. Anawalt 1981:11, 55–56.

106. Broda 1978:121–23.

107. Broda 1978:126; Pasztory 1983:278.

108. Acosta 1604, 2:441 [bk. 6, chap. 26]; Durán 1967, 1:115 [chap. 11].

109. Martyr d'Anghera 1970, 2:202 [decade 5, bk. 10].

110. Kampen 1972:162.

111. See *láminas* 79–81 of *Códice Vaticano* 1964–65:178–83.

112. Anawalt 1984.

113. Anawalt 1981:50–52; Sullivan 1972:164–65, 176–77.

114. Anonymous Conqueror 1963:169; Durán 1967, 1:114 [chap. 11].

115. The illustrations in the *Codex Mendoza* depicting the ehuatl with long sleeves is, in fact, a copyist error, as can be seen by comparing it with the earlier *Matrícula de tributos* (1980), on which it is based (Anawalt 1984).

116. Miller 1973:109.

117. Joyce 1920:289.

118. Casas 1967, 1:347 [bk. 3, chap. 66]; Clavigero 1787, 1:365; Torquemada 1975–83, 4:330 [bk. 14, chap. 5].

119. Acosta 1604, 2:441 [bk. 6, chap. 26]; Casas 1967, 1:347–48 [bk. 3, chap. 66]; Díaz del Castillo 1908–16, 2:65 [bk. 6, chap. 91]. Contra Hagen (1962:172) and Vaillant (1966:220), the headgear was not primarily decorative but was a functional, protective piece of the combat uniform.

120. Anonymous Conqueror 1963:169; Durán 1967, 2:91 [chap. 10]. See the example of a late classic warrior from present-day Veracruz wearing a helmet over a garment—presumably of cotton—resembling the arming cap, a padded cap worn under the medieval helmet to distribute its weight and as head protection (Sotheby's 1984:lot 135).

121. Clark 1938, 1:21; Durán 1967, 1:115 [chap. 11]; Martyr d'Anghera 1970, 2:202 [decade 5, bk. 10].

122. Anawalt 1981:24.

123. Clark 1938, 1:21; Martyr d'Anghera 1970, 2:202 [decade 5, bk. 10].

124. Motolinía 1950:206.

125. Sahagún 1963:111.

126. Díaz del Castillo 1908–16, 2:137 [bk. 6, chap. 104].

127. Linné 1939.
128. E.g., *Codex Fejérváry-Mayer* 1971:28, 38; *Codex Vaticanus* 1972:43–48; *Códice Borbonico* 1980; *Códice Borgia* 1980, 3:19; *Códice Laud* 1964–65:359; *Códice Selden* 1964–65:85, 87; *Códice Tudela* 1980: 31–38; *Códice Vaticano* 1964–65:87; Nuttall 1903:37–45; 1975:20, 57.
129. Hefter 1968:6.
130. The Maya are reported to have used axes in combat (Landa 1973:52), but this appears unlikely, for functional reasons.
131. E.g., *Códice Tudela* 1980:31–38; Nuttall 1903:37–45.
132. *Códice Borgia* 1980, 3:12.
133. *Códice Laud* 1964:318–19.
134. Coe 1975:26–27. However, their use as military weapons by the Maya cannot be ruled out completely. For example, see Euw (1977:11) and I. Graham (1979:93, 125).
135. Martyr d'Anghera 1970, 2:202 [decade 5, bk. 10]; Sahagún 1954:53. See the examples in Pasztory 1983:264.

Chapter 7

1. Durán 1967, 2:319 [chap. 41]. Where feasible, frontal assaults might be completely avoided, and undefended targets might be attacked. For example, in the battle of Xilotepec, while the armies of Tetzcoco, Tlacopan, Xochimilco, and Chalco skirmished with the enemy, the Aztecs followed a secret path into the city, where they captured and burned the main temple.
2. Aguilar 1963:140; *Códice Ramírez* 1975:127; Cortés 1971:60 [letter 2]; *Crónica mexicana* 1975:421 [chap. 52].
3. Ixtlilxóchitl 1975–77, 1:329.
4. Cortés 1971:59 [letter 2], 199 [letter 3].
5. Cortés 1971:319 [letter 4]; Ixtlilxóchitl 1975–77, 1:322.
6. Díaz del Castillo 1908–16, 1:284 [bk. 4, chap. 78]; Durán 1967, 2:258 [chap. 33]; Ixtlilxóchitl 1975–77, 2:36 [chap. 14].
7. Cortés 1971:214 [letter 3].
8. Cortés 1971:169, 183, 211 [letter 3]; Díaz del Castillo 1908–16, 4:3 [bk. 10, chap. 137]. For example, smoke signals were used by the Aztecs throughout the Spaniards' battle for Tenochtitlan.
9. Durán 1967, 2:272 [chap. 35]. During a battle with the Spaniards, smoke signals came from Citlaltepetl (the Hill of the Star) near Ixtlapalapan (Ixtapalapa), gathering the canoes to repulse Cortés's fleet, and these signals were answered by smoke from all the cities around the lake (Díaz del Castillo 1908–16, 4:108–109 [bk. 12, chap. 150]). Similarly, signal from the main temple at Tlatelolco called all the warriors to come and give assistance (Díaz del Castillo 1908–16, 4:119 [bk. 12, chap. 151]).
10. Díaz del Castillo 1908–16, 4:294 [bk. 13, chap. 166].
11. For example, the armies of Tenochtitlan, Tetzcoco, and Tlacopan marched by separate routes to converge on Xiuhtepec (Torquemada 1975–83, 1:208 [bk. 2, chap. 42]).
12. *Crónica mexicana* 1975:643–44 [chap. 98]; Torquemada 1975–83, 1:247–48 [bk. 2, chap. 58].

13. For example, in the war on Tepeyacac, the Aztec army gathered near Tepeyacac, and then divided into four parts. One part went to Tecalco, one to Cuauht-Inchan (Cuauhtinchan), one to Acatzinco, and one remained at Tepeyacac. The four armies attacked on signal at dawn and conquered all four cities (*Códice Ramírez* 1975 : 127).

14. *Crónica mexicana* 1975 : 634–35 [chap. 96]. And in the battle for Tenochtitlan, the Spaniards were subjected to coordinated combat assaults by land troops and those in canoes (Díaz del Castillo 1908–16, 4 : 75–76 [bk. 11, chap. 145], 4 : 125 [bk. 12, chap. 151]).

15. Anonymous Conqueror 1963 : 169; Díaz del Castillo 1908–16, 1 : 114 [bk. 2, chap. 32].

16. Casas 1967, 1 : 347 [bk. 3, chap. 67]; *Crónica mexicana* 1975 : 345–46 [chap. 34], 421 [chap. 52], 525–26 [chap. 72], 543 [chap. 76]; Durán 1967, 2 : 81 [chap. 9], 2 : 166 [chap. 19]; Hernández 1946 : 66 [bk. 1, chap. 20]; Mendieta 1971 : 130.

17. Díaz del Castillo 1908–16, 2 : 253 [bk. 8, chap. 128].

18. This line of reasoning has found some acceptance (e.g., Du Solier 1950 : 52; F. Peterson 1952 : 58–59).

19. Hernández 1946 : 66.

20. For example, López de Gómara (1965–66, 2 : 113) states that in Tlaxcallan the standard was carried in the rear during battle, and was brought forward where everyone could see it when the battle was over. But this doubtless referred to the army standards and not to the standards of tactical units: these entered battle with unit leaders. However, López de Gómara's account is second hand and is not a reliable source for such matters. The obvious functions of the standard would seem to demand its use as a signaling device or its abandonment.

21. E.g., Sotheby's 1984:Lot 135.

22. *Códice Vaticano* 1964–65 : 186–87.

23. Clavigero 1787, 1 : 371; *Crónica mexicana* 1975 : 377 [chap. 40]; Mendieta 1971 : 130; Motolinía 1971 : 347 [bk. 2, chap. 13].

24. Motolinía 1971 : 347 [bk. 2, chap. 13]. For example, Díaz del Castillo reported that in one engagement the warriors loosed such a hail of arrows, darts, and stones that more than seventy of the Spaniards were wounded during the first assault (1908–16, 1 : 118 [bk. 2, chap. 34]).

25. Durán 1967, 2 : 120 [chap. 14].

26. The depiction of an unshielded archer leading shielded warriors, each with a macuahuitl, in the *Códice Fernández Leal* (Peñafiel 1895:*lámina* 6), probably reflects the sequence of battle and not an actual charge, as such would be suicidal for the archer.

27. See pictures; Sahagún 1979, 3 : 450r, 461r, 463r, 467r, 468r.

28. E.g. Maudsley 1889–1902, 3:plates 49–51.

29. Kubler (1984 : 83) states that part of the headdress attire of the giant carved warriors at Tollan (Tula) consisted of a quiver of atlatl darts. This an unlikely suggestion. First, the item of costume he identifies as a dart quiver may simply be decorative. Second, I know of no evidence elsewhere in Mesoamerica to support this interpretation, but there are numerous examples of warriors entering battle with bare atlatl darts clutched in the left hand be-

hind the shield. Third, a quiver hanging from the left side of the headband makes retrieving a dart with the left hand very awkward. Fourth, it seems unlikely that a warrior would go into combat with several pounds of darts hanging from one side of his head, thereby seriously imbalancing him. And fifth, these figures are holding atlatl darts in their left hands along with clubs, so also placing them in a headband quiver is unlikely.

30. There are numerous depictions of warriors with a macuahuitl in their right hand and a shield and atlatl darts in their left. See *Códice Telleriano-Remensis* 1964–65:269, 279, 281, 287, 289, 291, 299, 309, 311, 313, 315; *Códice Vaticano* 1964–65:245, 247, 253, 255, 257, 271, 279, 281, 283, 285.

31. Mendieta 1971:130.

32. Muñoz Camargo 1981:258v; Chavero 1979: *lámina* 13, 48; Clark 1938, 2:63v; *Códice de Huamantla* in *Códices de México* 1979:79. In a drawing in room 22 of Las Monjas at Chichen Itza a Mayan warrior is shown carrying an atlatl in the right hand and a shield in the left. This shield is held in place by two straps, one passing over the forearm and the other over the palm, so that the shield rests against the back of the hand. The top of the strap goes across the palm between the thumb and forefinger. This leaves the open hand relatively unencumbered, and the warrior is depicted holding several atlatl darts in that hand. These darts extend horizontally in front and behind the warrior, which would permit the hand to accommodate other items as well (Bolles 1977:205). However, some shields had a single broad strap that enabled the user to wear it on the arm without encumbering the hand, such as those depicted at present-day Cacaxtla, Tlaxcala (Kubler 1980:168, 170), even to the extent that the shield hand could be used to wield other weapons—in this instance, a knife (Barrera Rubio 1980:179).

33. See Nuttall 1975:20.

34. Turney-High 1949:12–15; Díaz del Castillo 1908–16, 1:118 [bk. 2, chap. 34]. Projectile fire alone was sometimes sufficiently effective to drive off the enemy (Chimalpahin 1965:93 [relación 3]), particularly when combined with an advantageous tactical situation. For example, 400 Tlaxcaltec archers were able to hold a bridge against the Aztecs (Cortés 1971:243 [letter 3]).

35. Díaz del Castillo 1908–16, 1:118 [bk. 2, chap. 34]; Muñoz Camargo 1892:17.

36. The warriors at Chichen Itza are depicted holding a curved or gunstock-shaped device that is described as "the curved stick with which darts can be batted out of their deadly course" (Morris, Charlot, and Morris 1931, 1:252). This identification is erroneous. The battle scene (Morris, Charlot, and Morris 1931, 2:plate 139) shows warriors with battle dress, shields, and their "fending sticks" but with no offensive arms in this interpretation (which is very unlikely), while others, also clad for battle, carry these sticks and atlatl darts. This curved device is depicted elsewhere at Chichen Itza (Morris, Charlot, and Morris 1931, 2:passim) in a context that makes its martial use obvious. The device is clearly a club of some sort, probably inlaid with obsidian blades, as evidenced by a sacrifice scene (Morris, Charlot, and Morris 1931, 2:plate 145) and the parallel lines drawn inside

its edges (however, see the questionable example of a fending stick in Coggins and Shane 1984:49). The same device is also depicted in carvings at Tollan, and in the context of atlatl and darts (Diehl 1983:51, 62). Since the atlatl-wielding warriors carried these clubs in the left hand with their darts, and the atlatl in the right hand, and since some warriors have only clubs, it indicates the initial use of the atlatl, followed by use of the club in the subsequent hand-to-hand combat. Corroboration of this point is offered in the *Códice Borgia* (1980, 3:13, 49, 63, 64, 70), where these weapons are also grouped together (and where the curved club is definitely shown to be studded with blades) and by a depiction of Tezcatl-Ihpoca, who is shown wielding an atlatl in his right hand while in his left he holds a shield, darts, *and* a curved bladed club (*Códice Borgia* 1980, 3:17). The *Codex Nuttall* depicts similar scenes of warriors holding shields, darts, and clubs (also shown are an atlatl and bow and arrows) in one hand and a variety of weapons in the other, including the atlatl, thrusting spear, and axe (Nuttall 1975:10, 20, 39, 52, 70, 75, 77). Also, see the mural in the church at Ixmiquilpan of macuahuitl-wielding warriors also wearing arrow quivers (B. Smith 1968:178–79). Depictions of warriors holding a macuahuitl or club and shields and bows are also present in the *Códice Telleriano-Remensis* (1964–65:289) and in the *Códice Vaticano* (1964–65:255). Warriors carrying thrusting spears, shields, and quivers are also depicted in the *Códice Telleriano-Remensis* (1964–65:279) and in the *Códice Vaticano* (1964–65:2450). Although stela 5 at Uaxactun does show one example of an atlatl being used with a club, Tollan offers the first example of the widespread use of clubs in combat. This would necessitate shifting battle tactics from skirmishing with spears to closing for a decisive hand-to-hand battle. It is likely that this was the technological and tactical change that offered the Toltecs an advantage in their conquest of the Maya at Chichen Itza and not simply the use of bows and arrows.

37. Durán 1967, 1:114–15 [chap. 11].

38. Sahagún 1954:88.

39. *Crónica mexicana* 1975:359 [chap. 38]; Durán 1967, 2:166–67 [chap. 19].

40. Acosta 1604, 2:495 [bk. 7, chap. 17]; Cortés 1971:200 [letter 3]; *Crónica mexicana* 1975:359 [chap. 37], 402 [chap. 48], 542 [chap. 76]; Durán 1967, 2:166 [chap. 19].

41. Díaz del Castillo 1908–16, 4:35 [bk. 11, chap. 141].

42. Clavigero 1787, 1:355; Durán 1967, 2:319 [chap. 41]; Sahagún 1954:52.

43. Clavigero 1787, 1:371; Martyr d'Anghera 1970 2:135 [decade 5, bk. 5]. While the foregoing was ideally true, it was not always adhered to in the heat of battle. During the Tepanec war the victorious Aztecs became so excited that their soldiers mixed with the enemy instead of remaining in their units (Durán 1967, 2:81 [chap. 9]), although this appears to have had no adverse effect on the rout of the Azcapotzalcas.

44. Although not directly cited, this analysis owes much to John Keegan's *The Face of Battle.*

45. Mendieta 1971: 130.

46. Aguilar 1963: 140; Díaz del Castillo 1908–16, 1: 232 [bk. 4, chap. 63], 2: 251 [bk. 8, chap. 128]; Tapia 1963: 23; Torquemada 1975–83, 1: 277 [bk. 2, chap. 70].

47. Díaz del Castillo 1908–16, 4: 73 [bk. 11, chap. 145].

48. On one occasion when the Tlaxcaltecs were fighting the Spaniards, an army of 10,000 warriors began firing arrows and atlatl darts at the Spaniards from three sides, while they were quickly charged on the fourth by warriors with macuahuitl (Díaz del Castillo 1908–16, 1: 242 [bk. 4, chap. 66]).

49. Martyr d'Anghera 1970, 2: 202 [decade 5, bk. 10]. For a depiction of killing an enemy warrior with a stone knife see the murals at present-day Cacaxtla, Tlaxcala (Barrera Rubio 1980: 179).

50. Díaz del Castillo 1908–16, 1: 229 [bk. 4, chap. 62].

51. Cortés 1971: 294 [letter 4]; Díaz del Castillo 1908–16, 4: 25 [bk. 10, chap. 140], 4: 44 [bk. 11, chap. 142].

52. Acosta 1604, 2: 484 [bk. 7, chap. 14]; Casas 1967, 1: 350 [bk. 3, chap. 67]; Clavigero 1787, 1: 371; Díaz del Castillo 1908–16, 2: 231 [bk. 8, chap. 126]; Hernández 1946: 67 [bk. 1, chap. 20].

53. Mendieta 1971: 131.

54. Torquemada 1975–83, 1: 236 [bk. 2, chap. 54], 4: 325 [bk. 14, chap. 2].

55. *Códice Ramírez* 1975: 128; Durán 1967, 2: 167 [chap. 19].

56. *Crónica mexicana* 1975: 403–404 [chap. 48].

57. The most famous instance of assassination for military purposes—the Tepanec killing of the Aztec King Chimalpopoca—probably did not occur at all (see Chapter 9) (Durán 1967, 2: 71 [chap. 8]).

58. Acosta 1604, 2: 481 [bk. 7, chap. 13]; Mendieta 1971: 131.

59. *Crónica mexicana* 1975: 422 [chap. 52]; Díaz del Castillo 1908–16, 4: 129 [bk. 12, chap. 151]; Durán 1967, 2: 283 [chap. 37]. Consequently, the number of men held in reserve varied: in the Tepanec war, half were held back (Acosta 1604, 2: 481 [bk. 7, chap. 13]), while in one battle against the Spaniards, the Aztecs sent 2,000 canoes of warriors to attack from one direction, "another" 10,000 warriors by land to attack from a different direction, and 10,000 more warriors held in reserve, yielding a combatant-to-reserve ratio of 2: 1 (Díaz del Castillo 1908–16, 4: 75 [bk. 11, chap. 145]).

60. *Crónica mexicana* 1975: 422 [chap. 52]; Muñoz Camargo 1892: 15; Torquemada 1975–83, 1: 197 [bk. 2, chap. 36].

61. Díaz del Castillo 1908–16, 1: 24 [bk. 1, chap. 4].

62. Díaz del Castillo 1908–16, 2: 230 [bk. 8, chap. 126], 4: 117 [bk. 12, chap. 151], 4: 154 [bk. 12, chap. 153].

63. Martyr d'Anghera 1970, 2: 134 [decade 5, bk. 5].

64. Díaz del Castillo 1908–16, 1: 112 [bk. 2, chap. 31], 1: 119 [bk. 2, chap. 34].

65. Chimalpahin 1965: 93 [relación 3].

66. Cortés 1971: 59 [letter 2].

67. Hernández 1946: 24 [bk. 1, chap. 20].

68. Díaz del Castillo 1908–16, 4: 32 [bk. 11, chap. 141]; Torquemada 1975–83, 1: 207 [bk. 2, chap. 42].

69. *Crónica mexicana* 1975:644 [chap. 98].

70. For example, the Tepanec war lasted three years but involved numerous inconclusive battles and the conquest of many towns before a final victory was certain (Torquemada 1975–83, 1:155 [bk. 2, chap. 19]). The battle for Azcapotzalco lasted 114 days until the Aztecs and their Tetzcoca and Huexotzinca allies defeated the Tepanecs (Ixtlilxóchitl 1975–77, 2:79–80 [chap. 31]). And Ixtlilxochitl defended Tetzcoco from the Tepanecs for 50 days before he was killed and the city fell (Ixtlilxóchitl 1975–77, 2:44–49 [chaps. 17–19]).

71. For example, the Aztecs conquered Xochimilco in eleven days, the Tetzcocas conquered Acolman in three days, and the battle for Mazatlan was over by noon (*Crónica mexicana* 1975:553 [chap. 78]; Ixtlilxóchitl 1975–77, 1:378; Torquemada 1975–83, 1:207 [bk. 2, chap. 42]).

72. Cortés 1971:319 [letter 4].

73. Acosta 1604, 2:484 [bk. 7, chap. 14], 485 [chap. 15], 496 [chap. 18]; *Crónica mexicana* 1975:404 [chap. 48], 526–27 [chap. 72], 608 [chap. 91]; Dibble 1980, 1:91; Durán 1967, 2:429 [chap. 56]; Torquemada 1975–83, 1:198 [bk. 2, chap. 36], 1:208–9 [bk. 2, chap. 42].

74. Durán 1967, 2:128 [chap. 15].

75. Durán 1967, 2:320 [chap. 41].

76. Durán 1967, 2:273 [chap. 35].

77. Durán 1967, 2:439 [chap. 58].

78. *Crónica mexicana* 1975:584 [chap. 84].

79. *Crónica mexicana* 1975:335–37 [chap. 33].

80. *Crónica mexicana* 1975:527 [chap. 72].

81. In the Tepanec war, for example, the Tetzcocas burned all the defeated cities allied with the Tepanecs (Ixtlilxóchitl 1975–77, 2:42 [chap. 16]; Torquemada 1975–83, 1:155 [bk. 2, chap. 19]), and the Aztecs likewise burned Azcapotzalco (Durán 1967, 2:81 [chap. 9]). However, the people of Tzotzollan burned their own city and fled rather than submit to the Aztecs (Durán 1967, 2:437 [chap. 57]). When Ixtlilxochitl defeated the Tepanec puppet regime of his home city of Tetzcoco, he burned the entire town (Ixtlilxóchitl 1975–77, 2:80 [chap. 31]), and the Aztecs set fire to the town of Cuauhquechollan when they discovered the entry of a sizable force of Spaniards (Cortés 1971:151 [letter 2]).

82. Cortés 1971:254 [letter 3].

83. For example, when Cortés encountered the city of Cuauhquechollan with a population of 5,000 to 6,000, it was encircled by a stone and mortar wall 7.3 meters (24 feet) high on the outside and almost level with the ground on the inside, and along the top there were battlements three feet high. Entry was gained through four gateways large enough for a horseman to enter, but each entrance had three or four turns and was protected by a battlement (Cortés 1971:153 [letter 2]).

Quetzaltepec was also encircled by defensive walls, but it had six rather than one. The outermost wall was 5 brazas wide and 3 wide (1 braza = 1.67 meters or 5.49 feet (Carrera Stampa 1949:10)), or about 8.4 meters (27.5 feet) high and 5 meters (16.5 feet) wide, as were the second, third, fourth, and fifth walls, while the sixth and innermost wall was 2 brazas high and 6 brazas wide, or about 3.3 meters (11 feet) high and 10 meters (33 feet) wide (*Crónica mexicana* 1975:606 [chap. 90]).

84. *Crónica mexicana* 1975:310 [chap. 28]; Torquemada 1975–83, 1:309 [bk. 2, chap. 85].

85. Cortés 1971:156 [letter 2].

86. Cortés 1971:132 [letter 2], 181, 199 [letter 3], 4:217 [letter 3]; Díaz del Castillo 1908–16, 2:5 [bk. 5, chap. 83], 2:233 [bk. 8, chap. 126], 2:288 [bk. 9, chap. 134], 4:29 [bk. 10, chap. 140], 4:46 [bk. 11, chap. 142], 4:72 [bk. 11, chap. 145], 4:106 [bk. 12, chap. 150], 4:151 [bk. 12, chap. 152]; Sahagún 1975:59.

87. Anonymous Conqueror 1963:179; Casas 1967, 1:270 [bk. 3, chap. 51]; Cortés 1971:132 [letter 2], 218 [letter 3].

88. Cortés 1971:73 [letter 2].

89. Díaz del Castillo 1908–16, 4:59–62, 63–64 [bk. 11, chap. 144].

90. Torquemada 1975–83, 1:296 [bk. 2, chap. 79].

91. Cortés 1971:211 [letter 3].

92. Torquemada 1975–83, 1:285 [bk. 2, chap. 75].

93. Cortés 1971:245 [letter 3].

94. The number of warriors who emerged from Cuauhquechollan was put at 30,000 (Cortés 1971:151 [letter 2]), which is probably an exaggeration.

95. Suárez de Peralta 1949:11.

96. *Crónica mexicana* 1975:526–27 [chap. 72].

97. *Crónica mexicana* 1975:634–35 [chap. 96].

98. Durán 1967, 2:110–11 [chap. 12].

99. *Crónica mexicana* 1975:606–607 [chap. 90].

100. Aguilar 1963:151.

101. However, Miller (1977:215, and see also Coggins and Shane 1984: 165) notes the existence of structures depicted in mural 1 of the North Group in the Temple of the Jaguars at Chichen Itza that he identifies as siege towers. This is in the Mayan area and is centuries before the Aztecs, and while Miller's interpretation has met with some acceptance (e.g., Kubler 1984:316–18), it is problematic. There are several explanations for this structure. A nonmilitary explanation is that the structure is construction scaffolding, but most Mesoamerican buildings are not tall enough to require it, and although pyramids are, their inward slope reduces the usefulness of a vertical scaffold. There are several military possibilities, however. First, the three depicted towers (of three and four stories) could be used by leaders to oversee the battle and issue directions, but relaying orders from the top of the towers to combatants below over the din of battle seems difficult and unlikely. Second, they could be used to breach fortifications, but this idea meets the same difficulties as the construction theory: Mesoamerican walls are not high enough to require anything more elaborate than ladders to scale them, and pyramids slope inward and cannot be reached from the upper levels of the vertical tower. Moreover, there are no bridges from the towers on which men could cross. The third and likeliest explanation is that the structures were built solely for the purpose of pouring fire on the target pyramid. In the scene depicted, archers and slingers are absent: only atlatls are being

used. Thus, on level ground their range of about 60 meters (200 feet) was probably inadequate for the attacking troops, although it was more than sufficient for the elevated defenders. Without other assistance the attackers would have to climb a pyramid, with as few as a single avenue of attack. The defenders could thus concentrate their forces and use their atlatls effectively, while the attackers would have to limit their forces and ascend through a hail of darts without being able to answer the fire effectively. In that circumstance, the construction of a fire tower would greatly reduce the danger of attacking the pyramid by providing the attackers with an effective, and even superior, vantage point from which to fire on the defenders, suppressing return fire and providing cover for the attackers. This describes the events depicted, but they remain highly unusual, probably as a result of the evolution of tactics. By the late postclassic, assaults integrated archers and slingers in the attacks. The vastly superior range of these weapons completely eliminated the need for fire towers in attacking higher targets, as they were now within range from the ground. There is evidence of other Mayan scaffolding, but it is of uncertain size and appears to be in a sacrificial context (Coe 1975:26–27).

102. Aguilar 1963:152; Cortés 1971:130 [letter 2].

103. Sahagún 1954:53.

Chapter 8

1. Sahagún 1961:38; translation by J. Richard Andrews.

2. Garibay 1973:73; Hernández 1946, 1:64 [bk. 1, chap. 20]; Sahagún 1954:53.

3. Sahagún 1954:54.

4. Casas 1967, 2:400 [bk. 3, chap. 215]; Hernández 1946, 1:66 [bk. 1, chap. 20].

5. Durán 1967, 2:319 [chap. 41].

6. Garibay 1973:73.

7. Sahagún 1954:53.

8. Sahagún 1954:54, 74.

9. Sahagún 1952:53.

10. Sahagún 1951:166.

11. Hernández 1946:66 [bk. 1, chap. 20].

12. Díaz del Castillo 1908–16, 1:112 [bk. 2, chap. 31], 1:119 [bk. 2, chap. 34].

13. Durán 1967, 1:114 [chap. 11].

14. Cortés 1971:245 [letter 3].

15. Ixtlilxóchitl 1975–77, 2:36 [chap. 14].

16. Cortés 1971:153–54 [letter 2].

17. Aguilar 1963:155.

18. Hernández 1946:65–66 [bk. 1, chap. 20].

19. Hernández 1946:65 [bk. 1, chap. 20].

20. Ixtlilxóchitl 1975–77, 2:41 [chap. 16], 2:166 [chap. 65].

21. Torquemada 1975–83, 1:155 [bk. 2, chap. 19]. When the Azcapotzalcas were finally overthrown, all the rebel cities joined in sacking it (Tor-

quemada 1975–83, 1:198 [bk. 2, chap. 36]). Xochimilco was sacked when its inhabitants fled into the mountains after battling for eleven days (Torquemada 1975–83, 1:207 [bk. 2, chap. 42]). Similarly, when the vanquished Chalcas fled their city, it was sacked (Torquemada 1975–83, 1:227 [bk. 2, chap. 50]), as was Huexotzinco under similar circumstances (Torquemada 1975–83, 1:254 [bk. 2, chap. 61]).

22. Durán 1967, 2:112 [chap. 12].

23. Anonymous Conquerer 1963:168; Torquemada 1975–83, 1:199 [bk. 2, chap. 37].

24. Thus, Azcapotzalco submitted to Tetzcoco when it was within a few hours of being destroyed (Ixtlilxóchitl 1975–77, 1:336).

25. In the war with Cuetlachtlan, for example, the Aztecs apparently entered the city and were killing the elderly, women, children, and infants until the town's nobles begged for mercy and pledged to become tributaries (*Crónica mexicana* 1975:331 [chap. 32]). In another instance the civilian populace of Coaixtlahuacan fled, and the Aztecs burned the main temple before the people begged them to stop and promised to become tributaries (*Crónica mexicana* 1975:337 [chap. 33]). Similar sequences of events occurred elsewhere (*Crónica mexicana* 1975:468 [chap. 62], 541 [chap. 75]).

26. Cortés 1971:259 [letter 3].

27. *Relación de Michoacán* 1977:242–45 [chap. 22].

28. Cortés 1971:199 [letter 3].

29. Cortés 1971:246–47 [letter 3].

30. Clavigero 1787, 1:372.

31. Martyr d'Anghera 1970, 2:64 [decade 5, bk. 1].

32. Chimalpahin 1965:102–3 [relación 3].

33. *Crónica mexicana* 1975:614–20 [chaps. 92–93]; Durán 1967, 2:437 [chap. 57].

34. Acosta 1604, 2:481 [bk. 7, chap. 13]; Cortés 1971:196 [letter 3]; López de Gómara 1965–66, 2:257–58.

35. Acosta 1604, 2:346 [bk. 5, chap. 20], 352 [bk. 5, chap. 21]; Casas 1967, 1:346 [bk. 3, chap. 66].

36. Díaz del Castillo 1908–16, 4:192 [bk. 12, chap. 156].

37. Soustelle (1970:210) asserts that "specialists with ropes followed the fighting-men in order to bind those who had been overthrown before they could recover consciousness." However, his statement is based on a French translation of the *Crónica mexicana* (Tezozomoc 1853, 1:257) which states: ". . . ils étaient suivis de gens qui liaient avec des cordes tous ceux qu'ils avaient renversé, et coupaient les blessés en morceaux." The Spanish version (*Crónica mexicana* 1975:403 [chap. 48]) reads: ". . . y los que venian mas atras de los mexicanos, comenzaron á atar, prender y cautivar á los delanteros, haciendo pedazos cabezas, brazos y piernas." Neither version offers full support for Soustelle's contention. The described events occurred during Axayacatl's battle for Matlatzinco and may have been unique to that battle, but a likelier explanation is that having troops bind captives was a general occurrence in Mesoamerican battles but was part of the secondary and relief soldiers' obligations, not a function of specialized troops.

38. *Crónica mexicana* 1975:606 [chap. 90]; Durán 1967, 2:168 [chap. 19].

39. Sahagún 1954:73; Torquemada 1975–83, 1:259 [bk. 2, chap. 63].
40. Durán 1967, 2:115 [chap. 13].
41. Anonymous Conqueror 1963:168.
42. Clark 1938, 2:64r, 65r.
43. Acosta 1604, 2:443 [bk. 6, chap. 27]; Durán 1967, 1:49–50 [chap. 5].
44. In the war with Chalco a nobleman and cousin of the king was captured. But knowing he was of noble blood, the Chalcas, rather than killing him, decided to free him and make him their king. When he heard this, he killed himself rather than be freed while the other Aztec prisoners were being sacrificed (Durán 1967, 2:146–47 [chap. 17]).
45. Acosta 1604, 2:352 [bk. 5, chap. 21]; Casas 1967, 1:347 [bk. 3, chap. 67].
46. Casas 1967, 1:350 [bk. 3, chap. 67]; Hernández 1946:67 [bk. 1, chap. 20]. A possible depiction of a rope carried to take captives is in *Códice Laud* 1964–65:329.
47. Sahagún 1954:53.
48. Durán 1967, 2:359–60 [chap. 46].
49. Stevenson 1897:98.
50. Stevenson 1897:295, 317, 328.
51. Stevenson 1897:252–54.
52. Stevenson 1897:98–101.
53. Díaz del Castillo 1908–16, 1:120 [bk. 2, chap. 34].
54. The following are figures from a variety of campaigns, both successful and unsuccessful: 12,000 Matlatzincas captured at the cost of 1,000 Aztec dead (Ixtlilxóchtil 1975–77, 2:144–45 [chap. 53]); 11,060 Xiquipilcas captured at the cost of 106 Aztec dead (Torquemada 1975–83, 1:251 [bk. 2, chap. 59]); 44,200 captives from Alahuiztlan and Oztoman versus an unspecified number of Aztec dead (*Crónica mexicana* 1975:527 [chap. 72]); 2,800 warriors dead in the war between the Aztecs and Atlixco (Ixtlilxóchtil 1975–77, 2:179 [chap. 71]); 700 warriors captured from Tepeyacac versus 204 Aztec dead (Torquemada 1975–83, 1:228 [bk. 2, chap. 50]); 460 Tlatelolcas dead versus an unspecified Aztec (from Tenochtitlan) loss (Torquemada 1975–83, 1:248 [bk. 2, chap. 58]); 10,000 Aztec and allied dead versus an unspecified Huexotzinca loss (*Crónica mexicana* 1975:624 [chap. 94]); 2,800 Teuctepeca captives, of which the Aztecs took 400 prisoners, Chalco 200, and Coatlalpan, the lowland cities, and Chinampan 200; 1,332 captives from Quetzalapan versus 95 Aztec dead (Torquemada 1975–83, 1:296 [bk. 2, chap. 79]); Coatlalpan 140; Matlatzinco 180; Mexicatzinco, Huitzilopochco, Colhuacan, and Ixtlapalapan 120; Acolhuacan 800 versus unspecified losses by the Aztecs and their allies (*Crónica mexicana* 1975:635–36 [chaps. 96–97]); Tlatelolcas took 100 Tlaxcaltec prisoners and killed 370 versus unspecified losses of their own (*Crónica mexicana* 1975:651 [chap. 99]); 21,900 Aztec and allied dead versus unspecified Tarascan losses (Durán 1967, 2:284–85 [chap. 37]); 40 captives from Metztitlan versus an Aztec loss of 300 (Durán 1967, 2:304 [chap. 40]); and 8,200 Aztec dead versus "many" Chololtec dead and unspecified losses for Tliliuhqui-Tepec (Durán 1967, 2:448 [chap. 59]).
55. Mendieta 1971:131.

56. Díaz del Castillo 1908–16, 1:234 [bk. 4, chap. 63], 1:239 [bk. 4, chap. 65].

57. Sahagún 1954:53; 1975:57.

58. Sahagún 1954:53.

59. *Crónica mexicana* 1975:613 [chap. 92].

60. *Crónica mexicana* 1975:613–14 [chap. 92].

61. *Crónica mexicana* 1975:360 [chap. 38], 544–45 [chap. 76], 620 [chap. 93], 626 [chap. 94].

62. Sahagún 1954:53, 72–73.

63. Durán 1967, 2:170 [chap. 19].

64. *Crónica mexicana* 1975:300–302 [chap. 25].

65. Sahagún 1975:57.

66. Acosta 1604, 2:316 [bk. 5, chap. 8].

67. *Crónica mexicana* 1975:625 [chap. 94], 633 [chap. 96].

68. Sahagún 1957:69–70.

69. Sahagún 1952:47–48; 1969:11–15.

70. Durán 1967, 2:169 [chap. 19].

71. Hernández 1946:65 [bk. 1, chap. 20].

72. For example, from the Matlatzincas, King Axayacatl personally captured two warriors and their wives and children (Torquemada 1975–83, 1:251 [bk. 2, chap. 59]). But the noncombatants would have required little skill to capture and could not have counted for purposes of status enhancement.

73. The typical number of captives in a campaign is unclear, but numerous accounts present specific, though perhaps atypical, numbers. Almost 100,000 captives were taken by King Ahuitzotl in the Huaxyacac area (Ixtlilxóchitl 1975–77, 2:155 [chap. 59]); 16,400 captives were taken from Tecuantepec (Ixtlilxóchitl 1975–77, 2:166 [chap. 65]); 6,000 captives from Cuetlachtlan (Torquemada 1975–83, 1:225 [bk. 2, chap. 49]); more than 700 captive warriors from Tepeyacac (Torquemada 1975–83, 1:228 [bk. 2, chap. 50]); 11,060 captives from Xiquipilco (Torquemada 1975–83, 1:251 [bk. 2, chap. 59]); 1,200 captives from Tlacuilollan (Torquemada 1975–83, 1:267 [bk. 2, chap. 67]); 3,200 captives from Cuauhquechollan (Torquemada 1975–83, 1:290 [bk. 2, chap. 76]); 12,210 captives to be sacrificed from Tlachquiauhco, leaving no one in the town, 200 captives from Yopitzinco, 140 captives from Nopallan, and 1,332 captives from Quetzalapan (Torquemada 1975–83, 1:295–96 [bk. 2, chap. 79]); 2,000 Tzapotecs, 3,000 Tlappanecs, 2,000 Huexotzincas, 3,000 Xiuhcoacas, and 600 more captives, all from the war with Xiuhcoac (Chimalpahin 1965:221 [relación 7]); half the people were killed at Acotepec and the other half taken captive (*Crónica mexicana* 1975:660 [chap. 101]); 3,860 captives from Icpatepec, 140 from Malinaltepec, and 400 from Izquixochitlan (Torquemada 1975–83, 1:293 [bk. 1, chap. 78]); and in the war with Teuctepec and Coatlan, the Aztecs took 160 captives, Acolhuas 180, Tepanecs 200, Chalcas 40, people of the lowland cities 20, Chinampanecs 60, Cuauhtlalpanecs 40, Nauhtecs 20, and Matlatzincas 80, totaling 800 captives (*Crónica mexicana* 1975:625–26 [chap. 94]).

74. *Crónica mexicana* 1975:541 [chap. 75]; Durán 1967, 2:359 [chap. 46].
75. *Crónica mexicana* 1975:583 [chap. 84].
76. Durán 1967, 2:133–37 [chap. 16].
77. Sahagún 1951:46.
78. Acosta 1604, 2:352 [bk. 5, chap. 21]. Although sacrifice was the fate of most war captives, Bosch García (1944:38) states that some were used to ransom captives (based on Torquemada 1975–83, 4:326 [bk. 14, chap. 3]), and González (1979:87) maintains that others became slaves.
79. Acosta 1604, 2:352 [bk. 5, chap. 21].
80. Durán 1967, 1:31 [chap. 3].
81. Motolinía 1971:68 [bk. 1, chap. 21].
82. Sahagún 1970:32.
83. Durán 1967, 2:172 [chap. 20]; Sahagún 1951:3–4.
84. Durán 1967, 1:33 [chap. 3].
85. Sahagún 1957:25–26.
86. Chimalpahin 1965:229 [relación 7]; Durán 1967, 2:453–54 [chap. 60].
87. Sahagún 1957:12.
88. Sahagún 1957:2.
89. Torquemada 1975–83, 1:263 [bk. 2, chap. 66].
90. Durán 1967, 2:439 [chap. 58]; Sahagún 1951:168.
91. Sahagún 1951:179, 169.
92. Sahagún 1951:176.
93. Durán 1967, 1:98–100 [chap. 9], 2:172–73 [chap. 20]; Sahagún 1951:48–59; 1954:84–85. For a possible interpretation of the individual significance of these sacrifices, see Clendinnen 1985.
94. Durán 1967, 2:278–79 [chap. 36]; Sahagún 1951:46–47.
95. Motolinía 1971:74 [bk. 1, chap. 26].
96. In a xochiyaoyotl with Tlaxcallan, for example, the Tlatelolcas killed 370 of the enemy and captured only 100 (*Crónica mexicana* 1975:651 [chap. 99]). In a xochiyaoyotl with Chalco the Aztecs captured 500 warriors (Durán 1967, 2:143 [chap. 16]). In these battles, of course, noncombatants were not taken prisoners.

Chapter 9

1. Rounds 1979:74–75.
2. Rounds 1979:75–76. The actual origin of Acamapichtli is disputed (Davies 1973:55–64; 1980:30) and the various accounts sometimes conflict but they generally agree on his foreign or Aztec-foreign origin (Carrasco 1984a:57).
3. Carrasco 1984b:57–59; Rounds 1979:77.
4. Acosta 1604, 2:468; *Códice Ramírez* 1975:37; Durán 1967, 2:56 [chap. 6]; Torquemada 1975–83, 1:141 [bk. 2, chap. 13].
5. Several major difficulties exist in reconstructing martial events during the reigns of the early Aztec kings in addition to those of textual interpretation. First, the Aztecs were not independent but were tributaries of the

Tepanecs of Azcapotzalco at this time, so the conquests are often more appropriately considered to be those of the Tepanecs.

Second, what constituted a conquest under these conditions is not clear. Did it mean total abdication of sovereignty, merely the joining of battle, or something in between? And who had the right to claim such a victory—everyone engaged in it, so that a multinational force could claim as many victories as it had constituent armies, or only the dominant army? In the Mesoamerican case the former seems to have applied.

Third, there are no extant native sources of the period in question that discuss these conquests. While some accounts remain in indigenous codical format, some in Nahuatl, and still more in Spanish, none predates the Spanish conquest. And even if there once were such records, after they came to power, the Aztecs engaged in book burning and the conscious rewriting of history, so little faith can be placed in such accounts.

Fourth, the records of the preimperial Aztec kings are so inconsistent—some omitting conquests included by others and others placing them in the reign of a different king—that total acceptance of their veracity is impossible, even after textual analysis to reconcile conflicting statements. Often the result has been interpretations of conquests and reconquests rather than of a single conquest or perhaps, at best, a series of struggles in a lengthy campaign. While attempts have been made at reconciliation, they have produced a false precision belied by the textual sources. Consequently, while discussing the reconciliations I feel relatively confident about making, I will treat the preimperial reigns of Acamapichtli, Huitzilihhuitl, and Chimalpopoca largely in a single temporal unit within which the general patterns of Aztec conquests and martial participation can be seen, albeit darkly.

And fifth, there is a problem of chronology. Many different dates are given for the same events. Some of these events may be ambiguous and thus may not actually be in conflict, such as the "conquest" of a town when the war has been fought intermittently over a prolonged period. Others, however, are unambiguous, such as the death of a ruler, yet there is a lack of consistency among the historical sources in dating these events. One difficulty is in the numerous divergent calendrical traditions that operated simultaneously in the same general area (see Davies 1973:193–210).

Another difficulty in assessing the conquests of the preimperial kings (and consequently of the Tepanec Empire) is the ambiguity of the town names. While I have followed the majority view in assigning locations to the conquests named, this practice is not universally accepted (see Davies 1980:242–43). Nevertheless, given the ambiguities involved in the preimperial record, I feel that no reconstruction of the conquests of that period is likely to be definitive, nor is an erroneous one devastating to reconstructions of later conquests.

Recorded dates for specific conquests are not reliable, on the whole. While many sources give such dates (in the Julian system, the Mexican system, or both), they frequently conflict with other dates given for the same event in other sources—in absolute dates, in temporal order, and in time span. Furthermore, the timing of the campaigns introduces some dating difficulties. The usual campaign season followed the harvest in late fall and continued until planting and the rainy season of late spring and early summer, so that a single campaign could easily encompass part of two dated years.

Consequently, while I have used relative sequences of the various sources and attempted to reconcile them where possible, I have used significant events with generally agreed upon dates to place conquests in better sequence. Among these are the Tepanec war, the famine of 1454, the conquest of Tlatelolco, and the Spanish conquest, as well as the succession and death of kings. I have not placed significant reliance on absolute dating as a means of placing isolated conquests into general campaigns. Rather, I have placed primary reliance on the geopolitical logic of the military thrusts themselves.

I have attempted to evaluate the various claims by examining overall strategy and looking at the probable geographical constraints and thrusts of Aztec expansion. Furthermore, while the problem of several sources having borrowed their information from a single parent source may contaminate the quantitative test of authority, I have examined the conquests by kingly reign as reported in the historical sources and have attempted to establish a clustering of attributed conquests and to see whether those that deviated did so systematically. Such would be the case if all conquests were systematically displaced by a king or two, as would happen if a conquest were attributed to the wrong king initially but the same temporal sequencing was retained between all subsequent conquests; thus the sequences of conquests may play a more significant role than the attribution of conquests to specific kings, especially when examined in the context of all the sources. Consequently, a few towns mentioned in some of the early accounts are discounted when they contradict the majority of the sources, when their sequential ordering would place them more satisfactorily elsewhere even when their stated conqueror is ignored, or when there is no compelling reason to accept the validity of the claims and they contradict logical principles.

Unfortunately, the reverse is not always true. There may be towns for which false conquest claims were made, but where these fit into the logic of the conquest pattern, there is no way to weed them out, barring contradictory evidence. Consequently, the delineated conquests are conservative in that they include only those for which a reasonable argument of conquest can be made, but this reconstruction approach accepts at face value recorded conquests that do not otherwise contradict logical principles.

The issue of chronology is complex and unresolvable here. Therefore, in the interests of presenting as coherent and logical a sequence of conquests as possible, I will follow the standard chronology of central Mexico as given by Davies (1973, 1974, 1980).

6. Chimalpahin 1965: 82 [1376, 1 Tecpatl]. The struggle reportedly began at Techichco, near Colhuacan (*Anales de Cuauhtitlan* 1975: 32, 1 Tecpatl), and lasted either nine or twelve years. The primary chronicler, Chimalpahin (1965), does not reflect Aztec orthodoxy but records the events of the Chalco

area. Consequently Chimalpahin avoids the ethnocentrism of Aztec accounts but substitutes a Chalco bias. Thus while he records Chalca events in greater detail than do Aztec accounts, their significance is overemphasized.

7. Chimalpahin 1965:157 [relación 6].

8. Chimalpahin 1965:157 [relación 6].

9. Chimalpahin 1965:82 [relación 3]; 182 [relación 7].

10. The actual conquest of Chalco Atenco is more convincingly placed the reign of Huitzilihhuitl, as attested by numerous sources (*Anales de Cuauhtitlan* 1975:66; Berlin and Barlow 1980:53; Clark 1938, 1:28; Chimalpahin 1965:185; García Icazbalceta 1886–92, 3:251; *Leyenda de los Soles* 1975:128; Mendieta 1971:149; Mengin 1952:444; Paso y Troncoso 1939–42, 10:118). But Chimalpahin clearly records wars during the reigns of Acamapichtli (1965:82 [relación 3]) and Huitzilihhuitl (1965:185 [relación 7]) and, while neglecting to record their initial conquest, two other sources (Berlin and Barlow 1980:53; Mengin 1952:444) list the conquest under Huitzilihhuitl as resulting from rebellion by the Chalcas, implying their earlier subjugation. Consequently the war with Chalco can be assumed to have occurred, but it was a xochiyaoyotl without a conquest victor.

11. The conquests most prominently mentioned are of Xochimilco, Mizquic, Cuitlahuac, and Cuauhnahuac (*Anales de Cuauhtitlan* 1975:34, 66; Barlow 1949b:118; Berlin and Barlow 1980:51–52; Chimalpahin 1965:82; Clark 1938, 1:27; García Icazbalceta 1886–92, 3:250; *Leyenda de los Soles* 1975:128; Mendieta 1971:148; Mengin 1952:442–43; Paso y Troncoso 1939–42, 10:118), although neither the timing nor the sequence of these conquests is without contradictory data in the sources. Most of the sources (*Anales de Cuauhtitlan* 1975:34, 66; Barlow 1949b:118; Mendieta 1971:148; Paso y Troncoso 1939–42, 10:118) and all of those supplying dates for these events (Berlin and Barlow 1980:51–52; Chimalpahin 1965:82, 182; Mengin 1952:442–43) place the conquests in the sequence I have listed. Some sources list them as occurring in the same year (Clark 1938, 1:27, 1383, 8 Acatl), while others spread them out over an extended period (Berlin and Barlow 1980:51–52; Mengin 1952:442–43)—one by as much as fifteen years (García Icazbalceta 1886–92, 3:250). However, none of the sources offering dates for the conquests (however questionable those may be) includes Cuauhnahuac.

The Cuauhnahuac listed as a conquest of Acamapichtli has been identified as present-day Cuernavaca, Morelos, which indisputably bore the Nahuatl name Cuauhnahuac, and that identification has both its supporters (Davies 1973:111; 1980:226–27; Holt 1979:22) and opponents (Kelly and Palerm 1952:282n.2). The proponents of this identification believe that the conquest of the city at present-day Cuernavaca was feasible and accept the sources at face value. The opponents point to alternative sites bearing the in same name but located elsewhere. For example, Kirchhoff, Odena Güemes, and Reyes García (1976:177) place it near Xiquipilco northwest of the basin of Mexico. But Cuauhnahuac is invariably grouped with these southern cities, so that identification is unlikely as the town was conquered in the same campaign as the southern basin of Mexico lake cities.

Other opponents of the Cuernavaca, Morelos identification note a possible alternative in the work of Alonso de Santa Cruz that is consistent with the southern lakes conquests. In his famous map of the basin of Mexico, the label "Cuernavaca" is found on the site of Cuitlahuac, and the accompanying text (Santa Cruz 1920:538) includes "Cornavaca" between Xochimilco and Mizquic, suggesting that a Cuauhnahuac is in the basin.

Several factors support this. First, the repeated references to the four sites together indicate that they are somehow united—probably geographically. Second, at this stage of their expansion, it is unlikely that the Aztecs could have mounted a sufficiently large force or generated adequate logistical support to mount a successful campaign so far beyond the basin, so distant from the main thrust of their own expansion, and in an area that was not controlled by the Tepanecs. Third, even if the Aztecs had attempted to wage a war southward out of the basin, there are only two logical routes by which they could have approached what is now Cuernavaca, and both require a major ascent through mountain passes before descending to the temperate lands of present-day Morelos. The southwestern route has a more difficult ascent and goes through a narrower pass, but it is relatively short and enjoys the advantage of placing the already conquered Xochimilcas at the Aztecs' backs. The southeastern route requires a significantly smaller ascent, but it passes through lands held by the still-hostile Chalcas. And fourth, the logic of such a long and arduous campaign seems specious. The potential gains from conquering what is now called Cuernavaca were small, and the threat to the Aztecs' home city was great during their army's absence, since their homefront was not yet secure. Restricting campaigns to roughly within the basin was a safer course of action, because Tenochtitlan's army would be within recall distance should the city be attacked and there were many potential tributaries within the basin who could provide lucrative tribute goods and whose subjugation simultaneously removed them as threats during later, more distant campaigns when the bulk of the Aztec army was beyond effective recall.

The documentary evidence for the conquest of Cuauhnahuac (present-day Cuernavaca) during the reign of Acamapichtli is strong. But such a campaign lacks sound political, economic, or military logic. Thus I am convinced on the basis of that illogic, on the incongruous inclusion of Cuauhnahuac in a manifestly different group of conquests, and on Torquemada's (1975–83, 1:148–49 [bk. 2, chap. 17]) persuasive and detailed account of Cuauhnahuac's conquest during the reign of the next king, Huitzilihhuitl, that the sources erred in crediting it to Acamapichtli.

12. There is some evidence of a second campaign, into the northern areas of the basin of Mexico (Ixtlilxóchitl 1975–77, 2:33–36 [chaps. 12–14]), that resulted in the conquest of Xaltocan, Cuauhtitlan, and Tepotzotlan and extended as far as Xilotepec. However, the paucity of evidence for these conquests during this reign and the fuller evidence during that of Huitzilihhuitl indicate that they were not conquered at this time. Rather, this too is an apparent temporal confusion with later conquests. An additional town claimed as conquered at this time, Mazahuacan, is unidentified but appar-

ently refers to either a town or the area northwest of Tolocan centered on what is now called the Sierra de Tlalpujahua (standardized form, Tlalpoxahua) and occupied at that time by the ethnic Mazahuas (Durbin 1970:31). While there is no evidence attesting to this conquest during the reign of any of the preimperial Aztec kings, its location adjacent to Xilotepec and testamentary evidence (Ixtlilxóchitl 1975–77, 2:36 [chap. 14]) grouping Mazahuacan with the northern basin conquests (and emphasizing the primary role of the Tepanecs and the auxiliary role of the Aztecs) indicates that this conquest, too, belongs to the reign of Huitzilihhuitl.

13. Berlin and Barlow 1980:51–52, 2 Calli.

14. Cuauhhuacan is also mentioned as a conquest (Berlin and Barlow 1980:51–52, 6 Calli) after the southern lakes campaigns. The location of this site is uncertain but is presumably nearby in the basin of Mexico (see Kelly and Palerm 1952:282n.6).

15. Mengin 1952:442–43. Of the preimperial kings, this is mentioned only for the reign of Acamapichtli and is without contrary attestation elsewhere. Matlatzinco was an area west of the basin of Mexico between Tolocan and Malinalco (Durbin 1970: 23; Zorita 1963:194 [chap. 18]). This conquest is highly improbable as an Aztec venture but is possible if the Aztecs were serving as auxiliaries of the Tepanecs, who did control that area.

16. The recorded conquest of Cuauht-Inchan (*Anales de Cuauhtitlan* 1975:34, 10 Tochtli; Berlin and Barlow 1980:51–52, 3 Tochtli) is a problem. It was both far from the basin of Mexico (substantially farther than present-day Cuernavaca) and in a direction not in the Tepanec area of interest. Such a conquest does not fit into the pattern of campaigns at this time (i.e., limited to the basin) and there is no apparent reason for such a conquest despite the evidence in the historical sources.

One possible explanation of the "conquest" of Cuauht-Inchan lies in the distinction between having conquered a city and having fought people from that city. One source mentions Acamapichtli's conquests in two separate contexts: in one context Cuauht-Inchan is mentioned (*Anales de Cuauhtitlan* 1975:34), but in another (*Anales de Cuauhtitlan* 1975:66), Mizquic, Xochimilco, Cuauhnahuac, and Cuitlahuac are mentioned, yet Cuauht-Inchan is not. However, neither source attesting to its conquest (*Anales de Cuauhtitlan* 1975:34, 66; Berlin and Barlow 1980:51–52) mentions the city of Cuauht-Inchan. Rather, the term used is Cuauht-Inchan-tlaca—the people of Cuauht-Inchan. Given the great tactical and logistic constraints on conquering Cuauht-Inchan at this time, it seems highly unlikely that the Aztecs actually conquered the city, although the possibility still exists that the Aztecs engaged in a battle with the people of Cuauht-Inchan.

This explanation offers a satisfactory solution to this peculiar conquest. Unfortunately, however, the *Historia Tolteca Chichimeca* (Kirchhoff, Odena Güemes, and Reyes García 1976:218) specifically mentions the conquest of the city of Cuauht-Inchan in the year 10 Tochtli by Cuauhtlahtoa, ruler of Tlatelolco, which the editors (1976:218n.1) place during the reign of Acamapichtli. As a result of this battle the ruler's daughter was taken by Cuauhtlahtoa as his wife. There is, however, a problem with this account. This conquest occurs in the year 10 Tochtli, which is 120 years before the arrival of the Spaniards. At that time Cuacuauh was the king, not Cuauhtlahtoa, who was his grandson. Since the *Anales de Tlatelolco* (Berlin and Barlow 1980:52) lists Cuacuauh as the conqueror of Cuauht-Inchan, albeit in 3 Tochtli, and the time—120 years before the arrival of the Spaniards—fits his reign, the *Historia Tolteca Chichimeca* account is apparently correct, except for crediting the wrong participant. But given the physical constraints on the Aztecs, as well as the anomalous geopolitical location of Cuauht-Inchan from the Aztecs' point of view, it is unlikely that a legitimate conquest was involved. Rather, some ritualized combat may have occurred in which the daughter of one king was taken by another king as his wife, thereby establishing an alliance. Consequently, I suggest that while contact was clearly made with Cuauht-Inchan, it may have been a political conquest but was presented in the chronicles as a military one.

17. *Códice Ramírez* 1975:41.

18. Torquemada 1975–83, 1:148 [bk. 2, chap. 17].

19. *Códice Ramírez* 1975:41; Durán 1967, 2:66 [chap. 7]; Torquemada 1975–83, 1:151 [bk. 2, chap. 17].

20. Torquemada 1975–83, 1:146 [bk. 2, chap. 16].

21. Ixtlilxóchitl 1975–77, 1:322. This northern campaign has been attributed to Acamapichtli but actually occurred under Huitzilihhuitl. During this incursion Xaltocan, Xilotepec, and Tepotzotlan were conquered and probably also the nearby centers of Tollan, Cuauhtitlan, and Toltitlan (*Anales de Cuauhtitlan* 1975:66; Clark 1938, 1:28; García Icazbalceta 1886–92, 3:251; *Leyenda de los Soles* 1975:128; Paso y Troncoso 1939–42, 10:118).

However, Davies (1980:242–43) believes that Tollan refers to an *estancia* (a spatially distinct but politically incorporated calpolli of the main town) of Temazcalapan rather than to present-day Tula de Allende and that Xilotepec refers to present-day Jilocingo in the district of present-day Hueypoxtla rather than to present-day Jilotepec de Abasolo. If his interpretation is correct, the result would be a much smaller northern extension than is traditionally accepted.

The conquest of Tequixquiac is attested by only one source during this reign (García Icazbalceta 1886–92, 3:251) and placed in the following reign by many more, but the logic of its location in relation to the other conquered towns and the distance from other conquests in Chimalpopoca's reign argue strongly for its inclusion here. Tepanohuayan cannot be located with certainty, but Kelly and Palerm place it in the northern portion of the basin of Mexico just northeast of Toltitlan (1952:284n.1) and its conquest is also cited in the *Anales de Cuauhtitlan* (1975:36). While these towns are listed largely as undated conquests, they fit within the trajectory of the northern conquest and were easily accessible via treks on relatively level terrain.

22. Ixtlilxóchitl 1975–77, 2:36 [chap. 14].

23. Although clearly recorded as a conquest of Chimalpopoca, Chiapan (present-day Chapa de Mota) was conquered during the preimperial years and more convincingly fits into this time period than into that assigned by the *Anales de Tula* (1979:34). This reassessment of its position is made for two reasons. Geographically, this is the only major conquest into which it

would logically fall, while no other town near Chiapan was conquered during Chimalpopoca's reign. And temporally, this is the first conquest of any Aztec king listed by that source, albeit for Chimalpopoca. Thus it is probably an example of having amalgamated the early conquests into a coherent whole, but a whole that fails to pay proper attention to the regal temporal divisions. It is also during this campaign that the conquest of Mazahuacan properly belongs and not to that of the previous king, Acamapichtli.

Veytia (1944, 1:352–53) adds another conquered town—Chiucnauhtlan—seized during the march toward Xaltocan. However, his data seem to derive from Ixtlilxochitl, and he amplifies them considerably, interpreting as a conquest what Ixtlilxochitl may have intended to be a town passed in transit. Moreover, I have tried to rely on chroniclers and sources from the sixteenth and early seventeenth centuries, since later works derive from these and either embroider the facts or distort them by presenting them as a seamless whole. Consequently, I have not included either Clavigero's or Veytia's conquests here or throughout.

24. Cuauhximalpan, in the western portion of the basin of Mexico (García Icazbalceta 1886–92, 3:251), is solely attested during Huitzilihhuitl's reign and fits within a directly westward expansion. This expansion apparently took place after the northern campaign but does not appear to have been a significant effort. To the west of Cuauhximalpan lies Matlatzinco, which was already dominated by the Tepanecs and their Aztec auxiliaries, so taking Cuauhximalpan may have been merely a matter of securing questionable towns en route to the valley of Tolocan.

25. Ixtlilxóchitl 1975–77, 2:36 [chap. 14].

26. After the northern and western campaigns some attention seems to have been paid to the southern lake region. Berlin and Barlow (1980:15) are unique in placing the conquests of Xochimilco and Cuauht-Inchan in Huitzilihhuitl's reign and are joined only by Chimalpahin (1965:184 [relación 7]) in crediting him with Mizquic and Cuitlahuac. These alleged conquests clearly belong in the earlier reign, where the majority of sources place them, and their presence here is the result of erroneous repetition. The conquest of Cuauhnahuac, often listed as a conquest of Acamapichtli's, fits more convincingly into the reign of Huitzilihhuitl and is attested by Berlin and Barlow (1980:53), by Alvarado Tezozomoc (1975b:95), and especially by Torquemada (1975–83, 1:148–49 [bk. 2, chap. 17]).

As argued above, the illogic of undertaking a military conquest of what is now Cuernavaca, Morelos, is strong. Thus I do not accept the conquest of "Cuauhnahuac" (meaning present-day Cuernavaca) by the Aztecs. However, the strength of the written records is also compelling, and I accept their intended application to Cuernavaca, but I believe that the events recorded do not reflect normal conquest. The same limitations listed for Cuauhnahuac as present-day Cuernavaca during the reign of Acamapichtli apply here. It is unlikely that an actual military campaign could have been launched so far afield, and Huitzilihhuitl reportedly secured the daughter of Tezcacoatl, king of Cuauhnahuac, as his wife (Torquemada 1975–83, 1:148 [bk. 2, chap. 17]). However, accepting a wife from Tezcacoatl may have been construed in the retelling as a conquest. Consequently, I feel that present-day Cuernavaca was the town indicated in the records, but not as a military conquest.

27. Both of these towns are cited in the *Historia de los Mexicanos por sus pinturas* (García Icazbalceta 1886–92, 3:251), and the latter is also attested by Chimalpahin (1965:83 [relación 3]). Both towns were conquered as part of the struggle with Chalco which was subdued the following year. Chimalpahin (1965:185 [relación 7]) refers to the revolt of the Chalcas, but the nature of the political relationship between the Chalcas and the Aztecs up to this time is not entirely clear.

28. Ixtlilxóchitl 1975–77, 1:327–28.

29. Ixtlilxóchitl 1975–77, 2:40 [chap. 15].

30. *Anales de Cuauhtitlan* 1975:66; Clark 1938, 1:28; García Icazbalceta 1886–92, 3:251; Ixtlilxóchitl 1975–77, I:322, 2:40 [chap. 15]; *Leyenda de los Soles* 1975:128; Paso y Troncoso 1939–42, 10:118. Although rather distant from the other conquests, Tollantzinco, in present-day Hidalgo, is also listed by the same sources, indicating that it was part of this campaign. This city was far from Tenochtitlan and thus may have been subject to the same limitations as Cuauhnahuac and Cuauht-Inchan. However, Tollantzinco was conquered during a wider conflict that placed many intervening towns in Aztec hands that could have provided logistical support en route and secured their line of march, and the entire route of march was through gentle terrain. Tetzcoco, the most significant target of this campaign, was not conquered until after the death of Huitzilihhuitl (Davies 1974:53).

31. These included Azcapotzalco, Tlatelolco, Tenochtitlan, Colhuacan, Tlacopan, Xochimilco, Cuitlahuac, Mizquic, Ixtlapalapan, Mexicatzinco, Huitzilopochco, and Coyohuacan (Coyoacan), but not Chalco.

32. Ixtlilxóchitl 1975–77, 1:329–30.

33. Ixtlilxóchitl 1975–77, 1:330.

34. A few additional towns listed as conquests appear anomalous. Colhuacan is mentioned by Sahagún (1954:1), but since he lists no previous conquests for any Aztec king, and since Colhuacan was the previous patron city of Tenochtitlan, this may be a reference to their severance of that tie. However, the *Anales de Tlatelolco* (Berlin and Barlow 1980:53) mentions the sacrifice of Aztecs to the sun occurring in Colhuacan in the year 10 Tochtli. So while outright conquest of Colhuacan is not borne out by the documentation, some serious disruption of ties may have occurred.

Azcapotzalco is also mentioned (*Anales de Cuauhtitlan* 1975:66; Mengin 1952:444), but this is unquestionably erroneous. A last conquest is that of Ahuilizapan (present-day Orizaba, Veracruz) (Berlin and Barlow 1980:54; Mengin 1952:444). But the distance of this town from Tenochtitlan renders its conquest at this time extremely unlikely, vastly more so than the logistical and military constraints that barred actual military conquest of either Cuauht-Inchan or Cuauhnahuac. However, Davies (1973:146–47), half-heartedly suggests that perhaps this was executed by Aztec merchants.

35. *Códice Ramírez* 1975:42.

36. Chimalpopoca is recorded as having conquered several towns in the northern basin—Toltitlan, Cuauhtitlan, Otompan, and Tollantzinco, by the

Anales de Tlatelolco (Berlin and Barlow 1980:16), with the conquest of Cuauhtitlan further supported by the *Codex Mexicanus* (Mengin 1952: 444). However, both of these sources fail to note the conquests of these same locations during the reign of Huitzilihhuitl, as indicated by most of the sources. Thus, this listing probably represents a simple temporal misplacement of the same conquests and not actual reconquests at all.

37. García Icazbalceta 1886–92, 3:251; Ixtlilxóchitl 1975–77, 2:53; Torquemada 1975–83, 1:155 [bk. 2, chap. 19]. Tequixquiac is also widely attested as having been conquered during this reign (Barlow 1949b:121; Clark 1938, 1:29; *Leyenda de los Soles* 1975:128; Mendieta 1971:149). However, given the temporal confusion between his and the preceding reign, the logical fit it has with the earlier northern campaign, and its distance from any current conquests, there is a strong argument for placing it within the reign of Huitzilihhuitl, which is even more clearly the case with Cuauhtitlan.

For their aid in the Acolhua war, King Tetzotzomoc of Azcapotzalco gave the Aztecs the sites of Teopancalco, Atenchicalcan, and Tecpan (*Anales de Cuauhtitlan* 1975:37), identified as being near Cuitlahuac (Kelly and Palerm 1952:286n.1). Since these rewards were bestowed for having taken part in a campaign that began in the reign of Huitzilihhuitl (Torquemada 1975–83, 1:155 [bk. 2, chap. 19]), many of the conquests that occurred before the succession of Chimalpopoca but within the campaign ending in his reign, appear to have been restatements on the occasion of a new king's succession (García Icazbalceta 1886–92, 3:251), giving rise to a certain amount of confusion over credit.

38. Ixtlilxóchitl 1975–77, 1:322.

39. Torquemada 1975–83, 1:154 [bk. 2, chap. 19].

40. Ixtlilxóchitl 1975–77, 1:332–41.

41. Torquemada 1975–83, 1:155 [bk. 2, chap. 19].

42. Ixtlilxóchitl 1975–77, 1:332–41. Veytia (1944, 1:403) states that the siege lasted only four months (of 20 days each, totaling 80 days).

43. Ixtlilxóchitl 1975–77, 2:43–49 [chaps. 17–19].

44. Ixtlilxóchitl 1975–77, 1:332–41; 2:43–49 [chaps. 17–19]; Torquemada 1975–83, 1:156 [bk. 2, chap. 19].

45. Chimalpahin 1965:189 [relación 7].

46. Chimalpahin 1965:189 [relación 7]; Ixtlilxóchitl 1975–77, 2:53–55 [chaps. 21–22].

47. Ixtlilxóchitl 1975–77, 1:346–47.

48. Chimalpahin 1965:190 [relación 7].

49. Barlow 1949b:121; Clark 1938, 1:29; *Leyenda de los Soles* 1975:128; Mendieta 1971:149; Mengin 1952:444, 446.

50. Chimalpahin 1965:89 [relación 3]; 189 [relación 7].

51. Acosta 1604, 2:473–74; Durán 1967, 2:71 [chap. 8].

52. Durán 1967, 2:72 [chap. 8].

53. *Anales México-Azcapotzalco* 1903:49.

54. There are also a number of anomalous "conquests" of this period. First, Ahuilizapan is listed (Berlin and Barlow 1980:16) but probably belongs to the reign of Huitzilihhuitl. Second, Xaltocan is also listed as a conquest but Torquemada (1975–83, 1:153 [bk. 2, chap. 18]) failed to list this conquest

during the previous reign where it is overwhelmingly attested, so this is another instance of temporal misplacement with the conquest belonging to the previous king. Third, the conquest of Chiapan is listed for Chimalpopoca and for no prior king (*Anales de Tula* 1979:34), but given the town's location in the northwestern basin far removed from his other conquests, this seems unlikely. Rather, it appears to fit more easily into Huitzilihhuitl's campaign into that section of the basin, an interpretation buttressed by the fact that this is the first conquest listed for any of the Aztec kings by this source. Thus, I believe that another instance of temporal misplacement has occurred.

55. Alvarado Tezozomoc 1975b:104; Chimalpahin 1965:190 [relación 7]; Durán 1967, 2:71–72 [chap. 8]; García Icazbalceta 1886–92, 3:298; Herrera 1934–57, 6:207 [decade 3, bk. 2, chap. 12]; Torquemada 1975–83, 1:167–77 [bk. 1, chaps. 25–28]; Vázquez de Espinosa 1942:142 [bk. 3, chap. 12].

56. Davies 1974:61; 1980:306–309.

57. *Anales México-Azcapotzalco* 1903:50. However, this source is an earlier part of Chimalpahin's work (Gibson and Glass 1975:372) which is generally hostile to the Aztecs and may not be as accurate for the western area of the basin of Mexico as its name implies.

By some accounts (e.g., Alvarado Tezozomoc 1975b:104), Xihuitl-Temoc ("He-descends-like-a-comet"), a son of Chimalpopoca, ruled Tenochtitlan for sixty days. If true, Tenochtitlan would doubtless have been governed by a regent in his stead, but that Xihuitl-Temoc ruled at all is not generally accepted and I have omitted him. See also Carrasco 1984b:60.

Chapter 10

1. Itzcoatl, Chimalpopoca's successor, became the first Aztec king to whom independent conquests can be assigned. This does not mean that the Aztecs pursued their wars unassisted, since they did have help from other city-states—notably from their two partners in the Triple Alliance, Tetzcoco and Tlacopan—but rather that they played a major, if not exclusive, role in determining the thrust of those conquests.

The conquests of the imperial kings are recorded by many historical sources, but there are inconsistencies in both the sequence and number of conquests. Moreover, none of the conquest histories or enumerations of a given king's victories is comprehensive. One major distinction in the sources affecting their consequent assessment is between chronological recountings and conquest enumerations. Many of the conquests included in the conquest lists are not mentioned in the chronicles. The reverse is also true, although this is less often the case. Many towns were conquered during the various campaigns, and it is not unexpected that the different accounts would mention some and overlook others. Moreover, these accounts were recorded by people from different towns and they reflect their respective interests and foci. In Chimalpahin's account of the Chalca region, for instance, minor local towns take on a major emphasis unreflected in any other chronicle.

While variation in recorded conquests is expected, it does cause some problems in assessing them. For instance, are two towns with different names actually the same town when they occupy the same position in different conquest lists that are otherwise quite similar? Are all listed towns to be included in a maximal list of conquests, or must some selection process choose between them?

But these variations also offer some assistance in interpreting the conquests and assessing their significance. The more significant events (the overthrow of the Tepanec Empire in 1427 or the conquest of Tlatelolco in 1473, for example) are almost unanimously mentioned. This bears not only on their authenticity but also on their significance, at least to the recorders, and thus provides some indication of the relative importance of these conquests.

Towns included in the lists (as opposed to the chronological accounts) are recorded as conquests. Since the sources draw a distinction between the conquests of a particular king and the extent of his empire, actual conquest and not mere dominance is reflected in these lists. While it is tempting to interpret the lists as possibly reflecting something other than conquest, pictographic examples such as the *Codex Mendoza* use a conquest glyph (a destroyed and burning temple) for each conquered town listed. Nevertheless, many towns listed (and depicted in glyphs) are of notably less significance than others, judging by the references (or lack thereof) to them in other accounts. This variation in significance springs not from a difference between conquest and voluntary submission but from the considerable variation in what is regarded as a conquest by the Aztecs.

Conquest involved the army, but the actual destruction of the opposing army and its home city was not a necessary element. Conquest spanned a considerable spectrum from simply appearing before the target city and demanding its surrender to actually engaging in combat, destroying its army, razing the town, and massacring its populace. At any intermediate point surrender was usually possible. This, then, raises the prospect of campaigns and conquests of varying significance—at least in terms of their effort if not in terms of their strategic importance.

The chronicled campaigns tend to be those in which the army fought major battles or carried out particularly savage reprisals. Conquests in which the target cities submitted easily were important and were clearly credited as conquests to specific kings, but they were merely listed and not chronicled. Thus, in assessing the campaigns undertaken by the various kings, the way they are recorded makes it possible to rank their importance.

Accounts that only enumerate conquests make no claims for temporal sequence, but they may nevertheless have a chronological component. Sometimes, chroniclers apparently listed towns in the order they were conquered, much as I would list the countries I visited in the order I did so. Consequently, these data are occasionally used to assess the chronicled sequences, particularly when trying to place conquests not recorded in the chronicled sequences in their proper sequence.

2. Carrasco 1984b:59–61; Rounds 1979.

3. For a consideration of succession systems and their limitations, see Burling (1974).

4. Torquemada 1975–83, 1:148 [bk. 2, chap. 17]; 1:186 [bk. 2, chap. 32].
5. Ixtlilxóchitl 1975–77, 2:71–75 [chaps. 27–28].
6. Ixtlilxóchitl 1975–77, 2:77 [chap. 30].
7. Torquemada 1975–83, 1:188–90 [bk. 2, chap. 33].
8. Durán 1967, 2:74 [chap. 8].
9. Acosta 1604, 2:477–80; Durán 1967, 2:78 [chap. 9].
10. Chimalpahin 1965:93 [relación 3]; Ixtlilxóchtitl 1975–77, 2:80 [chap. 31].
11. Torquemada 1975–83, 1:201 [bk. 2, chap. 39].
12. Acosta 1604, 2:482 [bk. 7, chap. 13]; Alvarado Tezozomoc 1975b:108; *Anales de Cuauhtitlan* 1975:66; Barlow 1949b:121; Berlin and Barlow 1980:16; Chimalpahin 1965: 90. 93 [relación 3], 192 [relación 7]; Clark 1938, 1:30; *Códice Ramírez* 1975:51; *Códice Telleriano-Remensis* 1964–65:268; *Crónica mexicana* 1975:249 [chap. 91]; Dibble 1981:10; Durán 1967, 2:80–81 [chap. 9]; Paso y Troncoso 1939–42, 10:118; García Icazbalceta 1886–92, 3:252; Herrera 1934–57, 6:210 [decade 3, chap. 13]; Ixtlilxóchitl 1975–77, 2:79–80 [chap. 31]; *Leyenda de los Soles* 1975:128; Mendieta 1971:150; Mengin 1952:446; Sahagún 1954:1; Torquemada 1975–83, 1:198 [bk. 2, chap. 36].
13. Torquemada 1975–83, 1:190 [bk. 2, chap. 34], 1:198 [bk. 2, chap. 36]. The battle for Azcapotzalco is usually recorded as occurring in 1428 (Berlin and Barlow 1980:55; Chimalpahin 1965:93 [relación 3]; Dibble 1981:10), but other dates are also recorded: 1429 (Chimalpahin 1965:192 [relación 7]) and 3 Tochtli, which would be 1430 (*Anales de Cuauhtitlan* 1975:48).
14. Acosta 1604, 2:481 [bk. 7, chap. 13]; Torquemada 1975–83, 1:198 [bk. 2, chap. 36].
15. Torquemada 1975–83, 1:198–99 [bk. 2, chaps. 36–37].
16. Chimalpahin 1965:192 [relación 7]; *Códice Ramírez* 1975:51–52; Durán 1967, 2:82–83 [chap. 9].
17. *Crónica mexicana* 1975:256 [chap. 11]; Durán 1967, 2:86–87 [chap. 10].
18. Acosta 1604, 2:483–84 [bk. 7, chap. 14]; *Códice Ramírez* 1975:56; *Crónica mexicana* 1975:258–60 [chap. 12]; Durán 1967, 2:85–96 [chap. 10].
19. Berlin and Barlow 1980:55; Chimalpahin 1965:92 [relación 7]; Torquemada 1975–83, 1:203 [bk. 2, chap. 40].
20. The specific sequence of subsequent conquests varies in the historical sources, but the evidence indicates a planned and coherent campaign involving the subjection of Tepanec cities to consolidate the power of the Triple Alliance (*Anales de Cuauhtitlan* 1975:48; Chimalpahin 1965:193; Ixtlilxóchitl 1975–77, 2:80 [chap. 31]; Torquemada 1975–83, 1:202–203 [bk. 2, chaps. 39–40]). Ixtlilxochitl goes further and claims additional towns for this campaign—Tenanyocan, Tepanohuayan, Toltitlan, Cuauhtitlan, and Xaltocan—but these appear to belong to the later expansion into the north. Other sources listing conquests but no sequences indicate the conquest of Atlacuihuayan, Teocalhueyacan, and Mixcoac (Barlow 1949b:121; Clark 1938, 1:30; *Leyenda de los Soles* 1975:128; Mendieta 1971:150; Mengin 1952:449; Paso y Troncoso 1939–42, 10:118).
21. Rounds 1979:81.

22. Rounds 1979:79–80.

23. *Crónica mexicana* 1975:243 [chap. 7].

24. Acosta 1604, 2:480–81; Durán 1967, 2:75–77 [chap. 9].

25. *Códice Ramírez* 1975:57–58; *Crónica mexicana* 1975:268–69 [chap. 15]; Durán 1967, 2:99 [chap. 11], 2:103 [chap. 11].

26. Durán 1967, 2:103–104 [chap. 11].

27. This is in contrast to the situation elsewhere in central Mexico, where any of the alliance members could break away and find other allies to the lee of the alliance core.

28. Chimalpahin 1965:95 [relación 3], 192 [relación 7]. This probably occurred after the Tepanec war and the conquests in the west of the basin, but this sequence is uncertain (it is recorded as taking place in 1431). In any case the reason for this war is unclear, as is its outcome. And despite being listed as a conquest of Itzcoatl in other sources (Clark 1938, 1:30; García Icazbalceta 1886–92, 3:252; *Leyenda de los Soles* 1975:128), Tlatelolco's apparent freedom from strictures as well as its later definitive conquest by King Axayacatl argue against full acceptance of this as a conquest, although some conflict did no doubt occur.

29. Berlin and Barlow 1980:84; Chimalpahin 1965:190–91 [relación 7].

30. Torquemada 1975–83, 1:200 [bk. 2, chap. 38].

31. *Anales de Cuauhtitlan* 1975:47; Durán 1967, 2:122 [chap. 14]; Paso y Troncoso 1905–48, 6:212, 221, 229, 234; Torquemada 1975–83, 1:200 [bk. 2, chap. 38].

32. Torquemada 1975–83, 1:207 [bk. 2, chap. 42].

33. Durán 1967, 2:105–106 [chap. 12].

34. Durán 1967, 2:109–10 [chap. 12].

35. Barlow 1949b:121; Clark 1938, 1:30; *Crónica mexicana* 1975:249 [chap. 9], 274 [chap. 16], 280 [chap. 18]; Paso y Troncoso 1939–42, 10:118; Herrera 1934–57, 6:210 [chap. 13]; *Leyenda de los Soles* 1975:128; Sahagún 1954:1. Some sources indicate a series of separate and relatively unrelated wars in the southern basin, at least insofar as stated causes are concerned (Acosta 1604, 2:486 [bk. 7, chap. 15]; Chimalpahin 1965:95–96 [relación 3], 192 [relación 7]; *Códice Ramírez* 1975:58, 61; Durán 1967, 2:111–12 [chap. 12], 122 [chap. 14]; Ixtlilxóchitl 1975–77, 2:80 [chap. 31]; Torquemada 1975–83, 1:207 [bk. 2, chap. 42]).

36. Durán 1967, 2:110–11 [chap. 12].

37. Acosta 1604, 2:485–86; *Crónica mexicana* 1975:273–77 [chaps. 16–17]; Torquemada 1975–83, 1:207 [bk. 2, chap. 42].

38. Durán 1967, 2:112 [chap. 12].

39. Chimalpahin 1965:96 [relación 3], 192 [relación 7]. One source (Chimalpahin 1965:96 [relación 3]) lists Cuauhquechollan as then having been conquered, but that appears extremely unlikely, for several reasons. First, it would have required a considerable ascent through the pass in the southeastern part of the basin, which was dominated by the hostile Chalcas. Second, it would have entailed a further journey of some length through potentially hostile areas. Third, there seems to have been little military, political, or economic advantage in so doing. And fourth, there were no other nearby conquests.

40. Acosta 1604, 2:486 [bk. 7, chap. 15]; *Códice Ramírez* 1975:61.

41. *Crónica mexicana* 1975:278–80 [chap. 18]; Durán 1967, 2:117–18, 122 [chap. 14].

42. *Crónica mexicana* 1975:278–80 [chap. 18]; Durán 1967, 2:119 [chap. 14].

43. Acosta 1604, 2:486–87 [bk. 7, chap. 15]; *Códice Ramírez* 1975:60; Durán 1967, 2:119–21 [chap. 14]. The battle allegedly took place the year following the conquest of Mizquic and lasted seven days (Torquemada 1975–83, 1:207 [bk. 2, chap. 42]). These conquests were apparently fought in late autumn because of the roles played by the lake. At this time the lakes in the basin of Mexico still lacked extensive hydraulic works, so the combination of seasonal rain and a high evaporation rate meant that the lakes underwent enormous fluctuations in water level, with the nadir in late spring (Hassig 1985:137–39). Thus the effective employment of a canoe assault was most feasible during the autumn, with declining possibilities through winter and into spring.

44. Acosta 1604, 2:487; *Códice Ramírez* 1975:61–62; Durán 1967, 2:125–31 [chap. 15].

45. Chimalpahin 1965:96 [relación 3]; Durán 1967, 2:125–31 [chap. 15]. As a minority dissent from this interpretation, Ixtlilxochitl (1975–77, 2:87 [chap. 34]), a chronicler and embellisher of Tetzcoco's history, records that the Tetzcocas fought a real war with the Aztecs at Tepeyacac for seven days but that the Tetzcocas lost and made peace with the Aztecs.

46. Although the data are muddled regarding the precise sequence of events, some sources place the conquest of Tetzcoco before the conquests in the southern basin (Chimalpahin 1965:192 [relación 7]; Ixtlilxóchitl 1975–77, 2:80 [chap. 31]). But they probably confuse this "conquest" with the reconquest of the Acolhua domains, and most historical sources put the submission of Tetzcoco later (*Anales de Cuauhtitlan* 1975:66; *Códice Ramírez* 1975:61; *Crónica mexicana* 1975:249 [chap. 9]; *Leyenda de los Soles* 1975:128; Paso y Troncoso 1939–42, 10:118).

47. One source indicates that the Aztecs won the war and conquered Chalco but that it rebelled immediately (Ixtlilxóchitl 1975–77, 2:107 [chap. 39]). But it is clear that the war continued intermittently for decades, with victories and defeats on all sides.

48. Carrasco 1984a.

49. *Anales de Cuauhtitlan* 1975:50, 66; Dibble 1981:14; Ixtlilxóchitl 1975–77, 2:80 [chap. 31]; Torquemada 1975–83, 1:209 [bk. 2, chap. 42].

50. *Crónica mexicana* 1975:250 [chap. 9]. With the exception of Chiapan, all of the latter towns are located to the west of the mountains ringing the basin of Mexico, while the former towns all lie to the east, which could easily define a logical campaign area. However, none of these towns is listed as a conquest of the subsequent king, Moteuczomah Ilhuicamina, although they are included in lists of the towns within his empire (Durán 1967, 2:205 [chap. 25]). Thus the slight evidence of their prior conquest by Itzcoatl's reign must be accepted. The fact that these towns formed part of Moteuczomah Ilhuicamina's empire (Durán 1967, 2:205 [chap. 25]), plus some additional evidence (*Códice Telleriano-Remensis* 1964–65:278) and the *Crónica*

mexicana's general pattern of attributing Moteuczomah Ilhuicamina's conquests to Itzcoatl, argue for their inclusion in Itzcoatl's campaigns.

51. Clark 1938, 1:30; *Leyenda de los Soles* 1975:128; Paso y Troncoso 1939–42, 10:118. While these towns apparently formed a less significant part of this campaign, their locations indicate that they were conquered en route.

52. The route of this campaign is uncertain, but all of the towns were within easy reach of Tenochtitlan. Only a single difficult passage was required for those to the west—over the mountains from the basin of Mexico—before entering the level lands of the valley of Tolocan. Those to the north were accessible via interconnected valleys either from the valley of Tolocan or by going directly north from Tenochtitlan.

53. *Anales de Cuauhtitlan* 1975:66; Clark 1938, 1:30; *Leyenda de los Soles* 1975:128; Paso y Troncoso 1939–42, 10:118. The area was accessible via a pass running directly south from the valley of Tolocan into the conquest area and then along a series of interconnected valley floors.

54. Paso y Troncoso 1905–48, 6:148.

55. Davies (1980:241–44) points out that there are two schools of thought concerning the size of the Tepanec Empire, one claiming extensive areas and the other accepting a more modest size. But both accept some penetration of the area of present-day Morelos and Guerrero.

56. Maurice 1930:212.

57. Hassig 1985:73–84.

58. *Anales de Cuauhtitlan* 1975:48; Barlow 1949b:121; Berlin and Barlow 1980:55; Chimalpahin 1965:96 [relación 3], 195 [relación 7]; Clark 1938, 1:30; *Códice Aubin* 1980:66; Durán 1967, 2:122 [chap. 14]; Ixtlilxóchitl 1975–77, 2:106 [chap. 39]; *Leyenda de los Soles* 1975:128; Paso y Troncoso 1939–42, 10:118; Torquemada 1975–83, 1:208 [bk. 2, chap. 42].

59. Torquemada 1975–83, 1:208–209 [bk. 2, chap. 42]. Ixtlilxochitl (1975–77, 2:107 [chap. 39]) offers some muddled data that suggest additional conquests may have taken place in this area in conjunction with the conquest of Cuauhnahuac, and he is unique in listing "Tepozotlan" as a conquest. While this conforms to the general pattern of expansion in the northern area during that campaign, the reference is in conjunction with Huaxtepec, which indicates a southern location. Thus he probably intended to record Tepoztlan in present-day Morelos, which would be a logical target in any campaign against Cuauhnahuac. Kelly and Palerm (1952:289–90n.18) feel that Tepoztlan was intended, as apparently does Holt (1979:93). While either Tepoztlan or Tepotzotlan could have been conquered during Itzcoatl's campaigns and both possibilities would fit his general conquest patterns, given the context of the reference I agree that Tepoztlan was meant and that Ixtlilxochitl's entry was an error.

However, even if Ixtlilxochitl intended to record Tepoztlan rather than Tepotzotlan, there is the further question of whether Tepoztlan was, in fact, conquered. Ixtlilxochitl is unique in crediting Itzcoatl with this conquest and with that of Huaxtepec. Moreover, several other sources place the conquest of Tepoztlan and Huaxtepec in the reign of Moteuczomah Ilhuicamina (Clark 1938, 1:31; *Leyenda de los Soles* 1975:128). Support for these southern conquests has been assumed by examining which other towns were conquered. Tetellan is listed as one of Itzcoatl's conquests (Paso y Troncoso 1939–42, 10:118) and has been assumed to refer to present-day Tetela del Volcán, Morelos, which, as a logical extention eastward from Cuauhnahuac by way of Tepoztlan and Huaxtepec, would support the claim for a larger southern expansion. However, Barlow (1947:217) interprets Tetellan as refering to present-day Tetela del Río, Guerrero, and by examining the place of Tetellan in the recorded sequence of conquered towns, it becomes obvious that he is correct. Once Tetellan is removed as supporting an eastward expansion from Cuauhnahuac, there is little evidence that Tepoztlan and Huaxtepec were conquered during the reign of Itzcoatl, and they should be understood as belonging to the next king.

There are several other enumerated conquests that present specific problems in interpretation and others that offer general difficulties in acceptance. There is one indication (Durán 1967, 2:122 [chap. 14]) that Itzcoatl also conquered Huexotzinco, but there is little supporting evidence. A battle with Huexotzinco also occurred during the reign of Moteuczomah Ilhuicamina (*Anales de Cuauhtitlan* 1975:56; *Códice Telleriano-Remensis* 1964–65:280; Mengin 1952:451; Torquemada 1975–83, 1:222–23 [bk. 2, chaps. 48–49]), so Itzcoatl's battle may be a confusion with that of Moteuczomah Ilhuicamina's. However, Huexotzinco was (or became) a traditional foe of Tenochtitlan and was involved in numerous xochiyaoyotl battles. As a result it is difficult to deny the validity of any recorded battle with Huexotzinco, as each may be a separate event and not merely the misplaced record of a single event.

Additional conquests are credited to Itzcoatl that appear unlikely, for several reasons. They are so farflung that they would be very difficult logistically, if feasible at all. They violate the patterns of conquest demonstrated by the more reliably recorded campaigns. And also, neither Ixtlilxochitl's (1975–77, 2:106 [chap. 39]) nor the *Crónica mexicana*'s (1975:249–50 [chap. 9]) reported conquests in part of present-day Morelos (Tepoztlan, Huaxtepec) southern Puebla (Itzyocan, Tecalco, Teohuacan, Cozcatlan, Xolotlan, Cualtepec, Tepeyacac), Oaxaca (Coaixtlahuacan, Pochtlan, Tecuantepec, Huaxyacac, Xoconochco), Guerrero (Tlalcozauhtitlan), and Veracruz (Cuetlachtlan, Ahuilizapan, Tozapan, Izhuatlan, Cuauhtochco, Tochpan) find support from other sources. In fact, all indications are that these conquests took place during the reign of Moteuczomah Ilhuicamina instead. The two exceptions are the town of Tozapan, in Veracruz, and Totomihuac, in southern Puebla, which are listed as conquests of Itzcoatl (Berlin and Barlow 1980:56). However, these are attested nowhere else and fit more convincingly with the conquests of Moteuczomah Ilhuicamina. Consequently, I regard these farflung "victories" as erroneous.

Chapter 11

1. Torquemada 1975–83, 1:209 [bk. 2, chap. 43].

2. For a fuller discussion of the economic and political significance of the structure of the Aztec Empire, see Hassig 1985:3–150.

3. *Anales de Cuauhtitlan* 1975:56; Chimalpahin 1965:99 [relación 3]; García Icazbalceta 1886–92, 3:306. The feigned war with Tetzcoco is also cited by two sources (*Crónica mexicana* 1975:284 [chap. 19]; Durán 1967, 2:130 [chap. 15]) as occurring during this reign. However, the conquest of all these cities is well attested as having taken place under the previous king, Itzcoatl. Consequently, these conquests can be interpreted either as erroneous or as reflecting something less than armed combat. In the latter case they probably reflect the expected acknowledgment of vassalage after the succession of a new king.

4. Torquemada 1975–83, 1:210 [bk. 2, chap. 44].

5. Chimalpahin 1965:98 [relación 3]; *Crónica mexicana* 1975:287–89 [chap. 21]; Durán 1967, 2:133–35 [chap. 16].

6. *Crónica mexicana* 1975:287–89 [chap. 21]; Durán 1967, 2:135–38 [chap. 16].

7. In a minority opinion Torquemada (1975–83, 1:210–11 [bk. 2, chap. 44]) states that one provocation for war with Chalco was the killing of two of Nezahualcoyotl's children who had entered Chalca lands. Whether or not this occurred, it cannot be considered either the precipitating cause of the conflict or its underlying rationale.

8. *Crónica mexicana* 1975:292 [chap. 22].

9. Acosta 1604, 2:488–89; *Crónica mexicana* 1975:293–94 [chap. 23].

10. This series of conquests in present-day Morelos and Guerrero is usually placed next, although it lacks a firm place in the conquest chronology (Barlow 1947:218; Holt 1979: 98; Kelly and Palerm 1952:267). There is support for a southward thrust after the Chalca war (*Códice Ramírez* 1975:64), but it is unclear that all of the conquests in the Guerrero and Morelos areas should be linked into a single campaign merely because of propinquity.

11. The chronicle accounts of the campaigns do not list the present-day Morelos conquests with those of present-day Guerrero, nor are all of the Guerrero conquests listed together. Thus, Torquemada (1975–83, 1:218–19 [bk. 2, chap. 46]) records one campaign in which Cohuixco, Oztoman, Cuezallan, Ichcateopan, Teoxahuallan, Poctepec, Tlachco, and Tlachmalacac (Tlachmallac) were conquered. Then he records that Moteuczomah Ilhuicamina launched a second campaign, during which he conquered Chilapan, Cuauhteopan, and Tzompanhuacan. This division seems unlikely both from accounts of other sources and because of the relative positions of the towns listed. Instead, a single campaign into Guerrero is probable, including the towns listed above (*Anales de Cuauhtitlan* 1975:67; Ixtlilxóchitl 1975–77, 2:109 [chap. 40]; *Leyenda de los Soles* 1975:128; Paso y Troncoso 1939–42, 10:118; Torquemada 1975–83, 1:218–19 [bk. 2, chap. 46]).

12. Torquemada 1975–83, 1:218–19 [bk. 2, chap. 46].

13. The probable conquest route ran west from Tenochtitlan into the valley of Tolocan and then southward through the pass at Tenanco and into the series of valleys containing the target cities. This was the route Itzcoatl had followed in his incursion of the area, so it was familiar and offered crucial logistical support, making the campaign more feasible than an extended thrust into unconquered territory.

14. *Anales de Cuauhtitlan* 1975:67.

15. Clark 1938, 1:31; *Leyenda de los Soles* 1975:128; Paso y Troncoso 1939–42, 10:118; Sahagún 1954:1.

16. If the present-day Morelos cities were captured as a separate campaign, the logical route would have been through the pass at the southwestern end of the basin of Mexico, to Ocuillan, then to Cuauhnahuac, Xiuhtepec, Yauhtepec, Huaxtepec, Yacapichtlan, then southeast down the valley to Tecpantzinco and on to Itzyocan, before doubling back to Atlatlauhyan, Totolapan, and Tepoztlan.

The location of "Tecpatzinco" is in some doubt. Both Kelly and Palerm (1952:292) and Holt (1979:155) locate Tecpatzinco in Morelos between Tepoztlan and Yauhtepec, indicating a relatively small and insignificant place. Kelly and Palerm give the present-day name for this site as Tepetzingo, Morelos, but Tepetzingo is located about ten kilometers (6 miles) south southeast of present-day Cuernavaca, which is not the location indicated on the maps of either Kelly and Palerm or Holt. At issue, then, is whether this relatively minor town was the one actually conquered by Moteuczomah Ilhuicamina. Another candidate is present-day Tepalcingo, Morelos, located approximately fifteen kilometers (9 miles) southeast of present-day Cuautla. The sole source for this town is the *Codex Mendoza* (Clark 1938, 1:31), and while the geographical proximity of Tepetzingo fits the Mendoza context, the significance of the town does not. The *Codex Mendoza* lists major towns, not minor ones. Tepalcingo, however, fulfills the criteria of both geographical proximity and urban significance and is the likely candidate. Consequently, the remaining portion of the conquest route is southeast down the valley to Tecpatzinco.

One other town was probably conquered during this campaign—Itzyocan. Only one chronicle lists the town (Ixtlilxóchitl 1975–77, 2:107 [chap. 39]), and then with the Tepeyacac campaign. However, two lists of conquests (*Anales de Cuauhtitlan* 1975:67; Paso y Troncoso 1939–42, 10:118) include it, but in the context of the Morelos towns. While the latter are not determinative, there are reasons to accept the conquest of Itzyocan at this time. First, the conquest of Tepeyacac would have been undertaken most easily via Itzyocan, which could explain its listing in Ixtlilxochitl. Second, if Tepeyacac was conquered late in Moteuczomah Ilhuicamina's reign, rather than early, it would fall after the conquest of Coaixtlahuacan, which in the context of the other towns conquered in that campaign virtually demands passage through Itzyocan. Third, the conquest of Itzyocan would require only a modest extension of the thrust to Tecpatzinco, and the town is easily accessible within the same level drainage basin. Consequently, I include both Tecpatzinco and Itzyocan in the Morelos campaign (and the conquest of Cuauhquechollan is likeliest here as well, even though it is credited to Itzcoatl (Chimalpahin 1965:96 [relación 3], 194 [relación 7])), which has important implications for the campaign into the Tepeyacac region.

It is possible that the Guerrero and Morelos conquests were undertaken as a single campaign rather than as two, but there is little direct evidence to support such a reading. While some of the conquest lists offer towns in both areas (e.g., Clark 1938, 1:31; *Leyenda de los Soles* 1975:128; Sahagún

1954:1), most offer only one (for Guerrero, see Paso y Troncoso 1939–42, 10:118; for Morelos, see *Anales de Tula* 1979:35), and there is little support in the chronicles for both together (for Guerrero, see Ixtlilxóchitl 1975–77, 2:106–109 [chaps. 39–40]; Torquemada 1975–83, 1:218–19 [bk. 2, chap. 46]).

Although it keeps the two areas of conquest separate, the *Anales de Cuauhtitlan* (1975:53) does list both. According to that source, the Matlatzincas were conquered one year; then two years later Ocuillan was conquered, as was Cuauhnahuac; and the following year Poctepec (in Guerrero) was conquered. However, this source is sketchy and at variance with the others. The most compelling argument favoring the conquest of both areas at the same time is their relative proximity.

The Aztecs usually did not conquer new cities both going and coming on a major campaign. Conquest was more frequent on the outward leg of the journey than on the return. To risk facing an unconquered and hostile region on the return without assurance that the primary campaign had been successful would put the entire enterprise at serious risk. Yet combining Guerrero and Morelos as a joint exercise would do precisely that, requiring entry into the Guerrero area, followed by an exit through the Morelos area (or possibly the reverse), with fighting taking place continuously. The successful movement of troops would depend on logistical support garnered en route by the successful prosecution of the campaign. Failure to conquer any major town would place the entire army in serious jeopardy. Whatever the case, both the Morelos and the Guerrero campaigns (either jointly or separately) followed the beginning of the war with Chalco.

There is considerable evidence that the next campaign was against the cities of the Tepeyacac region (*Códice Ramírez* 1975:127; *Crónica mexicana* 1975:306–308 [chap. 27]; Durán 1967, 2:154–56 [chap. 18]; Ixtlilxóchitl 1975–77, 2:107 [chap. 39]). However, I feel that these references are erroneous.

Some sources place the Tepeyacac campaign early in the reign of Moteuczomah Ilhuicamina, while others place it late. To reconcile confusing and conflicting data among the sources, Holt (1979:95) asserts that there were two campaigns in the Tepeyacac region, not just one. His interpretation rests on two pieces of evidence. The first evidence of this interpretation is the account in the *Lista de los reyes de Tlatelolco* (Berlin and Barlow 1980:4), which Holt interprets as recording the conquest of Tepeyacac twice. But there are difficulties with this.

One problem is the chronology. In the *Lista de los reyes de Tlatelolco* Tepeyacac is included among the towns conquered, without any chronological referent, and this is for King Cuauhtlahtoa of Tlatelolco, who ruled for 41 years from 1427 to 1467 (according to Berlin and Barlow 1980:86). His reign only partially overlapped with that of Moteuczomah Ilhuicamina, who ruled 29 years from 1440 to 1468. Therefore, if Tepeyacac was conquered twice, the first time may have been before Moteuczomah Ilhuicamina's reign. While the *Crónica mexicana* (1975:245 [chap. 9]) does list the conquest of Tepeyacac during the reign of Itzcoatl, it is not reliable, since Tepeyacac is listed as a conquest along with other cities that are equally unlikely candidates for conquest during that reign.

Another problem is with the interpretation of the *Crónica mexicana*. In the *Lista de los reyes de Tlatelolco*, the list of Cuauhtlahtoa's conquests records several towns, then "Tepeaca," followed by additional towns and then (after a break in the text of the original document, indicated by three dots in the published version) "Tepeyacac," followed by additional towns. Despite the peculiarity of corrupting Tepeyacac ("Mountain-nose-place") to a perfectly valid Nahuatl name, Tepeaca (Tepeacan; "Mountain-water-place"), Tepeyacac is generally considered to refer to present-day Tepeaca, apparently correctly except for an eastward shift of the present-day town (Gerhard 1972:280). If there is an absolute correspondence between the two names, there is no apparent reason for the two references under different names, even if it had been conquered twice.

The two different references do not refer to two different conquests of the same place but to conquests of two different places. Tepeyacac was a pre-Columbian city and a state (Gerhard 1972:278) and referred to an area in the latter capacity. Similarly, Tepeaca was the post-Columbian name, but of both a city and a province (e.g., *El libro de las tasaciones* 1952:399).

Without deciding which refers to town and which to region, the two different entries do, in fact, reflect this distinction, just as other conquests list areas, such as Mazahuacan, Matlatzinco, Cohuixco, and towns within those areas, such as Xocotitlan, Tolocan, and Chilapan, respectively (*Crónica mexicana* 1975:250 [chap. 9], Ixtlilxóchitl 1975–77, 2:109 [chap. 40]).

The second evidence of two Tepeyacac campaigns is Torquemada's (1975–83, 1:228 [bk. 2, chap. 50]) reference to Tepeyacac as having rebelled. However, Torquemada fails to list its prior conquest. The statement could simply be an error, but, assuming that it is not, it can be reconciled with the bulk of the historical accounts in at least two different ways. First, Tepeyacac's prior status is not necessarily one of subjugation. Rather, Tepeyacac may have been on peaceful terms with Tenochtitlan, so that any shift in relations could have been considered a rebellion. In fact, Aztec merchants traveled through the region without difficulty, and free transit was apparently a common feature of Mesoamerican polities, even for armies, as long as the transit areas were not the targets.

Second, the rebellion could have been directed toward the region designated by Tepeyacac and not toward the town. Such an interpretation could then encompass the actions of Cuauht-Inchan, which was, in some way, subjugated by the Aztecs during the reign of Acamapichtli and which figures prominently in the wars in the region during Moteuczomah Ilhuicamina's reign. The former interpretation appears likelier. Any resistance to Aztec domination was interpreted as rebellion, regardless of any previous political relationship between the cities. For example, the *Crónica mexicana* (1975:343 [chap. 34]) records Cuetlachtlan and Cempohuallan as having rebelled for a second time. Yet there is no record of more than one previous conquest—their initial armed resistance was apparently considered to be the first rebellion, and their initial overthrow of Aztec domination thus constituted the second rebellion. In short, references to rebellions by previously unconquered cities seem to reflect their initial armed resistance to Aztec domination and not to some previous conquest and its subsequent overthrow. Thus, the first source (Torquemada) contains no direct evidence of two conquests and is useful only in the context of such evidence. And the second source (*Lista de los reyes de Tlatelolco*) contains ambiguities about the conquest chronology and fails to record more than one conquest of Tepeyacac (the town).

A further difficulty with accepting the earlier campaign (and hence two campaigns) into the Tepeyacac area rests on the sources themselves. While this documentation (*Códice Ramírez* 1975:127; *Crónica mexicana* 1975:306–308 [chap. 27]; Durán 1967, 2:154–56 [chap. 18]) is impressive in its detail, it does not reflect three different accounts of the conquest sequence but only one since all three apparently derive from a common source—the hypothesized *Crónica X* (Barlow 1945). Thus these three must be assessed as one account when weighed against those containing the competing version of the later conquest of Tepeyacac (*Anales de Cuauhtitlan* 1975:54; Berlin and Barlow 1980:59; Chimalpahin 1965:103 [relación 3], 206 [relación 7]; Torquemada 1975–83, 1:228 [bk. 2, chap. 50]). (A fourth source [Ixtlilxóchtil 1975–77, 2:107 (chap. 40)] lists an earlier Tepeyacac conquest, though not a later one, but this account is confused and at variance with other accounts on a variety of conquests.) In addition to the difficulties addressed above in accepting the *Crónica X* version of the Tepeyacac campaign, Durán's (1967, 2:153 [chap. 18]) version also contains internal evidence pointing to a confusion between the "earlier" and later conquests. In the "earlier" campaign Tenochtitlan's armies were assisted by those of Tetzcoco, Xochimilco, the Tepanecs, and Chalco. An earlier Tepeyacac conquest would place it after the war began between Chalco and Moteuczomah Ilhuicamina's Tenochtitlan but before Chalco's definitive conquest, which occurred at the end of Moteuczomah Ilhuicamina's reign. It is highly improbable that this enemy state would have assisted the Aztecs in a further conquest. It is likelier that Durán has confused the temporal relationship of the Tepeyacac conquest, projecting factual details that belong later in the sequence of conquests onto an "earlier" (and nonexistent) campaign.

Taking all the evidence together, there is little support for the proposition that Tepeyacac suffered two conquests by Moteuczomah Ilhuicamina. Two campaigns are theoretically possible (and so reconstructing the conquests does ease the burden of reconciling confusing and contradictory data), but there is no more evidence supporting such an interpretation than in any other instance in which the various accounts put conquests at conflicting times in the king's reign. Consequently, I feel that Tepeyacac was conquered only once by Moteuczomah Ilhuicamina and that the campaign occurred near the end of his reign. Thus the Tepeyacac campaign will be discussed later, as appropriate.

17. Torquemada 1975–83, 1:219–20 [bk. 2, chap. 47].

18. Chimalpahin 1965:99 [relación 3].

19. See Hassig (1981) for a detailed consideration of this famine. See Berlin and Barlow 1980:57; Torquemada 1975–83, 1:220–22 [bk. 2, chaps.

47–48], but contra Ixtlilxochitl (1975–77, 2:109–10 [chap. 40]), who is generally unreliable for the conquests of Moteuczomah Ilhuicamina.

20. *Códice Ramírez* 1975:128; *Crónica mexicana* 1975:310 [chap. 28].

21. The status of this town is unclear at this time. Although the conquered towns in this area are listed as Aztec tributaries by the *Codex Mendoza* (Clark 1938, 1:31), they had apparently been conquered by King Nezahualcoyotl (Chimalpahin 1965:200 [relación 7]; Ixtlilxóchitl 1975–77, 1:446) and had formed a traditional part of the Acolhua domain.

22. *Crónica mexicana* 1975:312 [chap. 28].

23. Durán 1967, 2:168–69 [chap. 19].

24. *Códice Ramírez* 1975:128; *Crónica mexicana* 1975:314–18 [chaps. 29–30]; Durán 1967, 2:167 [chap. 19].

25. Ixtlilxóchitl 1975–77, 1:446.

26. Torquemada 1975–83, 1:228 [bk. 2, chap. 50].

27. *Anales de Cuauhtitlan* 1975:67; Clark 1938, 1:31; *Leyenda de los Soles* 1975:128; Paso y Troncoso 1939–42, 10:118; Sahagún 1954:1. Tepotzotlan, located in the same area, is also listed, but this is an error for Tepoztlan (Ixtlilxóchitl 1975–77, 2:107 [chap. 39]). The route to Xilotepec is relatively direct and over level land, but as no other towns are definitely chronicled as having been conquered, the other towns probably offered obedience after the defeat of Xilotepec, or else they quickly submitted when the Aztec army approached. This was probably all carried out during the same campaign.

Holt (1979:110) is correct in reading the *Códice Telleriano-Remensis* as reflecting a battle between the people of Xiquipilco and Michhuacan (Michoacan) and not as an Aztec conquest of Xiquipilco. The town had been conquered by Itzcoatl and may have received Aztec assistance, but it was not one of Moteuczomah Ilhuicamina's reconquests. The addition of Chiucnauhtlan, however, is untenable, since it was conquered by Moteuczomah Xocoyotl, not by Moteuczomah Ilhuicamina.

The actual extent and significance of the Huaxtec expansion is also debated. Barlow (1947:218) suggests a considerable conquest of the Huaxtec region, while Kelly and Palerm (1952:268) feel that the area was the object of only modest conquests. Holt (1979:108–12) describes the campaign as a major military excursion but includes the Tetzcoco expansion to the north in so doing. The actual incursion into the northern Totonacapan area appears to have been relatively slight, carrying out the apparent objective of penalizing the area that had killed the empire's merchants and conquering towns passed en route but with a net result of few conquests—Xiuhcoac, Tamachpan, Tochpan, Tozapan, Chapolicxitlan, Tlapacoyan, Cuauhchinanco, Pahuatlan, and Xolotlan.

Based on the reference to Tochtepec (located in present-day southern Veracruz) in Ixtlilxochitl (1975–77, 2:107 [chap. 39]) and Alvarado Tezozomoc (*Crónica mexicana* 1975:311), Kelly and Palerm (1952:268–70) reconstruct the Aztec conquests as then either continuing on from the Huaxtec region southward down the Gulf coast or as taking place in a separate but simultaneous thrust to the south. But Holt (1979:113) concludes (correctly, I believe) that, given the other associated towns in these two sources, Tochtepec is an error for Tochpan (Tuxpan) and that no southern incursion occurred at this time.

The next problematic campaign was the thrust toward Cuetlachtlan. Holt (1979:113–15) and Kelly and Palerm (1952:270–72) feel that it was the next campaign, following the Huaxtec incursion (and the thrust into the southern Gulf coast region, according to Kelly and Palerm). As all acknowledge, however, there is a problem in the data.

Most sources record these Gulf area conquests, but the order in which they occurred is in doubt. All three sources offering the best descriptive evidence (Durán 1967, 2:185 [chap. 22]; *Códice Ramírez* 1975:129; *Crónica mexicana* 1975:328–31 [chap. 32]) place the Cuetlachtlan campaign next, before the Huaxyacac incursion. Other sources (Berlin and Barlow 1980:57; Torquemada 1975–83, 1:222–25 [bk. 2, chaps. 48–49]) place the Cuetlachtlan campaign after the Huaxyacac area campaign. While none of the lists reflects more than a single conquest of the Cuetlachtlan region, the three sources claiming priority for the Cuetlachtlan conquest also record a second conquest of that area following the Huaxyacac campaign. Thus, Holt (1979:113–17) and Kelly and Palerm (1952:268–72) feel that there were, in fact, two campaigns and that the sources that mention only one are referring to the second and simply fail to list the first.

Accepting the maximum number of conquests more easily reconciles the conflicting data, and the quality of the data describing two conquests is compelling. But all of these sources derive from a single original source—the *Crónica X*—and thus merely represent three variations of a single account. And there are reasons to doubt that version. First, the *Crónica X* accounts also erred (I believe) in their accounts of the Tepeyacac campaign (as spelled out above). They uniformly place that campaign earlier than it should be, leading to the conclusion that they probably did the same for Cuetlachtlan. Second, there were indeed two campaigns into the Cuetlachtlan region, but other accounts place the first in the reign of Moteuczomah Ilhuicamina and the second in the reign of his successor, Axayacatl. And third, rebellions tended to occur following the death of a ruler and the installation of his successor as a kind of test of his martial and political resolve. While this was not invariably the case, it does suggest that the rebellion is likelier to have occurred after the death of Moteuczomah Ilhuicamina.

Consequently, it is likely that the two-campaign accounts unjustifiably compress the temporal sequence, placing the actual campaign (of Cuetlachtlan and of Tepeyacac) earlier in the reign of Moteuczomah Ilhuicamina and then putting the later conquest of Cuetlachtlan (by Axayacatl) into this reign as well. Thus I accept the conquest of the Cuetlachtlan area, but only one later in the reign following the Coaixtlahuacan campaign.

28. *Crónica mexicana* 1975:311 [chap. 28], 315 [chap. 29]. Tozapan (Tuzapan) and Xolotlan in the Huaxtec area were erroneously attributed to King Itzcoatl (*Crónica mexicana* 1975:250 [chap. 9]). Another listed town that fits into this campaign is Tlapacoyan (*Anales de Cuauhtitlan* 1975:67; Clark 1938, 1:31; *Leyenda de los Soles* 1975:128; Paso y Troncoso 1939–42, 10:118).

29. Durán 1967, 1:95–103 [chap. 9], 2:172–74 [chap. 20]. Chalco was also listed, but erroneously.

30. *Anales de Cuauhtitlan* 1975:52; *Anales de Tula* 1979:35; Berlin and Barlow 1980:57; Chimalpahin 1965:100 [relación 3], 202 [relación 7]; Clark 1938, 1:31; *Códice Ramírez* 1975:129; *Crónica mexicana* 1975:334–37 [chap. 33]; Durán 1967, 2:185 [chap. 22]; *Leyenda de los Soles* 1975:128; Paso y Troncoso 1939–42, 10:118; Torquemada 1975–83, 1:222 [bk. 2, chap. 48].

31. Chimalpahin 1965:100 [relación 3], 202 [relación 7].

32. Torquemada 1975–83, 1:222 [bk. 2, chap. 48].

33. *Códice Ramírez* 1975:129; *Crónica mexicana* 1975:334–37 [chap. 33]; Durán 1967, 2:185 [chap. 22].

34. Torquemada 1975–83, 1:220–22 [bk. 2, chaps. 47–48]. Chalco, Huexotzinco, and Chalollan are also listed as helping the Aztecs, but erroneously.

35. *Códice Ramírez* 1975:129; *Crónica mexicana* 1975:335–37 [chap. 33].

36. Torquemada 1975–83, 1:222 [bk. 2, chap. 48], 228 [bk. 2, chap. 50]. Holt (1979:117) includes Texopan (Texupa) among the conquests of this campaign, based on the *Relación de Texupa* (Paso y Troncoso 1905–48, 4:55). But Texopan cannot be reliably included as a conquest at this time on textual evidence alone, since the *Relación* merely lists the town as subject to Moteuczomah, without distinguishing between the two rulers of that name. Its location on the probable campaign route makes its conquest a logical possibility, but many other towns on the same route were not conquered at this time, so there is insufficient reason to claim Texopan as a conquest.

Further extension of this campaign is uncertain, with few attestations in the sources. By Torquemada's account the Aztecs and their allies conquered not only Coaixtlahuacan but also Tochtepec, Tepzol, Tzapotlan, Tototlan, Tlatlactetelco, and Cuauhnochco (Torquemada 1975–83, 1:222–23 [bk. 2, chap. 48]). However, the latter towns were doubtless conquered in the following campaign against Alahuiztlan.

Tamazolapan is also listed as a conquest (Ixtlilxóchitl 1975–77, 2:109 [chap. 40]) but in a context that makes it doubtful. The city of Huaxyacac (Oaxaca), too, is listed as a conquest (*Códice Ramírez* 1975:131–32; *Crónica mexicana* 1975:355–60 [chaps. 37–38]; Durán 1967, 2:230 [chap. 28]), the result of more Aztec merchants having been killed. Although three accounts substantiate this conquest, they are all *Crónica X* accounts and hence represent a common version that is doubtful in this reign, if my earlier analysis of the Cuetlachtlan and Tepeyacac conquests is accurate. The *Origen de los Mexicanos* (in García Icazbalceta 1886–92, 3:300) does list Huaxyacac as one of Moteuczomah Ilhuicamina's conquests, but this apparently refers to the region (where conquests were made) rather than to the city (which is doubtful). Thus the conquest of the city of Huaxyacac appears at variance with other accounts and cannot be accepted as reliable.

37. *Crónica mexicana* 1975:335 [chap. 33].

38. Durán 1967, 2:194 [chap. 23].

39. Torquemada 1975–83, 1:223 [bk. 2, chap. 49].

40. Durán 1967, 2:211–14 [chap. 26].

41. Durán 1967, 2:195 [chap. 23].

42. If, as discussed above, there was only a single overall Gulf coast campaign (referring to the conquest of Cuetlachtlan), it occurred at this time, after the conquest of the Coaixtlahuacan area and before the final subjugation of Chalco. However, it is unclear how long this campaign took. Some sources place the conquests together without any appreciable temporal span, but others indicate a conquest lasting several years (Berlin and Barlow 1980:57; Torquemada 1975–83, 1:222–25 [bk. 2, chaps. 48–49]). And if Tlatlauhqui-Tepec is included, as it should be on geopolitical grounds, a campaign of some duration is indicated, albeit one that may have continued after the initial main thrust at an intermittent low level between and during other campaigns. Since, as discussed above, I feel that those sources listing two conquests of Cuetlachtlan during this reign are presenting its actual conquest early in Moteuczomah Ilhuicamina's leadership and incorporating the conquest by Axayacatl into the later years of the reign, I shall use otherwise unsubstantiated material from those sources only for the first conquest.

43. Muñoz Camargo 1892:113. As Davies (1968:104) notes, Huexotzinco was more important than Tlaxcallan at this time, and the numerous references to the latter can generally be considered as reflecting that city's later importance.

44. *Crónica mexicana* 1975:331 [chap. 32].

45. Torquemada 1975–83, 1:224 [bk. 2, chap. 49].

46. Berlin and Barlow 1980:57; *Códice Ramírez* 1975:128–29; *Crónica mexicana* 1975:325–31 [chaps. 31–32]; Durán 1967, 2:185 [chap. 22]; Torquemada 1975–83, 1:224–25 [bk. 2, chap. 49].

47. *Anales de Cuauhtitlan* 1975:67; Barlow 1949b:122; Clark 1938, 1:31; *Códice Aubin* 1980:72; García Icazbalceta 1886–92, 3:253; *Leyenda de los Soles* 1975:128; Paso y Troncoso 1939–42, 10:118; Torquemada 1975–83, 1:222–28 [bk. 2, chaps. 48–50]. Teohuacan (Ixtlilxóchitl 1975–77, 1:106 [chap. 39]) may have belonged to this campaign as well, as probably did Cozcatlan and Izhuatlan, despite having been credited to Itzcoatl (*Crónica mexicana* 1975:250 [chap. 9]). Maxtlan was also likely included here despite having been credited to Itzcoatl.

48. There is no indication of the route taken in this campaign. Ahuilizapan and Cuetlachtlan are listed as the primary conquests (Barlow 1949b: 122; Chimalpahin 1965:104 [relación 3]; *Códice Ramírez* 1975:129; *Códice Vaticano* 1964–65:244; *Crónica mexicana* 1975:331 [chap. 32]; Ixtlilxóchitl 1975–77, 1:107 [chap. 39]; Torquemada 1975–83, 1:223 [bk. 2, chap. 49]) and if Ahuilizapan was the first target, the route probably followed that of previous conquests, southeast out of the basin of Mexico to Itzyocan; from there southeast to Acatlan; and then striking toward Teohuacan. Another possibility for the route between Itzyocan and Teohuacan is east through the Tepeyacac region (or skirting it on the south) and then southeast to Teohuacan. The Tepeyacac region had not been conquered, but its rela-

tions with the Aztecs were not hostile so passage through the area was possible. From Teohuacan the route runs northeast up a valley through Coxolitlan to Ahuilizapan. Thereafter the Aztecs would have followed the terrain north, conquering towns en route as far north as Tzapotlan. From the northernmost conquest (Tzapotlan or Tlatlauhqui-Tepec) the journey back to Tenochtitlan may have taken any of several routes, the likeliest of which entered the level area to the south, allowing an easy march to the Teohuacan area.

Tlatlauhqui-Tepec is frequently listed as Moteuczomah Ilhuicamina's last conquest (*Anales de Tula* 1979:36; Chimalpahin 1965:103 [relación 3]; Durán 1967, 2:248 [chap. 31]). On geopolitical grounds, however, that conquest belongs with this campaign, although the campaign may have taken place over some considerable time span. The towns listed as conquests but not included in the chronicles of the campaign may have been physically conquered, but if so they were not overly important conquests. It is likelier that they submitted with the approach of the victorious Aztec army.

If they were physically conquered, the Totonac towns of the coastal lowlands present no difficulties in transit and could have been approached at any time during the campaign, although the most probable time would have been after Ahuilizapan or immediately after Tzapotlan. However, the recorded conquest of Cuetlachtlan appears to refer to the general region and not to the town per se. Moreover, the other lowland towns—Oceloapan, Cempohuallan, and Quiahuiztlan—are given only on conquest lists and not in chronicles, possibly indicating their nonresisting submission but certainly their secondary status in the campaign. It is probable that they submitted and were not physically conquered. This would obviate the necessity of the Aztec army making the arduous coastal descent and ascent.

49. Listing Teotitlan as a conquest during the reign of Moteuczomah Ilhuicamina is the sole exception I have made to my general practice of listing only those conquered towns for which a time—at least a specific reign—can be established in reconstructing the sequence of Aztec conquests. However, Barlow's (1949a) influential assessment of the extent of the Aztec Empire, based on the *Codex Mendoza* and the *Relaciones geográficas* of 1579–85, maintains that Teotitlan was an independent kingdom, unconquered by the Aztecs. And while a specific record of such a conquest is lacking, I concur with Davies' (1968:14–15) position that the city was not independent.

A sixteenth-century record of Aztec tributaries (Paso y Troncoso 1939–42, 14:120–21) lists Teotitlan, and the *Relación geográfica* of 1581 for Teotitlan (Paso y Troncoso 1905–48, 4:216) admits an alliance with the Aztecs, although it denies the payment of tribute. But clearly by the time of King Ahuitzotl, Aztec commercial interests along the route dominated by Teotitlan were enormous (Sahagún 1959:17, 22), to the extent that a merely casual relationship appears doubtful.

Enabling the army to transit vast distances was crucial to the maintenance of the empire—more so than the total domination of all intermediate settlements. As a result the way various towns were integrated into the empire differed. How tightly different communities were bound varied according to a number of considerations—their proximity and danger to Tenochtitlan, the availability of alternative logistical support, the level of resistance (actual or potential), and other nontribute benefits of the relationship. Trade was a major factor in the case of Teotitlan, which straddled the major routes into the lucrative Anahuac areas. Aztec interest in participating in this economic flow was doubtless balanced by Teotitlan's interest in retaining control of its own trade, position, and as much political autonomy as possible. In short, the rationale and evidence for Teotitlan having been incorporated into the Aztec Empire is persuasive; the timing of its incorporation is less clear, however. Massive commercial interests indicate the existence of such a relationship by the time of King Ahuitzotl, and the relative inactivity of Kings Axayacatl and Tizoc in the Teotitlan area, coupled with Moteuczomah Ilhuicamina's incursion into the region, argues strongly for its incorporation at this time. As with most of the Aztec tributaries to that point, the political relationship between Tenochtitlan and Teotitlan was asymmetrical, but unlike most, it was loose, the Aztecs finding it more advantageous to extract the benefits of trade, location, and control of market flow without the political and military disruptions that could have occurred through direct conquest and control of the city: it was better to tap into a compliant and mutually beneficial arrangement than to risk creating local hostility that could discourage trade completely. A more determined show of force was unnecessary, as logistical support could be obtained elsewhere en route or purchased in Teotitlan, and the benefits of the ongoing arrangement were obvious.

Although Teotitlan was brought into the Aztec sphere of influence, the main road it dominated into Anahuac does not appear to have been a major conquest route. This is not to say that Aztec armies did not march on that road—particularly when striving to transit the region speedily and without anticipating military engagements on the road. But it does not appear to have been used as a major artery from which the Aztecs struck at other towns. Other roads offer more convincing conquest routes, although the Teotitlan road could well have played a more significant role in consolidation, security, and maintenance of the conquered areas. Moreover, the Aztecs probably tried to minimize disruptions on this significant economic link.

50. *Crónica mexicana* 1975:333 [chap. 32].

51. *Anales de Tula* 1979:35, 1443; Chimalpahin 1965:98 [relación 3], 1446. As it stretched on, the fighting became more serious with the advent of arrow warfare (Chimalpahin 1965:99 [relación 3], 1453).

52. Itztompiatepec (Chimalpahin 1965:198–99 [relación 7], 1444), Panohuayan (Chimalpahin 1965:100 [relación 3], 201 [relación 7], 1456), Atezcahuacan (*Anales de Cuauhtitlan* 1975:53; *Anales de Tula* 1979:35, 1461; Chimalpahin 1965:100–101 [relación 3], 302 [relación 7], 1461), and Tzacualtitlan Tenanco (Chimalpahin 1965:101 [relación 3], 1464).

53. *Anales de Cuauhtitlan* 1975:53; Barlow 1949b:122; Chimalpahin 1965:101 [relación 3], 1464; Clark 1938, 1:31; *Códice Aubin* 1980:71; García Icazbalceta 1886–92, 3:306; Herrera 1934–57, 6:211; Ixtlilxóchitl 1975–77, 2:126 [chap. 45]; *Leyenda de los Soles* 1975:128; Paso y Troncoso

1939–42, 10:118; Sahagún 1954:1; Torquemada 1975–83, 1:226–27 [chap. 50].

54. Torquemada 1975–83, 1:227 [bk. 2, chap. 50].

55. *Anales de Cuauhtitlan* 1975:53; *Anales de Tula* 1979:35, 1465; Berlin and Barlow 1980:59; Chimalpahin 1965:102 [relación 3], 204–205 [relación 7], 1465; Durán 1967, 2:153 [chap. 18]; *Códice Telleriano-Remensis* 1964–65:280; 1465.

56. Chimalpahin 1965:39–48 [relación 3].

57. Calnek 1982:57. See also Carrasco 1984b. Specific rulers were removed, albeit temporarily in most cases, to be replaced by others who also possessed legitimate claims to local rulership and who were more amenable to Aztec demands. For example, when Huehueh Chimalpilli, the lord of Ecatepec, died in 1465, the Aztecs installed a military governor even though the town had long been an Aztec subject and had apparently posed no difficulties to their control.

58. Chimalpahin 1965:209 [relación 7].

59. Ixtlilxóchitl 1975–77, 2:112 [chap. 41]. The battle began at the hill of Tliliuhqui-Tepetl between Tetzcoco and Tlaxcallan (*Códice Telleriano-Remensis* 1964–65:282). This may indicate not only the location of the battle but also the likely participation of the town of Tliliuhqui-Tepec.

Various sources date this war differently, either before the final conquest of Chalco (Ixtlilxóchitl 1975–77, 2:111 [chap. 41], 126 [chap. 45]) or afterward (*Códice Telleriano-Remensis* 1964–65:280–82). Since this was not a formal campaign of conquest and it occurred roughly simultaneously with other military exploits, I do not consider the uncertainty of its sequential placement crucial, and its discussion here does not necessarily argue for this order.

60. In the Tepeyacac campaign the Aztec army apparently marched south from the basin of Mexico through the present-day Morelos area following the valley southeast to Tecpatzinco and thence to Itzyocan. Thereafter the army marched to Huehuetlan, which introduces a difficulty in this campaign.

Kelly and Palerm (1952:295n.4) say that the conquest of Huehuetlan is doubtful, having found their sole reference to this town in the *Códice Chimalpopoca*. However, this conquest is also supported by the *Anales de Tula* (1979:35), but there is a problem in establishing the town's location. As with many Mesoamerican towns, the names are common to several settlements, often in relatively close proximity to one another. In the case of Huehuetlan there are two possible candidates—present-day Huehuetlan el Chico, Puebla, and present-day Huehuetlan el Grande (also known as Santo Domingo Huehuetlan), Puebla. Kelly and Palerm (1952:291–92) identify the town as Huehuetlan el Chico but locate it at the site of Huehuetlan el Grande on their map. Thus, the identification of Huehuetlan is probably erroneous, but the location is the one they intend. Holt (1979:156) places the town at the site at Huehuetlan el Grande without comment. Both sources that list Huehuetlan put its conquest after the subjection of Chalco.

Two sources list the conquest of Huehuetlan, the *Anales de Cuauhtitlan* (1975:53) and the *Anales de Tula* (1979:35), both in 12 Calli, the year before the conquest of Tepeyacac. Itzyocan is listed by only one source (Ixtlilxochtil 1975–77, 2:107 [chap. 39]), which puts its conquest before Tepeyacac and after Chalco. Taken together, these sources indicate a sequence of conquests following the final subjugation of Chalco, proceeding to Tepeyacac by way of Itzyocan and Huehuetlan (or perhaps the reverse, depending on which location actually refers to Huehuetlan).

The historical sources show that the conquests of Itzyocan and Huehuetlan precede that of Tepeyacac, but because they are listed by separate sources, no temporal or geographical priority can be assigned between Itzyocan and Huehuetlan. Consequently, either site for Huehuetlan is potentially correct if only the written sources are considered. However, I agree that the conquered city was probably Huehuetlan el Grande rather than Huehuetlan el Chico, since passage from the basin of Mexico through Itzyocan is indicated for the campaign in the Huaxyacac region (which would require passing through Huehuetlan el Chico), while the conquest of Huehuetlan is mentioned in conjunction with that of Tepeyacac. Thus Huehuetlan el Grande, which is on the route to Tepeyacac (although not on the best route, which was straddled by Tenochtitlan's enemies Atlixco and Chalco) is a likelier candidate than Huehuetlan el Chico, which is on the route to present-day Oaxaca.

To assume an earlier conquest of the Tepeyacac region would require the forces of Tenochtitlan to have passed through major expanses of unconquered territory, which the sequence presented above does not. Thus, while there may have been some earlier disturbance at Tepeyacac, the basic sequence of conquest appears to be an extension through the previously conquered Morelos area to Itzyocan, Huehuetlan, Tepeyacac, Tecalco (Tecali), Cuauht-Inchan, Acatzinco, Tecamachalco, Coatepec, Yohualtepec, Oztoticpac, and Tetl-Icoyoccan (Tetlcoyocan) (*Anales de Cuauhtitlan* 1975:54, 67; Berlin and Barlow 1980:56, 59; Chimalpahin 1965:102 [relación 3], 206 [relación 7]; Clark 1938, 1:31; *Códice Ramírez* 1975:127; *Crónica mexicana* 1975:306, 308 [chap. 27]; Durán 1967, 2:150–51 [chap. 17]; Ixtlilxóchitl 1975–77, 2:107 [chap. 39]; *Leyenda de los Soles* 1975:128; Paso y Troncoso 1939–42, 10:118; Torquemada 1975–83, 1:228 [bk. 2, chap. 50]). All of these cities were actually conquered. Tetl-Ianallan (Tetlanallan) (Berlin and Barlow 1980:4) may also be a conquest in this area but is unlocated.

61. *Códice Ramírez* 1975:127; *Crónica mexicana* 1975:306–307 [chap. 27]; Durán 1967, 2:157–58 [chap. 18].

62. *Códice Ramírez* 1975:131; *Crónica mexicana* 1975:354–55 [chap. 37]; Durán 1967, 2:225 [chap. 28].

63. *Crónica mexicana* 1975:359 [chap. 38].

64. *Códice Ramírez* 1975:131; *Crónica mexicana* 1975:346 [chap. 34], 354 [chap. 37], 360 [chap. 38]; Durán 1967, 2:230 [chap. 28]; García Icazbalceta 1886–92, 3:300; Ixtlilxóchitl 1975–77, 2:109 [chap. 40]; Torquemada 1975–83, 1:223 [bk. 2, chap. 49], 1:228 [bk. 2, chap. 50].

65. *Códice Ramírez* 1975:131. Tecuantepec is listed as a conquest (García Icazbalceta 1886–92, 3:306), but it was not. Rather, the area *to* Tecuantepec was conquered, probably reflecting much of the route between Mictlan and Quetzaltepec. Torquemada (1975–83, 1:228 [bk. 2, chap. 50]) and Ixtlilxochitl (1975–77, 2:109–10 [chap. 40]) both provide extensive lists of

towns conquered in the area of this campaign, including Cuextlan, Tlahuitollan, Tamazollan, Acatlan, Piaztlan, Tetl-Icoyoccan, Xilotepec, Tochoco (Tozoco), Otlaquiquiztlan, and Xochipalco. However, they both seem to derive from an earlier common source that has muddled several campaigns. Many of these towns fit so convincingly into earlier conquest sequences and so poorly into one directed at the present-day Oaxaca-southern Veracruz area that they must be disregarded. Consequently, I include only those listed towns for which there is substantiation elsewhere or that fit into the probable march areas.

66. Little is known about the conquest route, but there are two likely alternatives. A direct route proceeds southeast out of the basin of Mexico along an established conquest itinerary via Itzyocan and Piaztlan to Tamazollan and then on to Huaxyacac (478 km. or 296 mi.; 15 to 25 days' march). From there the probable route runs to Mictlan (50 km. or 31 mi.; 2 to 3 days' march), then to Miahuatlan (85 km. or 53 mi.; 3 to 4 days) before partially doubling back and passing through the Tecuantepec region. The route then goes to Quetzaltepec (230 km. or 143 mi.; 7 to 12 days' march) and onto the lowland Gulf plain, from which Tochtepec (150 km. or 93 mi.; 5 to 8 days), Otlatlan (15 km. or 9 mi.; 1 day) and Cozamolapan (33 km. or 20 mi.; 1 to 2 days) are all accessible. From there the likely return route goes north, enters the highlands at Ahuilizapan, and follows the previous conquest route to Itzyocan and then into the basin of Mexico 523 kilometers or 324 miles; 16 to 27 days' march; this brings the total to 1,564 kilometers (970 miles), or 49 to 81 days' march, excluding days for rest, combat, and regrouping. Although this is the likely direction of the campaign, reversing the sequence is equally plausible.

67. *Códice Ramírez* 1975:133; Durán 1967, 2:238–39 [chap. 29].

Chapter 12

1. Durán 1967, 2:250 [chap. 32]. As was the case with the previous kings, the historical sources present conflicting information about which cities were conquered, when, and in what sequence. Which cities Axayacatl conquered is clearer than for the earlier kings, but there is less consensus about the dates of the campaigns, and those that are recorded are frequently inconsistent. Thus, rather than placing reliance on dates, I stress conquests in a sequence of events.

2. There are two different accounts of Axayacatl's preinaugural conquests. One claims that the conquest was of Tlatlauhqui-Tepec to the northeast. But the better supported account places the conquest far to the south. Axayacatl led an army to the Tecuantepec region, defeated its armies, and conquered the entire area as far south as Cuauhtolco (Huatulco) (*Códice Ramírez* 1975:68; Herrera 1934–57, 6:215; Torquemada 1975–83, 1:238–39 [bk. 2, chap. 55]; Vázquez de Espinosa 1942:143). Xochitepec was probably conquered during this incursion, based on both time of conquest and location (Torquemada 1975–83, 1:243 [bk. 2, chap. 58]). Another source (*Códice Ramírez* 1975:68) states that the people of Tecuantepec had killed merchants and royal tribute collectors and that this was the reason for their

conquest. However, the reference is brief, and it is unclear that it reflects this particular conquest.

3. Acosta 1604, 2:494; Torquemada 1975–83, 1:238–39 [bk. 2, chap. 55].

4. After conquering Cuauhtolco and Xochitepec, the army could have returned to the coastal lowland and marched northwest to the Papagayo River drainage. At that point the army could have marched up the Omitlan River to either Ohuapan or, likelier, Chilapan, both of which had been conquered by Moteuczomah Ilhuicamina and offered no difficulties throughout the reign of Axayacatl. From either of these towns, the army could have retraced the previous king's conquest route to Tepecuacuilco, Tlachco, and probably through Cuauhnahuac and from there into the basin of Mexico.

5. In carrying out this conquest, Axayacatl's likeliest route followed that of his predecessor south out of the basin of Mexico and along valleys and through the previously conquered towns of Cuauhnahuac, Tecpantzinco, Itzyocan, Acatlan, Huaxyacac, and Mictlan. There the route formed a loop that could be followed in either direction but is more likely to have followed the valley floors to Tecuantepec (720 km. or 446 mi.; 23 to 38 days' march) and then west along the Pacific coastal lowlands to Cuauhtolco. The route then probably followed a valley to the town of Xochitepec, which was conquered, through a pass to the previously conquered Miahuatlan, on to Mictlan, and then back to Tenochtitlan by reversing the route (totaling 1,365 km. or 846 mi.; 43 to 71 days' march, exclusive of rest days, combat, and regrouping days).

Sahagún (1954:2) is unique in listing the town of Teotzacualco as a conquest. This town is in present-day southern Oaxaca and, if a valid conquest, was probably conquered at this time, as it is located not too far from the main conquest route. However, the context in which he lists it indicates a location in the southern Matlatzinca area and he has no other support in this claimed conquest. Consequently, I do not include it here but list it as an unidentified town in the latter area.

6. Durán 1967, 2:265 [chap. 34]; Torquemada 1975–83, 1:239 [bk. 2, chap. 55].

7. *Anales de Cuauhtitlan* 1975:67; *Anales México-Azcapotzalco* 1903:67; Chimalpahin 1965:104 [relación 4]; Clark 1938, 1:33; *Códice Ramírez* 1975:69; *Códice Telleriano-Remensis* 1964–65:288; *Códice Vaticano* 1964–65:254; García Icazbalceta 1886–92, 3:253; Mengin 1952:452; Paso y Troncoso 1939–42, 10:119; Torquemada 1975–83, 1:243 [bk. 2, chap. 58]. Other sources say that the campaign in the region was initiated by Moteuczomah Ilhuicamina but was incomplete and was finished by Axayacatl (Chimalpahin 1965:104 [relación 3]).

8. *Códice Ramírez* 1975:129–31; Durán 1967, 2:197–203 [chap. 24].

9. Tlahuililpan is unlocated but was apparently near Oztoticpac and Poxcauhtlan. *Anales México-Azcapotzalco* 1903:67; *Anales de Cuauhtitlan* 1975:55; *Anales de Tula* 1979:36; Berlin and Barlow 1980:17; Chimalpahin 1965:104 [relación 3]; Dibble 1981, 1:24.

10. *Anales de Cuauhtitlan* 1975:67; Berlin and Barlow 1980:17; Clark

1938, 1:33; Paso y Troncoso 1939–42, 10:119. It is tempting to consider most of these conquests as examples of Axayacatl merely taking credit for completing the subjugation of the area begun by Moteuczomah Ilhuicamina, particularly since all the towns listed as conquered en route to Ahuilizapan, except for Matlatlan, had been conquered previously by Moteuczomah Ilhuicamina. However, reconquest fits into the fragile nature of the Mesoamerican alliance system, and this campaign does make important additions to these previous conquests in the Cuetlachtlan area and was probably waged by Axayacatl in his own right.

11. The route taken on this campaign is not given, but the likeliest one went south out of the basin of Mexico via Cuauhnahuac, Tecpantzinco, and Itzyocan to the Tepeyacac area and then via Tetl-Icoyoccan to Matlatlan, Ahuilizapan, and Cuetlachtlan. Cuezcomatl-Iyacac and Tototlan are close and relatively easily accessible to the north of this route, while Poxcauhtlan, Tlaollan, Mixtlan, and Quetzaloztoc are all clustered just to the south. The route thus may have run directly to Cuetlachtlan, with side trips for ancillary conquests. But since Cuetlachtlan refers to the area rather than just to the town of the same name, the conquest of all the towns in the region can be accounted for more satisfactorily by two side trips, north and south (or a very truncated loop), which may not have even reached the towns at either extreme to accomplish its purpose. Such a route has the advantage of shortness and of avoiding any major descents or ascents.

12. *Anales de Tula* 1979:36; *Anales México-Azcapotzalco* 1903:67; Chimalpahin 1965:104 [relación 3], 208 [relación 7]; Mengin 1952:453. Cuauhxoxouhcan (Coaxoxouhcan) is identified by Kelly and Palerm (1952: 297) as Cuaxoxoca in the present-day state of Mexico, which is a reasonable placement based on the single source used in their reconstruction. However, its context in all four sources and its identification with Totonacapan Cuauhxoxouhcan makes clear that it refers to a region rather than to a city and puts it in the Cuetlachtlan campaign. Only Xochitlan (*Anales México-Azcapotzalco* 1903:67; *Códice Aubin* 1980:73; Chimalpahin 1965:104 [relación 3]; Mengin 1952:453, *planche* 69) and Chiapan (also called Tepeticpac) (Chimalpahin 1965:104 [relación 3], 208 [relación 7]) remain attested.

Since three additional accounts—Chimalpahin (1965:105–106 [relación 3], 208–11 [relación 7]), the *Codex Mexicanus* (Mengin 1952:452–54), and the *Códice Telleriano-Remensis* (1964–65:284–94)—place the initial incursion into the Matlatzinca area before the conquest of Tlatelolco, they reflect this limited incursion, which may have resulted from unrest following the death of Nezahualcoyotl, who had conquered much of the area, rather than the major thrust following the conquest of Tlatelolco.

The conquests during this limited incursion probably occurred together, with the army marching into the relatively level areas north of the basin of Mexico. The line of march probably proceeded almost directly north, first to Xochitlan and then Chiapan (both during campaign season 1472–73) before returning home. Xilotepec is in the line of march and was probably conquered at this time. However, only one source claims such a conquest at this time (Chimalpahin 1965:104 [relación 3]), but even considering the possibility of two separate conquests of that town during Axayacatl's reign, as Chimalpahin indicates, that source's often garbled chronology and the weight of the contrary data argue strongly against it.

13. *Anales de Tula* 1979:36; *Anales México-Azcapotzalco* 1903:67; Barlow 1949b:123; Berlin and Barlow 1980:59; Chimalpahin 1965:104 [relación 3], 208 [relación 7]; *Códice Telleriano-Remensis* 1964–65:286; *Códice Vaticano* 1964–65:252; *Crónica mexicana* 1975:391 [chap. 45]; Dibble 1981, 1:22–23; Durán 1967, 2:262–63 [chap. 34]; García Icazbalceta 1886–92, 3:253; Mengin 1952:453.

14. There are recorded battles between them in the reigns of Itzcoatl, Moteuczomah Ilhuicamina, and even one earlier in the reign of Axayacatl, when the Tlatelolcas attacked the Tenochcas at night but were defeated (Durán 1967, 2:258–59 [chap. 33]). Axayacatl's initial conflict with Tlatelolco seems to have begun after his first year of rule (Chimalpahin 1965:207 [relación 7]).

15. Ixtlilxochtil 1975–77, 2:135–36 [chaps. 49–51]. An alternative explanation for this war is that Tenochtitlan sought to control the increasingly important pochtecah of Tlatelolco, but there is no direct evidence to support this possibility.

16. Torquemada 1975–83, 1:249 [bk. 2, chap. 59].

17. Torquemada 1975–83, 1:244–48 [bk. 2, chap. 58].

18. *Crónica mexicana* 1975:375–76 [chap. 41]. Torquemada includes Huexotzinco among those who promised to aid Tlatelolco, but this appears unlikely given both the contrary statement in the *Crónica mexicana* and the context in which it was made (Torquemada 1975–83, 1:244–48 [bk. 2, chap. 58]).

19. Torquemada 1975–83, 1:246–49 [bk. 2, chap. 58].

20. Acosta 1604, 2:495–96 [bk. 2, chap. 34]; Torquemada 1975–83, 1:244–48 [bk. 2, chap. 58].

21. Torquemada 1975–83, 1:246–49 [bk. 2, chap. 58].

22. Torquemada 1975–83, 1:249–50 [bk. 2, chap. 59]. Ixtlilxochitl's account (1975–77, 2:144 [chap. 53]) maintains that Xihuitl-Temoc aided the Aztecs.

23. Chimalpahin 1965:209 [relación 7].

24. *Anales de Cuauhtitlan* 1975:56; *Anales de Tula* 1979:36; Dibble 1981, 1:23.

25. Carrasco 1984b.

26. *Crónica mexicana* 1975:400–401 [chap. 47]; Durán 1967, 2:267–69 [chap. 35].

27. *Crónica mexicana* 1975:402 [chap. 48].

28. *Crónica mexicana* 1975:402–404 [chap. 48]; Torquemada 1975–83, 1:251 [bk. 2, chap. 59].

29. Durán 1967, 2:272 [chap. 35].

30. *Anales de Cuauhtitlan* 1975:55–57; *Anales de Tula* 1979:36; Barlow 1949b:123; Berlin and Barlow 1980:59; Chimalpahin 1965:105–106 [relación 3], 208–11 [relación 7]; Clark 1938, 1:33; *Códice Telleriano-Remensis* 1964–65:284–94; *Crónica mexicana* 1975:398–424 [chaps. 47–52]; Durán

1967, 2:267–93 [chaps. 35–38]; García Icazbalceta 1886–92, 3:253; Ixtlilxóchitl 1975–77, 2:145 [chap. 53]; *Leyenda de los Soles* 1975:128; Mengin 1952:452–54; Paso y Troncoso 1939–42, 10:119; Torquemada 1975–83, 1:250–51 [bk. 2, chap. 59]; Sahagún 1954:2. Calli-Imanyan is recorded as conquered a year or two after this series of conquests, but I have included it here for three reasons. First, the time span between it and the other conquests is relatively small; second, it is very close to Tolocan, even closer than other conquests made at this time; and third, it was not on the route to any other conquest.

31. *Anales de Cuauhtitlan* 1975:67; Berlin and Barlow 1980:17; Clark 1938, 1:33; *Crónica mexicana* 1975:402 [chap. 48]; *Leyenda de los Soles* 1975:128; Paso y Troncoso 1939–42, 10:119; Sahagún 1954:2.

32. *Anales de Tula* 1979:36; Berlin and Barlow 1980:59; Chimalpahin 1965:105 [relación 3], 208 [relación 7]; *Códice Telleriano-Remensis* 1964–65:288; Mengin 1952:454.

33. These two towns are sequentially recorded during the same year (Chimalpahin 1965:208 [relación 7]).

34. *Anales de Cuauhtitlan* 1975:56; *Anales de Tula* 1979:36; Chimalpahin 1965:105 [relación 3], 208 [relación 7]; Ixtlilxóchitl 1975–77, 2:145 [chap. 53]; Mengin 1952:454.

35. *Anales de Cuauhtitlan* 1975:67; Clark 1938, 1:33; Paso y Troncoso 1939–42, 10:119; Sahagún 1954:2. Coatepec (present-day Coatepec de Harinas, near Cuitlapilco) was also conquered, probably at the same time (Ixtlilxóchitl 1975–77, 2:144–45 [chap. 53]; Paso y Troncoso 1905–48, 6:116, 149; Sahagún 1954:2; Torquemada 1975–83, 1:248 [bk. 2, chap. 58]).

Two other conquered towns—Neucatepec and Cimatepec—are of uncertain location, apparently on the southwest side of what is now called the Sierra Nevada de Toluca (*Crónica mexicana* 1975:426 [chap. 51]; Ixtlilxóchitl 1975–77, 2:144 [chap. 53]). Their relative isolation presents some difficulties in assigning them to either the valley of Tolocan or the southern campaign. Nevertheless, the area was definitely conquered, according to an account from nearby Temazcaltepec (Paso y Troncoso 1905–48, 7:20). Access is difficult from either the valley of Tolocan (which would require a movement southwestward through a mountain pass from Tolocan) or the Chontalcoatlan area, but the latter route is easier, going up a valley from the Cuitlapilco area to Neucatepec and then crossing more mountainous areas to Temazcaltepec and on to Cimatepec. The army could then either backtrack or proceed to Tolocan, but given the apparent entry (Ocuillan) and exit (Tenantzinco) of the southern campaign, the former is more likely.

36. *Anales de Cuauhtitlan* 1975:56, 67; *Anales de Tula* 1979:36; Barlow 1949b:123; Berlin and Barlow 1980:17; Chimalpahin 1965:105 [relación 3], 208 [relación 7]; Clark 1938, 1:33; *Códice Telleriano-Remensis* 1964–65:288; *Códice Vaticano* 1964–65:254; Durán 1967, 2:293 [chap. 38]; Ixtlilxóchitl 1975–77, 2:144 [chap. 53]; Mengin 1952:454; Paso y Troncoso 1939–42, 10:119; Sahagún 1954:2; Torquemada 1975–83, 1:250 [bk. 2, chap. 58]).

37. Chimalpahin 1965:209 [relación 7].

38. Chimalpahin 1965:210 [relación 7].

39. *Anales de Cuauhtitlan* 1975:57; *Anales de Tula* 1979:36; Barlow 1949b:123; Chimalpahin 1965:105 [relación 3]; Clark 1938, 1:33; *Códice Telleriano-Remensis* 1964–65:290; *Códice Vaticano* 1964–65:254; Dibble 1981, 1:24; Durán 1967, 2:293 [chap. 38]; Ixtlilxóchitl 1975–77, 2:145 [chap. 53]; Mengin 1952:453–54; Torquemada 1975–83, 1:250 [bk. 2, chap. 58]; Sahagún 1954:2). Xiquipilco is too distant from the earlier conquests in the valley of Tolocan to have been a probable conquest then, and it fits conveniently into the pattern of the northern conquests. Consequently, I am placing it here on geopolitical grounds in disregard of its recorded conquest date. Tlahuililpan is also listed as a conquest (Berlin and Barlow 1980:17), but it is unclear which town is meant. One likely candidate is the Tlahuililpan between Tollan and Atocpan, but the context in which the conquest is listed implies a location in the Cuetlachtlan area, and I have accordingly included it there.

40. *Crónica mexicana* 1975:413 [chap. 50].

41. *Crónica mexicana* 1975:412 [chap. 49]. It is not entirely clear when these events took place, and indeed, since no army was involved, they could have occurred at any time. Neverthless, these events are recorded as having occurred immediately prior to the Michhuacan war and are best placed at this time. But because such "requests" were made without using force, it is unlikely that the other towns listed as conquered in that region during the reign of Axayacatl (but otherwise without dates) were incorporated as a result of this event.

42. Chimalpahin 1965:105 [relación 3].

43. Herrejón Peredo (1978:26–27) suggests that the area was taken by the Tarascans and that Axayacatl replaced the local ruler with a military ruler after the region was reconquered.

44. The war with the Tarascans occurred after the conquest of the Matlatzinca territory and the capitulation of Cempohuallan and Quiahuiztlan (*Crónica mexicana* 1975:421 [chap. 52]). This does not necessarily mean that the conquests to the south and north of the valley of Tolocan were completed at this time. In fact, one source (Barlow 1949b:123) indicates that perhaps the conquest of the entire area was not complete, with the conquest of Tolocan following the Tarascan war, but that source lacks a reliable chronology. Moreover, given the size and strength of the Tarascan Empire, the Aztec pattern of attempted encirclement of significant enemies, and the general strategic wisdom of securing these areas before projecting further afield, it is likely that the Michhuacan war took place at this time (campaign season 1479–80), following the completion of the Matlatzincas' conquests and those to the south and north as well.

45. *Crónica mexicana* 1975:421–24 [chap. 52].

46. *Crónica mexicana* 1975:421–24 [chap. 52].

47. Durán 1967, 2:281–83 [chap. 37].

48. Chimalpahin 1965:209 [relación 7]; Durán 1967, 2:281–84 [chap. 37]; Sahagún 1954:2.

49. *Anales de Cuauhtitlan* 1975:67; Chimalpahin 1965:104 [relación 3]; Clark 1938, 1:33; *Crónica mexicana* 1975:423 [chap. 52]; Paso y Troncoso 1939–42, 10:119. Tlaximaloyan lies along the probable route of march into the Tarascan territory, as does Malacatepec, which was also probably conquered during the entry (Ixtlilxóchitl 1975–77, 2:144 [chap. 53]; Torquemada 1975–83, 1:250 [bk. 2, chap. 58]).

50. Herrejón Peredo (1978:22) asserts that the Tarascan campaign march went from Tenochtitlan to Neucatepec, over the Sierra de Angangueo, to Tlaximaloyan (Tlaximaroa), and then to Matlatzinco, with the retreat going to Tlaximaloyan and back to Tzinacantepec. I am unable to concur with this sequence. The specific data are too thin to fill out this march definitively, and the route specified is too tortuous to be either logical or feasible.

51. I am indebted to Neil Goldberg for this analysis.

52. *Anales de Cuauhtitlan* 1975:57; *Crónica mexicana* 1975:429–30 [chap. 54]; Durán 1967, 2:293 [chap. 38].

53. Durán 1967, 2:265 [chap. 34].

54. The actual route taken by the Aztecs in this campaign is uncertain, but access to the area posed few difficulties. The most direct route went up the Teotihuacan Valley, either to Tollantzinco and then east or due east and then north. From Tliliuhqui-Tepec, Zacatlan was a short, easy trip, but it is likelier that this battle was fought at a border location and not actually at either of these towns.

The exact location of Tliliuhqui-Tepec is uncertain, but it is conventionally placed to the north of Tlaxcallan at present-day Chignaupan, Puebla (Gerhard 1972:390). Its location implies the possibility of an alliance with the other independent states of the present-day Puebla/Tlaxcala Valley, such as Tlaxcallan, Huexotzinco, Atlixco, and Chololłan, which the Triple Alliance fought for decades (Davies 1968: map 3). Given the intermittent nature of the wars in this area, the fact that they were often flower wars, and the absence of indication that the city was conquered, it is likely that the war with Tliliuhqui-Tepec was also a xochiyaoyotl.

55. *Anales de Cuauhtitlan* 1975:67; Barlow 1949b:123; Berlin and Barlow 1980:17; Clark 1938, 1:33; Paso y Troncoso 1939–42, 10:119; Torquemada 1975–83, 1:251 [bk. 2, chap. 59].

56. *Anales de Cuauhtitlan* 1975:67; Berlin and Barlow 1980:17; Clark 1938, 1:33; Paso y Troncoso 1939–42, 10:119. Chimalpahin (1965:106 [relación 3], 211 [relación 7]) is unique in recording the conquest of Tochcalco (unlocated) in 1479, which may refer to a town in this region, or may be an error for Tochpan. Torquemada (1975–83, 1:251 [bk. 2, chap. 59]) also records the reconquest of Tototlan, where some merchants had been killed, but it is unclear whether any of these reflect actual conquests during Axayacatl's reign or whether they extended into that of his successor, Tizoc.

Chapter 13

1. The meaning of "Tizoc" is uncertain, but as written (or in its variant form of Tizocicatzin), the name is meaningless. If the *i* in Tizoc can be inter-

preted as a variant of *e*, as occurs in other words, then the name would be Tezoc, which would derive from *te-zo*, "to bleed someone, to draw blood by piercing or sticking someone." Thus, the name would mean "He-has-bled-people," "He-has-pricked-people [or someone]," or "He-pricked-people [or someone]." This interpretation is supported by the name glyph for this king, which shows a leg that has been punctured by a thorn. The reading is still uncertain, however, and I present it cautiously. Moreover, I have retained the traditional spelling of Tizoc throughout.

2. Durán 1967, 2:295–97 [chap. 39].

3. Acosta 1604, 2:491.

4. Carrasco 1984b:70. However, he had been the tlacochcalcatl under King Itzcoatl. See chap. 10.

5. Durán 1967, 2:186 [chap. 22].

6. Torquemada 1975–83, 1:252 [bk. 2, chap. 60].

7. Durán 1967, 2:235 [chap. 39].

8. Durán 1967, 2:311 [chap. 40]; Herrera 1934–57, 6:212–13 [decade 3, bk. 2, chap. 13]; Ixtlilxóchitl 1975–77, 2:154 [chap. 58]; Sahagún 1954:2. However, Barlow (1947:220) dissents from this position.

9. Alvarado Tezozomoc 1975b:117; *Crónica mexicana* 1975:441 [chap. 57]; Durán 1967, 2:303 [chap. 40].

10. *Crónica mexicana* 1975:441 [chap. 57].

11. Durán 1967, 2:303–304 [chap. 40]; Herrera 1934–57, 6:212–13 [decade 3, bk. 2, chap. 13].

12. *Anales de Cuauhtitlan* 1975:67; Berlin and Barlow 1980:17; Clark 1938, 1:35; Paso y Troncoso 1939–42, 10:119.

13. As an example, Tzapotlan and Tochpan are not recorded as having been conquered, but they began paying tribute to Tenochtitlan at this time, an act of submission, doubtless as a result of this campaign (Chimalpahin 1965:107 [relación 3]).

14. Part of the route to the Metztitlan region is known. Marching separately from their home cities, the allied armies met at Tetzontepec, a site easily accessible to all the assembled forces via valley floors. The combined army then marched through the previously conquered towns of Tecpantepec and Atocpan to Atotonilco, also a previous conquest. From there the route is uncertain, but it led to the head of the Metztitlan Valley. The Aztecs' return trip was quick and doubtless retraced the outward route.

15. Acosta 1604, 2:493; *Crónica mexicana* 1975:441–45 [chaps. 57–58].

16. Among those attending were the lords of Cuetlachtlan, Ahuizilapan, Cempohuallan, Tochpan, Xiuhcoac, Cuauhnahuac, Yauhtepec, Huaxtepec, Yacapichtlan, Coaixtlahuacan, Huitzoco, Tepecuacuilco, Tlachmalacac, Nochtepec, Tzacualpan, Tlachco, Iztapan, Chiauhtla, Piaztlan, Teotlalco, Cuitlatenanco, Cuauhapazco, Xochihuehuetlan, Olinallan, Tlalcozauhtitlan, Matlatzinco, Tlacotepec, Calli-Imanyan, Tepemaxalco, Teotenanco, Malinalco, and Ocuillan (*Crónica mexicana* 1975:446–47 [chap. 58]; Durán 1967, 2:304–305 [chap. 40]).

17. Chimalpahin 1965:107 [relación 3], 216 [relación 7].

18. Chicpantlan's location is unknown. Berlin and Barlow 1980:59.

19. García Icazbalceta 1886–92, 3:253.

20. Berlin and Barlow 1980:59.

21. Barlow 1949b:125; García Icazbalceta 1886–92, 3:253; Mengin 1952:455. One source (Chimalpahin 1965:107–10 [relación 3]) indicates that there were two separate incursions or reconquests into the Matlatzinco area as a result, in 1484 and 1485, but the other chronicle sources indicate only one campaign (*Códice Telleriano-Remensis* 1964–65:294; García Icazbalceta 1886–92, 3:253; Mengin 1952:455).

22. Chimalpahin 1965:107 [relación 3]; *Códice Telleriano-Remensis* 1964–65:294.

23. Torquemada 1975–83, 1:252 [bk. 2, chap. 60].

24. *Anales de Cuauhtitlan* 1975:67; Berlin and Barlow 1980:17; Clark 1938, 1:35; Paso y Troncoso 1939–42, 10:119; Torquemada 1975–83, 1:252 [bk. 2, chap. 60].

25. The likely route for the Matlatzinca conquests was directly west out of the basin of Mexico to Tzinacantlan and then back to Tlacotepec.

26. *Anales de Cuauhtitlan* 1975:67; Berlin and Barlow 1980:17; Clark 1938, 1:35; García Icazbalceta 1886–92, 3:253; Paso y Troncoso 1939–42, 10:119; Torquemada 1975–83, 1:253–54 [bk. 2, chap. 61].

27. *Anales de Cuauhtitlan* 1975:67; Berlin and Barlow 1980:17; Clark 1938, 1:35; Paso y Troncoso 1939–42, 10:119.

28. Chimalpahin 1965:110 [relación 3].

29. Torquemada 1975–83, 1:252 [bk. 2, chap. 60].

30. Acosta 1604, 2:493 [bk. 7, chap. 18]; Durán 1967, 2:311 [chap. 40]; Vázquez de Espinosa 1942:143 [bk. 3, chap. 12].

31. Durán 1967, 2:311 [chap. 40].

32. Torquemada 1975–83, 1:257 [bk. 2, chap. 63].

33. Torquemada 1975–83, 1:255 [bk. 2, chap. 62].

Chapter 14

1. Unlike the way the other kings' names have been treated in this book, "Otter" is not a literal translation, nor is there a satisfactory literal translation. One possible translation is "water thornness" from *a-* (*atl*, water), *-huitz-* (*huitztli*, thorn), and *-yotl* (-ness), but this makes no apparent sense. Another possible derivation is from the unattested verb *huitzoa* (to become thorny, to become like a thorn) in a manner similar to other such Nahuatl constructions (e.g., Andrews 1975:241, 242, 358). This may present a more satisfactory construction, but its meaning is no more transparent. The name is usually translated as "water creature" or "water monster" (e.g., Pasztory 1983:53; Soustelle 1970:17–18), apparently influenced by Ahuitzotl's name glyph (see fig. 27) which shows a doglike creature with water on its back (see Nicholson and Keber 1983:120 for a discussion of the glyph). However, in his sixteenth-century natural history of Mexico, Hernández (1959, 2:393) lists *ahuitzotl* as the name for an otter, an animal indigenous to the basin of Mexico (Leopold 1972:461–64; Memoria de las obras 1975, 1:152–53). Thus, I have translated Ahuitzotl directly as "Otter," which is what it signifies, rather than attempting to give its literal meaning.

2. *Crónica mexicana* 1975:457 [chap. 60].

3. *Anales de Cuauhtitlan* 1975:58; Berlin and Barlow 1980:17; Clark 1938, 1:37; *Códice Telleriano-Remensis* 1964–65:298; *Crónica mexicana* 1975:462–68 [chaps. 61–62]; Durán 1967, 2:319 [chap. 41]; Ixtlilxóchitl 1975–77, 2:155 [chap. 59]; Paso y Troncoso 1939–42, 10:119; Sahagún 1954:2; Torquemada 1975–83, 1:257 [bk. 2, chap. 63].

4. Durán 1967, 2:319 [chap. 51].

5. Durán 1967, 2:320 [chap. 51].

6. *Anales de Cuauhtitlan* 1975:58; Barlow 1949b:126; Berlin and Barlow 1980:17; Clark 1938, 1:37; *Códice Telleriano-Remensis* 1964–65:298; *Códice Vaticano* 1964–65:264; Paso y Troncoso 1939–42, 10:119; Torquemada 1975–83, 1:258 [bk. 2, chap. 63].

7. Durán 1967, 2:323 [chap. 52].

8. Durán 1967, 2:324–25 [chap. 52].

9. *Códice Vaticano* 1964–65:264.

10. *Crónica mexicana* 1975:480–83 [chap. 65]; Durán 1967, 2:327 [chap. 42]; Torquemada 1975–83, 1:257 [bk. 2, chap. 63].

11. *Anales de Cuauhtitlan* 1975:58; *Anales de Tula* 1979:37; Berlin and Barlow 1980:60; Chimalpahin 1965:111 [relación 3], 220 [relación 7]; *Códice Vaticano* 1964–65:264; Dibble 1981, 1:29; Ixtlilxóchitl 1975–77, 2:155 [chap. 59].

12. *Anales de Cuauhtitlan* 1975:67; Berlin and Barlow 1980:17; Chimalpahin 1965:115 [relación 3], 224 [relación 7]; Clark 1938, 1:37; *Crónica mexicana* 1975:481 [chap. 65]; Durán 1967, 2:341 [chap. 43]; Paso y Troncoso 1939–42, 10:119; Sahagún 1954:2; Torquemada 1975–83, 1:263 [bk. 2, chap. 66].

13. Torquemada 1975–83, 1:267 [bk. 2, chap. 67].

14. The army probably marched from the basin of Mexico by way of the Teotihuacan Valley and proceeded northeast to conquer Xolotlan before meeting the allied armies at Cuauhchinanco. Given the proximity of the conquered towns to the likely battle site, it is probable that they all submitted to the Aztec army and that a march to each town by the army was not necessary.

If such a trek were necessary, however, it was probably from the Cuauhchinanco area east down the Tecolotlan River drainage onto the coastal lowlands and on to Nauhtlan, then north again to Tozapan, Tetzapotitlan; and then to Tochpan, Tamapachco, and Micquetlan. Then the route began the ascent into the hills again, probably going up the Vinazco River valley and down the Calabozo River drainage to Tlatlauhqui-Icxic and Xiuhcoac and following the valley around to Huexotla. From there, that river's tributaries stretch almost to Mollanco, where the Amaxac River drainage runs close to Atocpan and the level areas of the central highlands, offering easy access to Tecpatepec and leading back to Tenochtitlan.

15. *Crónica mexicana* 1975:517 [chap. 70]; Durán 1967, 2:337–41 [chap. 43].

16. Durán 1967, 2:340 [chap. 43]. Other reports put the number of sacrificial victims substantially lower.

17. Chimalpahin 1965:39–48 [relación 3].

18. Chimalpahin 1965:111 [relación 3].

19. Chimalpahin 1965:222–23 [relación 7].
20. *Crónica mexicana* 1975:251–58 [chaps. 71–72]; Durán 1967, 2: 347–48 [chap. 44].
21. *Crónica mexicana* 1975:521–22 [chap. 71].
22. *Crónica mexicana* 1975:533–36 [chap. 74]; Durán 1967, 2:347–55 [chaps. 44–45].
23. *Crónica mexicana* 1975:526–28 [chap. 72]; Durán 1967, 2:348 [chap. 44].
24. *Crónica mexicana* 1975:533–35 [chap. 74]; Durán 1967, 2:351 [chap. 45].
25. Durán 1967, 2:354–55 [chap. 45]. The routes taken by the allied armies are uncertain, and they did not unite until they reached Teticpac. Thus some marched south from the valley of Tolocan, while others probably went through the Cuauhnahuac area and then west. From Teticpac the joint army marched to Teloloapan, probably going almost due south by the shorter more rugged route in preference to the easier but more circuitous route along the Balsas River drainage. From there the troops marched overland directly to Oztoman and then descended on nearby Alahuiztlan. The armies probably retraced their steps on the return journey.
26. Durán 1967, 2:354 [chap. 45].
27. E.g., Herrejón Peredo 1978; Stanislawski 1947.
28. Stanislawski 1947:53–54.
29. Stanislawski 1947:49–50.
30. Brand 1971:644; Stanislawski 1947:51.
31. I do not take seriously Stanislawski's (1947:50) claims that the Tarascans were the aggressors in the Oztoman region but were on the defensive in the valley of Tolocan area simply because the Aztecs had a fortified site in the first area and none in the second.
32. Herrejón Peredo (1978:30) suggests a matching set of "bulwarks" by the Aztecs and their allies, but there is little evidence that they were specialized fortifications similar to those of the Tarascans. Although Oztoman faced Cutzamala (58 km. or 36 mi. apart, or 2 to 3 days' march), Cutzamala was apparently fortified after Oztoman became an Aztec outpost. Thus two different strategic postures were adopted by these competing empires: the Aztec hegemonic empire versus the Tarascan quasi-territorial empire.
33. *Relación de Michoacán* 1977:173–78, 186–97.
34. Vargas Rea 1944–46:7/3:101–103, 109–10; 7/4:128–31; 7/5:26; 7/8:21, 27.
35. Some of the towns in the subsequent Guerrero campaign had apparently been the objects of conquest previously (Chimalpahin 1965:113 [relación 3], 223 [relación 7]), but others had not and were not within the area of previous Aztec influence (Chimalpahin 1965:113 [relación 3], 223 [relación 7]; Dibble 1981, 1:30).
36. *Anales de Cuauhtitlan* 1975:67; Chimalpahin 1965:113 [relación 3], 224 [relación 7]; Clark 1938, 1:37; Paso y Troncoso 1939–42, 10:119.
37. *Anales de Cuauhtitlan* 1975:67; Berlin and Barlow 1980:17; Chimalpahin 1965:113 [relación 3], 223 [relación 7]; Clark 1938, 1:37; Dibble 1981, 1:29; Durán 1967, 2:341 [chap. 43]; Ixtlilxóchitl 1975–77, 2:155 [chap.

59]; Paso y Troncoso 1939–42, 10:119; Sahagún 1954:2. However, while the early conquests (Tlappantzinco, Cuauhtepec, Totoltenco, and Atl-Chayahuacan) apparently involved battles, none of the later conquests did to any notable extent, and the subjugation of the region probably proceeded peacefully. Writing from the Tarascan perspective, Brand (1971:644–48) believes these Pacific coast conquests to be unlikely, but this is a decidedly minority view.

38. The probable route for such a campaign was south from the basin of Mexico, through Cuauhnahuac and along the Amacozac River to the Mexcallan River and Tlalcozauhtitlan (188 km. or 117 mi.; 6 to 10 days). By going up the drainage of the Mexcallan and Tlappanec rivers, the army reached Tlappan (113 km. or 70 mi.; 4 to 6 days). At that point the journey could have taken one of two likely routes, going in either direction on a single large loop. The army could have gone to Tlappantzinco (45 km. or 28 mi.; 2 days), and then to Pochtlan (68 km. or 42 mi.; 2 to 3 days), Iztac-Tlallocan (63 km. or 39 mi.; 2 to 3 days), and Tototepec (65 km. or 40 mi.; 2 to 3 days). From there the route would follow the coast to Cuauhtepec (165 km. or 102 mi.; 5 to 9 days) and Nexpan (30 km. or 19 mi.; 1 to 2 days), where a division may have occurred. The army probably proceeded up the Omitlan River drainage to Acatl-Iyacac (75 km. or 47 mi.; 2 to 4 days) and then back to Tlappan (48 km. or 30 mi.; 2 days) before backtracking to Tenochtitlan.

If the Iztac-Tlallocan conquests were a separate thrust, they were easily accessible from Tlappantzinco by crossing a small mountain range and entering the Río de la Cuehara drainage, which passes Pochtlan, Iztac-Tlallocan, and Tototepec. The last town is on the coastal plain and permits easy access to all other coastal areas. If these conquests were part of the overall Guerrero thrust, a simple continuation to the northwest would bring the army to Cuauhtepec and the remaining towns.

Towns in the coastal region also became tributaries, as far up the coast as Acalecan (383 km. or 237 mi.; 10 to 20 days), although it is not clear that the army actually penetrated that far. The entire army may not have been needed, and it would have posed a major additional logistical challenge. An expansion that incorporated Acapolco (85 km. or 53 mi.; 3 to 4 days, from Nexpan) and Cihuatlan (143 km. or 89 mi.; 5 to 7 days farther) would probably have been sufficient, with the other cities acceding. The return via Tetellan (del Río) (375 km. or 233 mi.; 12 to 20 days, from Acalecan) would involve crossing the lower Sierra Madre del Sur, probably north of Acapolco, into the Iyetlan River drainage, which runs directly to Tetellan. From there the Balsas River drainage provides an almost direct route to Cuauhnahuac and the basin of Mexico. The side trek to Acalecan was an additional 1,600 kilometers (1,000 miles), requiring an added 50 to 84 days of army march time, although emissaries alone could have accomplished the trip in significantly less time.

39. Torquemada 1975–83, 1:258 [bk. 2, chap. 63].

40. Chimalpahin 1965:113 [relación 3], 224 [relación 7]; Ixtlilxóchitl 1975–77, 2:155 [chap. 59]; Torquemada 1975–83, 1:258 [bk. 2, chap. 63], 263 [bk. 2, chap. 66]. Although Totomihuacan and Xicochimalco are dated a little later, their geographical location and sequential listing argue for the

inclusion of both (*Anales de Cuauhtitlan* 1975:58; *Códice Telleriano-Remensis* 1964–65:300; *Códice Vaticano* 1964–65:266; Chimalpahin 1965:115 [relación 3], 224 [relación 7]). Torquemada's claim that Cuauhpilollan was conquered during this campaign and also that the campaign extended as far as (but did not include) the province of Cuezalcuitlapillan is unlikely, and other sources place this conquest more reasonably in the following campaign in the Huaxyacac area.

The route of this conquest probably led southeast out of the basin of Mexico to Chinantlan before turning northeast toward Cualtepec (265 km. or 164 mi.; 8 to 14 days). The historical accounts indicate the conquest of the people of the Cuetlachtlan area. Thus, a general battle may have been fought, resulting in the conquest of Quimichtlan, Acatlan, Tlallocatepec, and Coyolapan (78 km. or 48 mi.; 3 to 4 days, if fought in the vicinity of Ahuizilapan). Alternatively, each of these cities may have been conquered individually, with thrusts both north and south, but a general battle was likelier. The return to Tenochtitlan could have been made by reversing the trek through the lowlands to Ahuilizapan and then going west to the basin of Mexico by way of Totomihuacan.

41. *Anales de Cuauhtitlan* 1975:58; *Anales de Tula* 1979:37.

42. *Anales de Cuauhtitlan* 1975:58; *Anales de Tula* 1979:37; Chimalpahin 1965:113 [relación 3], 223–24 [relación 7]; Dibble 1981, 1:30–31; Ixtlilxóchtil 1975–77, 2:160 [chap. 61]; Torquemada 1975–83, 1:258 [bk. 2, chap. 63].

43. Chimalpahin 1965:223 [relación 7].

44. Chimalpahin 1965:113 [relación 3].

45. Dibble 1981, 1:32.

46. *Códice Telleriano-Remensis* 1964–65:300.

47. *Anales de Cuauhtitlan* 1975:58, 67; *Anales de Tula* 1979:37; Berlin and Barlow 1980:17; Chimalpahin 1965:115 [relación 3], 224–25 [relación 7]; Clark 1938, 1:37; *Códice Telleriano-Remensis* 1964–65:300–302; *Códice Vaticano* 1964–65:266–68; Ixtlilxóchitl 1975–77, 2:163 [chap. 63]; Paso y Troncoso 1939–42, 10:119 Torquemada 1975–83, 1:263 [bk. 2, chap. 66].

The probable route of this campaign led out of the basin of Mexico and went south by way of Cuauhnahuac and then southeast to Acatlan. From there the route probably crossed over into the plain where Mizquitlan and Tlacotepec were located, proceeded down the valley to Xaltepc and then to Ayotochcuitlatlan (Cuicatlan), and continued southeast to Huaxyacac, Teotzapotlan, and Mictlan. Then the route probably continued into the Tecuantepec area (the province of Quetzalcuitlapillan mentioned by Torquemada) and on to Cuauhpiloayan (800 km. or 500 mi.; 25 to 42 days). The return could have been a reversal of the outward route; or the army may have continued north on the Gulf coastal plain and reentered the highlands at Ahuilizapan before returning to the basin of Mexico along established and shorter routes (650 km. or 400 mi.; 20 to 34 days).

48. *Anales de Tula* 1979:37; Chimalpahin 1965:119 [relación 3]. During the same year, and apparently unattached to any other campaign, "Tliltepec" is mentioned as a conquest by two sources (*Anales de Cuauhtitlan*

1975:58; Ixtlilxóchitl 1975–77, 2:163 [chap. 63]). Although the conquest of Tliltepec (present-day San Miguel Tliltepec, Oaxaca) has been accepted (Holt 1979:228; Kelly and Palerm 1952:305), there are sound reasons not to do so. Tliltepec is distant from Tenochtitlan and an unlikely target for apparently unassisted Tetzcocas; both Tliliuhqui-Tepec and Tliltepec are recorded (but by different sources) as having been fought in the same year, with many Tetzcocas dying in both; and this war is mentioned in conjunction with a battle with Huexotzinco, which would tend to favor both a xochiyaoyotl and a location closer to the basin of Mexico (*Anales de Cuauhtitlan* 1975:58). Another consideration here is the confusion between the two names, Tliliuhqui-Tepec and Tliltepec. While there appears to be a considerable difference between the two names, there is little in Nahuatl. They are variant forms of the same thing, "Black-hill-place," and a minor lapse in orthography is easily understood. As a result, while the occurrence of a xochiyaoyotl between Tetzcoco and Tliliuhqui-Tepec is easily supported, a conquest of Tliltepec is not and is likely a *lapsus calami*.

49. *Códice Telleriano-Remensis* 1964–65:302; *Códice Vaticano* 1964–65:268. Zoltepec was easily accessible by going west from Tenochtitlan into the valley of Tolocan and then south via Tenantzinco to Malinaltenanco before going a short distance west to the town.

50. *Crónica mexicana* 1975:537–38 [chap. 75]; Durán 1967, 2:357–62 [chap. 46].

51. This army included soldiers from Coyohuacan, Xochimilco, Mizquic, Cuitlahuac, Colhuacan, Ixtlapalapan, Mexicatzinco, Huitzilopochco, Chalco, Tlahuic, the lowlands, the Matlatzinco region, the mountains of Tenantzinco, Malinalco, Ocuillan, Xilotepec, Chiapan, Xocotitlan, Mazahuacan, Xiquipilco, Cuauhhuacan, Tollantzinco, and the Otomies (*Crónica mexicana* 1975:538–39 [chap. 75]). Metztitlan is unconvincingly listed as forming part of this army, but some people from the mountains of that region may have participated.

52. *Crónica mexicana* 1975:541 [chap. 75]; Durán 1967, 2:360 [chap. 46].

53. Torquemada 1975–83, 1:267 [bk. 2, chap. 67].

54. *Crónica mexicana* 1975:541–44 [chaps. 75–76].

55. *Anales de Cuauhtitlan* 1975:58; *Anales de Tula* 1979:37; Berlin and Barlow 1980:60; Chimalpahin 1965:119 [relación 3], 225 [relación 7]; *Códice Vaticano* 1964–65:270; *Crónica mexicana* 1975:544 [chap. 76]; Durán 1967, 2:357–62 [chap. 46]; Ixtlilxóchitl 1975–77, 2:155 [chap. 59], 163 [chap. 63]; Mengin 1952:456; Torquemada 1975–83, 1:265–67 [bk. 2, chaps. 66–67].

56. *Anales de Cuauhtitlan* 1975:67; Berlin and Barlow 1980:17; Clark 1938, 1:37; Ixtlilxóchitl 1975–77, 2:166 [chap. 65]; Paso y Troncoso 1939–42, 10:119; Torquemada 1975–83, 1:258 [bk. 2, chap. 63]. These towns are given only in conquest lists. The references made by the sources here to Ayotlan and Xolotlan are errors and refer to the subsequent Xoconochco campaign.

In recording the first major conquest of the next king, Moteuczomah Xocoyotl, two sources describe the conquest of the Tecuantepec region. This campaign to the south began because Aztec merchants were killed by the people of Xaltepec, Cuatzonteccan, and Icpatepec (*Crónica mexicana* 1975: 597–99 [chap. 88]; Durán 1967, 2:417–22 [chap. 55]). Moteuczomah Xocoyotl led the Triple Alliance army on the campaign and conquered Xaltepec and Cuatzonteccan, and as a result the lords of Tecuantepec, Miahuatlan, and Izhuatlan also became tributaries.

While ostensibly describing the campaign of Moteuczomah Xocoyotl, the latter half of this account precisely parallels the one cited above for Ahuitzotl. Moreover, there is a complementary distribution of accounts, with these sources citing these conquests in the next reign, while most sources place it here. For these reasons, and the presence of two conflicting accounts for Moteuczomah Xocoyotl's first major campaign (of which this is one), I feel the account describes Ahuitzotl's exploits and properly belongs here.

57. *Crónica mexicana* 1975:546–47 [chap. 77]. The route for this conquest was doubtless along the established conquest route into the Huaxyacac area and then southeast from Mictlan to the area of Tecuantepec. From there, all the conquered cities are easily accessible along the lowland coastal plain of the Pacific.

58. Sahagún 1959:6.

59. Berlin and Barlow 1980:60; Dibble 1981, 1:34; Torquemada 1975–83, 1:264 [bk. 2, chap. 66].

60. The pochtecah claim that they had already completed the conquests of these towns by the time the Aztec army arrived (Sahagún 1959:3–6) is improbable considering their training, numbers, and opposition. Rather, at the approach of the Aztec forces, which had now proved their ability and resolve to project force that far, the hostile towns probably submitted, possibly to the pochtecah as the only immediate representatives of the empire, and thus avoided outright destruction.

61. *Crónica mexicana* 1975:550–53 [chap. 78].

62. *Crónica mexicana* 1975:550–55 [chaps. 78–79]; Durán 1967, 2: 383–89 [chap. 50].

63. *Anales de Cuauhtitlan* 1975:67; Berlin and Barlow 1980:17; Clark 1938, 1:37; *Crónica mexicana* 1975:544 [chap. 75]; Paso y Troncoso 1939–42, 10:119; Sahagún 1954:2. Huehuetlan, located near Huitztlan, was also part of this campaign. As discussed above, there are numerous towns named Huehuetlan: Barlow (1947) locates this one in present-day Guerrero, Kelly and Palerm (1952:305) locate it either in Guerrero or in Chiapas, but Holt (1979:236, 271–72) places it here; the context in which it is listed argues strongly for that interpretation.

Chillan was conquered in 1499 (Chimalpahin 1965:226–27 [relación 7]), and Xaltepec is recorded as having revolted and been reconquered in 1500 (*Anales de Cuauhtitlan* 1975:58; *Anales de Tula* 1979:37; Chimalpahin 1965:119–20 [relación 3], 227 [relación 7]; Ixtlilxóchitl 1975–77, 2:166 [chap. 65]; Torquemada 1975–83, 1:267 [bk. 2, chap. 67]). Both of these conquests are recorded as isolated occurrences, but the sources listing them fail to mention the Xoconochco campaign. Moreover, 1499 and 1500 are probably not as distant as they seem, but are in the same campaign season. Thus these two towns were probably conquered as part of the Xoconochco campaign, Chillan first and Xaltepec later.

This trek covered 2,300 kilometers (1,425 miles) round trip, requiring 72 to 119 days, exclusive of days required for combat, rest, and regrouping. Of this, the final loop beyond preexisting logistical support areas covered 700 kilometers (435 miles), or 22 to 36 days. The route taken for this campaign doubtless duplicated that of the earlier Tecuantepec campaign, as all the conquered towns are easily accessible once the Pacific lowlands have been reached.

Several towns listed as conquered during the rule of Ahuitzotl remain unlocated: Cuauhxayacatitlan (associated with present-day Jico Viejo and Coyulapa), Huipillan (possibly present-day La Huipililla, Guerrero), Cahuallan (in present-day Guerrero or Chiapas), Iztatlan (in present-day Guerrero or Chiapas), Chiltepec, Icxolotlan (possibly a repetition of Xolotlan), and Cuaxotlatlan. Several other towns can be tentatively located but cannot be convincingly placed chronologically. These include Coyolapan (present-day Cuilapan, Oaxaca [Barlow 1949a:118–19], not the town located in Puebla [contra Kelly and Palerm 1952:304–305, and Holt 1979:267]), and Tlilapan. For Tlilapan, there are two plausible alternatives, but in the recorded context—Tlilapan, Tochpan, Tziccoac; (García Icazbalceta 1886–92, 3:302–303—the location near Ahuilizapan is favored, but is not conclusive. Totolapan appears to have been associated with Huexotzinco (Chimalpahin 1965:223 [relación 7]).

64. Ixtlilxóchitl 1975–77, 2:177 [chap. 70].

65. Durán 1967, 2:391 [chap. 51].

Chapter 15

1. *Crónica mexicana* 1975:568 [chap. 81].

2. Torquemada 1975–83, 1:267 [bk. 2, chap. 68].

3. The preinaugural raid took place to the south, but there are two divergent accounts of precisely where. One account records Atlixco, a traditional enemy, as the target and maintains that the campaign was a success, with many prisoners taken even though many warriors and captains died (Torquemada 1975–83, 1:269–70 [bk. 2, chap. 69]). The second set of accounts lists Nopallan and Icpatepec as the targets. These towns had refused to pay tribute to the Aztecs, so Moteuczomah Xocoyotl gathered an army and conquered them, taking care to secure captives for his coronation (*Crónica mexicana* 1965:578–85 [chaps. 83–84]; Durán 1967, 2:407 [chap. 53]).

The second set of cities—Icpatepec and Nopallan—was the likelier target, as several factors militate against selecting Atlixco as the initial target. The precoronation campaigns had three main purposes. The first purpose, obtaining sacrificial war captives, was only one, and a lesser one at that. The second purpose was for the king-elect to demonstrate his skill and bravery as the war leader. The third was overwhelmingly political. The king-elect selected cities that had rebelled or otherwise given offense, permitting the Aztecs to demonstrate the consequences of such disobedience. Moreover, none of the previous kings had chosen a xochiyaoyotl foe for their precoronation campaign.

Given the reasons a xochiyaoyotl was fought (the inability or expense of outright conquest), selecting a xochiyaoyotl opponent for the precoronation campaign would not be effective. Such cities were enemies, not rebels, and they were unlikely to be subdued outright. Thus while martial skill might be demonstrated, the political consequences of rebellion would not be. A newly selected king had everything to lose and little to gain by selecting such a foe and was unlikely to do so. While there may have been a battle with Atlixco, and captives from that city may have formed part of the sacrifices for the coronation ceremony, I do not think that Atlixco was a primary target of the precoronation campaign.

4. The issue of which towns in the Huaxyacac region were conquered during the reign of Moteuczomah Xocoyotl is problematic. While many conquests are temporally specified in the documents, numerous others are not. Thus, the distribution of these conquered towns among the various campaigns can only be approximated. The specific time of a conquest cannot be given with assurance, since the conquerors passed through the region repeatedly, and their practice did not include the necessary conquest of all cities in seriatim.

5. *Crónica mexicana* 1975:582 [chap. 84].

6. *Crónica mexicana* 1975:583–84 [chap. 84].

7. *Crónica mexicana* 1975:584–85 [chap. 84]. There are several alternative routes available to the site of these conquests, most fairly direct, but the historical accounts lack sufficient information to select one with a reasonable degree of certainty. The most direct route left the basin of Mexico, proceeded through Cuauhnahuac, and followed the tributaries of the Mexcallan River southeast before crossing a pass, following the Río de la Cuehara and then the Atoyac River to the vicinity of Icpatepec and Nopallan. The return journey would have approximated the outward trek. The campaign stretched 975 kilometers (605 miles) round trip and would have required 30 to 51 days of march, exclusive of days for combat, rest, and regrouping.

8. Durán 1967, 2:411–12 [chap. 54].

9. Durán 1967, 2:403–404 [chap. 53].

10. Durán 1967, 2:211–12 [chap. 26].

11. Durán 1967, 2:211–12 [chap. 26].

12. Sahagún 1954:87.

13. Cortés 1971:109.

14. Carrasco 1984b.

15. Another account describes the southern campaign beginning over the killing of Aztec merchants by the people of Xaltepec, Cuatzonteccan, and Icpatepec (*Crónica mexicana* 1975:597–99 [chap. 88]; Durán 1967, 2:417 [chap. 55]). Moteuczomah Xocoyotl led the Triple Alliance army on the campaign and conquered Xaltepec and Cuatzonteccan, and as a result the lords of Tecuantepec, Miahuatlan, and Izhuatlan also became tributaries. However, the cities were conquered by Ahuitzotl, and the latter half of this description merely mislabels the king. Consequently, I have placed the Tecuantepec portion with Ahuitzotl's conquests, but retain the Xaltepec-

Cuatzonteccan-Icpatepec part here, where it should logically fit. The route for this campaign was the established one into the Huaxyacac area and posed no difficulties.

On this campaign Moteuczomah Xocoyotl raised an army, and the Tlatelolcas supplied their tributary arms and provisions so generously that Tlatelolco was once again allowed to march to war as an autonomous city (Durán 1967, 2:420 [chap. 55]).

16. Durán 1967, 2:421 [chap. 55].

17. *Crónica mexicana* 1975:598–99 [chap. 88].

18. Berlin and Barlow 1980:61; Dibble 1981, 1:35; Torquemada 1975–83, 1:270–71 [bk. 2, chap. 69].

19. *Anales de Cuauhtitlan* 1975:67–68; Berlin and Barlow 1980:18; Clark 1938, 1:41; Paso y Troncoso 1939–42, 10:119; Sahagún 1954:3.

20. *Anales de Cuauhtitlan* 1975:68; Berlin and Barlow 1980:18; Clark 1938, 1:41; Ixtlilxóchitl 1975–77, 2:108 [chap. 71]; Paso y Troncoso 1939–42, 10:119.

21. The somewhat confusing chronology of various xochiyaoyotl during the reign of Moteuczomah Xocoyotl is discussed as greater length by Davies (1968:136–49). Torquemada (1975–83, 1:272–77 [bk. 2, chaps. 70–71]) is unique in attributing a xochiyaoyotl at this time (probably 1504), but given the long-term, intermittent nature of this conflict between the Triple Alliance and Tlaxcallan, such a war at this time is completely plausible.

22. Torquemada 1975–83, 1:278–79 [bk. 2, chap. 72]. Holt (1979:276–78) places the conquest of all the towns in the present-day Veracruz area at this time as a separate campaign. However, the documentation for this is unclear and rests on only three dated sources: the *Codex en Cruz*, the *Códice Telleriano-Remensis*, and the *Relación* of Chimalpahin. All three of these sources contain some indication of a Veracruz conquest, but all require assessment.

The evidence of a Huaxtec conquest in the *Codex en Cruz* is marginal. In his interpretation for the year 12 Tecpatl (1504), Dibble (1981, 1:36) concludes in his somewhat abbreviated commentary, "The warrior, a conquest into the Huastec region? No interpretation is ventured." Similarly, the evidence is thin in the *Códice Telleriano-Remensis* (1964–65:304). The textual commentary for 11 Acatl (1503) refers only to Tlachquiauhco: while the modern Spanish commentary accompanying the codex says that one of the two place glyphs appears to be Atocpan, it is uncertain. Thus, in the case of the two pictoral codices, the interpetation of a Veracruz campaign is slight at best. This leaves only the chronicle account of Chimalpahin (1965:229 [relación 7]), which records the conquest of Pipiyoltepec (13 Calli, 1505).

There is no doubt that there were widespread conquests in the Veracruz area during the reign of Moteuczomah Xocoyotl, but when is unclear. One permissible interpretation is that there was a major campaign during which most of the listed Veracruz towns were conquered. If so, this is the likeliest time for its occurrence, although the data are slim. However, these Veracruz conquests may have equally been parts of various campaigns or piecemeal reconquests as the occasions arose. If the latter is the case, another interpretation would tie the two dated Veracruz conquests to a later campaign, such as that into the Huaxyacac area, since one likely route into the area is via the Gulf coast.

There is no other recorded campaign into which the undated conquests into the Veracruz area could easily fit. As a result, a campaign into Veracruz at this time is an acceptable interpretation, but a tentative one.

23. Torquemada 1975–83, 1:281 [bk. 2, chap. 73]. This is recorded as a separate event without other conquests, but it is equally possible that it was part of the following Huaxyacac campaign. The location of the other towns relative to Cuauhnelhuatlan indicates that there were, indeed, two separate campaigns.

24. The route of this conquest probably followed established routes out of the basin of Mexico by way of Itzyocan, Huehuetlan, and southeast past Teohuacan; via Teotitlan to Cuauhnelhuatlan; and returning the same way. Mazatlan and Huauhtlan were also likely conquered at this time (Berlin and Barlow 1980:18; Torquemada 1975–83, 1:286 [bk. 2, chap. 71]). The campaign stretched 800 kilometers (500 miles) round trip and would have required 25 to 42 days of march, exclusive of days for combat, rest, and regrouping.

25. *Crónica mexicana* 1975:602–603 [chap. 89]; Durán 1967, 2:425–31 [chap. 56]. By another account (Torquemada 1975–83, 1:285–87 [bk. 2, chap. 75]) the entire Huaxyacac region that held the Aztec fortresses and garrisons was rebellious. The Aztec garrison at the town of Huaxyacac was given a fiesta and afterward was ambushed by the lord of Tzotzollan. On being told of this by another of his governors, Moteuczomah Xocoyotl raised the army and marched on the region. Arriving in Huauhtlan (since Torquemada distinguishes between the two, this reference is probably to San Miguel Huauhtlan and not to Cuauhnelhuatlan, and its proximity indicates a location closer than Cuauhnelhuatlan), the Aztecs fought and won a battle, probably against Coaixtlahuacan. Neither Tzotzollan nor its lord was captured at this time, however. The more expansive conquests attributed to this battle logically belong later in the campaign.

26. *Crónica mexicana* 1975:602–605 [chaps. 89–90]; Durán 1967, 2:426–27 [chap. 56].

27. *Crónica mexicana* 1975:605–606 [chap. 90].

28. Durán 1967, 2:431 [chap. 56]. The conquest route probably followed that of the previous incursions into the area, passing through Huaxyacac. The campaign stretched 1,300 kilometers (800 miles) round trip and would have required 41 to 68 days of march, exclusive of days for combat, rest, and regrouping.

29. *Crónica mexicana* 1975:610–13 [chaps. 91–92]; Durán 1967, 2:433–35 [chap. 57]; Torquemada 1975–83, 1:288–89 [bk. 2, chap. 76].

30. Durán 1967, 2:434 [chap. 57].

31. *Crónica mexicana* 1975:610–14 [chaps. 91–92].

32. Durán 1967, 2:436 [chap. 57].

33. Torquemada 1975–83, 1:285–87 [bk. 2, chap. 75].

34. Durán 1967, 2:437 [chap. 57].

35. Berlin and Barlow 1980:61; Chimalpahin 1965:120 [relación 3]; *Códice Telleriano-Remensis* 1964–65:308; *Códice Vaticano* 1964–65:278;

Crónica mexicana 1975:614–20 [chaps. 92–93]; Ixtlilxóchitl 1975–77, 2:179 [chap. 71]; Mengin 1952:457; Torquemada 1975–83, 1:287 [chap. 75].

36. *Crónica mexicana* 1975:606–608 [chaps. 90–91].

37. *Crónica mexicana* 1975:606–608 [chaps. 90–91].

38. *Anales de Cuauhtitlan* 1975:67; Berlin and Barlow 1980:17–18; Clark 1938, 1:41; Ixtlilxóchitl 1975–77, 2:180 [chap. 71]; Paso y Troncoso 1939–42, 10:119; Torquemada 1975–83, 1:285 [bk. 2, chap. 75].

39. *Anales de Cuauhtitlan* 1975:68; Berlin and Barlow 1980:18; Clark 1938, 1:41; Paso y Troncoso 1939–42, 10:119; Torquemada 1975–83, 1:288 [bk. 2, chap. 76].

40. Berlin and Barlow 1980:61; Chimalpahin 1965:120 [relación 3], 228–29 [relación 7]; *Crónica mexicana* 1975:634–35 [chap. 96].

41. Of the captives taken, the Aztecs took 400 prisoners; Chalco 200; Coatlalpan, lowland towns, and Chinampan 200; Coatlalpan 140; Matlatzinco 180; Colhuacan, Huitzilopochco, Ixtlapalapan, and Mexicatzinco 120; Acolhuacan 800; Tlalhuacpan 300; the raw recruits another 200; and the new tequihuahqueh 260 (*Crónica mexicana* 1975:634–36 [chaps. 96–97]; Durán 1967, 2:439–40 [chap. 58]). Colhuacan, Huitzilopochco, Ixtlapalapan, and Mexicaltzinco were not mentioned explicitly. Rather, the reference was to Nauhteuctli, which refers collectively to those four tlahtohqueh (Gerhard 1972:178).

42. This has been interpreted as referring to "Totontepec" because of its location (Davies 1968:199–200) and based on the assumption that there were two campaigns. If these two are merged into a single one, Tototepec's proximity to Huauhtlan is less compelling, and the more obvious Tototepec can be considered as a conquest because of the inclusion of Teuctepec and Tzollan. Presumably, Tecozauhtepec (unidentified, but probably in present-day northern Oaxaca near the other towns listed as conquered during this campaign) was also conquered, as captives from Tzotzollan, Teuctepec, and Tecozauhtepec were sacrificed during the New Fire Ceremony (Chimalpahin 1965:229 [relación 7]; Durán 1967, 2:454 [chap. 60]). Other likely candidates for this campaign include Tzollan and Mictlan, although the sources are not consistent of the dating or sequence of these conquests (*Códice Telleriano-Remensis* 1964–65:308; Torquemada 1975–83, 1:290 [bk. 2, chap. 76]).

43. *Anales de Cuauhtitlan* 1975:67; Berlin and Barlow 1980:17–18, 61; Clark 1938, 1:41; Paso y Troncoso 1939–42, 10:119; Sahagún 1954:3; Torquemada 1975–83, 290 [bk. 2, chap. 76], 312 [bk. 2, chap. 87].

44. Much of this campaign took place along traditional conquest routes into the Huaxyacac region as far as Mictlan. From there thrusts were made both east to Quetzaltepec and southwest along valleys as far as Teuctepec and Tototepec. The return was probably along another established conquest route.

45. *Crónica mexicana* 1975:623–25 [chap. 94].

46. Ixtlilxóchitl 1975–77, 2:179 [chap. 71].

47. Torquemada 1975–83, 1:290 [bk. 2, chap. 76].

48. Clark 1938, 1:41.

49. Paso y Troncoso 1939–42, 10:119.

50. Berlin and Barlow 1980:61; Ixtlilxóchitl 1975–77, 2:184 [chap. 73]; Torquemada 1975–83, 1:290 [chap. 76].

51. Precisely where this occurred is unclear: Amatlan is in the mountainous zone south of Huaxyacac, but a blizzard en route from Tenochtitlan is likelier in the higher mountains surrounding that city than in the lower hills around Amatlan. If that was the case, however, an immediate return home would be expected, but since that did not happen, the setback probably occurred near the objective.

52. Chimalpahin 1965:120 [relación 3], 232 [relación 7]; *Códice Telleriano-Remensis* 1964–65:308.

53. Ixtlilxóchitl 1975–77, 2:181 [chap. 72].

54. Torquemada 1975–83, 1:293–94 [bk. 2, chap. 78]). By recording the conquests in two places with only a partial overlap of the town names, Torquemada makes it appear as though there were two separate campaigns for these towns. However, the listing of these towns in the same year and the separation of these conquests and the next by two years indicates that they were, in fact, conquered in a single campaign in 1511 (Chimalpahin 1965: 120 [relación 3], 232 [relación 7]).

55. Barlow 1949b:127; Berlin and Barlow 1980:61; Clark 1938, 1:41, 58; *Códice Aubin* 1980:80; *Crónica mexicana* 1975:599 [chap. 88]; Dibble 1981, 1:41; Ixtlilxóchitl 1975–77, 2:180 [chap. 71]; Torquemada 1975–83, 1:285 [bk. 2, chap. 75].

56. *Anales de Cuauhtitlan* 1975:67; Berlin and Barlow 1980:18; Clark 1938, 1:41; Paso y Troncoso 1939–42, 10:119.

57. Burgoa's (1934, 2:341–45) seventeenth-century description of Tzapotec resistance to a seven-month Aztec siege at Guiengola, resulting in a marital alliance with the Aztecs rather than conquest, is inconsistent with Aztec practice elsewhere. Marital alliances were made, but prolonged sieges were not carried out, for reasons already discussed. If a determined effort had been made by the Aztecs, as at Quetzaltepec, Guiengola could have been conquered. However, destroying the garrison would not necessarily have ended the site as a locus of harassment, endangering passage through the valley and hindering military movements. Instead, a more satisfactory resolution for the Aztecs was one guaranteeing pacification of the area, and for this, limited transit rights were conveyed in tribute, but the relationship between the Aztecs and Tzapotecs was assuredly asymmetrical.

58. *Anales de Cuauhtitlan* 1975:67; Barlow 1949b:127; Berlin and Barlow 1980:18; Clark 1938, 1:41, 58; Ixtlilxóchitl 1975–77, 2:180 [chap. 71]; Paso y Troncoso 1939–42, 10:119; Torquemada 1975–83, 1:293 [bk. 2, chap. 78]. The probable route went from the basin of Mexico and traversed the well-traveled road to Huaxyacac, thereafter dropping southeast through the Tecuantepec area before doubling back through Xochitepec and Icpatepec and heading northwest through the Malinaltepec area. The entire campaign stretched 2,000 kilometers (1,240 miles) and required 63 to 104 days of march (probably more toward the high end, since the terrain was particularly difficult on this route), exclusive of days for combat, rest, and regrouping.

59. Torquemada 1975–83, 1:295–96 [bk. 2, chap. 79].

60. The *Anales de Cuauhtitlan* (1975:61) lists Quimichtlan, but in a context that would place it in this region, and the citation more properly refers to Quimichtepec.

61. The probable route ran directly to Tlachquiauhco and then to Alotepec; doubled back through Quimichtepec, Nopallan, and the Yopitzinca area; and returned to the basin of Mexico (*Anales de Cuauhtitlan* 1975:61; Chimalpahin 1965:120 [relación 3], 232 [relación 7]; *Códice Telleriano-Remensis* 1964–65:310–12; *Códice Vaticano* 1964–65:280–82; Dibble 1981, 1:41; Mengin 1952:458; Torquemada 1975–83, 1:295 [bk. 2, chap. 79]).

62. Chimalpahin 1965:120 [relación 3], 233 [relación 7].

63. Chimalpahin 1965:232 [relación 7]; Torquemada 1979–83, 1:293 [bk. 2 chap. 78].

64. Torquemada 1975–83, 1:296 [bk. 2, chap. 79].

65. *Anales de Cuauhtitlan* 1975:67; Berlin and Barlow 1980:18; Chimalpahin 1965:229 [relación 7]; Clark 1938, 1:41, 58; *Crónica mexicana* 1975:599 [chap. 88]; Paso y Troncoso 1939–42, 10:119; Sahagún 1954:3; Torquemada 1975–83, 1:296 [bk. 2, chap. 79].

66. *Anales de Cuauhtitlan* 1975:61; Berlin and Barlow 1980:61. Although Torquemada (1975–83, 1:287–89 [chap. 76]) places the conquest of the Iztecs and Itzcuintepecas with the earlier, initial thrust into the Huaxyacac area, the only other dated source, the *Anales de Cuauhtitlan* (1975:61), convincingly places them later. Since this campaign is the most geographically appropriate for this conquests, I include them here.

67. Torquemada 1975–83, 1:296 [bk. 2, chap. 79].

68. Muñoz Camargo 1892:126; Torquemada 1975–83, 1:301–302 [bk. 2, chap. 82].

69. *Anales de Cuauhtitlan* 1975:61; Chimalpahin 1965:120 [relación 3], 233 [relación 7]; Dibble 1981, 1:43; Ixtlilxóchitl 1975–77, 2:188 [chap. 75].

70. *Crónica mexicana* 1975:658 [chap. 51].

71. Ixtlilxóchitl 1975–77, 2:190–92 [chap. 76]; Sahagún 1954:10; Torquemada 1975–83, 1:303 [bk. 2, chap. 83]. The accounts of Durán (1967, 2:473–84 [chaps. 64–65]) and the *Crónica mexicana* (1975:658–61 [chap. 51]), both of which stem from the common *Crónica X* source, are at variance with other accounts over who Nezahualpilli's successor was and how the succession occurred, and they are apparently unreliable on this point.

72. Chimalpahin 1965:233 [relación 7]; Durán 1967, 2:459–62 [chap. 61]; Mengin 1952:458; Torquemada 1975–83, 1:311–12 [bk. 2, chap. 87]. Tlatlauhqui-Tepec is recorded as having been conquered at the same time or slightly earlier (Chimalpahin 1965:120 [relación 3], 233 [relación 7]). The relative proximity of Tlatlauhqui-Tepec to Tlaxcallan argues in favor of a connection between this conquest and that. However, such a conjunction in a xochiyaoyotl is unusual. If they were not conquered as part of the same campaign, there are two alternative explanations. First, there were two entirely separate campaigns, one against Tlatlauhqui-Tepec and another against Tlaxcallan; second, Tlatlauhqui-Tepec is an error. The *Anales de Tlatelolco* (Berlin and Barlow 1980:17) does list Tlatlauhqui-Tepec as an undated conquest, supporting the correctness of the Chimalpahin reading.

However, that name may have been an error for Tliliuhqui-Tepec, which was another of Tenochtitlan's xochiyaoyotl rivals and would have been a logical joint target with Tlaxcallan in such a war. On the data available the issue cannot be resolved, so I will accept the documents at face value, but I do so tentatively. If that interpretation is correct, the recorded conquest of Tepeyacac may have occurred later during the same campaign (Chimalpahin 1965: 121 [relación 3]).

73. Durán 1967, 2:460–62 [chap. 61].

74. *Anales de Cuauhtitlan* 1975: 60, 67; Berlin and Barlow 1980: 17–18; Chimalpahin 1965: 120 [relación 3]; Clark 1938, 1:41; Paso y Troncoso 1939–42, 10:119.

75. Davies 1968: 137.

76. Chimalpahin 1965: 233 [relación 7]; *Códice Vaticano* 1964–65: 284; *Crónica mexicana* 1975: 638–40 [chap. 97]; Durán 1967, 2:454–55 [chap. 60].

77. *Anales de Cuauhtitlan* 1975: 61–63; Berlin and Barlow 1980: 61; *Códice Telleriano-Remensis* 1964–65: 312; *Crónica mexicana* 1975: 660 [chap. 101]; Ixtlilxóchitl 1975–77, 2:192 [chap. 75]; Torquemada 1975–83, 1:312 [bk. 2, chap. 87].

78. *Anales de Cuauhtitlan* 1975: 67; Chimalpahin 1965: 121 [relación 3]; Clark 1938, 1:41, 58; Paso y Troncoso 1939–42, 10:119.

79. Durán 1967, 2:462 [chap. 62].

80. Durán 1967, 2:464–66 [chap. 62].

81. Cortés 1971: 70 [letter 2]; Díaz del Castillo 1908–16, 2:7 [bk. 5, chap. 83].

82. Torquemada 1975–83, 1:312 [bk. 2, chap. 87]. Several towns are listed as conquests that present difficulties in interpretation. Acalhuacan is listed as referring to Tetzcoco by Kelly and Palerm (1952: 313), but a town of that name, an *estancia* of Ecatepec (Gibson 1964: 74), was a subject of Tlatelolco. Also, Coatitlan was also an *estancia* of Ecatepec (Gibson 1964: 74). Thus their interpretations as corruptions of Acolhuacan and Cuauhtitlan are questionable. Chizquiyauhco (Chimalpahin 1965: 120 [relación 3]) may be Chiconquiauhco (Holt 1979: 290). Tetenanco may signify Teotenanco. Teconpatlan may be Tecpatlan. Chimalpahin (1965: 229 [relación 7]) lists Tecozauhtepecas, which is probably an error for Tecozauhtecs, which yields Tecozauhtlan, which is supported by Clark (1938, 1:41). Totollan (Chimalpahin 1965: 228 [relación 7]) was an area around Piaztlan (Gerhard 1972: 42). Tlanitztlan is in present-day Oaxaca near Tototepec and Sola de Vega (Kelly and Palerm 1952: 316n.7). I have been unable to locate the remaining towns (Acolnahuac, Huixachtitlan, Mazatzintlan in Chichimec territory, and Zacuantepec).

83. Clark 1938, 1:58; *Crónica mexicana* 1975: 623 [chap. 94].

84. *Colección de documentos inéditos . . . de ultramar* 1885–1932, 11:364; 13:221–22. Scholes and Roys (1968: 34–35), however, interpret the Aztec presence there as reflecting an Aztec merchant community, but they do so on the basis of Sahagún's account of events in the region, an account that is graphic in detail but all too inadequate in its breadth of events.

Chapter 16

1. E.g., Powell 1975 : 159.
2. *Códice Osuna* 1976: folio 8–470; García Icazbalceta 1971, 2 : 307–18; Powell 1975 : 159.
3. Soustelle 1970 : 214; Todorov 1984.
4. Aguilar 1963 : 138; Cortés 1971 : 23 [letter 1]; Díaz del Castillo 1908–16, 1 : 136 [bk. 3, chap. 38]; Tapia 1963 : 25.
5. Cortés 1971 : 57–58 [letter 2]; Díaz del Castillo 1908–16, 1 : 215–17 [bk. 3, chap. 57].
6. Cortés 1971 : 58–62 [letter 2]; Díaz del Castillo 1908–16, 1 : 233–37 [bk. 4, chaps. 63–65].
7. Technological explanations for imperial expansion have been posed (e.g., Cipolla 1965; Headrick 1981), but they appear to have little validity in this case, particularly if mechanical technology is the focus.
8. Díaz del Castillo 1908–16, 1 : 228 [bk. 4, chap. 62], 232 [bk. 4, chap. 63]; Tapia 1963 : 29.
9. Anonymous Conqueror 1963 : 169.
10. Helmut Nickel, personal communication. The existence of such breech-loading cannons in the fifteenth and sixteenth centuries is well attested (Tarassuk and Blair 1982 : 48–49, and illustrations of pages 51–52; Stevens 1965 : 18–19). Several of these cannons and their breech chambers were recovered from Spanish ships sunk in 1554 off present-day Padre Island, Texas (Arnold and Weddle 1978 : 240–50, and figs. 28–30, 71–74). Also, Cortés's expedition had not been provisioned for an overland trek. The cannons he used were taken from his ships.
11. Sahagún 1975 : 62.
12. Cortés 1971 : 178 [letter 3]; Díaz del Castillo 1908–16, 2 : 272 [bk. 9, chap. 130], 4 : 19 [bk. 10, chap. 139], 4 : 35 [bk. 11, chap. 141], 4 : 75 [bk. 11, chap. 145].
13. Díaz del Castillo 1908–16, 4 : 32 [bk. 11, chap. 141], 4 : 81 [bk. 11, chap. 145].
14. Aguilar 1963 : 152; Díaz del Castillo 1908–16, 4 : 11 [bk. 10, chap. 138].
15. Díaz del Castillo 1908–16, 4 : 45 [bk. 11, chap. 142].
16. Cortés 1971 : 70 [letter 2]; Díaz del Castillo 1908–16, 2 : 7 [bk. 5, chap. 83].
17. Díaz del Castillo 1908–16, 4 : 117, 123–25 [bk. 12, chap. 151].
18. Díaz del Castillo 1908–16, 2 : 12 [bk. 10, chap. 138].
19. Díaz del Castillo 1908–16, 4 : 36 [bk. 11, chap. 141], 4 : 125–26 [bk. 12, chap. 151].
20. Díaz del Castillo 1908–16, 4 : 75–76 [bk. 11, chap. 145], 4 : 125 [bk. 12, chap. 151].
21. Cortés 1971 : 247 [letter 3]; Díaz del Castillo 1908–16, 1 : 242 [bk. 4, chap. 66], 2 : 233 [bk. 8, chap. 126], 4 : 76 [bk. 11, chap. 145], 4 : 121–22 [bk. 12, chap. 151].
22. Díaz del Castillo 1908–16, 4 : 121–22 [bk. 12, chap. 151].

23. Aguilar 1963:142; Cortés 1971:67 [letter 2]; Díaz del Castillo 1908–16, 1:227 [bk. 4, chap. 75]; Tapia 1963:32.

24. Aguilar 1963:146; Cortés 1971:84 [letter 2]; Díaz del Castillo 1908–16, 2:44 [bk. 5, chap. 88]; Tapia 1963:38.

25. Cortés 1971:88–90 [letter 2]; Díaz del Castillo 1908–16, 2:94–95 [bk. 6, chap. 95]; Tapia 1963:42.

26. Díaz del Castillo 1908–16, 2:135–36 [bk. 6, chap. 104].

27. Cortés 1971:97–98 [letter 2]; Díaz del Castillo 1908–16, 2:121–22 [bk. 6, chap. 100].

28. Díaz del Castillo 1908–16, 2:146 [bk. 6, chap. 107].

29. Díaz del Castillo 1908–16, 2:149–50 [bk. 6, chap. 108].

30. Díaz del Castillo 1908–16, 2:224–25 [bk. 8, chap. 125]. Aguilar (1963:151) ignores the massacre and maintains that Moteuczomah Xocoyotl ordered the Indians to war on the Spaniards, stopping only when he learned of Cortés's victory over Narváez.

31. The traditional spelling, "Cuitlahuac," is a locative, not a name form.

32. Aguilar 1963:153; Cortés 1971:132 [letter 2]; Díaz del Castillo 1908–16, 2:237–38 [bk. 8, chap. 126].

33. Sahagún 1975:65n.1.

34. Aguilar 1963:154–57; Cortés 1971:139 [letter 2]; Díaz del Castillo 1908–16, 2:249–58 [bk. 8, chap. 128].

35. Aguilar 1963:157; Cortés 1971:145–46 [letter 2]; Díaz del Castillo 1908–16, 2:273 [bk. 9, chap. 128].

36. Díaz del Castillo 1908–16, 2:273–74 [bk. 9, chap. 128].

37. Díaz del Castillo 1908–16, 2:277–80 [bk. 9, chap. 131].

38. Cortés 1971:177 [letter 3]; Díaz del Castillo 1908–16, 4:5–8 [bk. 10, chap. 137].

39. Díaz del Castillo 1908–16, 4:10 [bk. 10, chap. 137].

40. Cortés 1971:174–75 [letter 3]; Díaz del Castillo 1908–16, 4:10–13 [bk. 10, chap. 138].

41. Cortés 1971:186–87 [letter 3]; Díaz del Castillo 1908–16, 4:30–37 [bk. 11, chap. 141].

42. Cortés 1971:178–79 [letter 3]; Díaz del Castillo 1908–16, 4:13–18 [bk. 10, chap. 139].

43. Díaz del Castillo 1908–16, 4:22–23 [bk. 10, chap. 139].

44. Cortés 1971:189–91 [letter 3]; Díaz del Castillo 1908–16, 4:39–51 [bk. 11, chaps. 141–42].

45. Cortés 1971:191 [letter 3]; Díaz del Castillo 1908–16, 4:51–53 [bk. 11, chap. 142].

46. Cortés 1971:196–98 [letter 3]; Díaz del Castillo 1908–16, 4:58–70 [bk. 11, chap. 144].

47. Cortés 1971:198–202 [letter 3]; Díaz del Castillo 1908–16, 4:70–86 [bk. 11, chap. 145].

48. Díaz del Castillo 1908–16, 4:103–8 [bk. 12, chap. 150].

49. Díaz del Castillo 1908–16, 4:155 [bk. 12, chap. 153].

50. Motolinía 1971:74 [bk. 1, chap. 26].

51. Díaz del Castillo 1908–16, 4:80 [bk. 11, chap. 145], 4:151 [bk. 12, chap. 152].

52. Díaz del Castillo 1908–16, 4:156–57 [bk. 12, chap. 153].

53. Cortés 1971:209 [letter 3]; Díaz del Castillo 1908–16, 4:165 [bk. 12, chap. 150]; Gardiner 1956.

54. Díaz del Castillo 1908–16, 4:161 [bk. 12, chap. 153].

55. Cortés 1971:242–43 [letter 3]; Díaz del Castillo 1908–16, 4:169 [bk. 12, chap. 155].

56. Díaz del Castillo 1908–16, 4:169–70 [bk. 12, chap. 155].

57. Aguilar 1963:160; Cortés 1971:264 [letter 3]; Díaz del Castillo 1908–16, 4:183 [bk. 12, chap. 156].

Chapter 17

1. For example, in a xochiyaoyotl with Huexotzinco, Atlixco, and Chollan, the Triple Alliance sent an army of 100,000 men. The army gathered at Atzitzihuacan, a subject of Papayocan, but the battle began with only 200 Aztec warriors, and the units fought sequentially; the Tetzcocas first, then the people of Tlacopan, then the Aztecs (Durán 1967, 2:434 [chap. 57]).

2. For example, the relative lack of wealth in Metztitlan was attributed to the fact that they fought against the Aztecs (*Colección de documentos inéditos . . . de América* 1864–84, 4:454).

3. Chimalpahin 1965:204 [relación 7].

4. Torquemada 1975–83, 1:287 [bk. 2, chap. 75].

5. Towns where local tlahtohqueh were replaced by Aztec governors but which were not mentioned in chronicle accounts of conquests include Coatepec (Paso y Troncoso 1905–48, 6:52), Tepechpan (Paso y Troncoso 1905–48, 6:234), Tlacotepec (Paso y Troncoso 1905–48, 6:123), Tetellan (Paso y Troncoso 1905–48, 6:134), Quetzallan (Paso y Troncoso 1905–48, 6:140), Apaztlan (Paso y Troncoso 1905–48, 6:143), Tlachco (Paso y Troncoso 1905–48, 6:276), Miahuatlan (Paso y Troncoso 1905–48, 4:127), Coatlan (Paso y Troncoso 1905–48, 4:133), Tlacotlalpan (Paso y Troncoso 1905–48, 5:2), Piaztlan (Paso y Troncoso 1905–48, 5:78), Texallocan (Paso y Troncoso 1905–48, 5:87), and Temazcaltepec (Paso y Troncoso 1905–48, 7:21).

6. Armillas 1951:80; Gorenstein 1966:53; Palerm 1956:194. However, fortifications have been widely reported in Mesoamerica, but not just in the postclassic (Armillas 1942–44, 1948, 1951; Davies 1972; Gorenstein 1966, 1973; Palerm 1956; D. Peterson 1974).

7. Palerm 1956:194.

8. De la Croix 1972; Finer 1975.

9. Palerm 1956:194–95.

10. Luttwak 1976:61–66.

11. When this reorganization of the tribute system took place is uncertain. The format of the *Matrícula de tributos* (1980) is not prehispanic, and it may have been compiled after the Spanish conquest (Berdan 1980a:9; Robertson 1959:72–77), but it indicates that the reorganization may have occurred as early as 1511–12, after the widespread revolts following the as-

tronomically induced quietus, a period during which the Aztecs are likely to have sought a more accurate means of assessing the political climate in their tributaries.

12. Barlow 1949a.

13. *Anales de Cuauhtitlan* 1975:64.

14. Berdan 1976:138; Borah and Cook 1963:45–50.

15. Broda 1976:39–57. Even if tribute was previously paid to Tetzcoco six times per year, the two additional months were the seventh and fourteenth, so they did not interfere with the military campaign season.

16. Hicks 1977.

17. Berdan 1980b:38–39; *Matrícula de tributos* 1980:11v.

18. As one indication of this lack of full support for Aztec undertakings, Díaz del Castillo (1908–16, 1:284 [bk. 4, chap. 78]) noted that the Aztec allies did not fight well and often warned the enemy of Aztec intentions.

19. See Hassig (1985:85–126) for an extended discussion of this point.

References

Acosta, Joseph de
1604 *The Natural and Moral History of the Indies.* 2 vols. New York: Burt Franklin Reprint.

Acosta Saignes, Miguel
1946 "Los teopixque." *Revista Mexicana de Estudios Antropológicos* 8:147–205.

Aguilar, Francisco de
1963 "The Chronicle of Fray Francisco de Aguilar." In Fuentes 1963.

Alvarado Tezozomoc, Hernando
1975a *Crónica mexicana y Códice Ramírez.* Mexico: Porrúa.
1975b *Crónica mexicayotl.* Mexico: Universidad Nacional Autónoma de México.

Anales de Cuauhtitlan
1975 "Anales de Cuauhtitlan." In *Códice Chimalpopoca* 1975.

Anales de Tula
1979 *Anales de Tula.* Graz, Austria: Akademische Druck-u. Verlagsanstalt.

Anales México-Azcapotzalco
1903 "Anales México-Azcapotzalco." *Anales del Museo Nacional de México* 7:49–74.

Anawalt, Patricia Rieff
1981 *Indian Clothing Before Cortés: Mesoamerican Costumes from the Codices.* Norman: University of Oklahoma Press.
1984 "Aztec Martial Apparel: A Comparative Analysis of Extant Depictions.: Paper presented at the 32d Annual Convention of the American Society for Ethnohistory, New Orleans, La., November 8–11.

Andrews, J. Richard
1975 *Introduction to Classical Nahuatl.* Austin: University of Texas Press.

Anonymous Conqueror
1963 "The Chronicle of the Anonymous Conqueror." In Fuentes 1963.

Antigüedades de México
1964–65 *Antigüedades de México.* 4 vols. Mexico: Secretaría de Hacienda y Crédito Público.

Armillas, Pedro
1942–44 "Oztuma, Gro., fortaleza de los Mexicanos en la frontera de Michoacán." *Revista Mexicana de Estudios Antropológicos* 6:165–75.
1948 "Fortalezas Mexicanas." *Cuadernos Americanos* 7:5:143–63.
1951 "Mesoamerican Fortifications." *Antiquity* 25:77–86.

Arnold, J. Barto, III, and Robert Weddle
1978 *The Nautical Archeology of Padre Island: The Spanish Shipwrecks of 1554.* New York: Academic Press.

Bandelier, Adolf F.
1880 "On the Art of War and Mode of Warfare of the Ancient Mexicans." *Reports of the Peabody Museum of American Archaeology and Ethnology* 2:95–161.

Barlow, Robert H.
1945 "La crónica X: versiones coloniales de la historia de los Mexica Tenochca." *Revista Mexicana de Estudios Antropológicos* 7: 65–87.
1947 "Conquistas de los antiguos mexicanos." *Journal de la Société des Américanistes* 36:215–22.
1949a "The Extent of the Empire of the Culhua Mexica." *Ibero-Americana* 28.

———, ed.
1949b "El Códice Azcatitlán." *Journal de la Société des Américanistes* 38:101–35.

Barrera Rubio, Alfredo
1980 "Mural Paintings of the Puuc Region in Yucatan." In Robertson 1980.

Baumbach, Otto Schöndube
1969 "El horizonte clásico." *Artes de México,* no. 119.

Benedict, Francis G., and Morris Steggerda
1937 *The Food of the Present-Day Maya Indians of Yucatan.* Carnegie Institution of Washington Publication no. 456. Washington, D.C.: Carnegie Institution.

Berdan, Frances F.
1976 "A Comparative Analysis of Aztec Tribute Documents." *Actas del XLI Congreso International de Americanistas* 2:131–42.
1980a "The Matrícula de Tributos—Introduction." In *Matrícula de tributos* 1980.
1980b The Matrícula de Tributos-Provincial Tribute. In *Matrícula de tributos* 1980.
1982 *The Aztecs of Central Mexico: An Imperial Society.* New York: Holt, Rinehart and Winston.

———, and Patricia R. Anawalt, eds.
N.d. *Codex Mendoza.* Forthcoming.

Berlin, Heinrich, and Robert H. Barlow, eds.
1980 *Anales de Tlatelolco*. Mexico: Ediciones Rafael Porrúa.

Bernal, Ignacio
1966 "Teotihuacán ¿Capital de imperio?" *Revista Mexicana de Estudios Antropológicos* 20:95–110.

Beyer, Herman
1925 "La tiradera (atlatl) todavía en uso en el Valle de México." *El México Antiguo* 2:220–22.

Boletín
1940 *Archivo General de la Nación, Boletín*. Mexico: Archivo General de la Nación.

Bolles, John S.
1977 *Las Monjas: A Major Pre-Mexican Architectural Complex at Chichén Itzá*. Norman: University of Oklahoma Press.

Bonampak
1955 *Ancient Maya Paintings of Bonampak, Mexico*. Carnegie Institution of Washington Supplementary Publication 46. Washington, D.C.: Carnegie Institution.

Boone, Elizabeth Hill
1983 *The Codex Magliabechiano and the Lost Prototype of the Magliabechiano Group*. 2 vols. Berkeley: University of California Press.

Borah, Woodrow, and Sherburne F. Cook
1960 "The Population of Central Mexico in 1548: An Analysis of the Suma de visitas de pueblos." *Ibero-Americana* 43.
1963 "The Aboriginal Population of Central Mexico on the Eve of the Spanish Conquest." *Ibero-Americana* 45.

Borgonio Gaspar, Guadalupe
1954–55 "Organización militar de los Tenochca." *Revista Mexicana de Estudios Antropológicos* 14:381–83.

Bosch García, Carlos
1944 *La esclavitud prehispánica entre los aztecas*. Mexico: El Colegio de México.

Bosch Gimpera, Pedro
1966 "Pueblos e imperios." *Revista Mexicana de Estudios Antropológicos* 20:9–39.

Brand, Donald D.
1971 "Ethnohistoric Synthesis of Western Mexico." In Ekholm and Bernal 1971b.

Bray, Warwick
1968 *Everyday Life of the Aztecs*. New York: G. P. Putnam's Sons.

Broda, Johanna
1976 "Los estamentos en el ceremonial mexica." In Carrasco and Broda 1976.
1978 "El tributo en trajes guerreros y la estructura del sistema tributario mexica." In Carrasco and Broda 1978.

Browne, Jim
1940 "Projectile Points." *American Antiquity* 5:209–13.

Brundage, Burr Cartwright
1972 *A Rain of Darts: The Mexica Aztecs*. Austin: University of Texas Press.

Burgoa, Francisco de
1934 *Geográfica descripción*. 2 vols. Mexico: Archivo General de la Nación.

Burling, Robbins
1974 *The Passage of Power: Studies in Political Succession*. New York: Academic Press.

Bushnell, D. I., Jr.
1905 "Two Ancient Mexican Atlatls." *American Anthropologist* 7:218–21.

Bustillos Carrillo, Antonio
1974 *El Sacbé de los Mayas*. Mexico: B. Costa-Amic.

Calnek, Edward E.
1976 "The Internal Structure of Tenochtitlan." In Wolf 1976.
1978 "The Internal Structure of Cities in America: Pre-Columbian Cities; The Case of Tenochtitlan." In Schaedel, Hardoy, and Kinzer 1978.
1982 "Patterns of Empire Formation in the Valley of Mexico, Late Postclassic Period, 1200–1521." In Collier, Rosaldo, and Wirth 1982.

Canseco Vincourt, Jorge
1966 *La Guerra Sagrada*. Mexico: Instituto Nacional de Antropología e Historia.

Caplow, Theodore
1968 *Two Against One: Coalitions in Triads*. Englewood Cliffs, N.J.: Prentice-Hall.

Carrasco, Pedro
1971 "Social Organization of Ancient Mexico." In Ekholm and Bernal 1971a.
1984a "The Extent of the Tepanec Empire." In Durand-Forest 1984.
1984b "Royal Marriages in Ancient Mexico." In Harvey and Prem 1984.

———, and Johanna Broda, eds.
1976 *Estratificación social en la Mesoamérica prehispánica*. Mexico: SEPINAH.
1978 *Economía política e ideología en el México* prehispánico. Mexico: Editorial Nueva Imagen.

Carrera Stampa, Manuel
1949 "The Evolution of Weights and Measures in New Spain." *Hispanic American Historical Review* 29:2–24.

Casas, Bartolomé de las
1967 *Apologética historia sumaria*. 2 vols. Mexico: Universidad Nacional Autónoma de México.

Caso, Alfonso
1947 Mapa de Popotla. *Anales del Instituto Nacional de Antropología e Historia*, época 5, 2:315–20.
1963 "Land Tenure Among the Ancient Mexicans." *American Anthropologist* 65:863–78.
1966 "La época de los señoríos independientes: 1232–1427." *Revista Mexicana de Estudios Antropológicos* 20:147–52.
———, ed.
1928 "Relación de Mistepeque." *Revista Mexicana de Estudios Históricos* 2:142–46.
Castillo Farreras, Victor M.
1969 "Caminos del mundo náhuatl." *Estudios de Cultura Náhuatl* 8:175–87.
Cervantes de Salazar, Francisco
1971 *Crónica de la Nueva España*. 2 vols. Madrid: Ediciones Atlas.
Chavero, Alfredo, ed.
1979 *El Lienzo de Tlaxcala*. Mexico: Editorial Cosmos.
Chimalpahin, Francisco de San Anton Muñón
1965 *Relaciones originales de Chalco Amaquemecan*. Mexico: Fondo de Cultura Económica.
Cipolla, Carlo M.
1965 *Guns, Sails and Empires: Technological Innovation and the Early Phases of European Expansion 1400–1700*. New York: Minerva Press.
Clark, James Cooper, ed.
1938 *Codex Mendoza: The Mexican Manuscript Known as the Collection of Mendoza and Preserved in the Bodleian Library Oxford*. 3 vols. London: Waterlow and Sons.
Clausewitz, Karl von
1943 *On War*. O. J. Matthijs, trans. New York: Random House.
Clavigero, Francisco
1787 *The History of Mexico*. 2 vols. Charles Cullen, trans. London.
Clendinnen, Inga
1985 "The Cost of Courage in Aztec Society." *Past and Present* 107:44–89.
Cline, Howard F., ed.
1975a *Handbook of Middle American Indians: Guide to Ethnohistorical Sources, Part 3*. Austin: University of Texas Press.
1975b *Handbook of Middle American Indians: Guide to Ethnohistorical Sources, Part 4*. Austin: University of Texas Press.
Coale, Ansley J., and Paul Demeny
1966 *Regional Model Life Tables and Stable Populations*. Princeton, N.J.: Princeton University Press.
Codex Fejérváry-Mayer
1971 *Codex Fejérváry-Mayer*. Graz, Austria: Akademische Druck-u. Verlagsanstalt.

Codex Ixtlilxochitl
1976 *Codex Ixtlilxochitl.* Graz, Austria: Akademische Druck-u. Verlagsanstalt.
Codex Vaticanus
1972 *Codex Vaticanus 3773 (Codex Vaticanus B).* Graz, Austria: Akademische Druck-u. Verlagsanstalt.
Códice Aubin
1980 *Códice Aubin.* Mexico: Editorial Innovación.
Códice Bodley
1964–65 *Códice Bodley.* In *Antiqüedades de México* 1964–65.
Códice Borbonico
1980 *Códice Borbonico.* Mexico: Siglo Veintiuno.
Códice Borgia
1980 *Códice Borgia.* 3 vols. Mexico: Fondo de Cultura Económica.
Códice Chimalpopoca
1975 *Códice Chimalpopoca: Anales de Cuauhtitlan y Leyenda de los Soles.* Mexico: Universidad Nacional Autónoma de México.
Códice de Huamantla
1984 *Códice de Huamantla.* 2 vols. Mexico: El Instituto Tlaxcalteca de la Cultura.
Códice Laud
1964–65 *Códice Laud.* In *Antiqüedades de México* 1964–65.
Códice Osuna
1976 *Pintura del gobernador, alcaldes y regidores de México "Códice Osuna."* 2 vols. Madrid: Ministerio de Educación y Ciencia.
Códice Quinatzin
1975 "Códice Quinatzin." In *Memoria de las obras* 1975. vol. 1.
Códice Ramírez
1975 *Códice Ramírez.* In Alvarado Tezozomoc 1975a.
Códice Selden
1964–65 *Códice Selden (A.2.).* In *Antiqüedades de México* 1964–65.
Códice Telleriano-Remensis
1964–65 *Códice Telleriano-Remensis.* In *Antiqüedades de México* 1964–65.
Códice Tudela
1980 *Códice Tudela.* Madrid: Ediciones Cultura Hispánica del Instituto de Cooperación Iberoamericana.
Códice Vaticano
1964–65 *Códice Vaticano 3738.* In *Antiqüedades de México* 1964–65.
Códices de México
1979 *Los Códices de México.* Mexico: Instituto Nacional de Antropología e Historia.
Coe, Michael D.
1975 *Classic Maya Pottery at Dumbarton Oaks.* Washington, D.C.: Dumbarton Oaks.
Coggins, Clemency Chase, and Orrin C. Shane III
1984 *Cenote of Sacrifice: Maya Treasures from the Sacred Well at Chichén Itzá.* Austin: University of Texas Press.

Colección de documentos inéditos . . . de América
1864–84 *Colección de documentos inéditos relativos al descubrimiento, conquista y organización de las antiguas posesiones españoles de América y Oceania.* 42 vols. Madrid.

Colección de documentos inéditos . . . de ultramar
1885–1932 *Colección de documentos inéditos relativos al descubrimiento, conquista y organización de las antiguas posesiones españoles de ultramar.* 25 vols. Madrid.

Coles, John
1979 *Experimental Archaeology.* New York: Academic Press.

Collier, George A., Renato I. Rosaldo, and John D. Wirth, eds.
1982 *The Inca and Aztec States, 1400–1800: Anthropology and History.* New York: Academic Press.

Conrad, Geoffrey W., and Arthur A. Demarest
1983 "Ideological Adaptation and the Rise of the Aztec and Inca Empires." In Leventhal and Kolata 1983.
1984 *Religion and Empire: The Dynamics of Aztec and Inca Expansion.* New York: Cambridge University Press.

Cook, Noble David
1981 *Demographic Collapse: Indian Peru, 1520–1620.* New York: Cambridge University Press.

Cook, Sherburne F., and Lesley Byrd Simpson
1948 "The Population of Central Mexico in the Sixteenth Century." *Ibero-Americana* 31.

Cook de Leonard, Carmen
1971 "Minor Arts of the Classic Period in Central Mexico." In Ekholm and Bernal 1971a.

Corona Núñez, José
1966 "Los Teotihuacanos en el occidente de México." *Revista Mexicana de Estudios Antropológicos* 20:111–16.

Corson, Christopher
1976 *Maya Anthropomorphic Figures from Jaina Island, Campeche.* Ramona, Calif.: Ballena Press.

Cortés, Hernán
1971 *Hernan Cortes: Letters from Mexico.* A. R. Pagden, trans. New York: Grossman Publishers.

Crónica mexicana
1975 *Crónica mexicana.* In Alvarado Tezozomoc 1975a.

Cuevas, P. Mariano, ed.
1975 *Documentos inéditos del siglo XVI para la historia de México.* Mexico: Porrúa.

Dahlgren, Barbro, ed.
1979 *Mesoamérica: Homenaje al doctor Paul Kirchhoff.* Mexico: SEPINAH.

Davies, Nigel
1968 *Los señoríos independientes del imperio azteca.* Mexico: Instituto Nacional de Antropología e Historia.

1972 "The Military Organization of the Aztec Empire." *Atti del XL Congresso Internazionale degli Americanisti* 4:213–21.
1973 *Los mexicas: primeros pasos hacia el imperio*. Mexico: Universidad Nacional Autónoma de México.
1974 *The Aztecs: A History*. New York: G. P. Putnam's Sons.
1977 *The Toltecs: Until the Fall of Tula*. Norman: University of Oklahoma Press.
1980 *The Toltec Heritage: From the Fall of Tula to the Rise of Tenochtitlán*. Norman: University of Oklahoma Press.
1983 *The Ancient Kingdoms of Mexico*. New York: Penguin Books.

De la Croix, Horst
1972 *Military Considerations in City Planning: Fortifications*. New York: George Braziller.

Denevan, William M.
1976a "Mexico: Introduction." In Denevan 1976b.
1976b *The Native Population of the Americas in 1492*. Madison: University of Wisconsin Press.

Díaz, Juan
1963 "The Chronicle of Juan Diaz." In Fuentes 1963.

Díaz del Castillo, Bernal
1908–16 *The True History of the Conquest of New Spain*. Alfred Percival Maudslay, trans. 5 vols. London: Hakluyt Society.

Dibble, Charles, ed.
1980 *Códice Xolotl*. Mexico: Universidad Nacional Autónoma de México.
1981 *Codex en Cruz*. 2 vols. Salt Lake City: University of Utah Press.

Diehl, Richard A.
1983 *Tula: The Toltec Capital of Ancient Mexico*. New York: Thames and Hudson.

Dobyns, Henry F.
1983 *Their Numbers Become Thinned: Native American Population Dynamics in Eastern North America*. Knoxville: University of Tennessee Press.

Dorantes de Carranza, Baltasar
1970 *Sumaria relación de las cosas de la Nueva España*. Mexico: Jésus Medina.

Dupuy, R. E., and T. N. Dupuy
1970 *Encyclopedia of Military History*. New York: Harper & Row.

Durán, Diego
1967 *Historia de las Indias de Nueva España e islas de la tierra firme*. 2 vols. Mexico: Porrúa.

Durand-Forest, J. de
1984 *The Native Sources and the History of the Valley of Mexico*. BAR International Series 204. Oxford.

Durbin, Thomas Edmond
1970 "Aztec Patterns of Conquest as Manifested in the Valley of

Toluca, the State of Mexico, Mexico." Ph.D. dissertation, University of California at Los Angeles.

Du Solier, Wilfredo
1950 *Ancient Mexican Costume*. Mexico: Ediciones Mexicanas.

Ekholm, Gordon F., and Ignacio Bernal, eds.
1971a *Handbook of Middle American Indians*. Vol. 10, Archaeology of Northern Mesoamerica, Part 1. Austin: University of Texas Press.
1971b *Handbook of Middle American Indians*. Vol. 11. Archaeology of Northern Mesoamerica, Part 2. Austin: University of Texas Press.

Engels, Donald W.
1978 *Alexander the Great and the Logistics of the Macedonian Army*. Berkeley: University of California Press.

Euw, Eric von, ed.
1977 *Corpus of Maya Hieroglyphic Inscriptions*, Vol. 4, part 1. Cambridge. Mass.: Peabody Museum.

Farfán, Augustín
1579 *Tractado breve de anothomia y chirvgia, y de algunas enfermedades, que mas comunmente suelen hauer en Nueva España*. Mexico.

Ferguson, R. Brian
1984a "Introduction: Studying War." In Ferguson 1984b.

———, ed.
1984b *Warfare, Culture, and Environment*. New York: Academic Press.

Fernández de Oviedo, Gonzalo
1979 *Sumario de la natural historia de las islas*. Mexico: Fondo de Cultura Económica.

Finer, Samuel E.
1975 "State- and Nation-Building in Europe: The Role of the Military." In Tilly 1975a.

Flannery, Kent V., and Joyce Marcus, eds.
1983 *The Cloud People: Divergent Evolution of the Zapotec and Mixtec Civilizations*. New York: Academic Press.

Florescano, Enrique
1969 *Precios del maíz y crisis agrícolas en México (1708–1810)*. Mexico: El Colegio de México.

Follett, Prescott H. F.
1932 "War and Weapons of the Maya." *Middle American Research Institute* no. 4.

Frías y Frías, Valentín
1906 *La conquista de Querétaro*. Querétaro, Mexico.

Fried, Morton H.
1967 *The Evolution of Political Society: An Essay in Political Anthropology*. New York: Random House.

Fuentes, Patricia de, ed.
1963 *The Conquistadores*. New York: Orion Press.
Furst, Peter T.
1978 *The Ninth Level: Funerary Art from Ancient Mesoamerica*. Iowa City: University of Iowa, Museum of Art.
García Icazbalceta, Joaquin, ed.
1886–92 *Nueva colección de documentos para la historia de México*. 5 vols. Mexico: Francisco Díaz de León.
1971 *Colección de documentos para la historia de México*. 2 vols. Mexico: Porrúa.
Gardiner, C. Harvey
1956 *Naval Power in the Conquest of Mexico*. Austin: University of Texas Press.
Garibay K., Ángel María
1973 *Teogonía e historia de los mexicanos: Tres opúsculos del siglo XVI*. Mexico: Porrúa.
Gay, Carlo T. E.
1972 *Chalcacingo*. Portland, Oreg.: International Scholarly Book Service.
Gemelli Careri, Giovanni Francesco
1976 *Viaje a la Nueva España*. Mexico: Universidad Nacional Autónoma de México.
Gerhard, Peter
1972 *A Guide to the Historical Geography of New Spain*. Cambridge: Cambridge University Press.
Gibson, Charles
1964 *The Aztecs Under Spanish Rule*. Stanford, Calif.: Stanford University Press.
1971 "Structure of the Aztec Empire." In Ekholm and Bernal 1971a.
———, and John B. Glass
1975 "A Census of Middle American Prose Manuscripts in the Native Historical Tradition." In Cline 1975b.
Glass, John B.
1964 *Catálogo de la colección de códices*. Mexico: Instituto Nacional de Antropología e Historia.
———, and Donald Robertson
1975 "A Census of Native Middle American Pictorial Manuscripts." In Cline 1975a.
Goldberg, Neil J., and Frank J. Findlow
1984 "A Quantitative Analysis of Roman Military Operations in Britain, Circa A.D. 43 to 238." In Ferguson 1984b.
Gómez de Orozco, Frederico, ed.
1927 "Descripción de Cholula." *Revista Mexicana de Estudios Históricos* 1:158–70.
González Rul, Francisco
1971 "El macuahuitl y el tlatzintepuzotilli: dos armas indígenas." *Anales del Instituto de Antropología e Historia*, época 7, 2:147–52.

González T., Yolotl
1979 "La esclavitud en la época prehispánica." In Dahlgren 1979.
Gorenstein, Shirley
1963 "The Differential Development of Military and Political Organization in Prehispanic Peru and Mexico." Ph.D. dissertation, Columbia University.
1966 "The Differential Development of New World Empires." *Revista Mexicana de Estudios Antropológicos* 20:41–67.
1973 "Tepexi el Viejo: A Postclassic Fortified Site in the Mixteca-Puebla Region of Mexico." *Transactions of the American Philosophical Society*, vol. 63, part 1.
Graham, Ian, ed.
1979 *Corpus of Maya Hieroglyphic Inscriptions*, Vol. 3, part 2. Cambridge, Mass.: Peabody Museum.
———, and Eric von Euw, eds.
1977 *Corpus of Maya Hieroglyphic Inscriptions*, Vol. 3, part 1. Cambridge, Mass.: Peabody Museum.
Grennes-Ravitz, Ronald A.
1975 "The Extrapolation of Preclassic Reality from Postclassic Models: The Concept of an Olmec Empire in Mesoamerica." *Actas del XLI Congreso Internacional de Americanistas* 1:378–83.
Hagen, Victor W. von
1962 *The Aztec: Man and Tribe*. New York: Mentor Books.
Hammond, Norman, ed.
1977 *Social Process in Maya Prehistory: Studies in Honor of Sir Eric Thompson*. New York: Academic Press.
Hardoy, Jorge E.
1973 *Pre-Columbian Cities*. New York: Walker.
Harvey, H. R., and Hanns J. Prem, eds.
1984 *Explorations in Ethnohistory: Indians of Central Mexico in the Sixteenth Century*. Albuquerque: University of New Mexico Press.
Hassig, Ross
1981 "The Famine of One Rabbit: Ecological Causes and Social Consequences of a Pre-Columbian Calamity." *Journal of Anthropological Research* 37:171–81.
1985 *Trade, Tribute, and Transportation: The Sixteenth-Century Political Economy of the Valley of Mexico*. Norman: University of Oklahoma Press.
Headrick, Daniel R.
1981 *The Tools of Empire: Technology and European Imperialism in the Nineteenth Century*. New York: Oxford University Press.
Hefter, Joseph
1968 "Crónica del traje militar en México, del siglo XVI al XX." *Artes de México*, no. 102.
Hernández, Francisco
1946 *Antigüedades de la Nueva España*. Joaquin García Pimentel, ed. Mexico: Pedro Robredo.

1959 *Historia natural de Nueva España*. 2 vols. Mexico: Universidad Nacional Autónoma de México.

Herrejón Peredo, Carlos
1978 "La Pugna entre mexicas y tarascos." *Cuadernos de Historia* 1:9–47.

Herrera, Antonio de
1934–57 *Historia general de los hechos de los castellanos en las islas y tierra firme del mar oceano*. 17 vols. Madrid.

Hicks, Frederic
1977 "Social Stratification and the Calpixque of Aztec Mexico." Paper presented at the 76th Annual Convention of the American Anthropological Association, Houston, Tex., December 3.
1979 "'Flowery War' in Aztec History." *American Ethnologist* 6: 87–92.

Holt, H. Barry
1976 "The Extent of the Dominance of Tenochtitlan During the Reign of Mocteuczoma Ilhuicamina." *Middle American Research Institute* no. 22:49–62.
1979 "Mexica-Aztec Warfare: A Developmental and Cultural Analysis." Ph.D. dissertation, University of Texas at Austin.

Howard, Calvin D.
1974 "The Atlatl: Function and Performance." *American Antiquity* 39:102–104.

Isaac, Barry L.
1983a "The Aztec 'Flowery War': A Geopolitical Explanation." *Journal of Anthropological Research* 39:415–32.
1983b "Aztec Warfare: Goals and Battlefield Comportment." *Ethnology* 22:121–31.

Ixtlilxóchitl, Fernándo de Alva
1975–77 *Obras Históricas*. 2 vols. Mexico: Universidad Autónoma Nacional de México.

Jiménez Moreno, Wigberto
1966 "Los imperios prehispánicos de Mesoamerica." *Revista Mexicana de Estudios Antropológicos* 20:179–95.

Jones, Christopher, and Linton Satterthwaite
1982 *The Monuments and Inscriptions of Tikal: The Carved Monuments*. University Museum Monograph 44, Tikal Report no. 33, part A. Philadelphia: University Museum, University of Pennsylvania.

Joyce, Thomas A.
1920 *Mexican Archaeology*. London: Philip Lee Warner.

Jubinal, Achille
1846 *La Armería real ou collection des principales pièces de la Galerie d'Armes Anciennes de Madrid*. Supplement. Paris: Dessins de M. Gaspard Sensi.

Kampen, Michael Edwin
1972 *The Sculptures of El Tajín, Veracruz, Mexico*. Gainesville: University of Florida Press.

Katz, Friedrich
1974 *The Ancient American Civilizations.* New York: Praeger Publishers.
Keegan, John
1978 *The Face of Battle.* New York: Penguin Books.
Kelly, Isabel, and Ángel Palerm
1952 *The Tajin Totonac, Part 1: History, Subsistence, Shelter, and Technology.* Smithsonian Institution, Institute of Social Anthropology, Publication no. 13. Washington, D.C.
Kirchhoff, Paul, Lina Odena Güemes, and Luis Reyes García, eds.
1976 *Historia Tolteca Chichimeca.* Mexico: Instituto Nacional de Historia e Antropología.
Korfmann, Manfred
1973 "The Sling as a Weapon." *Scientific American* 229:4:34–42.
Kubler, George
1980 "Eclecticism at Cacaxtla." In Robertson 1980.
1984 *The Art and Architecture of Ancient America.* New York: Penguin Books.
Landa, Diego de
1973 *Relación de las cosas de Yucatán.* Mexico: Porrúa.
1978 *Yucatan Before and After the Conquest.* William Gates, trans. New York: Dover.
Leopold, A. Starker
1972 *Wildlife of Mexico: The Game Birds and Mammals.* Berkeley: University of California Press.
Leventhal, Richard M., and Alan L. Kolata
1983 *Civilization in the Ancient Americas: Essays in Honor of Gordon R. Willey.* Albuquerque: University of New Mexico Press and Peabody Museum of Archaeology and Ethnology.
Leyenda de los Soles
1975 *Leyenda de los Soles.* In *Códice Chimalpopoca* 1975.
El libro de las tasaciones
1952 *El libro de las tasaciones de pueblos de la Nueva España: Siglo XVI.* Mexico: Archivo General de la Nación.
Linné, S.
1937 "Hunting and Fishing in the Valley of Mexico in the Middle of the 16th Century." *Ethnos* 2:56–64.
1939 "Blow-Guns in Ancient Mexico." *Ethnos* 4:56–61.
López de Gómara, Francisco
1965–66 *Historia general de las Indias.* 2 vols. Barcelona: Obras Maestras.
López de Velasco, Juan
1971 *Geografía y descripción universal de las Indias.* Madrid: Ediciones Atlas.
Luttwak, Edward
1976 *The Grand Strategy of the Roman Empire.* Baltimore, Md.: Johns Hopkins University Press.

McAfee, Byron, and R. H. Barlow
1946 "La guerra entre Tlatelolco y Tenochtitlán según el Códice Cozcatzin." *Memorias de la Academia Mexicana de la Historia* 5:188–97.

McNeill, William H.
1982 *The Pursuit of Power: Technology, Armed Force, and Society Since A.D. 1000.* Chicago: University of Chicago Press.

Macazaga, Ordoño, Cesar
1983 *Diccionario de indumentaria náhuatl.* Mexico: Editorial Innovación.

Martínez Cortés, Fernando
1974 *Pegamentos, gomas y resinas en el México prehispánico.* Mexico: Sepsetentas.

Martyr d'Anghera, Peter
1970 *De Orbe Novo: The Eight Decades of Peter Martyr D'Anghera.* Francis Augustus MacNutt, trans. 2 vols. New York: Burt Franklin.

Mason, Otis T.
1884 "Throwing-Sticks in the National Museum." *Smithsonian Annual Report* 2:279–89.

Matrícula de tributos
1980 *Matrícula de tributos (Códice de Moctezuma).* Graz, Austria: Akademische Druck-u. Verlagsanstalt.

Maudsley, Alfred Percival
1889–1902 *Biologia Centrali-Americana; or, Contributions to the Knowledge of the Fauna and Flora of Mexico and Central America.* 6 vols. London: R. H. Porter.

Maurice, F.
1930 "The Size of the Army of Xerxes in the Invasion of Greece 480 B.C." *Journal of Hellenistic Studies* 50:210–35.

Memoria de las obras
1975 *Memoria de las obras del sistema de drenaje profundo del Distrito Federal.* 3 vols and atlas. Mexico: Departamiento del Distrito Federal.

Mendieta, Gerónimo de
1971 *Historia eclesiástica indiana.* Mexico: Porrúa.

Mengin, Ernest
1952 "Commentaire du Codex Mexicanus Nos. 23–24." *Journal de la Société des Américanistes* 41:387–498.

Miller, Arthur G.
1973 *The Mural Painting of Teotihuacan.* Washington, D.C.: Dumbarton Oaks.
1977 "'Captains of the Itzá': Unpublished Mural Evidence from Chichén Itzá." In Hammond 1977.

Molina, Alonso de
1970 *Vocabulario en lengua Castellana y Mexicana y Mexicana y Castellana.* Mexico: Porrúa.

Monjarás-Ruiz, Jesús
1976 "Panorama general de la guerra entre los Aztecas." *Estudios de Cultura Nahuatl* 12:241–64.
Moriarty, James Robert
1969 "Ritual Combat. A Comparison of the Aztec 'War of Flowers' and the Medieval 'Mèlée.'" *Miscellaneous Series*, no. 9, Museum of Anthropology, Colorado State University, Fort Collins.
Morris, Earl H., Jean Charlot, and Ann Axtell Morris
1931 *The Temple of the Warriors at Chichén Itzá, Yucatan*. 2 vols. Carnegie Institution of Washington Publication no. 406. Washington, D.C.: Carnegie Institution.
Motolinía (Toribio de Benavente)
1950 *History of the Indians of New Spain*. Elizabeth Andros Foster, trans. Berkeley, Calif.: Cortes Society.
1971 *Memoriales o libro de las cosas de la Nueva España y de los naturales de ella*. Mexico: Universidad Nacional Autónoma de México.
Muñoz Camargo, Diego
1892 *Historia de Tlaxcala*. Mexico: Oficina Tip. de la Secretaría de Fomento.
1981 *Descripción de la ciudad y provincia de Tlaxcala de las Indias y del mar oceano para el buen gobierno y ennoblecimiento dellas*. Mexico: Universidad Nacional Autónoma de México.
Nelson, Edward William
1899 *The Eskimo About Bering Strait*. Bureau of American Ethnology, 18th Annual Report. Washington, D.C.: U.S. Government Printing Office.
Neumann, C.
1971 "A Note on Alexander's March-Rates." *Historia: Journal of Ancient History* 20:196–98.
Nicholson, H. B., and Eloise Quiñones Keber
1983 *Art of Aztec Mexico: Treasures of Tenochtitlan*. Washington, D.C.: National Gallery of Art.
Nickel, Helmut
N.d. "A Note on the *Macquauitl*." manuscript, Metropolitan Museum of Art, New York.
Noguera, Eduardo
1945 "El atlatl o tiradera." *Anales del Museo Nacional de Arqueología, Historia y Etnografía*, época 5, 3:205–38.
1958 *Tallas prehispánicas en madera*. Mexico: Editorial Guarania.
Nuttall, Zelia
1891a "The Atlatl or Spear-Thrower of the Ancient Mexicans." *Archaeological and Ethnological Papers of the Peabody Museum* 1:3:169–205.
1891b "On Ancient Mexican Shields." *Internationales Archiv für Ethnographie* 5:34–53.
1903 *The Book of the Life of the Ancient Mexicans*. Berkeley: University of California Press.

———, ed.
1975 *The Codex Nuttall.* New York: Dover.
Orozco y Berra, Manuel
1978 *Historia antigua y de la conquista de México.* 4 vols. Mexico: Porrúa.
Paddock, John
1966a "El fenómeno imperial: Algunos enfoques teóricos." *Revista Mexicana de Estudios Antropológicos* 20:69–81.
1966b "La idea del imperio aplicada a Mesoamérica." *Revista Mexicana de Estudios Antropológicos* 20:83–94.
1966c "Monte Albán: ¿Sede de Imperio?" *Revista Mexicana de Estudios Antropológicos* 20:117–46.
Palerm, Ángel
1956 "Notas sobre las construcciones militares y la guerra en Mesoamérica." *Ciencias Sociales* 7:189–202.
1973 *Obras hidráulicas prehispánicas en el sistema lacustre del Valle de México.* Mexico: Instituto Nacional de Antropología e Historia.
Paso y Troncoso, Francisco del, ed.
1905–48 *Papeles de Nueva España.* 9 vols. Madrid and Mexico.
1939–42 *Epistolario de Nueva España.* 16 vols. Mexico: Antigua Librería Robredo de José Porrúa e Hijos.
Pasztory, Esther
1983 *Aztec Art.* New York: Harry N. Abrams.
Peets, Orville H.
1960 "Experiments in the Use of Atlatl Weights." *American Antiquity* 26:108–10.
Peñafiel, Antonio, ed.
1895 *Códice Fernández Leal.* Mexico: Oficina Tipografica de la Secretaría de Fomento.
Peterson, David A., and Thomas B. MacDougall
1974 *Guiengola: A Fortified Site in the Isthmus of Tehuantepec.* Vanderbilt University Publications in Anthropology no. 10.
Peterson, Frederick A.
1952 "Warriors of Ancient Mexico." *Mexican Life* 28:6:13–14, 58–66.
1962 *Ancient Mexico: An Introduction to the Pre-Hispanic Cultures.* New York: Capricorn Books.
Phillips, David A., Jr.
1979 "The Growth and Decline of States in Mesoamerica." *Journal of the Steward Anthropological Society* 10:137–59.
Piho, Virve
1972a "La jerarquía militar azteca." *Atti del XL Congresso Internazionale degli Americanisti* 2:273–88.
1972b "Tlacatecutli, Tlacochtecutli, Tlacateccatl y Tlachochcalcatl." *Estudios de Cultura Nahuatl* 10:315–28.

1974 "Esquema provisional de la organización militar mexica." *Actas del XLI Congresso International de Americanistas* 2:169–78.

Pope, Saxton T.
1923 "A Study of Bows and Arrows." *University of California Publications in American Archaeology and Ethnology* 13:9: 329–414.

Porcacchi da Castiglione Arretino, Thomaso
1980 *Descripción de la gran ciudad e isla Temistitan*. Luz Maria Ziaurriz, trans. Mexico: Miguel Ángel Porrúa.

Powell, Philip Wayne
1975 *Soldiers, Indians and Silver*. Tempe: Center for Latin American Studies, Arizona State University.

Ramírez Cabañas, Joaquín, ed.
1943 *La ciudad de Veracruz en el siglo XVI*. Mexico: Universitaria.

Ramón y Zamora, Jerónimo
1897 *Repúblicas de Indias, idolatrias y gobierno en México*. Mexico: Victoriano Suárez.

Rees, Peter W.
1971 "Route Inertia and Route Competition: An Historical Geography of Transportation Between Mexico City and Vera Cruz." Ph.D. dissertation, University of California at Berkeley.

Relación de Michoacán
1977 *Relación de las ceremonias y ritos y población y gobierno de los indios de la provincia de Michoacán*. Morelia, Michoacán: Balsal Editores, S.A.

Robertson, Donald
1959 *Mexican Manuscript Painting in the Early Colonial Period: The Metropolitan Schools*. New Haven, Conn.: Yale University Press.

Robertson, Merle Green, ed.
1980 *Third Palenque Round Table, 1978*. vol. 5, part 2. Austin: University of Texas Press.

Rounds, J.
1979 "Lineage, Class, and Power in the Aztec State." *American Ethnologist* 6:73–86.

Sahagún, Bernardino de
1950–82 *General History of the Things of New Spain: Florentine Codex*. Arthur J. O. Anderson and Charles E. Dibble, trans. 13 vols. Salt Lake City: University of Utah Press.
1951 *The Ceremonies*. Book 2.
1952 *The Origin of the Gods*. Book 3.
1954 *Kings and Lords*. Book 8.
1957 *The Soothsayers*. Book 4.
The Omens. Book 5.
1959 *The Merchants*. Book 9.

1961 *The People*. Book 10.
1963 *Earthly Things*. Book 11.
1969 *Rhetoric and Moral Philosophy*. Book 6.
1970 *The Gods*. Book 1.
1975 *The Conquest of Mexico*. Book 12.
1977 *Historia general de las cosas de Nueva España*. Angel María Garibay, trans. 4 vols. Mexico: Editorial Porrúa.
1979 *Códice Florentino*. 3 vols. Mexico: Archivo General de la Nación.

Sanders, William T.
1970 "The Population of the Teotihuacan Valley, the Basin of Mexico and the Central Mexican Symbiotic Region in the Sixteenth Century." In Sanders, Kovar, Charlton, and Diehl 1970.

———, Anton Kovar, Thomas Charlton, and Richard A. Diehl
1970 *The Natural Environment, Contemporary Occupation and 16th Century Population of the Valley. The Teotihuacan Valley Project. Final Report*. Vol. 1. Occasional Papers in Anthropology, no. 3. Department of Anthropology, Pennsylvania State University.

———, Jeffrey R. Parsons, and Robert S. Santley
1979 *The Basin of Mexico: Ecological Processes in the Evolution of a Civilization*. New York: Academic Press.

Santa Cruz, Alonso de
1920 *Islario general de todas las islas del mundo*. Madrid: Imprenta del Patronato de Huérfanos de Intendencia e Intervención Militares.

Schaedel, Richard P., Jorge E. Hardoy, and Nora Scott Kinzer, eds.
1978 *Urbanization in the Americas from its Beginnings to the Present*. The Hague: Mouton Publishers.

Scholes, France V., and Eleanor B. Adams, eds.
1957 *Información sobre los tributos que los indios pagaban a Moctezuma: Año de 1554*. Mexico: José Porrúa e Hijos.

———, and Ralph L. Roys
1968 *The Maya Chontal Indians of Acalan-Tixchel: A Contribution to the History and Ethnography of the Yucatan Peninsula*. Norman: University of Oklahoma Press.

Séjourné, Laurette
1966 *Arquitectura y pintura en Teotihuacán*. Mexico: Siglo Veintiuno.

Sekunda, Nick
1984 *The Army of Alexander the Great*. London: Osprey Publishing.

Seler, Eduard
1939 *Selected Works*.
1960 *Gesammelte Abhandlungen zur Amerikanischen Sprach- und Altertumskunde*. 5 vols. Graz, Austria: Akademische Druck-u. Verlagsanstalt.

Sherwin-White, A. N.
1983 *Roman Foreign Policy in the East*. Norman: University of Oklahoma Press.

Siméon, Rémi
1981 *Diccionario de la lengua nahuatl o mexicana*. Mexico: Siglo Veintiuno.

Skinner, G. William
1977a *The City in Late Imperial China*. Stanford, Calif.: Stanford University Press.
1977b "Cities and the Hierarchy of Local Systems." In Skinner 1977a.

Smith, Bradley
1968 *Mexico: A History in Art*. New York: Harper & Row.

Solís y Rivadeneyra, Antonio de
1753 *The History of the Conquest of Mexico by the Spaniards*. 2 vols. London.

Sotheby's
1984 *Important Pre-Columbian Art*. New York: Sotheby-Parke Bernet.

Soustelle, Jacques
1970 *Daily Life of the Aztecs on the Eve of the Spanish Conquest*. Stanford, Calif.: Stanford University Press.

Stanislawski, Dan
1947 "Tarascan Political Geography." *American Anthropologist* 49: 46–55.

Stenzel, Werner
1976 "The Military and Religious Orders of Ancient Mexico." *Actas del XLI Congreso International de Americanistas* 2:179–87.

Stevens, Phillip H.
1965 *Artillery Through the Ages*. New York: Franklin Watts.

Stevenson, William Flack
1897 *Wounds in War: The Mechanism of Their Production and their Treatment*. London: Longmans, Green.

Suárez de Peralta, Juan
1949 *Tratado del descubrimiento de las Indias*. Mexico: Secretaría de Educación Pública.

Sullivan, Thelma D.
1972 "The Arms and Insignia of the Mexica." *Estudios de Cultura Náhuatl* 10:155–93.

Taagepera, Rein
1968 "Growth Curves of Empires." *General Systems* 13:171–75.
1978a "Size and Duration of Empires: Systematics of Size." *Social Science Research* 7:108–27.
1978b "Size and Duration of Empires: Growth-Decline Curves, 3000 to 600 B.C." *Social Science Research* 7:180–96.
1979 "Size and Duration of Empires: Growth-Decline Curves, 600 B.C. to 600 A.D." *Social Science History* 3:3/4:115–38.

Tapia, Andrés de
1963 "The Chronicle of Andrés de Tapia." In Fuentes 1963.
Tarassuk, Leonid, and Claude Blair, eds.
1982 *The Complete Encyclopedia of Arms and Weapons*. New York: Simon & Schuster.
Tezozomoc, Alvaro
1853 *Histoire de Mexique*. H. Ternaux-Compans, trans. 2 vols. Paris.
Thompson, J. Eric S.
1933 *Mexico Before Cortez*. New York: Charles Scribner's Sons.
Tilly, Charles
1975a "Reflections on the History of European State-Making." In Tilly 1975b.
———, ed.
1975b *The Formation of National States in Western Europe*. Princeton, N.J.: Princeton University Press.
Todorov, Tzvetan
1984 *The Conquest of America: The Question of the Other*. New York: Harper & Row.
Tolstoy, Paul
1971 "Utilitarian Artifacts of Central Mexico." In Ekholm and Bernal 1971a.
Torquemada, Juan de
1975–83 *Monarquía indiana*. 7 vols. Mexico: Universidad Nacional Autónoma de México.
Turney-High, Harry Holbert
1949 *Primitive War: Its Practice and Concepts*. Columbia: University of South Carolina Press.
U.S. Army
1971a *Foot Marches*. Field Manual No. 21–18. Washington, D.C.: Department of the Army.
1971b *The Infantry Battalions*. Field Manual No. 7–20. Washington, D.C.: Department of the Army.
Vaillant, George C.
1966 *Aztecs of Mexico: Origin, Rise, and Fall of the Aztec Nation*. Baltimore, Md.: Penguin Books.
Vargas Rea, Luis, ed.
1944–46 *Papeles de Nueva España coleccionados por Francisco del Paso y Troncoso*. Mexico.
Vázquez de Espinosa, Antonio
1942 *Compendium and Description of the West Indies*. Charles Upson Clark, trans. Smithsonian Miscellaneous Collections. Washington, D.C.: Smithsonian Institution.
Velasco Piña, Antonio
1979 *Tlacaelel: el Azteca entre los Aztecas*. Mexico: Jus.
Veytia, Mariano
1944 *Historia antigua de México*. 2 vols. Mexico: Editorial Leyenda.

Wicke, Charles R.
1971 *Olmec: An Early Art Style of Precolumbian Mexico.* Tucson: University of Arizona Press.
Wolf, Eric R., ed.
1976 *The Valley of Mexico.* Albuquerque: University of New Mexico Press.
Yadin, Yigael
1963 *The Art of Warfare in Biblical Lands.* 2 vols. New York: McGraw-Hill Book Co.
Zorita, Alonso de
1963 *Los señores de la Nueva España.* Mexico: Universidad Nacional Autónoma de México.
1971 *Life and Labor in Ancient Mexico.* Benjamin Keen, trans. New Brunswick, N.J.: Rutgers University Press.

Index

NOTE: Entries may have more than one referent.